CW01190977

COMPARATIVE CONSTITUTIONALISM

A. V. DICEY

EDITED BY J. W. F. ALLISON

LECTURES ON
COMPARATIVE
CONSTITUTIONALISM

A. V. DICEY

THE OXFORD EDITION OF DICEY

VOLUME II

EDITED BY J. W. F. ALLISON

OXFORD

UNIVERSITY PRESS

OXFORD
UNIVERSITY PRESS

Great Clarendon Street, Oxford, OX2 6DP,
United Kingdom

Oxford University Press is a department of the University of Oxford.
It furthers the University's objective of excellence in research, scholarship,
and education by publishing worldwide. Oxford is a registered trade mark of
Oxford University Press in the UK and in certain other countries

© Editorial matter, J. W. F. Allison 2013

The moral rights of the author have been asserted

First Edition published in 2013

Impression: 1

All rights reserved. No part of this publication may be reproduced, stored in
a retrieval system, or transmitted, in any form or by any means, without the
prior permission in writing of Oxford University Press, or as expressly permitted
by law, by licence or under terms agreed with the appropriate reprographics
rights organization. Enquiries concerning reproduction outside the scope of the
above should be sent to the Rights Department, Oxford University Press, at the
address above

You must not circulate this work in any other form
and you must impose this same condition on any acquirer

Crown copyright material is reproduced under Class Licence
Number C01P0000148 with the permission of OPSI
and the Queen's Printer for Scotland

Published in the United States of America by Oxford University Press
198 Madison Avenue, New York, NY 10016, United States of America

British Library Cataloguing in Publication Data
Data available

Library of Congress Control Number: 2013938386

ISBN 978–0–19–968581–3

Printed in Great Britain by
CPI Group (UK) Ltd, Croydon, CR0 4YY

Preface to *The Oxford Edition of Dicey*

In the late-nineteenth century and for much of the twentieth century, *The Law of the Constitution* by Albert Venn Dicey was the main doctrinal influence upon English constitutional thought. It was invoked in Parliament, likened to Blackstone's *Commentaries*, and more widely cited in English academic literature than any other constitutional authority. By its critics, it was still granted the status of orthodoxy and, by many others, it was treated as a canonical text embodying axiomatic principles or it was simply understood as indeed the law of the constitution, thus approximating to, or turned into, a kind of constitutional code for want of a written constitution.

In earlier works, I criticized both *The Law of the Constitution* and its reception. In my first book,[1] I sought to show, inter alia, how Dicey neglected political and historical context and how his neglect contributed to his own, and a more general Diceyan, rejection of an English administrative law that retarded, for decades, its development. In my second book,[2] I elaborated, inter alia, on Dicey's express adoption of an analytical legal view of the constitution, on his relegation of the historical view, and on his consequent focus on constitutional form, not formation, which rendered static his analytical scheme of rules and principles and of sets and distinctions. In proportion, I argued, to the considerable extent Dicey's analysis remained constant in necessarily multiple editions of the same analytical textbook, enjoyed influence or acceptance, and continued to be applied, it ossified or encapsulated a changing constitution.

The Oxford Edition of Dicey is intended to address the problematic extent to which *The Law of the Constitution* was canonized or had lasting authority conferred upon it, whether uncritically or despite extensive criticism. Volume One is intended to take readers first back to its pedagogical beginnings, by incorporating in Part I what simply were, as entitled, *Lectures Introductory to the Study of the Law of the Constitution*, and then to developments from those beginnings by incorporating in Part II the main addenda in later editions, which are particularly difficult to access in any one library at any one time. Volume Two is intended to take readers well beyond *The Law of the Constitution*'s canonical text by publishing lectures for changing versions of a comparative constitutional book that Dicey began but did not finish. It is to make readily accessible Dicey's largely unpublished comparative constitutional lectures, the manuscripts of which are in the Dicey Papers entrusted by Dicey's literary executor Robert S. Rait to the Codrington Library.[3] In other words, *The Oxford Edition of*

---

[1] *A Continental Distinction in the Common Law: A Historical and Comparative Perspective on English Public Law*, rev. pbk edn (Oxford: Oxford University Press, 2000), 18–23.
[2] *The English Historical Constitution: Continuity, Change and European Effects* (Cambridge: Cambridge University Press, 2007), especially 7 ff.
[3] All Souls College, Oxford, MS 323.

Dicey is designed to facilitate looking both back to and well beyond what became Dicey's canonical constitutional text and to suggest implications of what comes to light or more clearly into view. By facilitating access to additional sources, my aim is further to historicize and to complement or broaden understanding of domestic English and comparative constitutionalism as expounded by Dicey.

Intending the publication of Volume Two to facilitate access to Dicey's many unpublished comparative constitutional lectures, I am mindful of the primacy of Dicey's previously published works in Volume One. The contents of *The Oxford Edition of Dicey* have been subject, further, to an important limitation. They have been generally limited to what Dicey chose to expound in print or lecture. They do not include a selection from Dicey's extensive private correspondence, which is here given little attention and only occasional mention by way of reference to the existing biographical studies. Although sources of considerable biographical insight and interest,[4] Dicey's private letters differed much—in deliberation, elaboration, and real and expected publication—from his expositions in print or lecture. Often expressed in passing or in reaction to a recent occurrence, the thoughts evident in Dicey's private correspondence varied with context and correspondent. If thoughts or views he expressed there were, on the one hand, yet to be expounded in print or lecture, they were more open to development and could later be readily changed or deviated from. If, on the other hand, those thoughts related to what Dicey had already expounded in print or lecture, Dicey could assume or take for granted his existing exposition, on which his privately expressed thoughts could be expected to have a varying and complicated, conceivably dialectical, bearing—perhaps corrective and/or defensive, proud and/or diffident, obstinate and/or apologetic. In editing these volumes, I have been keen to avoid providing an uncritical extension of Dicey's already extensive body of constitutional writings into one in which coherence is more elusive and from which dubious authority is nonetheless derived for some or other highly selective, normative or ideological interpretation therefore more readily made to recreate Dicey in the image of its maker.

In finding for Volume One the materials that were published abroad and not in English, namely the Prefaces for the French edition of *The Law of the Constitution* and Sir Paul Vinogradoff's Foreword to the two Russian editions, I am grateful to the Squire Law Library, to David Wills the Librarian, and especially to Lesley Dingle for her expertise, efficiency, and invariable willingness to help. I am also grateful to librarians in the Peace Palace Library in The Hague and in the Russian State Library in Moscow. Mark Walters kindly sent me a translation of Vinogradoff's Foreword to the second Russian edition and put me in touch with Eric Myles, who translated

---

[4] On these sources and their use, see generally R. S. Rait (ed.), *Memorials of Albert Venn Dicey, being chiefly Letters and Diaries* (London: Macmillan, 1925); R. F. Shinn and R. A. Cosgrove (eds), *Constitutional Reflections: the Correspondence of Albert Venn Dicey and Arthur Berriedale Keith* (Lanham, MD: University Press of America, 1996); R. A. Cosgrove, *The Rule of Law: Albert Venn Dicey, Victorian Jurist* (Chapel Hill, NC: University of North Carolina Press, 1980); D. Sugarman, 'The Legal Boundaries of Liberty: Dicey, Liberalism and Legal Science', Review of *The Rule of Law: Albert Venn Dicey, Victorian Jurist* by R. A. Cosgrove, (1983) 46 MLR 102; M. D. Walters, 'Dicey on Writing the *Law of the Constitution*' (2011) 31 OJLS 1.

the Foreword as published in the first Russian edition. To both Mark and Eric, I am much indebted.

For first drawing my attention to the Dicey Papers in the Codrington Library of All Souls College, I would like to express thanks to the late Michael Taggart. In working towards his book entitled *An Index to Common Law Festschriften*,[5] he sent me Geoffrey Hand's chapter 'A. V. Dicey's Unpublished Materials on the Comparative Study of Constitutions' in the *Festschrift* for L. Neville Brown.[6] Mike was, I seem to remember, drawing my attention to significant statements by Dicey on the separation of powers but was perhaps also suggesting that I give the Dicey Papers substantial attention, which I am now pleased to have given them in selecting and introducing the contents of Volume Two.

I am grateful to OUP's two referees who recommended that OUP approach me to edit the comparative constitutional lectures from the Dicey Papers, and to Professor Ian Maclean, the Fellow Librarian of All Souls College, and the other members of the College's Governing Body, for granting permission to publish from those Papers entrusted to the College. I would also like to give special thanks to Vernon Bogdanor for his interest, encouragement, and advice, based in part on his own leading work on the Dicey Papers for the All Souls-*Public Law* Seminar, where in 1985, on the centenary of the publication of *The Law of the Constitution*'s first edition, he first drew attention to those Papers.[7]

For friendly assistance in the Codrington Library and for taking numerous digital photographs of the Dicey Papers at OUP's request for the purposes of this project, I am grateful to Norma Aubertin-Potter and Gaye Morgan. In making research trips to Oxford and obtaining a computer with sufficient capacity to cope with dense digital images, I benefited from Yorke Fund Grants and am accordingly grateful to the Fund's Managers. I would like to thank OUP's Production Editor Matthew Humphrys for his efficiency and friendliness and Penny Dickman for the quality of her indexing. To Alex Flach and Natasha Flemming at OUP, I would like to express particular thanks for their initiative, drive, and sustained support in this unusual, difficult, and protracted project. On editing issues, I was fortunate to benefit from useful discussions with Richard Rex and other Fellows of Queens' College. Finally, I would like to thank my family and friends for all their support.

---

[5] Oxford: Hart, 2006.

[6] In G. Hand and J. McBride (eds.), Droit Sans Frontières: *Essays in Honour of L. Neville Brown* (Birmingham: Holdsworth Club, 1991), 77–93.

[7] See 'All Souls-*Public Law* Seminar: Dicey and the Constitution' [1985] PL 583; V. Bogdanor, 'Dicey and the Reform of the Constitution' [1985] PL 652, especially 672, n.

Contents of Volume II

EDITOR'S INTRODUCTION TO VOLUME II   xi

PART I THE COMPARATIVE STUDY OF THE CONSTITUTION*

Introduction   3
1 General Characteristics of Existing English Constitutionalism   16
2 Constitutionalism of the Commonwealth   29
3 English Constitutionalism under George III   60
4 American Constitutionalism   75
5 French Constitutionalism (with Appendix, *Droit Administratif* and
   Constitution of Year VIII, Art. 75)   89
6 Prussian Constitutionalism   105
7 Party Government   122
8 Parliamentarism   137
9 General Conclusions   151

PART II THE COMPARATIVE STUDY OF CONSTITUTIONS†

Introduction—Nature of Comparative Study of Constitutions (analysis)   169
1 Historical [Constitutions] and Non-Historical Constitutions
   (analysis and full text)   171
2 Ancient Constitutionalism and Modern Constitutionalism
   (analysis and full text)   192
3 Representative Government (analysis and full text)   214
4 The Separation of Powers (two analyses)   229
5 Divisions of Constitutions (analysis and full text)   232
6 The Judiciary in Relation to the Executive and Legislative Powers
   (two analyses)   249
7 Local Government and Centralization (two analyses)   253
8 Federal Government (analysis)   255
9 Federal Government (continued): The Australian
   Commonwealth (analysis)   257

---

* Part I's title has been derived from the first page, and the chapter/lecture headings and their sequence have been derived from the second page (headed 'Old forms of Mss Lectures'), of a four-page manuscript entitled 'Comparative Study of the Constitution: List of Papers etc', Dicey Papers, All Souls College, Oxford, Codrington Library, MS 323 (see Editor's Introduction, pp xvii f. below). On that page, the Introduction and chapters 1, 4, 5, 6 and 9 were dated May 1897, chapter 2 was dated June 1897, chapter 3 was not dated, and chapters 7 and 8 were dated July 1898 and August 1898 respectively. Most of the original lecture manuscripts were also dated and, if so, their dates have been footnoted at the start of chapters. These dates are the dates when lecture texts were first written, rewritten, or re-used.

† Part II's title, the chapter/lecture headings (excluding the Introduction), and their sequence have been derived from a manuscript lecture schedule headed 'Easter & Trinity Terms 1900: Comparative Study of Constitutions', Dicey Papers, All Souls College, Oxford, Codrington Library, MS 323 (see Editor's Introduction, pp xvii f. below). In later manuscript notes, the schedule was recorded as a 'New Series', and 'written 1900' was added beneath the titles to chapters/lectures 1, 2, 3, and 5, marking those lectures that had been written out in full. Dates written on the original manuscripts of lecture texts and analyses have been footnoted at the start of chapters.

APPENDIX—COMPARATIVE CONSTITUTIONALISM*

I	Memorandum on English Party System of Government	261
II	Lecture 4: Comparison between English [Executive] and other Executives *or* Parliamentary and Non-Parliamentary Executives (analysis and full text); Lecture 5: Comparison [between] English Executive [and] other Executives (continued) (analysis and full text)	274
III	Note 2: Self-Government	299
	Note 3: Self-Government and Local Self-Government	302
IV	Modes of Changing or Amending a Constitution (analysis)	303
V	Authorities and Questions for *The Comparative Study of Constitutions*	305
VI	Note 17: Conclusions as to French *Droit Administratif*	307
VII	Why Universal Suffrage Suits France (full text)	315
VIII	Scheme of Lectures, 1906	320
IX	Scheme of Lectures, 1908	333

Index   341

---

* These materials from the Dicey Papers were not incorporated in the lecture scheme and schedule from which the contents of Parts I and II respectively have been derived. They have been put in chronological order in so far as that order has been ascertained. Dates written on the original manuscripts of Appendix items have been footnoted below. On the selection of items, see Editor's Introduction, pp xix f. below.

Editor's Introduction to Volume Two

The comparative constitutional lectures in this volume have been derived from lecture and related manuscripts that were entrusted by Albert Venn Dicey's literary executor R. S. Rait to All Souls College and are known as the Dicey Papers.[1] In editing this two-volume edition, the challenge they have posed has been the converse of that posed by Dicey's canonical text *The Law of the Constitution*. In the first volume, the challenge was to historicize Dicey's multi-edition textbook, which, in being attributed canonical status, became viewed as a single authoritative text—'a smooth-surfaced entity known as "Dicey"'—detached from its context.[2] In this second volume, the challenge has been an ageing assortment of long-forgotten and little-known papers that happen to be Dicey's. It has been to understand, make accessible, and suggest the significance of wide-ranging, poorly ordered, and largely unpublished manuscripts.

To meet the challenge posed by the Dicey Papers, the task undertaken in this volume has been twofold. On the one side, it has been to select lecture and related manuscripts from the assortment of Papers and to arrange and reproduce them so as to create a coherent, comprehensive, and accessible whole that is true to the manuscripts and Dicey's changing overview of his lectures, insofar as is possible. On the other side, it has been to suggest and explain their significance to understanding Dicey's constitutional thought and implications for English constitutionalism as reflected in Dicey's work and developing under, or in opposition to, his influence. In this Introduction, I will seek to explain the one side of the task and carry out the other. Mindful of the timing and variation of Dicey's comparative constitutional lectures and of the formal features of the Dicey Papers, I will first explain why and how I have edited the lecture manuscripts. I will then suggest the significance of Dicey's comparative constitutional lectures for understanding Dicey's constitutional thought and their broader implications for English constitutionalism.

Dicey's Comparative Constitutional Lectures

From 1895 to 1900, and then again for a few years before his retirement from the Vinerian Professorship in 1909, Dicey delivered various courses of comparative constitutional lectures, first at Oxford but also at the London School of Econom-

---

[1] All Souls College, Oxford, Codrington Library, MS 323. In this volume they will be cited simply as the Dicey Papers.
[2] The phrase is that of S. Collini, *Public Moralists: Political Thought and Intellectual Life in Britain, 1850–1930* (Oxford: Oxford University Press, 1991), 288.

ics and later in the United States.[3] On the invitation of President Eliot of Harvard University, Dicey visited Cambridge Massachusetts in the autumn of 1898 to give lectures on the 'Development of English Law during the Nineteenth Century in connection with the Course of Public Opinion in England' and, at the same time, he delivered a course of comparative constitutional lectures at the Lowell Institute in Boston, which he had adapted from his comparative constitutional lectures for Oxford and the LSE.[4] Before his visit to the United States, Dicey's comparative constitutional lectures were centred on English constitutionalism, were entitled *The Comparative Study of the Constitution*, and approximated in content to what is published in Part I below. In the two years after his visit, Dicey's lectures became more generally comparative and less focused on English constitutionalism, were entitled *The Comparative Study of Constitutions*, and resembled what is published in Part II below.

In what Dicey called a 'sort of Diary' of his visit to the United States, he expressed the thought that both his Harvard lectures and his Lowell Institute lectures 'ought to be the foundation of readable books if I live long enough to complete them'.[5] From about 1897 Dicey had contemplated a comparative book and he was still thinking about a possible book in the summer of 1900. He dictated lectures accordingly and, in a letter to James Bryce, called their subject 'comparative constitutionalism', from which this volume's title has been derived:

> I am writing, or rather dictating, the lectures which I gave at the beginning of the Term on what I suppose one must call for want of a better name, Comparative Constitutionalism. They are dull enough. But as life gets on and one's friends die off, one gets a desire to gather together the fragments of one's work so as at least to leave evidence behind one of having tried to do something. I should like to put these lectures into not probably quite a final form but into such a shape that they might be published as remains if I die before doing more at them.[6]

---

[3] Dicey began dictating the lectures in 1894, and there is evidence in the Dicey Papers of lecture schemes for 1895. The first page of the manuscript from which the Introduction to Part I below has been derived was dated 16 November 1894. A further, four-page, manuscript headed 'Comparative Study of the Constitution: List of Papers etc' lists on its first page various lecture schemes, the first of which was dated May 1895 and the third was dated 'Oct. & Dec. 1897 (London School of Economics)' and corresponds with a similarly noted lecture schedule elsewhere in the Dicey Papers. The Dicey Papers do not contain lecture schemes or schedules, or references to such schemes or schedules, dated between 1901 and 1904, which is the period during which Dicey delivered the lectures in Oxford that were to become *Lectures on the Relation between Law and Public Opinion in England during the Nineteenth Century* (London: Macmillan, 1905), pp vii f. They contain only further lecture schemes and schedules for the Easter and Trinity Terms in 1905, 1906, and 1908 (see pp 320 ff, 333 ff below).

[4] R. S. Rait, *Memorials of Albert Venn Dicey, being chiefly Letters and Diaries* (London: Macmillan, 1925), ch. 10, especially 145. The back page of an attached bundle of lecture synopses or analyses in the Dicey Papers was dated 1 August 1898 and labelled 'Scheme for Lectures at Lowell Institute'. The bundle contains synopses under the following headings: Introduction; Nature of Comparative Study of Constitutions (see pp 169 f. below); Historical Constitutions; Flexible & Rigid Constitutions; Constitutions with Parliamentary & Non-Parliamentary Executives; Position of Judiciary under Different Constitutions; Parliamentary Government & the Party System; Parliamentarism; Remedies for Parliamentarism (see pp 137 f. below); General Conclusions.

[5] Extract, 2 November 1898, Rait, *Memorials*, n. 4 above, 159.

[6] Letter to Bryce, 4 June 1900, ibid. 184–7, especially 186. The original manuscript for this letter is not indexed as being in the James Bryce Papers, Bodleian Library, Oxford, could not be found there, and may not have survived.

Dicey did not finish and publish the book he had contemplated, but he did leave his comparative constitutional lectures in shape for posthumous publication to be possible, as he had envisaged. The melancholy, diffidence, and lack of enthusiasm expressed in his letter would seem part of the explanation for his not turning his lectures into a book. The feelings Dicey expressed in the letter, however, were attributable, in part, to the serious illness of his friend Henry Sidgwick, to whom he referred at the start of the letter and who was to die three months later.[7] That Dicey was finding his comparative constitutional lectures particularly problematic is likely. In another letter to Bryce a few years earlier, Dicey had complained of difficulties with definition in dealing with their subject, which may well, later, still have impeded his progress, dampened his enthusiasm, or reduced his confidence in their value.[8] Whether because of theoretical or methodological difficulties and/or relative lack of enthusiasm for the comparative lectures he had given, inter alia, at the Lowell Institute in Boston, Dicey did not develop them into a book, stopped working on them, and turned his attention to the Harvard course of lectures he had given on the same visit to the United States he had given his Lowell Institute lectures.[9] His Harvard course of lectures he used for similar courses at Oxford and developed into *Law and Public Opinion in England*, which was first published in 1905.[10] His comparative constitutional lectures he left unpublished but they again, under his earlier title *The Comparative Study of the Constitution*, formed the basis of courses in 1905 and 1906 and once more in 1908, the year before his retirement from the Vinerian Professorship.[11]

---

[7] Ibid.

[8] In the letter Dicey complained of how difficult it was to define what one really means by a constitution's spirit, a notion that featured prominently in various lectures published in Part I below: letter to Bryce, 16 March 1897, James Bryce Papers, Bodleian Library, Oxford, Bryce 2, fols 240–3. See pp xxiii ff below.

[9] Rait, *Memorials*, n. 4 above, 189. Richard Cosgrove, who was unaware of the Dicey Papers, mistakenly suggested that Dicey had already, in late 1897, abandoned writing a comparative constitutional book after he had encountered methodological difficulties: R. A. Cosgrove, *The Rule of Law: Albert Venn Dicey, Victorian Jurist* (Chapel Hill, NC: University of North Carolina Press, 1980), 170. If there was a particular time when Dicey turned his attention away from his comparative constitutional lectures and to the lectures that became *Law and Public Opinion in England* (n. 3 above), it is difficult to establish from the Dicey Papers when exactly it occurred. Geoffrey Hand suggested that it was after March 1901 on the evidence of the four-page manuscript headed 'Comparative Study of the Constitution: List of Papers etc' in the Dicey Papers. He called that list the 'Summer 1901 List' because the last of the materials to which it referred was dated March 1901 and because it listed on its fourth page books and other reading materials relating to Dicey's comparative project. Hand concluded that it 'seems likely that the list is of items Dicey wanted to have by him that summer' with the dominant intention of working on his comparative study: G. Hand, 'A. V. Dicey's Unpublished Materials on the Comparative Study of Constitutions' in G. Hand and J. McBride (eds), *Droit sans Frontières: Essays in Honour of L. Neville Brown* (Birmingham: Holdsworth Club, 1991), 77–93, 93. The fourth page of the manuscript, however, has the caption 'Taken by Prof. Dicey to Tun-Wells'. It was therefore a list of what were taken or had previously been taken rather than of what Dicey wanted or planned to have with him that coming summer. An alternative, more plausible, view of the manuscript is of it as a rough inventory or catalogue of papers, lecture schemes, and past reading materials that was drawn up after Dicey had stopped, or when he was about to stop, working on his comparative lectures so as to facilitate a return to them at some future point. Whether or not that view is correct, in 1900 (according to later manuscript notes to the lecture schedule from which the contents of Part II below have been derived), Dicey dictated the last of his comparative constitutional lectures in the Dicey Papers that were dictated and, later that year or in the following year, he devoted his full attention to the lectures that were to become *Law and Public Opinion in England*.

[10] *Law and Public Opinion in England*, n. 3 above, pp vii f.

[11] For the 1906 and 1908 lecture schemes, see apps VIII and IX, pp 320 ff, 333 ff below.

The Dicey Papers

In 1931, shortly before Rait entrusted the Dicey Papers to the college in his role as Dicey's literary executor, he wrote a letter to the Fellow Librarian of All Souls College. He explained that Dicey had 'himself refrained (for many years) from printing' the lectures in the Papers and added that 'I advised that they should not be printed after his death, but should be presented to the Library of All Souls for the use of any future worker who may care to consult them'.[12]

For more than fifty years, no one seems to have consulted the Dicey Papers or drawn attention to them. Richard Cosgrove in writing his biography on Dicey and initially Geoffrey Hand were unaware of their existence.[13] Credit is due to Vernon Bogdanor for discovering them when he was preparing his contribution for the All Souls-*Public Law* seminar 'Dicey and the Constitution' in 1985, the centenary of the publication of *The Law of the Constitution*'s first edition.[14] After he had consulted the Dicey Papers, he added a note to them in which he summarized their contents and concluded that the 'material in this collection seems to me of great value to students of constitutional law and constitutional history'.[15] On being informed of the Papers by Owen Hood Phillips, who had also participated in the All Souls-*Public Law* seminar, at which he would have heard Bogdanor refer to them, Hand wrote his chapter 'Dicey's Unpublished Materials on the Comparative Study of Constitutions'.[16] Hand also rearranged the Dicey Papers in accordance with a note of Dicey's own that he had found amongst them.[17] In the twenty years since then, they have attracted the attention of a few scholars,[18] their order seems to have been altered unintentionally but to an unknown extent, and they have remained largely unpublished.[19]

---

[12] Letter of R. S. Rait to C. Oman, 20 April 1931, Dicey Papers.

[13] See Cosgrove, *Albert Venn Dicey*, n. 9 above; G. Hand, 'The Book Dicey Didn't Write; or, The Subject Law Faculties Don't Teach', (1982) 7 Holdsworth Law Review 128 (Essays in Honour of Owen Hood Phillips); Hand, 'Dicey's Unpublished Materials on the Comparative Study of Constitutions', n. 9 above, 77, n.

[14] See V. Bogdanor, 'Dicey and the Reform of the Constitution' [1985] PL 652, especially 672, n. On being asked how he learnt of the existence of the Dicey Papers, Vernon Bogdanor replied as follows: 'I can't now remember. But probably the answer is this. I was asked to participate in the 1985 seminar. I therefore wrote—I suspect out of the blue—to the Codrington Library to ask if there were any Dicey papers available. I was told that there were a couple of parcels which had not been untied since Dicey's death! I really can't think of any more detail. It is the only discovery I have ever made', email exchange with the Editor, 28 January 2013. See also V. Bogdanor, 'Conclusion' in V. Bogdanor (ed.), *The British Constitution in the Twentieth Century* (Oxford: Oxford University Press, 2003), 689–720, especially 718–9; V. Bogdanor, *The New British Constitution* (Oxford: Hart, 2009), 12.

[15] Note, 29 July 1985, Dicey Papers.

[16] Note 9 above, 78, n.

[17] As reported in Hand's letter to the Librarian of All Souls College, P. S. Lewis, 16 September 1986, Dicey Papers. Hand stated elsewhere that he 'ventured to rearrange the materials themselves... very broadly according to the... plan' of the book he suggested Dicey intended to write: 'Dicey's Unpublished Materials on the Comparative Study of Constitutions', n. 9 above, 77, n.

[18] See, e.g., S. Cassese, 'Albert Venn Dicey e il diritto amministrativo' (1990) 19 Quaderni Fiorentini per la storia del pensiero giuridico moderno 5, 12 f.; M. D. Walters, 'Dicey on Writing the *Law of the Constitution*' (2011) 31 OJLS 1, 21 ff.

[19] Six were published in P. Raina (ed.), *A. V. Dicey: General Characteristics of English Constitutionalism, Six Unpublished Lectures* (New York: Peter Lang, 2009).

For various reasons, comprehensive publication of the comparative constitutional lectures in the Dicey Papers is now warranted, despite Dicey's own reluctance and Rait's advice that they only be made available to those who might wish to consult them. The historical significance of the lectures has increased greatly with the passing of more than a century since they were written. Further, apart from their value in the study of constitutional law and constitutional history as noted by Bogdanor, they amount to a pioneering venture in comparative constitutionalism, interest in which has surged in recent decades. Finally, to the extent the lectures deal with English constitutionalism, they are a fertile source with which to reconsider Dicey's constitutional thought and assess implications for the kinds of response Dicey's exposition in *The Law of the Constitution* has elicited.

The Dicey Papers kept in the Codrington Library consist of unpublished materials used for lecture courses given in various institutions over a number of years more than a century ago. Part of the challenge of editing Dicey's comparative constitutional lectures for publication is posed by their consequent formal features, five of which are of particular significance. The first and most obvious of these features is that the lectures were not previously developed into a book, remained largely unpublished in print, and were made public only in being delivered as lectures. They are therefore largely unknown and have received little critical attention. They were termed 'lectures' or 'chapters' interchangeably by Dicey, as they are in this volume, because, although only delivered as lectures, they were also seen as potential chapters of a future book.

The second formal feature of the Papers is that the manuscripts were dictated by Dicey. The lecture manuscripts were therefore in spoken rather than written English, both in being dictated and in being delivered as lectures. According to Rait, '[a]ll his books, ... and many of his letters, were dictated to Mr. Edmund North, his faithful and attached clerk for fifty years'.[20] For Dicey, dictation was necessitated by his inability to write legibly and general slowness at work attributed to a lack of muscular control and general physical deficiencies, of which there is repeated mention in Rait's *Memorials*.[21] The illegible or barely legible notes or corrections very occasionally added to the manuscripts appear to have been Dicey's own. The many legible revisions seem to have been those of his clerk or scribe. In addition, the lecture manuscript 'Historical and Non-Historical Constitutions' (incorporated as the first lecture in Part II below) was stated on its title page in a later manuscript note in red ink to have been 'Rev. by Miss C. E. S.', who was presumably his cousin Caroline Emilia Stephen, a friend from childhood,[22] and who must have helped him on occasion, as evident in the similar red notes added to the lecture scheme of Easter and Trinity Terms 1900 according to which the contents of Part II below have been derived.

The third formal feature of the Dicey Papers is heterogeneity of manuscript. They include not only lecture manuscripts, numbered and often renumbered, but also

---

[20] Rait, *Memorials*, n. 4 above, 300. See also ibid. 145, 163.
[21] See, e.g., ibid. 6, 18, 21 f., 217, 288 f.
[22] Ibid. 23.

bundles of notes, the occasional paper or unnumbered lecture manuscript, various lecture synopses or analyses, and numerous lecture schemes and schedules. The Papers appear to have been a stock of draft lecture and other materials, which Dicey developed and from which he drew in delivering his changing comparative constitutional lecture courses from 1895 to 1908.

The fourth formal feature of the Papers is wide variation in the degree to which the lecture and other manuscripts were revised or redrafted and are distinct, overlapping, or repeated. They therefore vary greatly in the extent to which they approximated to what would have been their final form had they gone to press.

The Papers' fifth formal feature is their generally disordered state, lack of overall arrangement, and assortment of internal references consisting of various headings, dates, and chapter or lecture numbers, often altered and inconsistent. When editing for this volume began, the contents of the first of the two boxes containing the Dicey Papers in the Codrington Library were in the following order: the notes of Rait, Bogdanor, and Hand, 'English Constitutionalism under George III' (undated and the third lecture of Part I below), 'Memorandum of English Party System of Government' (dated 6 August 1889 and Appendix I below), 'Introduction' (dated 16 November 1894 and preliminary to the lectures in Part I below), 'General Characteristics of Existing English Constitutionalism' (dated March 1897 and the first lecture of Part I below), miscellaneous notes to particular pages of the lecture on party government, 'Party Government' (dated July 1898 and the seventh lecture of Part I below), 'Comparison between English and Other Executives' (undated and one of the two successive lectures in Appendix II below), a stray synopsis page, an undated paper on Puritanism pages of which had been transferred elsewhere, etc. Only a very rough chronological order of contents is apparent and reflected in the fact that in the Dicey Papers manuscripts used for Part I below generally precede those used for Part II.

In view of the Papers' formal features, Geoffrey Hand had good reason to describe his attempt to establish the contents of Dicey's comparative constitutional book in his early work on the Papers as having 'the character of detective work upon successive and incomplete versions of a jigsaw puzzle'.[23]

Editorial Approach

Apart from appreciating the desirability of some formal continuity with Volume One of this edition, I have approached the task of editing the manuscripts in the Dicey Papers with three main concerns in mind. They correspond with the concerns expressed in the Editor's Introduction to Volume One but, as directed to the formal features of the Dicey Papers, they differ in emphasis, implication, and the extent to which they have been competing or contradictory. The first concern has been to keep the alteration of the original manuscripts to a minimum and to explain any significant change that has

---

[23] Hand, 'Dicey's Unpublished Materials on the Comparative Study of Constitutions', n. 9 above, 79.

been made in editing them. The originals to which fidelity has been sought, however, have not been the manuscripts in their original form when first written but the manuscripts as corrected or refined by Dicey or by his scribe on his instruction. Fidelity to the latest available form of the lecture manuscripts has been chosen, on the one hand, out of respect for the editing or improving that Dicey managed to get done with a view to possible future publication and, on the other hand, out of having to rely often on surviving lecture manuscripts in which earlier, superseded, sections had been deleted or omitted and thus become unavailable. Further, what was evidently altered by Dicey has not been recorded as such but, so as to limit distractions in the reading of the text, simply deleted and the text changed according to Dicey's alteration.

The second concern in editing this volume has been with relevance and ease of access for modern readers of unfinished and variously refined lecture manuscripts. Showing their relevance to Dicey's constitutional thought as expressed in *The Law of the Constitution* and related controversies about English constitutionalism has been one of this Introduction's main purposes. In respect of the pages below another purpose has been to ensure (for a modern reader) easy readability of unfinished lecture texts that are unencumbered by many textual distractions. Ensuring easy readability has necessitated compromise with the first concern above: for example, excluding what has remained evident but was already deleted in the original manuscripts. Further, in this volume concern with ease of access has also been to enable comprehensive access to whatever is available in the Dicey Papers that might be of relevance, use, or interest to modern readers. Comprehensive access has been sought because of the general inaccessibility of the Papers, the substantial uncertainty about what Dicey would have included in a comparative constitutional book had he produced one, and the reason he once gave for why he was dictating his comparative constitutional lectures, namely to leave them as 'fragments' of his work in shape for posthumous publication, which is how he left many of them.[24]

The third concern in editing this volume has been with thematic coherence. That concern, however, has not been with the pedagogical or educational themes of the first volume of this edition. Whereas some formal consistency with the first volume's presentation has been sought, the substantive thematic coherence with which this volume has been concerned is, on the one hand, the significance of Dicey's comparative constitutional lectures for understanding Dicey's constitutional thought and the kinds of response it has elicited. It is, on the other hand, the coherence to be found in the varying schemes of the comparative constitutional courses Dicey gave and the book he contemplated at different times.

The main editorial decision was for two schemes of Dicey's comparative constitutional lectures to be published, one in Part I, the other in Part II. The first scheme consists of a complete set of fully written lectures, is entitled *The Comparative Study of the Constitution*, and predates Dicey's 1898 visit to the United States, when he lectured at the Lowell Institute. The second scheme consists of an incomplete set of

---

[24] Letter to Bryce, 4 June 1900, Rait, *Memorials*, n. 4 above, 184–7, especially 186. See pp vii f. above.

fully written lectures, is entitled *The Comparative Study of Constitutions*, and postdates his visit. My approach has differed from that of Geoffrey Hand who, in his contribution to the *Festschrift* for L. Neville Brown ('Dicey's Unpublished Materials on the Comparative Study of Constitutions'), speculated so as to establish a 'plausible table of contents' for the single book Dicey would have settled on had he finished it.[25] That approach has not been adopted here for various reasons. What comparative book Dicey would or might have finished is highly uncertain and also unascertainable because Dicey did not come sufficiently close to finishing it. At most, when he was dictating several comparative constitutional lectures both in 1897 and in 1900, he contemplated publication at some future point, either before or after his death. Further, Dicey contemplated two, clearly distinguishable, basic lecture schemes—one before and one after his 1898 visit to the United States—which overlapped to a minimal extent.[26] To select one scheme would not have enabled access to the other, and to combine both would not have been true to either. Therefore, both have been included below: the one kept distinct in Part I, the other in Part II, and each entitled as in each of Dicey's two basic lecture schemes.

The versions of the two lecture schemes that have been selected for publication are the schemes, from those available in the Dicey Papers, that were in date the last, and therefore presumably the most developed, in each of the two periods, one before and one immediately after his visit to the United States, when Dicey dictated various lectures as chapters, contemplated a book, and came closest to producing one. The first scheme has been derived from the second page (entitled 'Old forms of Mss Lectures') of the four-page manuscript in the Dicey Papers headed 'Comparative Study of the Constitution: List of Papers etc'. The scheme was not dated but was presumably originally compiled in late 1898 or 1899 because it lists lectures dated to have been written mainly in 1897 but also as late as August 1898. Hand's considerable contribution was to identify the importance of that four-page manuscript to understanding the Dicey Papers.[27] The second scheme of lectures published in Part II below has been derived from a manuscript lecture schedule headed 'Easter & Trinity Terms 1900: Comparative Study of Constitutions', which recorded in later manuscript notes in red ink that all the full lecture texts in Part II below had been written in 1900, itself dates back to that year, and is as such the last lecture schedule available in the Dicey Papers before Dicey turned his attention away from his comparative constitutional lectures.

The Dicey Papers contain many lecture synopses or analyses (including reading lists), from which Dicey lectured unless and until replaced by full lecture texts.[28] Still

---

[25] Note 9 above, especially 78.

[26] On the interface of Dicey's two schemes, the lectures 'Party Government' and 'Parliamentarism' illustrate overlap. They were listed on the second page of the four-page manuscript entitled 'Comparative Study of the Constitution: List of Papers etc' under 'Old forms' of his lectures from which the contents of Part I below have been derived. The same or similar lectures were also part of the scheme for Dicey's lectures on *The Comparative Study of Constitutions* at the Lowell Institute (see n. 4 above).

[27] 'Dicey's Unpublished Materials on the Comparative Study of Constitutions', n. 9 above, 93.

[28] As Dicey indicated in a letter to Bryce, 16 March 1897, Bryce Papers, n. 8 above, MS Bryce 2, fols 240–3.

reproduced after a full lecture text had been written,[29] and occasionally copied almost exactly from those for a previous course, they may well have also been for direct student use. For various reasons, they have been incorporated below (together with their reading lists, here published not before analyses, as in the original manuscripts, but after them). Where lectures were not fully written, they are the record of their contents. Where lectures were fully written, they facilitate overall understanding of the lecture texts, much in the way that Dicey's marginal notes have facilitated understanding of *The Law of the Constitution*, only more necessarily here because numerous lecture texts were left unrefined. They are entitled 'Analyses' below because Dicey used the term 'Analysis' to entitle their equivalent at the start of his new Introduction to *The Law of the Constitution*'s eighth edition.[30] By 'analysis' is meant a synopsis or statement of the complex resolved into simple elements, or into simpler and more accessible components. Analyses have been derived from manuscripts that approximated in date, insofar as has been possible and dates ascertainable, to their accompanying lecture texts, corresponding lecture schemes, or the substantial redrafting of lecture texts where that is evident. Where a full lecture text has not been available, two Analyses from different schemes have been provided, if available, so as to give a better idea of the lecture's content. The particular manuscripts from which both full lecture texts and Analyses have been derived are explained in footnotes on their title pages as published below.

The Appendix has been compiled to provide easy access to lecture texts and other materials (including Analyses, Notes, and Dicey's last two lecture schemes) that were not incorporated in the lecture scheme and lecture schedule from which the contents of Parts I and II respectively have been derived. The materials have been selected for two main reasons: first, because their general availability would seem important and their content illuminating or revealing and, secondly, because they may have been incorporated in the comparative book Dicey contemplated but did not complete. For, example, the first item in the Appendix, which has been arranged in chronological order insofar as that order has been ascertained, is Dicey's 'Memorandum on English Party System of Government', dated 6 August 1889 on the manuscript's title page. In the Memorandum, Dicey subjected the party system to radical early criticism and advocated a modified form of referendum as a corrective to its evils.[31] His advocacy preceded that which he expressed in his 1890 article in the *Contemporary Review*—confirming him as the referendum's 'first English advocate'—and remains relevant to current debates about recourse to a referendum in Britain.[32] Also included in the Appendix are Notes, which reveal, for example, the extent to which Dicey actually admired French *droit administratif* and was ignorant of the English

---

[29] See, e.g., the 1908 scheme of lectures, app. IX, pp 333 ff below.
[30] See *The Oxford Edition of Dicey*, i, *The Law of the Constitution*, 417 f.
[31] See pp 270 ff below.
[32] Bogdanor, 'Dicey and the Reform of the Constitution', n. 14 above, especially 658; A. V. Dicey, 'Ought the Referendum to be Introduced into England?' (1890) 57 *Contemporary Review* 489. See generally R. Weill, 'Dicey was not Diceyan' [2003] CLJ 474.

prerogative writs,[33] and which, together with the Analyses and lecture schemes and texts as drafted and redrafted, illustrate the stages in Dicey's production of his principal works.[34] Further, in recognition of Volume One's educational theme, a list of questions for students has been included, illustrating Dicey's pedagogic preoccupation with questions of meaning, historical comparison, and jurisdictional contrast, as well as his liberal educational expectation that students assess for themselves the merits and demerits of institutions.[35]

Apart from the main decisions on this volume's contents, lesser editorial decisions have been made regarding punctuation, capitalization, and the ordering of headings, which vary greatly in the manuscripts. These have been standardized in the texts published below for ease of comprehension, and thus of access to readers. They were mostly not Dicey's but the punctuation, capitalization, and headings of his scribe to whom he dictated and, as such, were subject to minimal oversight and seem seldom to have been subsequently corrected by Dicey or on his instruction. Standardization would, further, have occurred in the editing of the texts for publication. In determining what to standardize, relevant considerations have been readability, continuity with Volume One, and keeping departures from the original texts to a minimum. Further, such departures have been restricted for reasons particular to punctuation and capitalization in the Dicey Papers. An attempt has been made to retain, in places, punctuation that reflects the spoken character of Dicey's lectures, dictated and delivered as lectures, such as the frequent comma before a conjunction, grammatically intrusive but suggesting a pause for breath and/or rhetorical emphasis on a final point to be added. Dicey's own capitalization, as evident in the editions of *The Law of the Constitution* that were published in his lifetime, express his own, late-nineteenth century, basic judgements of value and institutional importance, such as the capitalization of King, Courts, and Parliament, as of Parliamentary sovereignty, and has therefore been retained. To avoid a text full of unusual and unattractive markings that would distract and annoy readers, alteration of punctuation, capitalization, and the ordering of headings has been bracketed only in cases of significant doubt about Dicey's intended meaning. All word changes, however, as apparent departures from Dicey's dictated words, which may be more than alterations of the scribe's record, have been bracketed.

The Implications and Significance of Dicey's Comparative Constitutional Lectures

For decades, Dicey constitutional thought has been commonly understood through the reading, teaching, and later recollection of *The Law of the Constitution*. As shown in Volume One,[36] the main responses to it have varied in orientation and have usually

---

[33] App. VI, pp 307 ff below.
[34] See Rait, *Memorials*, n. 4 below, 88 f.
[35] App. V. See Allison (ed.), *The Oxford Edition of Dicey*, i, *The Law of the Constitution*, pp xxi ff.
[36] See Allison (ed.), *The Oxford Edition of Dicey*, i, *The Law of the Constitution*, pp xvi ff.

been of one or more of the following kinds. Commentators have responded, first, to Dicey's method: usually either to what is seen as his analytical, scientific, or Austinian formalism or to what is seen as his highly questionable use of comparative and historical materials to abstract, explain, and illustrate the legal principles in *The Law of the Constitution*'s classificatory scheme of sets and distinctions. Commentators have responded, secondly, by criticizing Dicey's institutional focus—his preoccupation with Parliament and the common law courts and his relative inattention to government. Thirdly, both approving and critical responses have been oriented to Dicey's main constitutional principles, namely parliamentary sovereignty and the rule of law, the second of which has long been the subject of debate, and the first of which has more recently become so. Fourthly, responses have been oriented to the relationship between Dicey's constitutional thought as expressed in *The Law of the Constitution* and its context, either when Dicey's book was first published or, in later decades, when the principles that it retained largely unchanged in edition after edition continued to be applied, readily accepted, or treated as axiomatic despite many changes to law and government. Dicey's comparative constitutional lectures have implications for each of these kinds of response to his constitutional thought as expressed in *The Law of the Constitution*.

Dicey's Method

Mere inspection of this volume's wide-ranging contents, which cover various kinds of constitutionalism in the present and from the past—English, American, French, Prussian, and that of the English Commonwealth—as well as the functioning (or failing) of governing institutions through representative government, parliamentarism, party government, types of executive, etc, dispels any sense that Dicey's constitutional method was restricted to the abstraction of principles and their authoritative presentation in an Austinian analytical or classificatory scheme of sets and distinctions. Dicey's concern to classify is apparent but seemingly confined to his lectures 'Historical and Non-Historical Constitutions' and 'Divisions of Constitutions'.[37] Rather, this volume's contents would suggest that Dicey devoted much attention to comparative and historical context and that, in differentiating kinds of constitutionalism, appreciated by implication the societal and historical contingency of constitutional arrangements. Further, in *The Law of the Constitution*, Dicey's method was profoundly affected by his educational concerns and mission, expressed in his Inaugural Lecture, to implement a compromise by which English law was to be taught at the universities but university legal education and related professorial legal literature were to be tailored to the pressing, residual, educational needs of practitioners in legal practice.[38] In delivering his comparative constitutional lectures in

---

[37] Pt. II below, lects 1, 5.
[38] 'Can English Law be Taught at the Universities?', *The Oxford Edition of Dicey*, i, *The Law of the Constitution*, app. I. See Editor's Introduction, ibid., pp xxiv ff, xxxiv ff.

university courses and contemplating their publication, however, Dicey widened or went beyond his educational mission.[39] Dicey's multi-edition textbook *The Law of the Constitution* and general professorial success may well have helped both to build and to maintain the 'very narrow ledge' for university law teachers to stand on, but it was a ledge that became wider than it has been taken to be or was one on which Dicey himself did not always stand.[40] His comparative constitutional lectures derive some of their significance from the extent to which and the relative success or failure with which, at the time, Dicey left that ledge or stood on one of its edges in promoting, using, and teaching a broad comparative-constitutional method appreciative of societal and historical contingency.

Dicey's comparative constitutional lectures do not shed much further light on his historical method. In being intended and presented as the outcome of the comparative, not the historical, method,[41] they provide little with which to contradict William Holdsworth's view that Dicey's 'gifts as a legal historian were equal to his gifts as a lawyer'[42] or, apart from his carelessness about crucial dates,[43] to confirm Richard Cosgrove's view that Dicey dispensed with detailed historical research and imposed a reductionist legal method on historical materials.[44] They do, however, illustrate Dicey's comparative method and afford much further evidence upon which to focus and with which to avoid assessing his method solely on the basis of his flawed treatment of French *droit administratif* (in using it for pedagogical reasons to demonstrate by way of contrast the English rule of law and its value in *The Law of the Constitution*).[45] In his comparative constitutional lectures, Dicey first vigorously promoted the value of the comparative method and then, in an early and innovative comparative venture, confronted and grappled with a few of its basic problems, which may still seem all too familiar to comparativists now.

As in *The Law of the Constitution*, where Dicey initially demarcated the true nature of constitutional law by distinguishing legal, historical, and political views of the constitution,[46] Dicey introduced the comparative method by distinguishing it from

---

[39] In a letter to Bryce, Dicey stated that he was considering making the spirit of the constitution the subject of the last three or four lectures in his course *The Comparative Study of the Constitution* to 'give some variety to myself, rather than to my pupils': 16 March 1897, Bryce Papers, n. 8 above, MS Bryce 2, fols 240–3. Dicey may have widened, or went beyond, his educational mission as much for his own sake as for that of his students.

[40] See generally D. Sugarman, 'Legal Theory, the Common Law Mind and the Making of the Textbook Tradition' in W. Twining (ed.), *Legal Theory and Common Law* (Oxford: Basil Blackwell, 1986), 26–61, 29 ff, 48 ff, especially 33.

[41] 'Introduction', pp 3 ff below.

[42] W. S. Holdsworth, 'Charles Viner and the Abridgments of English Law', Inaugural Lecture, All Souls College, 25 November 1922, (1923) 39 LQR 17, 19.

[43] See, e.g., 'Constitutionalism of the Commonwealth', pp 49 f., 57 below.

[44] Albert Venn Dicey, n. 9 above, especially ch. 8.

[45] See generally Allison (ed), *The Oxford Edition of Dicey*, i, *The Law of the Constitution*, pp xvii f., xxxv f.; R. Errera, 'Dicey and French Administrative Law: A Missed Encounter?' [1985] PL 695; J. W. F. Allison, *A Continental Distinction in the Common Law: A Historical and Comparative Perspective on English Public Law*, rev. pbk. edn (Oxford: Oxford University Press, 2000), 18–23. See the praise for Dicey's treatment of Swiss federalism and the depth of his innovative insight into 'the cultural conditions of constitutional law' in D. A. Brühlmeier, 'Dicey and the Swiss Constitution' [1985] PL 708, especially 711.

[46] *The Oxford Edition of Dicey*, i, *The Law of the Constitution*, 9 ff.

the analytical and the historical methods at the start of his course *The Comparative Study of the Constitution*. The comparative method he described as 'the elucidating of existing institutions or laws and in our case of the English constitution by comparison with analogous institutions or laws which have existed in other times or which now exist in other lands', or even with institutions that have not had 'an actual historical life' but have been 'constructed by the fancy of philosophers or poets'.[47] For Dicey, comparison was thus to be both historical and non-historical and, although it could only supplement the analytical and historical methods, it had 'immense recommendations of its own'.[48] These included, on the one hand, the illumination of what in one's own institutions escapes notice because it is customary, enabling erroneous views to be dispelled, and, on the other hand, 'the discovery of new affinities and new dissimilarities between different constitutions', enabling reclassification according to 'new principles'.[49] Dicey argued, further, that the comparative method suggested 'general conclusions' as well, relating, for example, to 'the true importance of constitutional arrangements' and variability of the institution that becomes the embodiment of the will of the nation.[50]

In his introductory lecture to *The Comparative Study of the Constitution*, Dicey explained that he was concerned to do more than just compare institutions or laws and that it was 'more profitable to compare the conceptions or ideas which underlie political arrangements'.[51] To do so, he developed the notion of the spirit of a constitution or of its institutions, which he initially identified with and seems to have derived from Montesquieu's notion of *l'esprit des lois*.[52] For Dicey, the spirit of institutions was essential to understanding, for example, the Queen's measure of influence or the authority accorded to the German Emperor. The difficulties with definition, however—of which Dicey complained in his letter to James Bryce (mentioned above) and which may have contributed to his loss of confidence in, or relative lack of enthusiasm for, a comparative book—were with defining what one really means by a constitution's 'spirit'.[53]

Dicey returned to that notion of a constitution's spirit in his third lecture of *The Comparative Study of the Constitution* to clarify the extent of underlying differences despite apparent resemblances between constitutionalism under George III and constitutionalism then existing under Queen Victoria. Dicey had already become aware of the difficulty in defining the term 'spirit', which he both acknowledged and emphasized. He claimed that few 'things are more difficult of definition'.[54] He had

---

[47] 'Introduction', p. 6 below.
[48] Ibid, pp 6 f.
[49] Ibid, p. 11.
[50] Ibid, pp 13 ff, especially 13. For Dicey's later treatment of the advantages of the comparative method, see his Analysis incorporated as the Introduction to *The Comparative Study of Constitutions*, p. 169 f. below.
[51] 'Introduction', p. 6 below.
[52] In a letter to Bryce, Dicey stated that he took the spirit of a constitution to be 'nearly equivalent' to Montesquieu's notion: 16 March 1897, Bryce Papers, n. 8 above, MS Bryce 2, fols 240–3.
[53] Ibid.
[54] 'English Constitutionalism under George III', p. 70 below.

also become aware that his notion of a constitution's spirit was different from Montesquieu's, which he therefore expressly distinguished. For Dicey, the term 'spirit' did not mean 'the end or final cause for which a constitution, or laws, or institutions generally exist or may be supposed to exist', which is the meaning he supposed Montesquieu had attributed to it.[55] Dicey's understanding of Montesquieu was limited. Montesquieu, through his emphasis on the relation between a people's laws and the variety of factors affecting a people such as 'the nature and the principle of the government', 'the climate', 'the properties of the terrain', 'the way of life of the peoples', etc., envisaged the spirit of the laws not as their end, final cause, or purpose but what today might be called the spirit of a society to which its laws should conform.[56] In contrast, with the term 'spirit of the constitution', Dicey referred 'to the way in which the persons of a given time look upon their institutions, the way in which they expect them to work or assume that they will work'.[57] For Dicey, the spirit of institutions was, in short, 'the subjective side of their working'.[58] He admitted that the term 'spirit' was 'an extremely vague one' but stressed that it conveyed 'a notion as indefinite as it is important'.[59]

In the lecture 'English Constitutionalism under George III' and in later lectures, Dicey applied his notion of a constitution's spirit to English, French, and Prussian constitutionalism of the late-nineteenth century. Dicey identified the spirit of the institutions of the English constitution (as he called it), commonly looked upon 'from a legal point of view', as legal and contrasted it, on the one hand, with the civil administrative spirit of the institutions of French constitutionalism and, on the other hand, with the military spirit of the institutions of Prussian constitutionalism, looked upon 'from the point of view of soldiers'.[60] For Dicey, the English constitution was viewed from the perspective of a people with 'a legal turn of mind', 'imbued with legalism and who import into their political arrangements that love of precedent and acquiescence in fictions which is proper to the law courts'.[61] Through 'a love for forms and precedents' the English constitution was characterized by formal, often fictitious, continuities.[62] Dicey characterized French constitutionalism by its 'administration carried on by civilians in a civil spirit and not an administration modelled on the principles of an army'.[63] He distinguished it by reference to the civil, 'authoritative and centralized'

---

[55] Ibid.

[56] Montesquieu, *The Spirit of the Laws* (A. M. Cohler, B. C. Miller, and H. S. Stone (eds and trs)) (Cambridge: Cambridge University Press, 1989), bk. 1, ch. 3, 8 f.

[57] 'English Constitutionalism under George III', p. 70 below.

[58] Ibid. In its emphasis on the subjective—the attitude of a people towards their institutions—Dicey's notion of spirit was closer to the nineteenth-century Germanic notion of the *Volksgeist* than it was to Montesquieu's notion.

[59] Ibid.

[60] Ibid.

[61] 'Historical Constitutions and Non-Historical Constitutions', pp 182, 181 f. below.

[62] Ibid., p. 182. Dicey's main example was 'the fiction that in 1649 Charles II immediately succeeded Charles I': ibid., p. 178. See pp xliii f. below.

[63] 'French Constitutionalism', especially p. 92 below. For a different but comparable emphasis on French 'sentiments or convictions of which French history is, in the main, the cause', see 'Why Universal Suffrage Suits France', app. VII, especially p. 316 below.

character of its administration and the width of that administration's executive, legislative, and judicial powers, through the exercise of the last of which administrative courts developed *droit administratif*.[64] In contrast, Dicey characterized the Prussian constitutionalism in the reign of King Wilhelm I by its unified, hierarchical, and disciplined administrative *corps* of soldier citizens who, as citizens, were subject to compulsory military service, and were headed by the King as a real, militarily trained, Commander-in-chief to whom they were subservient by oath of allegiance.[65]

Dicey used the notion of a constitution's spirit to emphasize the importance of the subjective—the attitudes of a people to their institutions—principally but not solely in comparing English, French, and Prussian constitutionalism. He did not similarly refer to the spirit of the Constitution of the United States but he did emphasize the crucial importance of 'the feelings which produced the Constitution', which 'in turn fostered and increased the feelings to which the Constitution owed its birth' and thus achieved 'the gradual predominance of national sentiment' that Dicey suggested was 'the ultimate cause of the prosperity of the Union'.[66] His emphasis on the subjective was not confined to national contrasts but also featured prominently in his explanation of why not only a Parliament but '[a]ny institution whatever may become the embodiment of a nation'.[67]

Dicey's notion of a constitution's spirit was left largely unrefined and now seems quaintly metaphysical. His general use of it, further, to attribute collective attitudes to entire peoples in a stark, monolithic, national contrast of the constitutionalism of England with that of Prussia and that of France now appears oversimplified and overstated. Suspect and unconvincing, it illustrates a late-nineteenth-century nationalist outlook and is contradicted by the extensive interaction of legal systems recognized in more recent scholarship.[68] Dicey's treatment of a constitution's spirit was a product of its time, but he was using it in an attempt to go beyond the superficial comparison of laws and institutions and to grasp the ideas underlying them and the social attitudes towards them. Whereas he looked to a constitution's spirit, comparativists today might look to legal or constitutional culture. He encountered problems, as do comparativists today in many of their uses of legal culture—whether assuming uniformity and continuity, pretending to explain but invoking a notion of culture that is itself in need of explanation, or suggesting an environment of attitudes that might be most influential when unnoticed and barely open to enquiry.[69] Further,

---

[64] 'French Constitutionalism', especially p. 92 below.
[65] 'Prussian Constitutionalism', pp 110 ff below.
[66] 'General Conclusions', p. 156 below. See also Dicey's elaboration on the legal spirit of federalism exemplified in the USA, *The Oxford Edition of Dicey*, i, *The Law of the Constitution* 92 ff.
[67] 'General Conclusions' pp 161 ff below, especially 161.
[68] For a critical elaboration on the role of all three spirits—the legal, the civil administrative, and the military—in the development of English legal and constitutional thought through European interaction during the twentieth century, see J. W. F. Allison, 'The Spirits of the Constitution' in N. Bamforth and P. Leyland (eds), *Accountability in the Contemporary Constituton* (Oxford: Oxford University Press, 2013) 27–56.
[69] See generally R. Cotterrell, *Law, Culture and Society: Legal Ideas in the Mirror of Social Theory* (Aldershot: Ashgate, 2006), especially ch. 5; J. S. Bell, *French Legal Cultures* (Cambridge: Cambridge University Press, 2001); D. Nelken (ed.), *Comparing Legal Cultures* (Aldershot: Dartmouth, 1997).

in his treatment of a constitution's spirit, Dicey's elaboration on the importance of attitudes towards institutions (although not his collective attribution of them to entire peoples) may usefully be understood in modern terms as a rudimentary and undeveloped antecedent of Lon Fuller's elaboration on the importance of supportive attitudes, convictions, and understandings to the conduct of law as a purposeful enterprise and their centrality to what Fuller regarded as the implicit law upon which explicit or made law depends.[70]

Dicey confronted and grappled not only with the notion of a constitution's spirit that was comparable to a modern notion of constitutional culture. He also did so with the problem of transplanting constitutional ideas or mechanisms, as had Montesquieu. In developing his notion of the spirit of the laws, Montesquieu had drawn attention to the hazards of legal transplantation. After making an initial concession to natural lawyers by declaring that law 'in general is human reason insofar as it governs all the peoples of the earth', he had immediately particularized that reason by adding that 'the political and civil laws of each nation should be only the particular cases to which human reason is applied'.[71] Montesquieu had suggested that successful transplantation was hazardous or extremely unlikely because, in the application of reason to particular societies, laws should conform to the variety of factors that together constitute 'the spirit of the laws', such as 'the nature and the principle of the government', 'the climate', 'the properties of the terrain', etc.[72]

In the last two lectures of *The Comparative Study of the Constitution*, Dicey showed a concern with the problem of legal transplantation similar to Montesquieu's but did not relate it specifically to his notion of a constitution's spirit. Rather, he explained the problem of legal transplantation in terms of civic virtue. In his lecture on 'Parliamentarism', which he presented as a 'newly discovered political disease' characterized by parliamentary factions and their discrediting of parliamentary government, Dicey suggested how the referendum might help cure the disease but warned against 'any mechanical change' through its introduction.[73] His reason was that constitutional changes could have only a limited effect because 'the working of constitutions depends at bottom upon the character of the citizens among whom they exist'.[74] In

---

[70] See, e.g., L. L. Fuller, *The Morality of Law*, rev. edn (New Haven: Yale University Press, 1969), 145; L. L. Fuller, *Anatomy of Law* (New York: Praeger, 1968), 91 ff. See generally J. W. F. Allison, 'Legal Culture in Fuller's Analysis of Adjudication' in W. J. Witteveen and W. van der Burg (eds), *Rediscovering Fuller: Essays on Implicit Law and Institutional Design* (Amsterdam: Amsterdam University Press, 1999), 346–63, especially 356 f.

[71] *Spirit of the Laws*, n. 56 above, bk. 1, ch. 3, 8.

[72] Ibid. 8 f.

[73] 'Parliamentarism', especially pp 139, 150 below.

[74] Ibid., p. 150. Benjamin Jowett, Dicey's Tutor at Balliol College, Oxford, was reported to have asked another Balliol student (Hilaire Belloc) the question '[u]nder what form of government is the state of man at its best?' This question was described by Belloc as 'always uppermost' in Jowett's mind and one 'which he believed all young men should consider'. To Belloc's reply, 'a Republic', Jowett answered '[y]ou cannot have a Republic without Republicans'. To Belloc, Jowett's answer was 'for terseness and truth and a certain quality of *revelation*...worthy of Aristotle': H. Belloc, *The Cruise of the 'Nona'* (London: Constable, 1925), 56. Jowett's view of the dependence of a republican form of government on the republican virtues of its people may well have made a similarly strong impression on Dicey, who referred to the democratic desire 'to found a Republic without Republicans' (p. 35 below) and expressed great indebtedness to Jowett for guiding him in the right direction and profoundly affecting

his following, concluding, lecture to *The Comparative Study of the Constitution*, he spelt out what he suggested was effectively a moral obstacle to successful constitutional transplantation—the want of appropriate civic virtues—which would result in only poor imitation:

> The institutions of the United States and of other countries have great merits, but they assuredly will not give to uncivilized or half-civilized people the virtues of Englishmen or of American citizens. The idea, for example, that the Federation of the United States can be transplanted to Spanish South America and there create a nation as powerful and orderly as the United States is an absurdity. The notion that the English constitution which is the product of very peculiar historical conditions would suit every country of civilized Europe is one of those delusions which is not ridiculous only because it has possessed the minds and guided the policy of statesmen otherwise entitled to deep respect…Wherever you find a good constitution that works well there you may be certain that there exists a people many of whom are endowed with high civic virtues.[75]

Dicey expressed his appreciation of the obstacle to successful constitutional transplantation in his conclusion that, if the constitution is seen as 'the vestment of a nation', a 'suit of armour will not change a weakling into a warrior, but the strength of a giant may be rendered useless by a strait waistcoat'.[76]

Readers have reason to regard Dicey's words in the lengthy passage quoted above as prejudiced and chauvinistic in their claim to superiority in civic virtue of what he conceived as the people of the civilized world. His words express views of the late-nineteenth century and were only partially ameliorated by a degree of relativism in his understanding of virtues as particular to peoples and by his emphasis on the 'very peculiar historical conditions' that produced the English constitution and thus rendered its general transplantation 'ridiculous'.[77] His emphasis on civic virtue illustrates or confirms his credentials as a public moralist,[78] made his analysis of transplantation unduly reductionist, and compares unfavourably with Montesquieu's account of the variety of factors that together constitute the spirit of the laws, to which the laws of a nation should conform, and which therefore render transplantation hazardous.[79] Dicey, however, has not been alone in emphasizing particular obstacles to legal or constitutional transplantation. Well before him Montesquieu had himself stressed the environmental obstacles to transplantation, and well after him Otto Kahn-Freund, at the height of the Cold War, stressed the importance of political obstacles to transplantation. Kahn-Freund argued that, through a process of 'political differentiation'

---

the course of his life: Rait, *Memorials*, n. 4 above, 27 f. Dicey once commented that it was through the Oxford tutorial system that students 'may carry away in their thoughts the truths, or at any rate the doctrines, which the tutor wishes to impress upon them': A. V. Dicey, 'Law Teaching, Oral and Written' in H. H. Henson (ed.), *A Memoir of the Right Honourable Sir William Anson* (Oxford: Oxford University Press, 1920), 84–101, especially 88.

[75] 'General Conclusions', pp 153 f. below. For examples of poor imitation, see 'Divisions of Constitutions', pp 241 f. below; 'Comparison between English Executive and other Executives', app. II, p. 280 below.
[76] 'General Conclusions', p. 156 below.
[77] Ibid., p. 153.
[78] See Collini, *Public Moralists*, n. 2 above, 287 ff.
[79] *Spirit of the Laws*, n. 56 above, bk. 1, ch. 3, 8 (see p. xxvi above).

and 'economic, social, cultural assimilation', the political—the proximity of relationship between transplant and power structure—had become more important than the environmental.[80] Dicey's own analysis serves as a reminder of the danger of reductionism in approaching transplantation and of the advantage of broad appreciation of the various features of a context that modern concepts of legal or constitutional culture facilitates. Dicey deserves credit, however, for at least confronting, more than a century ago, the problem of simply transplanting constitutions or constitutional ideas, which has contributed to many a constitutional failure since then. Further, in grappling with the problem of transplanting constitutional ideas, he was recognizing their contingency. Those who derive from Dicey's textbook *The Law of the Constitution* authority for constitutional ideas of universal or general validity need to address Dicey's own understanding of their contingency, expressed in his advocacy and use of the comparative method in his comparative constitutional lectures.

Within what Dicey in the nineteenth century assumed to be the civilized world, his whig historical and comparative references were far less celebratory of the English constitution than their equivalent in *The Law of the Constitution*.[81] Dicey showed greater objectivity and, adhering more consistently to an external, comparative, point of view,[82] he sought mainly to use comparison so as better to understand and assess variation in institutional or constitutional design. His fierce criticism in his lecture 'Party Government' was focused on the working of the English party system, and in his other lectures Dicey expressed high praise, at times, for Swiss, American, French, and Prussian people and for their institutions. Apart from his favouring of the Swiss referendum, Dicey emphasized the education and intelligence of the Swiss,[83] praised the Constitutional Convention in the United States as 'the very best form of law-making by the people',[84] described the French constitutions as 'typical products of French genius',[85] and admired Prussian constitutionalism for establishing good government, administrative efficiency, and German unity.[86] Assertions of English institutional superiority were not absent from his comparative constitutional lectures,[87] but they were fewer and less prominent than in *The Law of the Constitution* and were

---

[80] 'On Uses and Misuses of Comparative Law' (1974) 37 MLR 1, especially 8.

[81] On Dicey's whig history, see generally J. W. F. Allison, *The English Historical Constitution: Continuity, Change and European Effects* (Cambridge: Cambridge University Press, 2007), 165–84.

[82] Cf. Dicey's oscillation between internal and external points of view in furthering his legal educational purposes in *The Law of the Constitution*: Allison (ed.), *The Oxford Edition of Dicey*, i, *The Law of the Constitution*, pp xl ff.

[83] See, e.g., 'Representative Government', p. 227 below; 'Divisions of Constitutions', p. 242 below.

[84] 'American Constitutionalism', pp 86 ff, especially p. 86.

[85] 'French Constitutionalism', p. 95 below.

[86] 'Prussian Constitutionalism', especially pp 107 ff below. Dicey also supported Otto von Bismarck's stance in the constitutional conflict of 1862–6 between the Prussian Crown and Parliament: ibid., pp 116 ff.

[87] See, e.g., his assertion that the 'truth is that the constitutions of every civilized nation are at the present day all of them copies, though often poor copies, of the British constitution' and his claim that it 'is not...the English constitution which has made England strong, independent, and prosperous, but the English constitution which is the result of the independence and the vigour of the people of England': 'Historical and Non-Historical Constitutions', pp 183, 187 below.

supplemented by significant praise for the people and institutions of at least certain other countries.

In using the comparative method in his lectures, Dicey was developing, and encouraging his students to develop, comparative insights and subtlety. For example, he repeatedly drew attention to essential differences between constitutions despite apparent resemblances,[88] and was able nonetheless to appreciate instances of what would today be called constitutional convergence.[89] He also seemed to grasp and begin to use a notion approximating to that of an ideal type or model.[90] In his concluding chapter to *The Comparative Study of the Constitution*, he distinguished between 'three types of constitutionalism'—parliamentary, democratic, and monarchical—but recognized that they 'tend at times to blend one with the other'.[91] He explained that these three types 'though essentially different, tend to shade off into one another and one may easily find countries as to which one may fairly doubt whether they are governed on the parliamentary, the democratic, or the monarchical system'.[92] Further, in his lecture 'Ancient Constitutionalism and Modern Constitutionalism' he presented the objection to the 'merely chronological division of history' as follows: 'This objection is, in effect, that periods chronologically remote may be really analogous and that eras chronologically near to each other may have no real analogy to one another, and hence that the chronological division into ancient and modern conceals the essential similarities between corresponding periods of history'.[93] Dicey was developing an appreciation of the notion of an ideal type in respect of geographical or jurisdictional as well as historical comparison.

For the modern comparativist, Dicey's method illustrates a surprising degree of methodological sensitivity in deriving comparative insights, more than a century ago, and in confronting problems that remain familiar in modern comparative work. At the same time, various features of Dicey's comparative method now appear quaint, peculiar, or unusual. Those that now appear so include his notion of a constitution's spirit, the strength of his emphasis on the dependence of a constitution on the moral qualities or civic virtues of a nation's people, and his reliance on only a few sources in striking contrast to the mass of comparative material now available in our globalized age of easy publication and information overload. Further apparent peculiarities are the equivalence of his treatment of historical and geographical or jurisdictional comparison,[94] and an important borrowing from private law in comparative constitutional

---

[88] See, e.g., 'Prussian Constitutionalism', pp 119 ff below; 'General Conclusions', pp 156 ff below.

[89] See, e.g., his observation that 'the constitutions of England and of France tend towards increased resemblance': 'French Constitutionalism', p. 102 below, and that 'on the whole written or enacted constitutions are gradually superseding unwritten or conventional constitutions': 'General Conclusions', p. 157 below.

[90] See generally M. Weber, '"Objectivity" in Social Science and Social Policy' (first published in German in 1904) in E. A. Shils and H. A. Finch (eds and trs), *The Methodology of the Social Sciences* (New York: The Free Press, 1949), 49–112, especially 89 ff. See also Allison, *Continental Distinction in the Common Law*, n. 45 above, 31–3.

[91] 'General Conclusions', pp 158, 159 below.

[92] Ibid., p. 158.

[93] p. 202 below.

[94] See, e.g., the lectures 'Constitutionalism of the Commonwealth', 'English Constitutionalism under George III', and 'Comparison between English Executive and other Executives (continued)' (app. II, lect. 5).

law. For Dicey in his comparative constitutional lectures, the value of the historical method was comparative: 'Half the instructiveness of the historical method is that inquiry into the past compels us to realise the difference between it and the present. History is comparison, though comparison need not be history. The historical method is at its best an illustration of the comparative method.'[95] Dicey's treatment of the past was accordingly also the treatment of its relevance to the present.[96] The borrowing from private law was his extended use of the notion of agency to explain representative government, its delayed development, and the inherent 'tacit limit on the power of a representative assembly' or parliament.[97] This particular crossing of the public–private divide was made by Dicey in his lecture on 'Representative Government', which Geoffrey Hand rightly held in high esteem and regarded as reason to regret Dicey's failure to develop his comparative constitutional lectures into a book.[98] It is exemplary amongst the comparative insights interspersed with apparent peculiarities in Dicey's comparative constitutional lectures.

Dicey's Institutional Focus

'Representative Government' is one of several lectures in the Dicey Papers that call into question assumptions about Dicey's institutional focus. Commentators have in the past criticized his preoccupation with Parliament and the common law courts, and relative inattention to executive government, subject to a qualification. They have qualified their criticism with praise for Dicey's treatment of constitutional conventions as both innovative and consequential in bringing conventions to the forefront of constitutional thought and practice,[99] albeit solely as the object of the political view of the constitution which Dicey distinguished from the legal view and thus marginalized in legal study.[100] Critics of Dicey's institutional focus must now take account not only of his treatment of constitutional conventions but also of the attention he later gave in his comparative constitutional lectures to representative government,[101] party government, parliamentarism, and the basic distinction between parliamentary and non-parliamentary executives.

Dicey's earliest criticism of the party system of government available in the Papers preceded his 'Party Government' lecture and was expressed in his 'Memorandum on English Party System of Government', dated 6 April 1889 on the manuscript's title page and incorporated in the Appendix as Item I below. In the Memorandum, Dicey was radical and ferocious in his criticism of the evils of 'party government through

---

[95] 'Introduction', p. 5 below.
[96] See generally 'Ancient Constitutionalism and Modern Constitutionalism', pp 192 ff below.
[97] 'Representative Government', especially pp 218 f. below. See pp xxxvi f. below.
[98] 'Dicey's Unpublished Materials on the Comparative Study of Constitutions', n. 9 above, 82.
[99] See, e.g., W. I. Jennings, 'In Praise of Dicey 1885–1935' [1935] Public Administration 123, 130; E. C. S. Wade, *Introduction to the Study of the Law of the Constitution*, 9th edn (London: Macmillan, 1939), p. cxlvi. See Allison (ed.), *The Oxford Edition of Dicey*, i, *The Law of the Constitution*, pp xviii ff.
[100] *The Oxford Edition of Dicey*, i, *The Law of the Constitution*, 18 ff, 178, 185 ff.
[101] See pp xxxvi f. below.

a Cabinet'.[102] The first three evils he listed were the sacrifice of 'good administration to party exigencies', 'government by and for a party, and not by and for the nation', and that 'Cabinet government of the English type stimulates the demand for constitutional changes while it gives no guarantee that these changes shall be carried out by experts, or be the result of mature deliberation'.[103] His suggested remedies were divided into those that did not and those that did involve a formal change in the constitution. They included enhancement of the role of the Crown or of the House of Lords, fixed-term parliaments and cabinets, a rigid constitution, and the referendum, his innovative advocacy of which in the English context preceded that expressed in his 1890 *Contemporary Review* article.[104] Drafted mid-way between the introduction of Government of Ireland Bill 1886 and that of the Government of Ireland Bill 1893, the Memorandum reflects, in the third evil of the party system that he listed (stated above) and the general ferocity of his criticisms, Dicey's political struggle against Irish Home Rule and his concerns about related parliamentary decision-making.

After the failure of the Government of Ireland Bill 1893, Dicey dictated his 'Party Government' lecture (dated July 1898 on the manuscript's first page), which was more developed as well as more measured and balanced in style than his Memorandum. Dicey recognized the '[a]pparent advantages' of the party system, described the conditions necessary for its beneficial working (such as the loyalty of all parties to the constitution and real differences of principle between the parties), and concluded that those conditions were also 'the requirements under which alone popular government can flourish'.[105]

Dicey's treatment of the party system both in his Memorandum and in 'Party Government' was earlier, more direct, and more comprehensive that that in his new Introduction to *The Law of the Constitution*'s eighth edition, where Dicey dealt with the constitution's further development and four 'new constitutional ideas' that had arisen since the first edition's publication.[106] In his Introduction, he explained that the effect of new constitutional conventions, such as the use of the guillotine to end delay in the passage of Bills through Parliament, was 'to increase the power of any party which possesses a parliamentary majority', and he presented the main argument in favour of one of the four 'new constitutional ideas'—the referendum—as its strength in being able 'to curb the absolutism of a party possessed of a parliamentary majority'.[107] That the remedy of the referendum would be 'too feeble to cure the malady' that Dicey, particularly in his 1889 Memorandum, had diagnosed in dramatic and alarming terms may well be the conclusion of many readers.[108]

---

[102] 'Memorandum on English Party System of Government', p. 263 below.
[103] Ibid.
[104] Dicey, 'Ought the Referendum to be Introduced?', n. 32 above. See p. xix above.
[105] 'Party Government', especially pp 125, 135 below.
[106] *The Oxford Edition of Dicey*, i, *The Law of the Constitution*, 450 ff.
[107] Ibid., especially 447, 479.
[108] Bogdanor, 'Dicey and the Reform of the Constitution', n. 14 above, especially 670.

Sharing themes with Dicey's 'Party Government' lecture, such as advocacy of the referendum, was his 'Parliamentarism' lecture. For Dicey, parliamentarism was a 'disease of modern Parliaments'—'the formation of groups who place their own objects above the general interest of the nation'—manifest in parliamentary factions and related abuses, and generally discrediting parliamentary government, not only in England but in different ways and with different causes also in other nations, including France, Italy, and Germany.[109] Dicey considered but wholly rejected proportional representation as a cure for the disease, because of what he supposed was the attempt thereby to achieve the representation of national opinion:

> If the matter be explored to the bottom the fallacy of proportional representation lies in the idea that a legislative body such as the House of Commons exists primarily for the sake of discussion or for the formation of opinion. It is not a debating club; it is not a school; it is part of the government, and the decisive, even exaggerated, authority of majorities is a necessary condition for giving to a representative assembly the force needed for governmental action.[110]

Instead of proportional representation, Dicey advocated the referendum as a cure for the disease of parliamentarism but warned against its mechanical introduction, or what we might call its transplantation.[111]

In contrast to Dicey's explanation in *The Law of the Constitution* that the responsibility of ministers to Parliament depends on conventions of the constitution 'with which law has no direct concern',[112] Dicey consistently demonstrated in his comparative constitutional lectures an overriding concern with the character of a parliamentary executive and the distinction between it and a non-parliamentary executive. In 1893, Dicey introduced as the sole change to *The Law of the Constitution*'s fourth edition Note III on the distinction between the two forms of executive, and he added that the 'subject is one of some novelty, and will be found to possess considerable importance'.[113] Dicey retained Note III as such in *The Law of the Constitution*'s later editions that appeared in his lifetime, but E. C. S. Wade, in editing the next two editions, omitted it and all but two of the other Notes from the ninth edition, and all the Notes from the tenth edition. Wade explained that the Notes 'were in the nature of supplements to his lectures, and in the main dealt with topics upon which the student of to-day has easy access to more adequate material in his textbooks'.[114] He preferred to use the Appendix of the ninth edition and that of the tenth edition to provide up-to-date material on *droit administratif* and English administrative law. Because Dicey had introduced the subject of the executive's character only in a Note, presumably, as in the case of each of the Notes, so as to minimize alteration to the main text about the effect of which he expressed concern,[115] and because the Note was then omitted

---

[109] 'Parliamentarism', p. 147 below.
[110] Ibid.
[111] See pp xxvi ff above.
[112] *The Oxford Edition of Dicey*, i, *The Law of the Constitution*, 178. See also ibid., 18 ff.
[113] Preface, 4th edn, ibid., 289.
[114] *The Law of the Constitution*, 9th edn, n. 99 above, p. x.
[115] See *The Oxford Edition of Dicey*, i, *The Law of the Constitution*, 419.

from *The Law of the Constitution*'s current editions for more than half a century, what became an important feature of Dicey's constitutional thought was little noticed and has long been neglected. Quite how important that feature became to Dicey's constitutional thought was apparent in his comparative constitutional lectures.

In 'Divisions of Constitutions', the last of Dicey's full lecture texts in *The Comparative Study of Constitutions* in the order they are published below, Dicey presented the division between constitutions with a parliamentary executive and those with a non-parliamentary executive as one of four basic constitutional divisions (alongside those between written and unwritten, flexible and rigid, and responsive and irresponsive constitutions) apart from the division between historical and non-historical constitutions he had dealt with in his first lecture. Dicey explained that the English Cabinet had for centuries been a non-parliamentary executive, consisting of Crown servants actually appointed by the monarch, but that it had become parliamentary by way of convention. He emphasized the 'vital importance' to a constitution's character of whether its executive was parliamentary in that the 'ability to appoint or dismiss the executive' was really that of the parliament.[116] For Dicey, this ability was the basis of the 'practical power' of Parliament at Westminster, and 'possession of this right [was] the source of more than half the authority' that had then accrued to the House of Commons, in reality although not in name.[117] This ability was thus more important as a source of authority than Parliament's legal sovereignty 'in the technical sense' of being able to 'make and repeal any law whatever'.[118] Dicey devoted two further comparative lectures to the distinction between parliamentary and non-parliamentary executives, incorporated in the Appendix as Item II below, in which he further described and illustrated the two forms of executive and presented the comparative merits and demerits of each. Central to his understanding of the constitutionalism of the English Commonwealth, American constitutionalism, and Prussian constitutionalism, inter alia, was his characterization of their executives as non-parliamentary in each of his lectures on each of their forms of constitutionalism. For Dicey, their executives were therefore in striking contrast with the executive as it had become at Westminster and were similar only to the English executive in the distant past or the executive in a possible future if general elections were gradually to become the means by which the people, not Parliament, appointed the Prime Minister.[119]

Dicey's account of the parliamentary executive as central to the English constitution was of special importance. Through his comparative elaboration on its executive's parliamentary character, initially in Note III of *The Law of the Constitution*'s

---

[116] 'Divisions of Constitutions', pp 243, 239 below.
[117] Ibid., p. 239.
[118] Ibid.
[119] 'It is a matter of curious speculation whether a general election may not by degrees become something like the equivalent to the popular choice of a given statesman as Premier. Should this at any time become the constitutional rule the result would be that our executive would cease to be a parliamentary executive for it would no longer in fact be appointed by Parliament': 'Divisions of Constitutions', p. 241, n. below.

fourth edition and then at considerable length in his comparative constitutional lectures, Dicey complemented, by implication, the three 'guiding principles which pervade the modern constitution of England' that he had put forward in *The Law of the Constitution*, namely the legislative sovereignty of Parliament, the rule of law, and the dependence of conventions of the constitution on the law of the constitution.[120] He added, in effect, a fourth principle—the political responsibility of the executive to Parliament with the actual power to appoint and dismiss ministers.

Dicey's comparative constitutional lectures do not afford evidence with which to contradict the view that Dicey was preoccupied with Parliament, underestimated the growth of executive power in the late-nineteenth century, and overestimated the capacity of a representative Parliament to control it.[121] The executive with which Dicey was concerned in the English context was a parliamentary executive, headed by cabinet ministers responsible to Parliament. In his comparative lectures on the two forms of executive, as in *The Law of the Constitution* generally, Dicey was not dealing with the full reach of government through ministries, boards, commissions, corporations, etc. Similarly, his lectures on the party system, parliamentarism, and representative government were about parliamentary, not local, government. But his comparative constitutional lectures do afford evidence with which to contradict the view that Dicey marginalized executive government in his own thinking and teachings on the constitution when, in his textbook, he defined solely the law of the constitution as the subject of constitutional legal study and described constitutional conventions as the object of the political view he distinguished from the legal.[122] His preoccupation when *The Law of the Constitution* was first published was with legal constitutionalism, but English constitutionalism—as he understood it and as later evident in the institutional focus of the fourth edition's Note III, and especially of his comparative constitutional lectures on the working of representative government, the party system, parliamentarism, and the executive's parliamentary character—was both legal and political.

Dicey's institutional focus in his comparative constitutional lectures was considerably wider than it was in *The Law of the Constitution*, but the significance he attributed to institutions should not be exaggerated. Contradicting or qualifying his emphasis upon institutions and institutional design was Dicey's institutional scepticism evident in *The Comparative Study of the Constitution*'s two central themes. The one theme was that a constitution, however good its institutions, depends for its success on the civic virtues of its people. The other theme was that any institution, whether it be, for example, the Crown, the House of Lords, or the Church, and not necessarily a representative parliament such as the House of Commons, might become in national sentiment the embodiment of the national will, 'the emblem of

---

[120] *The Oxford Edition of Dicey*, i, *The Law of the Constitution*, 5, 25, especially 5.
[121] See P. P. Craig, 'Dicey: Unitary, Self-correcting Democracy and Public Law' (1990) 106 LQR 105.
[122] *The Oxford Edition of Dicey*, i, *The Law of the Constitution*, 18–25, 178, especially 23, 178.

the nation', 'the home, so to speak, of the national spirit'.[123] Both themes reflect Dicey's emphasis on the subjective—the attitudes of a people to their institutions—in his comparative method.[124] Through that emphasis and despite the broad institutional focus in his comparative constitutional lectures, Dicey regarded the English constitution's spirit as none the less legal because its institutions were looked upon 'from a legal point of view' by a people with 'a legal turn of mind and a love for forms and precedents'.[125]

Dicey's Constitutional Principles

Dicey's comparative constitutional lectures shed further light, but in various ways and of varying quality, on his two main principles of parliamentary sovereignty and the rule of law.[126]

In *The Law of the Constitution*, Dicey distinguished the 'theoretically boundless sovereignty of Parliament'—which in its legal sense meant absolute legislative supremacy, the lack of any legal limit to law-making—from its practical or political actuality as restricted by external and internal limits.[127] Dicey's comparative constitutional lectures have implications both for parliamentary sovereignty in its legal or theoretical sense of absolute legislative supremacy and for parliamentary sovereignty in its political or practical actuality.

On the one hand, as in *The Law of the Constitution*, Dicey categorically asserted the absolute legislative authority of Parliament in English constitutionalism when he compared it with the constitutionalism of the English Commonwealth under the Instrument of Government and with American and French constitutionalism.[128] For example, he anticipated that, had the Commonwealth under the Instrument of Government lasted, 'the position and authority of the English Courts would have undergone a complete change' because the Instrument was 'a rigid and a more or less written constitution'.[129] He contrasted what might have been with existing English law of which he said the 'primary doctrine...is now and long has been that no Court could

---

[123] 'Introduction', pp 14 f. below; 'General Conclusions', pp 152–6, 161 ff, especially 165 below. For Dicey, more than one authority could become supreme in the state, each in its own sphere, because 'supremacy depends at bottom on the capacity of each authority to command popular obedience': 'Comparison between English Executive and Other Executives', app. II, lect. 5, p. 294 below. Dicey would therefore have been unlikely to object to today's notion of bipolar sovereignty or, indeed, to that of tripolar sovereignty.

[124] See pp xxiii ff above.

[125] 'English Constitutionalism under George III', p. 70 below; 'Historical Constitutions and Non-Historical Constitutions', p. 182 below.

[126] See Allison (ed.), *The Oxford Edition of Dicey*, i, *The Law of the Constitution*, pp xx ff, xxxviii ff.

[127] Ibid., 27 ff, 41 ff, especially 46.

[128] 'Constitutionalism of the Commonwealth', pp 57 f. below; 'American Constitutionalism', pp 83 f. below; 'French Constitutionalism', p. 101 below; 'Divisions of Constitutions', p. 237 below; 'The Judiciary in Relation to the Executive and Legislative Powers', p. 249 below. See *The Oxford Edition of Dicey*, i, *The Law of the Constitution*, 28 ff, 38 f.

[129] 'Constitutionalism of the Commonwealth', p. 57 below. On the Instrument of Government as a written and rigid constitution, see ibid., pp 43 ff. See generally 'Divisions of Constitutions', pp 235 ff below.

treat an Act of Parliament as void'.[130] Despite expressions of Coke implying otherwise and although 'it is certain that judicial interpretation has at times in practice nullified the effect of statutory enactments', he claimed that 'it would I believe be impossible to point to a case of authority in which the Courts have treated a statute as a nullity on the ground of its being unconstitutional, or indeed on any ground whatever'.[131]

On the other hand, as in *The Law of the Constitution*, Dicey distinguished the practical exercise of the theoretically limitless legislative authority of Parliament but also recognized that it was much more of a practical reality at the end of the nineteenth century than it had been in the eighteenth century,[132] and suggested an inherent limitation absent from *The Law of the Constitution*. There Dicey did describe external and internal limits on the real power of the sovereign but, in his analysis, the external limit consisted of the prospect of disobedience or resistance, and the internal limit arose from 'the nature of the sovereign power itself' as a product of the society in which it is exercised.[133] He concluded by crediting representative government for being productive of coincidence between the external and internal limits.[134] In his comparative constitutional lecture on representative government, he made use of an extended analogy between agency in private law and representation by delegates of the people in a representative assembly or parliament. He acknowledged 'that very different degrees of authority may be conferred on representative bodies' and that 'the English Parliament [has] in theory been vested with complete sovereignty' but stated that its 'authority…is rather indefinite than absolute'.[135] He argued that an 'agent after all derives his power from the will of his principal and, just as no man can in private life constitute a universal agent who has the right to act for him and to bind him in all matters whatsoever, so the people of a country never will and never in reality can transfer to a representative assembly absolute, unlimited, irrevocable authority to act for the nation'.[136] His conclusion was that 'representation, being nothing else than agency, involves in its very idea a tacit limit on the power of a representative assembly…or Parliament'.[137] By elaborating on the notion of representation as agency, Dicey thus subordinated the sovereignty of a representative parliament to popular sovereignty. Towards the end of the lecture, Dicey listed the merits and the defects of representative government, the last of which was that 'parliamentary government gives undue authority to parliamentary majorities'.[138] His final sentence was simple and anti-climactic: '[a] Parliament may be wiser than the citizens who elect it, but a Parliament which does not represent its electors is not an assembly which illustrates the benefit of the representative system'.[139]

---

[130] 'Constitutionalism of the Commonwealth', p. 57 below.
[131] Ibid. See generally Allison, *English Historical Constitution*, n. 81 above, ch. 6.
[132] 'English Constitutionalism under George III', pp 70 f. below.
[133] *The Oxford Edition of Dicey*, i, *The Law of the Constitution*, 44 ff, especially 46.
[134] Ibid., 47 f.
[135] 'Representative Government', pp 218 f. below.
[136] Ibid., p. 218.
[137] Ibid., pp 218 f.
[138] Ibid., pp 219 ff, especially p. 226.
[139] Ibid., p. 228.

In his lecture on representative government, Dicey still contrasted a vesting of complete authority 'in theory' with a limit 'in reality' and made no mention of the courts or of any implication for their role.[140] His analysis of the limitation inherent in representation would therefore seem related to Parliament's sovereignty not in its legal or theoretical sense of absolute legislative supremacy but in its political or practical actuality. If so, Dicey conceived of a representative parliament's sovereignty as unlimited in its legal or theoretical sense but as subject in its political or practical actuality to a limit inherent in representation. Why the one should be unlimited legally or theoretically and the other limited not only practically or politically but also theoretically or inherently, through what was at least a quasi-legal 'tacit limit' involved in the 'very idea' of representation as agency,[141] is an anomaly Dicey did not address in his comparative constitutional lecture. In view of his extended use of a legal construct—agency in private law, effected legally and limited legally in private law—to explain the inherent limitation, and in view of the defects of representative government that he listed, Dicey had reason to avoid the anomaly and reach the further conclusion, which he did not quite reach, that a representative parliament's sovereignty is inherently and legally limited both in its political or practical actuality and in its legal or theoretical sense.

The Dicey Papers similarly shed light on how Dicey conceived of the rule of law. Whether his conception in *The Law of the Constitution* was formal or substantive has been the subject of debate.[142] Dicey's comparative constitutional lectures and a Note in the Dicey Papers (listed there and to be referred to here as Note 17) provide further evidence of its formality in three ways.

First, Dicey portrayed the very spirit of the English constitution as legal in being viewed from the perspective of a people with 'a love for forms and precedents' and 'imbued with legalism and who import into their political arrangements that love of precedent and acquiescence in fictions which is proper to the law Courts'.[143] Dicey's formal rule of law corresponded with the legal spirit—a predilection for forms and manifest in fictions—that he attributed to the English constitution itself.

Secondly, in his comparative constitutional lectures Dicey repeatedly depicted the limited relevance of law and the minimalism of judicial responses at times of constitutional conflict. He emphasized the law's limited relevance in the support he expressed for Otto von Bismarck's position in the constitutional conflict between the Prussian Crown and its parliament of 1862–1866.[144] He described how, as leading

---

[140] Ibid., especially p. 218.

[141] Ibid., pp 218 f.

[142] See Allison (ed.), *The Oxford Edition of Dicey*, i, *The Law of the Constitution*, pp xx, xxxix f.; P. P. Craig, 'Formal and Substantive Conceptions of the Rule of Law: An Analytical Framework' [1997] PL 467, 470 ff; T. R. S. Allan, *Constitutional Justice: A Liberal Theory of the Rule of Law* (Oxford: Oxford University Press, 2001), 18 f.; Allison, *English Historical Constitution*, n. 81 above, 158 ff, 209 ff.

[143] 'Historical Constitutions and Non-Historical Constitutions', pp 181 f. below. See also 'English Constitutionalism under George III', p. 70 below, and, e.g., pp xliii f. below. On his first visit to the United States, Dicey expressed the view that the USA was an opposite to England in that things there were what they appeared to be: Rait, *Memorials*, n. 4 above, 72 f.

[144] 'Prussian Constitutionalism', pp 116 ff below.

minister, Bismarck had effectively governed for five years in defiance of Parliament and its constitutional refusal to settle the budget for implementing a scheme of military reorganization. He observed that '[c]onstitutional conflicts are at bottom contests decided by policy and power rather than by argument or law' and regarded his observation as sufficiently important to warrant repeating the gist of it.[145] Elsewhere, Dicey opposed conferring upon courts a power actually to nullify (as opposed to treat as a nullity) an unconstitutional law. For Dicey, such a power would be worth 'very little' in practice because it would 'only be exercised at a crisis, just at a time... when the Courts are likely to have little real power as opposed to the legislature or the executive'.[146] Dicey fully appreciated the economy of the common law,[147] and of courts more generally, at times of constitutional conflict and crisis, although he did not use the expression. That economy is shown or achieved by judicial protection or intervention that is formal, justified on narrow procedural or other technical grounds, rather than by judicial protection that is substantive, relying upon or appealing to contentious principles of legal and political morality.

Thirdly, in his little known and almost unnoticed 'Note 17: Conclusions as to French *Droit Administratif*', incorporated in the Appendix as Item VI below, Dicey expressed considerable and reasoned admiration for French administrative law, in part because of its supposed remedial advantages over English law, and concluded that on 'the whole it appears to be true that if administrative law is to exist it is seen at its best as French *droit administratif*'.[148] Note 17's manuscript was not dated but is adjacent in the same bundle of notes to the manuscript for Note 16 (a list of references to other, presumably lost, Notes on French administrative law), which was dated 25 May 1899. As a rough undated Note, the purpose of which is uncertain, Note 17 needs to be treated with particular caution. The praise for developed *droit administratif* that Dicey expressed there was, however, similar in tone to the praise he gave in his preface to *The Law of the Constitution*'s French edition,[149] and accords with the naming of Dicey (together with Goodnow) by G. Jèze (who with A. Batut translated the French edition) as one of two foreign lawyers who best know French administrative law and who do not conceal their admiration for it.[150] From his familiarity with Dicey's own preface to the French edition, Jèze would have appreciated

---

[145] Ibid., pp 117 f.

[146] 'Divisions of Constitutions', p. 237 below.

[147] See Allison, *English Historical Constitution*, n. 81 above, 123 ff. See, e.g., Dicey's treatment of *Wolfe Tone's Case* (1798) 27 St. Tr. 614 in *The Oxford Edition of Dicey*, i, *The Law of the Constitution*, 164; Allison, ibid., Editor's Introduction, pp xxxix f.

[148] pp 307 ff, especially 307. Dicey's Note 17 reveals his puzzling neglect and partial ignorance or forgetfulness of the ancient English prerogative writs (especially the writ of *certiorari*) and his preoccupation with the writ of *habeas corpus*. See, e.g., *The Oxford Edition of Dicey*, i, *The Law of the Constitution*, 130, 170, 178. See generally Allison, 'The Spirits of the Constitution', n. 68 above, pp 38 ff. Cassese cited Note 17, and Hand referred to its 'constitutional importance': Cassese, 'Albert Venn Dicey', n. 18 above, 12 f.; Hand, 'Dicey's Unpublished Materials on the Comparative Study of Constitutions', n. 9 above, 93, n.

[149] *The Oxford Edition of Dicey*, i, *The Law of the Constitution*, 325 f. See also ibid., Editor's Introduction, pp xxxv f.

[150] G. Jèze, *Les principes généraux du droit administratif* (Paris: Berger-Levrault, 1904), 122, n. Cf. generally Errera, 'Dicey and French Administrative Law', n. 45 above, 704–7.

the admiration Dicey expressed there and that whatever criticism Dicey directed at *droit administratif* was principally for the pedagogical purpose of demonstrating to English students the contrasting character of the English rule of law. If Dicey actually admired, or learned to admire, the substantive working of developed *droit administratif*, as he claimed he did, his continuing demonstration in all of *The Law of the Constitution*'s editions, by way of contrast with France's specialized jurisdiction, was principally a demonstration of the English rule of law's formal, jurisdictional, equality of individuals and officials alike under the ordinary law applied by ordinary courts formally independent of the administration.

In his comparative constitutional lectures, Dicey complemented his two main principles of parliamentary sovereignty and the rule of law and his third principle of the dependence of constitutional conventions on the law of the constitution with a fourth principle, at least by implication, and elaborated further on what did not quite qualify as a fifth. Through his comparative institutional focus on the English constitution's parliamentary executive, he added, in effect, a fourth principle—the political responsibility of the executive to Parliament at Westminster—as argued above.[151] The other principle that did not quite qualify but on which he elaborated further was the separation of powers, not only in other jurisdictions but also in the English context. In *The Law of the Constitution*, Dicey barely mentioned the separation of powers as such and, where he did refer to it, it was the French separation to which he referred, and about that separation he was disparaging. In explaining French administrative law, he referred to its underlying 'so-called separation of powers' as a 'dogma' based on a 'double misconception'—Montesquieu's misunderstanding of the English constitution and the French revolutionaries' misunderstanding or misapplication of Montesquieu's doctrine.[152] Implicit in his analysis of the English rule of law, however, and his treatment of the French administrative jurisdiction as a contrast was a separation of powers involving judicial independence. Dicey repeatedly stressed the role of the ordinary English courts in all disputes whether they involve individuals or officials, and he regarded the French administrative jurisdiction as a contrast with the rule of law because of its formal association with the French administration.[153]

In his very early work on the Privy Council for his Arnold Prize Essay, Dicey had studied 'the gradual separation of judicial, political, and administrative functions' in the English context.[154] In his comparative constitutional lectures, he showed renewed interest. He incorporated a lecture on the separation of powers in *The Comparative Study of Constitutions*, dictated Analyses (but not a full lecture), and referred to the separation of powers in various other lectures. Showing the inconsistency and ambivalence that has been characteristic of English doctrinal treatment of the separation of powers,[155] he asserted that the 'separation exists under [the]

---

[151] See pp xxxii ff above. Cf. generally *The Oxford Edition of Dicey*, i, *The Law of the Constitution*, 5, 25.
[152] *The Oxford Edition of Dicey*, i, *The Law of the Constitution*, 104.
[153] Ibid., 95–119.
[154] A. V. Dicey, *The Privy Council: The Arnold Prize Essay 1860* (London: Macmillan, 1887), especially 147.
[155] See Allison, *English Historical Constitution*, n. 81 above, ch. 4, especially 78 ff, 83 ff, 86 ff.

English constitution' and that one merit of representative government was that it 'favours the separation of powers', but he also referred to the English separation as a 'nominal separation' and stated that the doctrine was 'not really carried out under [the] English constitution though more nearly in Montesquieu's time than in any other'.[156] In regard to the American adoption of the separation of powers, he observed that 'the inconsistency of Montesquieu's teaching with the actual working of the English constitution was less visible towards the end of the 18th than it is at the close of the 19th century'.[157] In elaborating, further, on English institutional continuity, he talked of the 'practical absurdity of Montesquieu's dogma' in consequence and of Montesquieu's 'artificial constitution of England'.[158] Dicey was inconsistent and ambivalent in his treatment of the separation of powers as such, but he did clearly affirm the separation of powers in its particular English form of judicial independence as the general doctrine's 'most important element'.[159] In short, the principle of judicial independence, which was largely implicit in his exposition of the English rule of law in *The Law of the Constitution*, he made explicit in his comparative constitutional lectures.

Dicey's Comparative Constitutional Thought and English Constitutionalism

In various usual ways, Dicey's comparative constitutional lectures reflected their context—doctrinal, institutional, political, etc.—as did *The Law of the Constitution*. Apart from Dicey's typical inconsistency and ambivalence towards the separation of powers as such in the English context, several other examples have already been mentioned. One example was Dicey's monolithic, nineteenth-century, national contrast of the constitutionalism of England with that of France and Prussia.[160] Another was his recognition, in explaining Prussian constitutionalism and in supporting Bismarck's position in the constitutional conflict of the Prussian Crown with its parliament, that '[c]onstitutional conflicts are at bottom contests decided by policy and power rather than by argument or law'.[161] His stark recognition of the rule of law's limited reach was expressed as a general truth or a matter of common sense and is

---

[156] 'The Separation of Powers (1899)', p. 230 f. below; 'Representative Government', p. 221 below. In a surviving manuscript listing authorities and questions for students, Dicey asked only about the doctrine's application in France and the United States, not of its application in England: 'Authorities and Questions', p. 306 below. For further ambivalence, see 'Comparison between English Executive and other Executives', app. II, lect. 4, pp 277, 281 f.

[157] 'American Constitutionalism', p. 79 below.

[158] 'Historical Constitutions and Non-Historical Constitutions', pp 176 f. below. See generally W. S. Holdsworth, *A History of English Law*, x (London: Methuen, 1938), 713–24.

[159] 'The Separation of Powers (1900)', p. 229 below. See also 'French Constitutionalism', pp 97 f. below; 'General Conclusions', pp 156 f. below.

[160] See *The Comparative Study of the Constitution*, lects 3, 5, 6. See pp xxiv ff above.

[161] 'Prussian Constitutionalism', p. 117 below.

a reminder not to romanticize Dicey's nineteenth-century constitutional thought,[162] nor to assume consistency in the English liberalism accompanying Empire.[163]

Apart from reflecting their context in various usual ways, Dicey's lectures in being the outcome of a comparative method demonstrated, further, a particular relation to their constitutional context, an indirect relation but purposeful and significant. That relation was indirect in that English constitutionalism was being understood by way of comparison. It was purposeful and significant in that, through using the comparative method, Dicey was seeking to demonstrate its 'immense recommendations'.[164] Of those recommendations, Dicey made special mention of two: first, that 'the comparative method as applied to the English constitution brings into light just those aspects of our institutions which we otherwise fail to notice'; secondly, that it 'leads to the discovery of new affinities and new dissimilarities between different constitutions', enabling reclassification according to 'new principles'.[165] In seeking to demonstrate those recommendations, Dicey expressed, on the one hand, new insights into English constitutionalism absent from or barely evident in *The Law of the Constitution* or, if evident, left largely unexplained. He elaborated further, on the other hand, upon a few old insights evident in characterizations that were commonplace but were of special comparative significance to the classification of constitutions. Two exemplary new insights were into the executive's parliamentary character, discussed above, and into what Dicey termed the constitution's responsiveness. Two illustrative characterizations on which he elaborated further were of the constitution as unwritten and of it as historical. They are discussed below.

Dicey actually presented his insight into the executive's parliamentary character as the exemplary product of the comparative method. Dicey explained that English thinkers, prepossessed by the House of Commons' authority and only its own history, were inclined to 'assume that a really representative body must of necessity exercise practical control over the executive' but claimed that 'our whole point of view' is changed by a comparative perspective on, for example, the American Congress and the German Reichstag.[166] In consequence, Dicey characterized English constitutionalism not only by the two main principles of parliamentary sovereignty and the rule of law expounded in *The Law of the Constitution*, but also by its parliamentary executive, the institutional outcome of what was suggested above to be the further implicit principle of the executive's political responsibility to Parliament.

Dicey expressed his insight into the English constitution's responsiveness mainly in his lecture 'Divisions of Constitutions'. By a responsive constitution, Dicey meant a constitution that was responsive to public opinion or popular feeling. In explaining the idea of responsiveness, he contrasted what he called the American constitution

---

[162] See generally Allison, 'Spirits of the Constitution', n. 68 above, 45 ff.
[163] See generally, e.g., *The Oxford Edition of Dicey*, i, *The Law of the Constitution*, 431–4, 466 ff.
[164] 'Introduction', pp 6 f. below.
[165] Ibid., pp 7, 11.
[166] Ibid., pp 7 f.

with the English. For Dicey, the American constitution, although obviously more democratic than the English constitution, was an 'irresponsive' constitution, in part, because its system of checks and balances restricts the directness and immediacy of the effect of public opinion upon the action of each of the different branches of government.[167] In contrast, the modern English constitution was exemplary in its responsiveness—the 'best example in existence and perhaps which has ever existed of a "responsive constitution".[168] He claimed that the constitution is 'an instrument which responds easily and immediately to the wishes of Englishmen' and that the 'Houses of Parliament, and especially the House of Commons, can constitutionally and do in fact give effect to the real or supposed wishes, one might even say, to the whims of the electorate'.[169] Responsiveness thus worked politically, or was brought about politically, through Parliament. Dicey's belief in the constitution's responsiveness was exaggerated and is vulnerable to criticism,[170] but the characteristic of responsiveness was absent from *The Law of the Constitution*. Dicey seems to have developed it specifically for his comparative constitutional lectures although its outcome in English law during the nineteenth century was the subject of the lectures, initially concurrent with his comparative lectures, that became *The Relation between Law and Public Opinion in England*.[171]

One commonplace characterization on which Dicey elaborated further was of the English constitution as unwritten. By that, he meant that it was the product not of enactment in a single document but of mainly legal decisions and was dependent for its working on 'understandings or conventions'.[172] He observed that written constitutions were 'gradually superseding unwritten or conventional constitutions' because 'tacit understandings' had become insufficient through the extension of the franchise beyond a limited class of people, and because of the need for a constitution to be written if it is to be new.[173] The characterization of the constitution as unwritten was evident in *The Law of the Constitution*,[174] has long been commonplace, and is unremarkable but for a further observation by Dicey and an expression of contempt. Dicey observed that the 'English constitution becomes as time goes on more of a written constitution than it was a century ago',[175] and, in his Introduction to *The Law of the Constitution*'s eighth edition, he later claimed that the Parliament Act 1911 'goes some way towards establishing in England a written or...enacted constitution'.[176] His claim was an early precursor to Vernon Bogdanor's claim that the British constitution is

---

[167] 'Divisions of Constitutions', pp 245 f. below.
[168] Ibid., p. 243.
[169] Ibid.
[170] See, e.g., Craig, 'Dicey: Unitary, Self-correcting Democracy and Public Law', n. 121 above; Allison, *English Historical Constitution*, n. 81 above, 164 f.
[171] *Law and Public Opinion in England*, n. 3 above. See generally pp xi ff above.
[172] 'General Characteristics of Existing English Constitutionalism', pp 22 f. below.
[173] 'General Conclusions', p. 157 below. See also 'Divisions of Constitutions', p. 233 f. below.
[174] *The Oxford Edition of Dicey*, i, *The Law of the Constitution*, 10, 24.
[175] 'French Constitutionalism', p. 102 below.
[176] *The Oxford Edition of Dicey*, i, *The Law of the Constitution*, 445.

'half way' to codification 'by piecemeal means' as a result of statutes such as the European Communities Act 1972 and the Human Rights Act 1998.[177] Dicey's expression of contempt was for written constitutions in comparison with historical constitutions 'framed to meet an actual want' and 'having endured have probably met the actual requirements of the time'.[178] Their doing so was, according to Dicey, 'a great deal more than can be said of the scores of paper constitutions which have been designed by theorists' and put into force since the late-eighteenth century.[179]

Another characterization, then commonplace, on which Dicey also elaborated further was of the constitution as historical. Partly out of a commonly voiced contempt for the paper constitutions proliferating elsewhere as the constitutional equivalent of paper money,[180] Dicey characterized the English constitution as first and foremost a historical one. Dicey made the constitution's historical character the first of its listed features to be dealt with in his first lecture of *The Comparative Study of the Constitution*, and the distinction between historical and non-historical constitutions was the subject of the first lecture of *The Comparative Study of Constitutions*. His analysis in the earlier lecture was embryonic or undeveloped. For Dicey in that lecture the constitution was historical in being historically and continuously developed and in being 'a work of native production'.[181] In the later lecture 'Historical and Non-Historical Constitutions', he provided four distinguishing characteristics of a historical constitution. They were, first, its 'antiquity', secondly, its 'continuity', thirdly, its 'spontaneity' (in the sense of its not being 'created at any given moment in accordance with any deliberate plan, design or principle'), and fourthly, its 'originality' (in the sense of 'absence of imitation').[182] The second and third characteristics warrant further attention for different reasons—the second for the difficulty in trying to apply it, the third for its general significance despite its late introduction to Dicey's analysis.

Dicey encountered difficulty in applying the second characteristic—continuity— both to the non-historical constitution he attributed to France and to the historical constitution he attributed to England. Despite the French revolution and various transitions from monarchical to republican to imperial forms of government, Dicey recognized a high degree of continuity in modern French history,[183] but his conclusion was ultimately that, in modern France, the French 'have revolutions' but 'no real restorations'.[184] In England, the problem in showing the characteristic of continuity was the interregnum from 1649 to 1660 between the reigns of King Charles I and King Charles II. Dicey tried to resolve the problem by emphasizing the legal

---

[177] Bogdanor, 'Conclusion', n. 14 above, 719.
[178] 'Historical Constitutions and Non-Historical Constitutions', p. 187 below.
[179] Ibid.
[180] Linda Colley, 'When did the British Constitution Become Unwritten?', Mark Pigott Lecture, 21 October 2010, Cambridge.
[181] 'General Characteristics of Existing English Constitutionalism', expecially p. 20 below.
[182] 'Historical Constitutions and Non-Historical Constitutions', especially pp 174, 183 below.
[183] See, e.g., 'French Constitutionalism', pp 90 f. below; 'Historical and Non-Historical Constitutions', pp 181 f.; 'Why Universal Suffrage Suits France', app. VII below. See also *The Oxford Edition of Dicey*, i, *The Law of the Constitution*, 101 ff, 368 ff.
[184] 'Historical Constitutions and Non-Historical Constitutions', p. 181 below.

fiction accompanying the Restoration, 'that in 1649 Charles II immediately succeeded Charles I', which 'blotted out from popular tradition the very memory of the Interregnum'.[185] Dicey explained that the fiction worked because 'it corresponded with national feeling' and the English 'love for forms and precedents'.[186] For Dicey, the English historical constitution was characterized by the continuity of its institutions because, even when clearly discontinuous, they were viewed as continuous by a people who accepted the fiction, again illustrating the importance Dicey attached to the subjective—the attitudes of a people to their institutions.[187] Dicey would have encountered less difficulty and avoided his heavy reliance on the subjective had he applied the characteristic of continuity less categorically, for example, by recognizing a historical constitution's general continuity despite occasional discontinuity, or by emphasizing a historical constitution's accommodation of change in its mode of development.[188]

The historical constitution's third characteristic—spontaneity—was absent from the 'Historical Constitutions and Non-Historical Constitutions' lecture Analysis (dated 1 May 1900) but was introduced to the main lecture text (dated 26 May 1900), initially as 'Undesigned creation' and then as 'Spontaneity' when the lecture text was later altered.[189] Dicey therefore appears to have developed the idea of spontaneity specifically for his comparative constitutional lectures. That a historical constitution was spontaneous in the sense of not being the product of a deliberate design or plan was significant to Dicey's overall assessment of historical and non-historical constitutions. For Dicey, the dispute as to which was preferable was 'only one form of an interminable controversy between two different views of life and philosophy'—between those who 'in morals or in politics...place their trust in instinct, in intuition, or generally in feeling' and those who place their trust 'in the reasoning powers of man, who believe that in politics as in every other sphere mankind ought to be guided by foresight and thought rather than by unconscious instinct or moral sentiment'.[190] Although Dicey recognized defects in the historical constitution, such as adaptations 'suggested by the circumstances of the moment' that are 'often misadaptations', and its retention of institutions that 'survive the causes which gave rise to and justified their existence', to which of the 'two different views of life and philosophy' he leaned in his comparative constitutional writings was clear.[191] Apart from meeting actual wants and needs, Dicey emphasized the historical constitution's merits of presumed suitability 'for the nation by whom it has been created' and conciliation of

---

[185] Ibid., p. 178.

[186] Ibid., pp 180, 182. 'The breach in the continuity of our constitutional history was, so to speak, filled up by popular sentiment. When lawyers proclaimed that Charles II ascended the throne on the death of his father, they propounded a patent absurdity which was not felt to be absurd because it corresponded with national feeling': ibid., p. 180.

[187] See pp xxiii ff above.

[188] Elsewhere, in advocating the English historical constitution's mode of development for the British Empire, Dicey emphasized development, not continuity: *The Oxford Edition of Dicey*, i, *The Law of the Constitution*, 470 f. Cf. generally Allison, *English Historical Constitution*, n. 81 above.

[189] See 'Historical Constitutions and Non-Historical Constitutions', p. 182, n., below.

[190] Ibid., pp 190 f.

[191] Ibid., pp 188, 190.

the 'good will and loyalty' of the people amongst whom it has long existed.[192] Viewing the English constitution as principally historical in character, Dicey later, in the last edition of *The Law of the Constitution* to be published in his lifetime, recommended its mode of development as a model to be followed in the development of the British Empire.[193]

Capacious Constitutionalism

A recurring explanation amongst various explanations for the appeal and influence of Dicey's constitutional thought as expressed in *The Law of the Constitution* has been its quality of capaciousness, contributing to its fertility as a source from which to seek authority.[194] Within a year from when it was first published, Frederick Pollock commented that 'Dicey's book, designed for peaceful uses, has become an armoury for political combatants' and doubted 'whether the untried weapons snatched out of it by untrained hands are altogether safe for those who wield them'.[195] Twenty-five years later, for example, during the Parliamentary debates that culminated in the Parliament Act 1911, weapons were being snatched from it and put to prominent use by adversaries from both sides of the House of Commons who cited Dicey as pre-eminent constitutional authority.[196]

The capaciousness of Dicey's constitutional thought has been attributed, inter alia, to the frequent ambivalence of his analysis arising from inapparent variation in his point of view in presenting, for example, 'purely analytical conclusions' that might also be 'statements of approval'.[197] Further, Dicey's bequest to future generations has memorably been likened to a tool kit:

> Dicey's contribution has been to design and bequeath to future generations of reformers and scholars a tool kit of concepts and analytical schema which has enabled debate to proceed on an orderly intellectual footing. It is hard to imagine meaningful constitutional discourse being possible without our having recourse to his seminal ideas about the Rule of Law, parliamentary sovereignty and constitutional conventions... There is something for everyone in Dicey's tool kit.[198]

For its capaciousness, Dicey's constitutional thought has thus been both criticized and praised.

---

[192] Ibid., p. 187.
[193] *The Oxford Edition of Dicey*, i, *The Law of the Constitution*, 470 f.
[194] On the various other reasons for Dicey's appeal and influence, see generally Allison (ed.), *The Oxford Edition of Dicey*, i, *The Law of the Constitution*, pp xii–xvi; Allison, *English Historical Constitution*, n. 81 above, 165 ff, 188 ff; Allison, *Continental Distinction in the Common Law*, n. 45 above, 22 f.
[195] F. Pollock, 'Oxford Law Studies' (1886) 2 LQR 453, 457.
[196] See Hansard, HC, vol. 24, cols 1108, 1117 (20 April 1911). See also ibid., cols. 1673 (25 April 1911), 1838–9 (26 April 1911). See Allison (ed.), *The Oxford Edition of Dicey*, i, *The Law of the Constitution*, p. xiii.
[197] E. Barendt, 'Dicey and Civil Liberties' [1985] PL 596, especially 596. On the variation of Dicey's pedagogical point of view, see Allison (ed.), *The Oxford Edition of Dicey*, i, *The Law of the Constitution*, xl ff.
[198] G. Drewry, 'Comment' [1985] PL 676, 676.

If capaciousness was a quality of Dicey's thought in *The Law of the Constitution*, it was all the more so of that in his comparative constitutional lectures. Apart from their wide-ranging, historical and non-historical, comparative scope and the breadth of their institutional focus, one of Dicey's main justifications for the comparative method was its bringing 'into light just those aspects of our institutions which we otherwise fail to notice'.[199] Dicey's use of the comparative method was productive of fresh insights into and emphasis upon aspects of English institutions that were left unnoticed or largely undeveloped in *The Law of the Constitution*. They related, in particular, to the constitution's responsiveness to popular feeling and its executive's parliamentary character, implicit in which was the principle of the executive's responsibility to Parliament. That responsiveness was brought about politically through Parliament and that responsibility of the executive to Parliament was political. Whereas *The Law of the Constitution* has long been both celebrated and criticized for its legal constitutionalism, Dicey's comparative constitutional lectures complemented its legal constitutionalism with much that was political. The outcome was a better balancing of the legal and the political in a more comprehensive and capacious constitutionalism, different aspects of which should appeal to both legal and political constitutionalists in the English context.

Apart from their legal and political constitutionalism, Dicey's comparative constitutional lectures afford at least five further striking examples of ambivalence, paradox, or contradiction, most of which will now make Dicey's constitutional thought all the more capacious in accommodating contrasting points of view. First, Dicey promoted and illustrated the 'immense recommendations' of the comparative method,[200] but did not actually develop his comparative constitutional lectures into the book he contemplated. Secondly, the legal educational mission he set himself in his Inaugural Lecture was to tailor university legal education to the pressing, residual, educational needs of practitioners in legal practice,[201] but in his comparative constitutional lectures he took a broad view of those needs or was willing to deviate from his mission. Thirdly, he devoted much attention to the institutions and mechanisms of government—representation, the referendum, the party system, the character of an executive, etc.—but then also emphasized the subjective—the attitude of a people towards them—and attributed a constitution's success, ultimately, not to its institutions and mechanisms but to the civic virtues of its people. Fourthly, he restated the absolute character of Parliament's sovereignty in its legal or theoretical sense of legislative supremacy but qualified a representative parliament's sovereignty, at least, in its political or practical actuality with a quasi-legal limitation inherent in its representativeness. Fifthly, he described the very spirit of the English constitution as legal,[202] but recognized that '[c]onstitutional conflicts are at bottom

---

[199] 'Introduction', p. 7 below.
[200] Ibid., pp 6 f.
[201] Allison (ed.), *The Oxford Edition of Dicey*, i, *The Law of the Constitution*, pp xxiv ff.
[202] See p. xxiv above.

contests decided by policy and power rather than by argument or law'.[203] Whether, or which of, these examples are of real or only apparent contradiction should interest and absorb readers of the pages below.

The capaciousness, inter alia, of Dicey's thought in *The Law of the Constitution* did, in some degree, contribute to its appeal and lasting influence by providing something for everyone in Dicey, that is, by serving as a tool kit or armoury from which useful principles, ideas, arguments, or mechanisms might be found, taken, and put to the use of persons varying in method, purpose, or political point of view. Insofar as it did so, Dicey's comparative constitutional lectures have the potential similarly to enhance that appeal and influence. If their potential were realized, debates about Dicey's constitutional thought would also be debates about the character and real or apparent contradictions of modern English legal and political constitutionalism under his influence. The comparative breadth of this volume's lectures by a pioneering contributor to legal education and related literature would, further, be reason to reconsider how fully to entertain such debates in university legal education unconfined or less confined by a narrow preoccupation with relevance to the needs of legal practice.

---

[203] 'Prussian Constitutionalism', p. 117 below.

PART I

THE COMPARATIVE STUDY OF THE CONSTITUTION

Introduction

Analysis*

A. Three Methods of Studying Constitution
  I. *Analytical method*
    1. This the natural method of legal exposition
    2. Deficiencies of method
  II. *Historical method*
    1. Its merits
      (i) Needed for explanation of existing state of things
      (ii) Involves incidentally comparison of different periods
    2. Its defects
      (i) Direction of attention to origins
      (ii) Confusion of history with apology
      (iii) Omission of periods falling out of line of development
  III. *Comparative method*
    1. Distinction between comparative method and other methods
    2. May be applied either to constitution generally, or to particular institutions
    3. Cannot be separated from analytical and historical method
B. Merits of Comparative Method
  I. *Elucidation of peculiarities of English constitutionalism*
  II. *Illustration of different types of constitutionalism*
  III. *Suggestion of new modes of classification*

Illustrations
  Connexion between legislation and taxation
  Connexion between legislative power and sovereign power
  The position of the judiciary
  The relation of the executive and the legislature

---

* Its contents have been derived from an undated manuscript attached to the lecture schedule headed 'Easter & Trinity Terms, 1897'.

Introduction[*]

There exist at least three modes or methods of studying the English, or for that matter any other, constitution.

The first may for convenience be termed the analytical or expository method.

This is the mode of treatment rightly adopted by the writers of legal commentaries on constitutional law, such as Blackstone and Stephen in England, or Story in America. The aim of such a commentator, if we confine our attention to the constitution of England, is to explain our existing scheme of government. He takes our institutions, such as the Crown, the Cabinet, the Houses of Parliament or our constitutional rights, such for example as the right of self-defence, or of public meeting, as they are. He tries to set forth in an intelligible form the character of English institutions and of the rights enjoyed by British citizens. His aim would be completely attained could he give an account of the constitution, using that word in its widest sense, expressed in a set of definite propositions placed in a logical order, accompanied by such commentary as sufficed to explain the full import and the precise meaning of what I may term the articles of the constitution. His object, in short, is to produce a constitutional code accompanied by illustrative comment. Neither the law nor the practice of the English constitution lends itself easily to codification. Still, the task of exposition has been achieved with more or less success and completeness by more than one eminent writer and there is no reason why we should not ultimately possess in England commentaries on the constitution equal to those with which Story has enriched the legal literature of America.

It is obvious, however, that English institutions being what they are an author who strictly confined himself to the use of the analytical method could not produce a satisfactory exposition of the English constitution. He must of necessity have some recourse to history. It would be impossible for instance for him to explain the present constitution of the House of Lords without casting an eye back on the growth of the Peerage and the events which have in one generation after another changed the component parts and modified the influence of the upper House. Who, again, could understand or expound the rules which determine the right to elect a member of Parliament without some reference to the Reform Act of 1832 and the condition of affairs to which that act put an end? How would it be possible to understand the presence in the House of Lords of elected peers without a knowledge of the Acts of Union with Scotland and Ireland? The analytical method requires for its completeness the aid, though only the subordinate aid, of a different mode of investigation.

This is the second, or the historical, method.

Its high repute at the present day, as well as the honour justly paid to authors such as Hallam, Stubbs, Freeman, or Gneist, by whom the growth of English institutions

---

[*] The manuscript's first page was dated 16 November 1894, and 'Delivered at Liverpool' was later noted. To the text, a title page was added and dated May 1897.

has been traced out from their earliest origin down to modern times, makes it almost needless to describe the character, or dwell on the merits, of the historical treatment of the constitution. The danger today is that the undoubted merits of this method should be exaggerated, or rather that its deficiencies should be overlooked. History may degenerate into antiquarianism, and we may pay so much attention to the origin of institutions as to neglect their recent developments, or their actual working. There are men of learning who can discuss with ability the origin of our land laws and yet would find it difficult to answer the simplest question about the laws which at the present day determine the succession to, or the sale of, land in England and who could give us a far more accurate account of the Parliaments of Edward I or Henry VIII than of the Parliaments of George III or Queen Victoria.

Another defect of the historical method is that it leads its votaries to confound historical explanation with moral or intellectual justification. To show how an institution came into existence is a very different thing from demonstrating that it ought to exist. Weeds have a history no less than useful plants, and it is as easy, I conceive, to account historically for disease as for health.

Another defect of the purely historical treatment of the constitution is that transactions which though full of instruction fall out of the line of development are apt to be overlooked. Slight is the study which eminent constitutionalists have devoted to the constitutionalism of the Commonwealth. A single chapter of Hallam covers the whole period between the abolition of the monarchy and the Restoration. You will meet many persons of more than average education who do not know that before the earliest of the Acts of Union both Scotland and Ireland had been united to England. Our ignorance of the Commonwealth keeps out of sight an experiment in constitution making full of interest to students of modern constitutionalism. Do not suppose for a moment that I underrate the immense benefits conferred upon us all by the masters of constitutional history. All I venture to assert—and this almost with bated breath—is that the historical method, like every other mode of study, has its defects to which I will venture to add one further observation; the service which the study of the history of institutions renders to constitutionalists is not itself historical. What we really gain from tracing the growth of an institution is a foundation for comparing the institution as it once was with the same institution as it now exists. He who knows what were the actual powers of the Crown in the time, say, of Elizabeth or of Anne acquires not only the knowledge of the past but additional understanding of the present. He can understand much better what the Crown is today from his knowledge of what it was in the sixteenth and seventeenth century. The kind of light which is attained by comparing the authority and position of Queen Victoria with the authority and position of Queen Anne may also be attained by comparing the authority and position of Queen Victoria with the powers possessed by Louis XIV, President Cleveland, or the German Emperor. Half the instructiveness of the historical method is that inquiry into the past compels as to realise the differences between it and the present. History is comparison, though comparison need not be history. The historical method is at its best an illustration of the comparative method.

Thirdly, [there is] the comparative method.*

What is the true meaning of this term? It is as its name imports the elucidating of existing institutions or laws and in our case of the English constitution by comparison with analogous institutions or laws which have existed in other times or which now exist in other lands. The comparison may be historical as when we compare the constitution under Charles I or the constitution under George III with the constitution under Victoria; it may be non-historical as where we compare the British Parliament with the American Congress, with the French National Assembly, or with the German Reichstag. The comparative study of the constitution has no direct connection with either past or present. You may compare the Crown of England with the American Presidentship, or with the Cromwellian Protectorate. Constitutions which have passed away, or which have never had any real life, such as the French Directorial Constitution, may to a student who pursues the comparative method be as instructive and throw by way of contrast or likeness as much light upon the polity of modern England as does the constitution of the German Empire or of the Swiss Confederation. Nor need he confine his attention to institutions which have had an actual historical life. He may learn much from the ideal or imagined polities, constructed by the fancy of philosophers or poets. The dreams of Rousseau had more permanence as they have more importance than the constitutional edifices erected by his revolutionary disciples, and the doctrines of Montesquieu had as much to do with the Institutions of the United States as had the experience of English government. Note further that it is not institutions or laws alone which are the proper subjects of comparison. It is even more profitable to compare the conceptions or ideas which underlie political arrangements, than to study the actual mechanism of politics. In the long run and in spite of all appearances to the contrary thoughts rule the world, and men's ideas guide or misguide human conduct. Know what is the conception which Germans entertain of the authority due to the Emperor; know what is the idea prevalent in America of the power which ought to be exercised by a President; what is the opinion which modern Englishmen entertain as to the measure of influence which belongs to the Queen, or how far English opinion will support the House of Lords in a conflict with the House of Commons, and you have learnt what Montesquieu would call the spirit of the German, American, or English institutions, and have gained a key to their working which cannot be supplied by any study however diligent of the letter or form of their constitutions.

The comparative method can only supplement, it cannot supersede other methods of study. Comparison is impossible until we know the main traits of our existing constitution, nor will mere comparison ever solve difficulties the answer to which must be supplied by history. We see that this is so if we apply our method to the elucidation of, say, the American Commonwealth. It is inapplicable until we have ascertained what are the articles of the Federal Constitution. Some of them will never be intelligible until we have learnt the historical conditions under which they came into existence. But though the comparative method is a mere supplement to other

---

* On Dicey's comparative method, see Editor's Introduction, pp xxii ff above.

modes of study it has immense recommendations of its own. On one or two of these I will specially dwell.

First, the comparative method as applied to the English constitution brings into light just those aspects of our institutions which we otherwise fail to notice.

It has often been remarked and with substantial proof that the Greeks were victims in their philosophical speculations to the influence of language. They were the slaves of words just because they knew no tongue but their own and came to regard distinctions of language as equivalents to differences of things. A similar doctrine may be applied to English constitutionalists. They fail to understand the peculiarities of the English constitution because they have given little attention to the institutions of other countries. We fail in speculation as in private life to note what is customary. Anything which is usual strikes us as a matter of course and therefore undeserving of notice. The political arrangements which exist around us, the way in which they work, the spirit that controls them—the very things which make up the essence of English public life—are matters to which we are accustomed and which seem therefore to require no explanation. No mere exposition of the rules of which English constitutional law consists will ever free us from this error. An enquiry into the growth of our system of government will do something to free us from the delusion that things must be as they are; for investigation is, after all, a comparison, but historians are apt to fancy that the way in which things have proceeded in England is the only path they could have followed, and mistake historical accidents for fundamental principles. For this misconception the only radical cure is the thoughtful study of institutions bearing some similarity to, but also differing from, the constitution of modern England.

Let me give you a few examples of the erroneous views which may be dissipated by the comparative method. There is no more marked trait of English constitutionalism than the connection between the right of Parliament to levy taxes and the right of Parliament to pass laws. The power to tax is, historically speaking, the foundation of Parliamentary supremacy. The right to refuse supplies was the weapon by which the House of Commons first extorted a share in the sovereignty and at last appropriated nearly the whole sovereign power of the Crown. There is intimate, and as it seems to most Englishmen, necessary connection between the granting of taxes and the right to make laws which governed the whole course of the long conflict between the Commons and the King. What for our present purpose is more important, it has determined for most Englishmen their way of looking at the relations between the legislature and the executive. To this source we must trace the dogma, which though now a little out of date, was once of high repute, that taxation involves representation. Hence flows the notion that a legislative assembly must of necessity be a taxing body, with which is connected the conclusion that the legislature must have a constitutional right so to use its control of the budget as to make any assembly which can be called a Parliament supreme in the state, and place in its hands both the appointment and the control of the executive. All these views seem to most Englishmen a matter of course. History tells them that the authority gained by the House of Commons is the prize of the long conflict with the Crown, but the teaching of history is obscured by more than one prepossession. A fictitious appeal to precedent fosters the belief that the acquisition of new power was the recovery of old rights. Thinkers who escape from this delusion fall more often than not into another error. They assume that a really representative body must of necessity exercise practical control over the executive. They see indeed that it was possible for the English Parliament to have failed in attaining any authority whatever. They did not perceive that it is not in the nature of things impossible that the development of parliamentary government should have taken an essentially different turn from that which [it] took in England, yet it is at any rate conceivable that a legislative assembly may exist and exert real authority, and yet not be the master of the executive. The plain truth is that as to the matters to which I have referred our whole point of view is changed from the moment we make use of the comparative method. The American Congress is a true legislature; it represents the American people, it votes taxes, yet it is not the sovereign nor anything like the sovereign of the United States. More than this it is not the superior, it is not always even the equal of the President. The American House of Representatives again, which corresponds with our House of Commons has like the House of Commons exclusive control of the budget. The Senate which corresponds to our House of Lords, can no more interfere directly with the budget than can our own upper House, yet for all this, the House of Representatives is not in reality the equal of the Senate. Turn again to the German Reichstag. It is a real Parliament, it can pass, or refuse to pass laws. It holds the taxing power. There is not the remotest reason to suppose that the German Emperor wishes to rid himself of the Reichstag's authority. It is in the highest degree doubtful whether, if he entertained the wish, he has the power to destroy the Reichstag. It is equally certain that the German Parliament, if I may use that term, cannot determine the policy of the Empire. It cannot appoint or remove Imperial Ministers. Here you have in short a true legislature which occupies nothing like the position of the English Parliament. We shall find exactly the same phenomenon if we turn from Germany to Switzerland. There again we shall discover a true Parliament, but a Parliament which is not, and does not pretend to be, the sovereign authority in the state. The plain truth is that it is the position of the modern Parliament of England, and not of the Parliaments of other countries, which is peculiar.

The dogma, again, that Parliament has constantly a right to extend its authority by the refusal of supplies, is a doctrine which has not obtained acceptance in all the countries which possess representative legislatures. The authority of this dogma was the real point at issue between Bismarck and the Parliament of Prussia. The constitutional contest which raged in Prussia between 1861 and 1866 excited keen interest among English Liberals. Its real import was hardly understood. Englishmen conceived that the King wished to establish a despotism. They were equally perplexed by the maintenance of the existence and the defiance of the authority of Parliament. It will now be acknowledged that Bismarck had no wish to destroy the Prussian legislature, or to govern by means of a *coup d'état*. What he did wish was that Parliament should legislate and not govern. His contention was that the right to settle the budget could not constitutionally be used so as to deprive the Crown of its admitted authority. The contest ended in something like a drawn battle. Practically the King and his Minister triumphed. The constitutional dogmas established by their success prevailed not only throughout Prussia, but throughout the German Empire. For the present, at any rate, the executive is neither in Prussia, nor in Germany, appointed or directly controlled by Parliament. English critics will say the result is unconstitutional. The wiser way of looking at the matter is to say that the ideas which prevail in Germany resemble those which prevail in the United States, and differ from the doctrines which now prevail in England.

I emphasise the expression 'now prevail'. One of the most interesting results of comparing our constitutionalism with the views prevalent in other times and other countries is to show conclusively that at one time it appeared probable that the English Parliament might continue to exist as a genuine power in the state, and yet might occupy a position not above the executive, but side by side with it. Let any man who doubts this turn to Cromwell's Instrument of Government—what we should now call the Constitution of 1653. It anticipates in some respects the theories of modern democracy, and especially the views entertained by the founders of the American Commonwealth, and though the assertion sounds paradoxical would have satisfied the ideas of Prince Bismarck far better than can the modern constitution of England. Through the whole of our modern constitutionalism there runs one assumption of which we make so much as a matter of course that we resent its being called an assumption. It is that the House of Commons represents the nation and the national authority in a way in which it is not represented by the Crown or the executive. We can easily see why this is so. My object now is to point out that the validity of the assumption is denied in many countries which enjoy parliamentary government. The President of the United States, the German Emperor, the Swiss Executive Council, perhaps even the French President claim to be as truly organs of the national will as the representative body, be it Congress, or Reichstag, or Federal Assembly, or National Assembly.

Consider again another aspect of constitutional law, the position of the Bench. To any Englishman the functions and position of our judges seem to be the only possible functions and position of the judicial bench. The judges, we know, are the expounders of the law, they are at once dependent and independent, any law passed by Parliament they must put into effect. A statute may at any moment extend or curtail their powers. There is no recorded instance in which they have claimed to set aside an Act of Parliament. It is in the highest degree improbable that they will ever make the claim. On the other hand the judicial bench has within legal limits uncontrolled authority. The judges possess within bounds more easily understood than defined, legislative functions. Their strict adherence to precedents has been the basis of their power. This enables them to construct rules which have legal authority and to build up independently of Parliament whole departments of law. Our judges, again, exercise no political functions. Their just pride is to keep apart from politics and partisanship. They nevertheless exercise over the executive a control which in ordinary times is hardly perceived, yet is real and important. By means of the writ of *habeas corpus* they can any moment check illegality on the part of the government, and can decide questions which in some foreign countries would be held to involve matters of high policy, and to be absolutely beyond the control of the law courts. It was but the other day that the Courts determined not only the meaning of the term 'offence of a political character', but the practical question whether the Swiss citizen who was guilty of treason and murder in Switzerland should be handed over for trial and punishment to the Swiss executive.

These things you will think so obvious that they do not need mention. The matter bears a very different aspect when we investigate the judicial systems of other countries. I say nothing for the moment of the old French Parliaments, which blended judicial, administrative, and political functions in a way which would seem to modern Englishmen almost inconceivable, were they not reminded that the anomalies of the French Parliaments still exist in Jersey. A careful study of the bodies which, with all their faults, were in France the last refuge of independence and public spirit would be of great value. But I pass the matter by, and for the moment direct your attention, not to the old French monarchy, but to modern constitutions, under which exist as much freedom as in England. The Supreme Court of the United States, as indeed the whole judicial system of America, is administered by lawyers influenced by English precedents, yet every Court throughout the American Commonwealth exercises a kind of authority which does not fall to any tribunal in England. The American judges treat as null any Act of Congress which violates the Constitution, and in fact play a part as protectors of the Constitution which against Parliament is never assumed by the English judicial bench. Look again at the tribunals of France. The French magistracy are entitled to the highest respect. They claim and maintain judicial independence, but their sphere of action differs from that of the English judiciary. They exert little, if any, influence in the way of judicial legislation, and respect for administrative law as well as the interpretation placed by Frenchmen of all classes on the so-called doctrine of the separation of powers have restrained the magistrates of France from any interference with the executive in affairs which could by the widest interpretation of the term be considered as matters of the state.

This is not the result of imperial or democratic despotism. During the reign of Louis Philippe France was, we suppose, governed in accordance with maxims borrowed from English constitutionalism, yet the Duchesse de Berri was kept in prison and ultimately sent out of the country not in accordance with any statute, and still less under the judgment of any court, but simply by virtue of authority inherent in the executive. I say authority rather than power, because though the grievances of the Duchesse roused parliamentary debate, no Frenchman of any party suggested that the courts had a right to liberate her from an imprisonment which in England would have been terminated in a day by the issue of a writ of *habeas corpus*.

I would ask you, did time allow, to investigate the singular mixture of judicial and executive functions exercised by the Swiss executive, the Ministry, to use English terms of the Confederation. Astonishing as the assertion sounds in English ears the Swiss Ministry are in many respects a law Court. The Cabinet, with the approval of the country, has determined the limits within which the Salvation Army may legally instruct, or disturb, the people of Switzerland. The Cabinet has decided what to Englishmen would appear a purely legal enquiry, whether the government at Ticino was, or was not, bound under the Constitution of that canton to submit certain proposals of constitutional reform to the approval or disapproval of the people. But on this subject I will say no more. The examples I have given you, of which it were easy to supply a far larger store, suffice to show that the position of English judges may be essentially different from the position of the judiciary in other free and even democratic countries.

Secondly, the comparative method leads to the discovery of new affinities and new dissimilarities between different constitutions, and this enables us to group them in accordance with new principles.

Take, for example, the division of so-called parliamentary governments in accordance with the relations existing between the executive and the legislature.

If we adopt this method of division, we shall find that the essential distinction which discriminates the constitution of one land from that of another is the parliamentary or extra-parliamentary character of the executive.

An executive is parliamentary in the full sense of the term when it is appointed, controlled, and removed, by the parliament or legislature.

An executive is extra-parliamentary when it is appointed and kept in power, not by the Parliament or legislature, but by some other person or body of persons standing outside, or at any rate, independent of Parliament.

Under the class of countries which possess parliamentary executives we find grouped together England, the whole body of constitutional monarchies, such as Italy and Belgium, and the existing French Republic, remarkable for being in name and appearance exactly what it is not in truth and reality. In theory the Ministry is the extra-parliamentary body consisting of the Crown's servants chosen by the Crown, in reality it is a parliamentary body consisting of legal parliamentary politicians appointed in fact by the party which commands a majority in Parliament. We shall find, again, if we look at things and not at words that it is often difficult to determine which is the group within which we ought to bring a given constitution. We shall find further that each type of executive has its peculiar merits and its peculiar defects, and that few subjects deserve more or have received less study than the attempts which have been made with occasional, but with rare, success to institute an executive which should have at once a parliamentary and an extra-parliamentary character. On this matter, however, I cannot on the present occasion deal further.

Thirdly, the comparative study shows us that the wide term 'parliamentary government' includes within it very different types of constitutionalism. Two main types deserve very special attention.

The first of these is the fully developed parliamentary constitutionalism of England. Its essential feature is the omnipotence of Parliament, and the decisive predominance of the representative body in the House of Commons. The House of Commons has by slow degrees arrogated or obtained a power hardly conceded either in theory or in fact to any other representative assembly. It has a main and decisive part in legislation, it in fact, through not in name, appoints the executive. More than this, it not only appoints, but controls the exercise of executive power. All this, we shall be told, is the result of our progress towards democracy. What I wish to insist upon, not as a politician (for with politics we have tonight no concern) but as a student of constitutional theory, is that this omnipotence of an elected assembly is not the result, or at any rate, the final result, of democratic progress or development, but the result of the peculiarities of English history. If we look either at the past history of England or at the institutions which exist around us in other countries we shall find that this decisive predominance of an elective legislature is an anomaly, though it well may be a salutary anomaly. Till times within the memory of men now living the House of Commons did not, with anything like its present directness, appoint the executive. At the beginning of the century the Crown as represented by George III had a great deal to say as to who should constitute the English Cabinet. The proof of this is decisive. We wonder sometime at the bitterness with which politicians fought out the question whether on the King's recurring madness there was to be a regency, and what were to be the powers of the Regent. The reason of the violence with which this constitutional question was debated is not far to seek. It was supposed that if the Prince of Wales had the authority which belonged to the Crown not only would the Cabinet be changed, but the whole policy of England might be turned in a new direction. It will perhaps be doubted in the light of later experience whether Tories and Whigs alike do not somewhat exaggerate the importance of the change which might be produced by the accession of the Prince of Wales to regal power, but the exaggeration if it existed is conclusive proof of the authority, which men far better acquainted with the English constitution of a century ago than can be their descendants, attributed to the Crown.

Turn to foreign countries and you will find that everywhere or almost everywhere a check of some kind or other is imposed upon the power of the elected legislators.

The American Congress is tight bound by the bonds of the Constitution, its authority is balanced by the power of the President, by the hands of the judiciary, and above all by the power of the electors who appoint the executive. It is now acknowledged on all hands that President Lincoln exercised, and exercised, I must add, for the salvation of the country, the authority of a public-spirited dictator. No Ministry in England has ventured for more than a century and no Ministry, while our present constitution lasts, will venture on such exertions of power. Sometimes at the moment, however, unpopular words were put forth by the President who saved the Union. Even in France where the executive and judiciary have less of independent authority than the Cabinet or the judges of England, where in fact you really have [a] parliamentary executive, you will yet find that a curious check is placed on the predominance of the Chamber of Deputies. Not a syllable of the constitutional laws can be changed except by a Congress, that is by the Senate and the Chamber of Deputies sitting together, and though the Chamber of Deputies practically appoint the Ministry it must be remembered that the President, who under the French Constitution certainly may exert very considerable influence, is appointed, not by the Chamber of Deputies, but by the Congress. If we want to know what this would mean, let us suppose that no constitutional change could be passed through Parliament unless it had received the sanction of an assembly composed of the combined House of Lords and House of Commons. At the present moment we are told that the head of the French government would not be President had it not been for the almost unanimous support of the Senate.

Turn from France to the most successful democracy of modern days, the democracy of Switzerland. There, again, you have an elective assembly whose authority is strictly limited. It is limited, on the one hand, by the necessity, as regards the appointment of the executive, of voting together with the Senate. It is limited, on the other hand, and far more effectually limited, by the fact that every constitutional change, every law of considerable importance must, before it is finally passed, obtain direct sanction of the people. The veto of the Crown which has expired in England, which formed a part of the old English constitution, has become a real, though suspensive, veto on the part of the American President, and had curiously reappeared in a new form in the most democratic of modern states as the effective veto of the nation.

I might give you other examples of my meaning. They might be interesting, but are, I think, needless. What I want to insist upon is this, that the comparative method brings to light the existence of two distinct constitutional types. The one is the parliamentary type which has received its full development in England; for the other type it is difficult to find a precise term. It might be described, however, as constitutionalism of a non-parliamentary type, under which the real legislature is confined to legislative functions, whilst the control of the executive or of the constitution is to a great extent placed beyond its power.

The comparative method, beyond what I may call its special recommendations, has the merit that the use of it suggests the general conclusions which ought to guide the whole study either of our own constitution or of other constitutions.

It, in the first place, suggests the true importance of constitutional arrangements. It is abundantly plain that there have been periods of history, and these not very distant from us, when not only popular opinion [but also] the judgment of men of great capacity attributed an importance to constitutions which they do not in reality possess. The whole French Revolutionary history, and to a certain extent the annals of the English Commonwealth bear traces of the conviction that a good constitution could of itself create a great and free nation. We all know now that forms of government, be they bad, or be they good, are of far less importance than human character, or than the circumstances social and economical of which forms of government are for the most part the outcome. Still the student of constitutions will soon convince himself that if a good constitution cannot create a free or prosperous people, it is quite possible that bad institutions may mar both the freedom and prosperity of the state. The powerlessness of Germany, though possessed as we now see of all the elements of power was caused for a considerable time by the vicious arrangements of the German Confederation. It is hardly too much to say that for fifty years and more the Northern States of America struggled against the artificial supremacy conferred by constitutional arrangements on the States of the South. The Constitution is after all something like the clothing of the state. You may clothe a man in armour, but you will not thereby give him either bravery or strength; but the force of a giant is useless if once you get him bound in a strait waistcoat.

Secondly, nothing appears more obviously true than that a freely elected assembly, especially if it be elected by the whole or the greater number of the citizens, must represent the wishes of the electors. This is the fact or supposed fact on which is grounded the authority for representative assembly. Till very recent times it was never, I suppose, doubted by democracies that a freely elected Parliament would necessarily express the will of the electors or, at any rate, the majority of them. When for any reason men were dissatisfied with the laws passed by Parliament they thought and alleged that the so-called representative assembly had not been rightly or fairly elected. Reformers quarrelled with the constitution of the constitutional bodies or else alleged that corruption or intimidation had falsified the result of their votes. This position is one which now no thoughtful man can unhesitatingly maintain. The experience of foreign countries shows conclusively that it may well happen that a freely elected assembly, and an elected assembly, I may add, consisting of persons by whom the electors are willing for many purposes to be represented, does not really represent the wish of the electorate. It has again and again happened, for example in Switzerland, that the Parliament has passed laws which the people negative, and that the people having vetoed the particular law send back the same representatives to sit in Parliament. The whole scheme of American constitutionalism rests now on the assumption that the very men appointed to draw up a constitution for a State, say for New York, may draw up a constitution, which the people of New York refuse to accept, and the assumption is well verified by the facts of American history.

Thirdly, one general reflection is suggested both by the constitutional history of any country whatever which we may choose for our study. It is so obvious that I scarcely like to dwell upon it, and yet is so rarely put into words that I do not like to leave it unnoticed. It is that almost any organ of the state or government may represent in a special manner the will of the nation. From a series of historical circumstances it becomes the embodiment for the time of the country. It is a natural English assumption that this special function of representing the nation must belong to the assembly which is technically representative. This assumption is unfounded. In England the Houses of Parliament, and especially the House of Commons, has on the whole, and as a rule, been the embodiment of the national will. Even in England we can only make this assertion with considerable limitations. Under the Tudors the Crown was the representative of the country quite as truly as the House of Commons, perhaps more truly. The long contests of George III with his Parliaments, with the Whigs, was really a contest as to whether the King was, or was not, entitled to be the representative of the nation in the same degree as the House of Commons. George III in fact claimed to occupy a position not unlike that of the American President or the German Emperor, and it is difficult to say that he did not succeed in making out his claim. It is quite certain that the opinions of the good old King had a weight with the nation resembling that which we now concede to a popular Prime Minister. In other countries at least we can easily perceive that it is not always the elective house which commands the confidence of the nation. In Germany it is the Emperor, in America it is often the President, it is often the Senate. Nor is it at all necessary that the nation should find its representative either in a monarchy or in a political assembly. The French Parliaments struggled vehemently, though their efforts ended in failure to become the representatives of the nation. In France the tendency has always been to make the executive the embodiment of national authority. In Scotland there was a Parliament, and a Parliament, which had at times real power, yet at one period the nobles or the King had more authority than the Parliament. From the time of the Reformation the true representation of Scotland was found, not in the Parliament, but in the Church Assembly, yet history teaches us that it is almost an accident what is the organ of the state which embodies the will of the nation. Never was there a Parliament in many respects less entitled to admiration, though its faults have, in some respect, been a good deal exaggerated, than the Parliament of Ireland. It never represented in reality more than one section of the nation, and this section it often misrepresented. It was a Parliament, moreover, with an extra-parliamentary executive, and an executive appointed, not in Ireland, but in England. Yet by one of the curious paradoxes of history this Parliament became the representative of Ireland in a sense in which the Parliament of Scotland had never, I conceive, fully represented the people of Scotland. A constitutionalist at least may be entitled to notice that the undeveloped parliamentary system of Scotland and the misdeveloped parliamentary system of Ireland are both full of instruction. They impress upon us the conclusion to which the whole comparative study of constitutions leads, that the real power and authority of any one organ of the state depends on its becoming in some way or other the representative of the nation, and whether King, Parliament, or Church represents the national will. It depends not nearly so much on constitutional arrangements as upon a long series of historical causes.

1

General Characteristics of Existing English Constitutionalism

Analysis*

A.   Constitution an **Historical** Constitution
  I.   An *historically* developed constitution
         (Contrast French, Italian, or Belgian Constitutions)
  II.   A *continuously* developed constitution
         (Contrast German Empire, Swiss Confederation)
  III.   Constitution the product of *historical conditions*

B.   Constitution an **Unwritten** Constitution
  I.   Not to be found in any *law* or *document*
  II.   Result of *legal decisions* or conflicts
  III.   The working of constitution depends on *conventions*

C.   Constitution a **Parliamentary** Constitution
  I.   *Parliamentary sovereignty*
  II.   *Parliamentary executive*

D.   Constitution a **Democratic** Constitution

E.   Constitution a **Unitary** Constitution

(See Bagehot, *The English Constitution*;
Boutmy, *Études de Droit Constitutionnel*;
Boutmy, *Le Développement de la Constitution*.)

---

* Its contents have been derived from an undated manuscript attached to the lecture schedule headed 'Easter & Trinity Terms, 1897'.

[General] Characteristics of Existing English Constitutionalism[*]

Let us look at the existing constitution from two or three different points of view.

A. The Modern Constitution of England is an *Historical* Constitution[†]

This is a statement which we all of us constantly make in one form or another and no one is the least tempted to deny, but of which it is more difficult than at first sight appears to appreciate the full meaning. In one sense every human institution and therefore every polity is historical. It has come into existence through a definite set of events. It connects in some way or other with the past. Thus, to take the French Republic which has existed for not more than a quarter of a century: it certainly is the product of history. The story of its formation is a very curious one. A student can hardly understand a line of the constitutional laws unless he bears in mind the events of 1870 and of the years which follow. The fall of the Second Empire, the German invasion of France, the conservatism of the Assembly at Versailles, the insurrection of the Commune, and many other well known events must be borne in mind if we are to explain either the proclamation of the Third Republic or the peculiar and fragmentary form of the laws governing the French commonwealth. Nor again can the working of French institutions be understood unless we go a good way back into the history of France, unless we take into account both the causes and the results of the great Revolution. Thus, to give one example, the power and the incapacities of the French magistracy or as Americans would say of the judiciary are demonstrably the result, though it may be the result by way of reaction, of the condition of the French *Parlements*. The French Constitution therefore is in one sense historical, but every one feels that it is not an historical constitution exactly in the sense or more strictly in the senses in which we apply the term to the English constitution, and the same remark applies to the Constitution say of Italy, of Belgium, of the German Empire, and indeed of almost any European state with the possible exception of Hungary.

If then every constitution has a history and has links with the past what do we mean when we apply the term 'historical' to English institutions as marking off a difference between them and the political arrangements of other lands?

The statement that our constitution is an historical constitution includes at least three ideas which, though often blended or confused together, are distinguishable.

---

[*] The manuscript was dated March 1897 (also 5 May 1897 in a later manuscript note), and 'General' was omitted in the title but has been added here for the sake of consistency with the title as stated elsewhere.

[†] For Dicey's more developed account of the four characteristics he later attributed to the historical constitution, see 'Historical Constitutions and Non-Historical Constitutions', pp 172 ff below. See generally Editor's Introduction, pp xlii ff above.

I. The English constitution has been historically developed

It has grown, that is to say, with the growth of the nation. The Crown, the Parliament, the Courts, the national Church, as they now exist are each of them the gradual creation of the course of events which make up the history of England. Thus it is absolutely impossible to explain either the constitution of the existing Parliament, or the position of the Church of England, without constant references to past history. No doubt in one sense this, as I have said, is true of all institutions at all times and everywhere, but it is not true of all institutions in the same sense. It is quite possible to state, for example, the constitution of the French Senate and to enumerate the powers of that body without going further back than the date at which the Senate was created. There is no need for tracing its descent from any prior assembly, as for example from the order of the *noblesse* in a States General, from the Senate of Napoleon I, from the House of Peers under the Bourbons or the Orléanist dynasty, or from the Senate of the Second Empire. I have said there is no need to trace this descent. I ought rather to have said there is no possibility of doing so. You cannot explore a genealogy where no genealogy exists. This difference between the House of Lords and the French Senate forms a distinction between the whole of the French and the whole of the English constitution. The one has not and the other has been the result of historical development.

II. The constitution has been continuously developed

There has been no break in the growth of the English Parliament and system.

The Parliament of today differs in material points from the Parliament of, say, Henry VIII just as the Parliament of Henry VIII differed from the Parliament of Edward I, or the Parliament of Edward I differed essentially from the *Magnum Concilium* of the first Norman Kings and the Great Council in its turn differed greatly from the *Witenagemót*, but each of the stages of parliamentary growth are linked together. You may say that the Parliament of one age is the same Parliament as the Parliament of the next, something in the same sense in which you may say that a man of 70 is the same person as the boy of 7 years old. You may of course point out eras at which the fabric of the English constitution has undergone changes or developments, such for example as the Revolution of 1688, the date of the Union with Scotland in 1706, or the date of the Union with Ireland in 1800, or the crisis which ended in the passing of the Reform Bill of 1832. But though you may point to changes, and great changes, you cannot point to any distinct break, with one possible exception, in the development of the constitution. Continuity it is true is not identity, but practically unbroken continuity is undoubtedly one of the features in the development of English institutions which makes them emphatically historical.

Contrast this unbroken growth of the English parliamentary system with the history of the modern German Empire or the modern Swiss Confederation. Both of them are in a very true sense historical constitutions. They are connected with the past history of Germany or of Switzerland respectively in a way in which the French

Republic is not connected with the past history of France. They give effect to ideas which have been working with more or less distinctness for centuries amongst the German and the Swiss people. The German Empire could not be what it is were it not for traditions and sentiments dating back to the Holy Roman Empire. It would be absolutely impossible to understand many of the anomalies in the Imperial Federation, for example the constitution and position of the Bundesrath, unless you took into account the state of things which existed under the Empire up to 1800 and further under the Confederation from 1815 to 1866. The Empire dates from 1871 but it is the result of tendencies which have been working for centuries. From one point of view it is the restoration or revival of an older state of things. The modern Swiss Republic dates indeed from 1848, but it is distinctly the result of that constant effort towards national unity which, amidst all the struggles and confusions which perplex any man who studies the annals of Switzerland, is the true note or mark of Swiss progress. Yet though the modern German Empire and the modern Swiss Republic are in one sense historical constitutions they each lack the characteristic of continuity. It is indeed quite conceivable that under different circumstances the German Imperial Constitution of today might have stood in unbroken connection with the Holy Roman Empire. It is even more easily conceivable that a process of gradual reform might without any break have transformed the Swiss Confederacy as it existed in 1789 into something like the modern Swiss Republic. But as a fact this gradual development did not take place. In each case the French revolution broke the line of historical continuity. The Holy Roman Empire ceased for a time to exist. The institutions by which it was replaced were not linked to it. Take the example of Switzerland which is a very striking one. You can say with truth that the habits and sentiments created by the old Confederacy gave birth to the modern Confederation, but it is impossible to deny that the French Republic and the Napoleonic Empire interrupted the course of Swiss constitutional development. The unitary Helvetic Republic modelled under the influence of French politicians and reproducing the ideas and institutions which prevailed in France in 1797 stands apparently at least unconnected with the Confederacy of the Thirteen Cantons and unacknowledged by the modern Republicanism of Switzerland. It occupies a position not absolutely unlike the position occupied by the Commonwealth of the Protectorate in the history of England. It is worth turning for a moment to the Commonwealth. It illustrates by way of contrast the matter under consideration. Had the Constitution of 1653 created by the Instrument of Government held its ground the country might have gained many and considerable advantages. But English constitutionalism would have lost its specially historical character. The political institutions of the country would have dated back to a definite year, and there would have been a district breach in their continuity. The artifices of lawyers can achieve much but it would have taxed and overtaxed their astuteness to show that the Parliament created by Cromwell and his officers with its single House and with its representation of England, Scotland, and Ireland descended from the last Parliament of Charles I. Even as it was the Rebellion did introduce a temporary break into the continuity of our constitutional development. The grotesque fiction by which Charles II was looked upon as immediately succeeding Charles I, the effort to blot out from a constitutional point of view every transaction which took place between 1649 and 1660, was due no doubt immediately to the violence of partisanship and of triumphant reaction, but it was also the expression of the instinctive resolution of Englishmen to maintain the historical continuity of their institutions.

III. *The constitution is a work of native production. It is the product of the special historical conditions of England*

By this statement is meant that the English constitution for good and bad is the result of events taking place in England and of the immediate wants and wishes of Englishmen. It is not in any sense a copy of any foreign polity. This cannot be asserted of any or at any rate of most of the constitutions now existing in Europe. They have all of them been more or less consciously influenced by the example of England. The bicameral system of Parliament admits of justification on grounds of policy and expediency but if we ask why it is that almost every modern legislature consists of neither more nor less than two Houses or Chambers, why in short we have not monocameral or tricameral Parliaments, the true answer is that it became the fashion to create Parliaments of two Houses because of the fame and the success of the English constitution under which there have always been two Houses.

If again we ask why it is that English constitutionalism is an article of purely native manufacture we are driven back to the conditions physical or political which have fixed the course of English progress. The small size of England, the insularity of the country, the easy accessibility of all parts thereof, the absence of Roman influence, and above all, the formation at a very early period of a government which could enforce its will throughout the whole land and could therefore establish uniformity of law and uniformity of administration, are some at any rate of the conditions which have given to the constitution of England its purely English character. Here however we touch upon matters belonging to the province of historians rather than of lawyers; all we need note is that the English constitution is historical in being in a special sense the immediate result of the conditions which govern English history.[1]

By way of contrast a student may notice the way in which the absence of some among the favourable conditions existing in England arrested the development of

---

[1] Mark the curious absence of all conscious attempts on the part of Englishmen to realize either historical or, except in the time of the Puritan revolution, political ideals. Tradition seems in England to have had as little influence as abstract political speculation. Contrast the attempts of the French revolutionists to carry out theories of equality; contrast also the Italian desire for unity or national independence and the German desire for the renewal of Imperial greatness. Few things are more perplexing than the absence from English history of tradition and its influence. Cromwell made Protestantism triumphant and preserved the unity of what is now the United Kingdom yet in England Cromwell never became a popular hero. There is no Cromwellian legend. The Jacobins, on the other hand, and Napoleon each left behind them a tradition strong enough to affect the whole course of French history. No Ministers ever commanded so much popularity as Chatham and his son, yet I doubt whether at Hayes there remains the least recognition of the two Pitts among the people who live there. I have been told that the name of Hampden is completely forgotten in the village where he lived and where there are tombs of the family. The only two events which seem to have left something like a tradition are the Gunpowder Plot and the Restoration, and even these are falling more and more out of ordinary memory.

Scotch constitutionalism. To begin with there was little essential difference between the political institutions of Scotland and the political institutions of England. In each country you find a mediaeval King and a mediaeval Parliament; in each country there is the mediaeval Church allied in the main politically with the King. Up moreover to the time of Edward I there was a strong tendency on the part of Scotch Kings and lawyers to imitate the institutions of England yet there was one essential difference. The Scotch King down to the Union of the two countries under James I never possessed anything like the uncontested power which belonged from the time of William the Conqueror to the English Crown. Owing partly to the geographical foundation of the country, partly to the existence of clanship, and partly to other causes, the authority of the Crown was balanced and all but overbalanced by the power of the nobility. Hence there never was established anything like that supremacy of the Royal Courts, which by the time of Edward I at any rate existed in England. Independent jurisdictions belonging to the nobles existed until after 1745, and until 1603 the authority of the Crown was even in the Lowlands extremely precarious and in the Highlands had hardly any existence. Hence two results.

Just because of the independence or unruliness of the nobles, Parliament, which represents the power of the Crown combined with, or transferred to, the peers and the representatives of the commons, never gained anything like the weight which it possessed in England long before England and Scotland were united under one Crown. To look at the same thing from another point of view the powerlessness of the Scotch Crown made it unnecessary for the nobles and the commons to unite and place regular and legal limitations on the authority of the King.

When again the movement against the Church of Rome which is known as the Reformation took place in Scotland as well as in England, the Crown was not in a position to guide and control it. It was carried out by a portion of the nobility and the people and resulted in the formation of a church system in which the vigorous portions of the nation were more truly represented than in Parliament. It is hardly an exaggeration to say that the Church Assembly was the true representative of the Scotch nation. No doubt the Crown rather than the Parliament came directly into conflict with the Church, but the authority of the Church Assembly was in reality fatal to the authority and development of Parliament. It is well even here to note that the Act of Union gave security to the Scotch Church and whilst it abolished the Parliament which did not represent[,] [it] preserved and safeguarded the Church Assembly which did represent[,] the nation. It was the relation between Church and Parliament which made the Union a possibility and a success. On this point however it is unnecessary to say more here. All that need be noted is that the absence in Scotland of certain favourable conditions which existed in England arrested the development of Scotch constitutionalism. The country with which to compare Scotland in constitutional matters is France. It is quite possible that but for the Union with England the Crown might ultimately have acquired in Scotland something like the authority it gained in France. It is equally possible that had the tendencies which made for Protestantism been as strong in France as in Scotland the French Calvinists might have acquired for the Protestant Church something like the independence and authority which the Scotch Calvinists gained for the Church of Scotland.

B. The Constitution is an *Unwritten* Constitution[*]

The expression 'unwritten constitution' is a lax and popular one. It does not mean that considerable parts of the constitution of England are not to be found in written documents, or even in enactments. The Magna Charta, the Bill of Rights, the Act of Settlement, the Acts of Union are written documents which do contain a great deal of the constitution.

When we call the constitution unwritten we mean three things.

(1) The articles of the constitution are not to be found, as are the articles of the Constitution of the USA, in any one definite document or enactment; there is in short no such thing as a written constitution of England in the sense in which there is a written constitution of the USA, of Italy or of Belgium. This however, be it remarked, is a mere matter of form. If the main provisions of the English constitution were reduced to the form of an Act passed by Parliament the substance of the constitution would remain unchanged, provided always that the Constitution Act could be changed or repealed in the same manner as other Acts of Parliament.

(2) The articles of the constitution are to a great extent the result either of legal decisions or of conflicts which resulted in something very like legal decisions.

The fundamental principle for example that the order of the Crown does not justify an illegal act, or that no tax can be imposed except by Act of Parliament, may now fairly be deduced from decisions, and the Petition of Right or the Bill of Rights comes very near to an authoritative decision on various points of constitutional law.

(3) The working of the constitution depends on understandings or conventions.

That this is the fact is undoubted. The rule that if a Ministry is defeated the Cabinet go out of office, the rule that the Queen assents to all Bills passed by Parliament, the rule that the House of Lords must ultimately yield to the House of Commons when it is shown that the [lower] House represents the will of the nation, are all mere understandings, but they are understandings on which every politician acts and which practically regulate the public life of England. What is the sanction which gives force to these conventions I have elsewhere tried to explain.[2] All that need here be noted is the existence of these conventions. They form a part no doubt of every civilized polity. They have in one or two respects completely modified the working of the Constitution of the USA. But

---

[2] *The Law of the Constitution*, ch. XV.

[*] See also 'Divisions of Constitutions', pp 233 ff below. See generally Editor's Introduction, pp xlii f. above.

conventions form a larger part of the English constitutional system than of the French or the Italian constitutional systems and are apt, it is conceived, to be of less importance under a written than under an unwritten constitution.

The statement that a constitution is an 'unwritten' constitution is often used as meaning something different from what the words naturally import, namely that it is a flexible constitution or in other words a constitution the articles of which can be changed by the ordinary legislative body or Parliament in the same way in which other laws are changed. This characteristic, however, of flexibility which belongs to the English constitution has no essential connection, or but a very slight connection, with the fact that a constitutional law of a country is unwritten or, in other words, is not to be found in any one or more definite enactment or enactments. The matter stands thus: where a constitution is written or enacted the articles thereof are frequently but by no means always 'rigid'; they cannot that is to say be changed by the ordinary legislative power in the ordinary course of legislation. Where, on the other hand, a constitution is unwritten or unenacted, it generally, though this does not appear to be necessary, is flexible, its articles, that is to say, can be changed by the ordinary legislative body in the ordinary course of legislation. The flexibility, however, of the English constitution which is only accidentally connected with its being unwritten or unenacted is best considered under our next head.

C. The Constitution is a *Parliamentary* Constitution

This statement again which appears a very simple one implies much more than the assertion that England in common with almost every modern civilized country has a Parliament by which term we roughly designate any national legislature consisting wholly or in part of persons elected to represent the citizens. When we call the English constitution parliamentary, we mean certainly to assert that in England laws are passed by a Parliament, but we mean more than this and, what is particularly to be noticed, in reality mean to combine together two or three different statements.

Let us try, as in other cases, to analyse all that is implied in the assertion that we have an emphatically parliamentary constitution.

I. *The English Parliament is a sovereign law-making body*[3]

Any law whatever, even the most fundamental laws of the land, can be legally changed by Parliament. No person or body of persons have according to English constitutional law a right to treat an Act of Parliament as invalid. Such an Act may be impolitic, may be immoral, may be unjust, but it cannot be called illegal, unconstitutional, or void. Contrast the position of Congress. Any law which exceeds the authority given to Congress under the Constitution is void and will be treated as

---
[3] See *The Law of the Constitution*, chs. I and II.

such by the American Courts. No law, again, to look at the same matter from the negative side is valid in England or throughout the British Empire which is opposed to or contravenes an Act of Parliament. The legislative sovereignty of Parliament is complete and absolute.

The matter may be looked at from another point of view. There is under the English constitution no way by which the people or the nation can exert supreme legislative authority except by an Act of Parliament. Our constitution knows of no appeal to the people. There is in England nothing like the so called *plebiscites* of the French Empire or the referendum as it exists in modern Switzerland or, though not under that name, in most of the States of America.

II. *The government of England is a parliamentary executive*

The English executive government is in reality, though not in name, the Cabinet. Now the English Ministry or Cabinet are not, it is true, directly chosen by Parliament and a somewhat erroneous impression is conveyed even by the statement now often made that they are indirectly elected by Parliament or rather by the House of Commons. What is true is that the government must consist of 'members of Parliament', if we use that term as including members of the House of Lords who command the confidence of the majority of the House of Commons, or, speaking generally, who are the leading men in Parliament among the party who command a majority in the House of Commons. It is therefore in the strictest sense true that the government is a parliamentary executive, its members are parliamentary leaders selected from persons who have seats in the House of Commons or the House of Lords; they derive their power from the confidence reposed in them by the House of Commons, and when this confidence is withdrawn they lose office. No King since the Revolution of 1688 has even attempted to form an extra-parliamentary government, and the very few cases in which a government has been kept for a time in office which did not command a majority in the Commons constitute exactly the exceptions of the kind which proves the rule.

It is natural for Englishmen to imagine that the real legislative authority of Parliament involves the existence of a parliamentary executive, but, as I shall show in later lectures, one of the most obvious and also one of the most important conclusions impressed upon us by the comparative study of constitutions is that legislative authority does not necessarily imply executive authority. I will give you but two examples of their severance. The English Parliament itself obtained supreme legislative authority and even legislative sovereignty long before it acquired the right practically to appoint the executive. None of the Stuarts directly disputed the legislative authority of Parliament; it was not till a considerable time after the Revolution of 1688 that Parliament obtained anything like complete control over the appointment of the executive. Cabinet government is the growth of modern times. The legislature of Imperial Germany has unlimited or all but unlimited authority in the field of legislation, but it is notorious and admitted that there does not exist in the German Empire a parliamentary executive.

III. Parliament is the centre, so to speak, of English political institutions

When we call our constitution parliamentary we have before our minds a fact which it is a little difficult to put into words. We all feel that Parliament and above all the House of Commons as the most powerful member of Parliament plays a part far greater than that which falls to any other English institution.

This is in part the result of history. Century after century the influence of Parliament has increased and the influence of every other power in the state has relatively decreased. The Houses of Parliament, and especially the lower House, have, so to speak, became the embodiment of the nation. We can hardly now imagine a state of things under which Parliament did not meet yearly and sit for a large portion of the year. This, be it always remembered, is as time is measured historically a recent phenomenon. No doubt long before the Revolution of 1688 a good King was expected to convene Parliament pretty frequently, but there was no reason to expect anything like the constant sessions of Parliament to which we are accustomed. It moreover has happened in England that every event and every contest has tended in one way or another to increase Parliamentary power. The Restoration marks the greatest reaction which is recorded in the political annals of England, but note that the Restoration was as much the victory of the Parliament as of the King. If Cromwell had put Charles I to death he had also dissolved by force the only legal Parliament in existence. The Restoration of the King was preceded by the reassembling of the Rump, that is of all that remained of the last legally elected Parliament. Add to this that the Restoration Parliament did not restore the system of administrative government which had existed from the accession of the Tudors to the fall of the Star Chamber. Parliament profited by legislation which as against Parliament had diminished the power of the Crown. Parliament again, as I have before pointed out, has never, excepting the Crown the power of which it has substantially appropriated, known any rival authority. The executive has never been as it still is in Germany and was for a long time in France, the representative of the nation. Parliament has not in England been checked as is Congress, by State rights which represent the authority of one sovereign and[,] still in one sense of the word, semi-sovereign state. Parliament has never found its power balanced, as is the power of the Swiss Federal Assembly, by the direct action of the people.

If you want to see how essentially our government is parliamentary you should consider how totally different would be the abolition of Parliament in England from the abolition of Parliament, say, in France or in Germany. In England it would mean a total change in our political institutions and in what one may call the habits of ordinary life. In France it would mean nothing like the same thing. Parliament was not in strictness abolished but it was, so to speak, silenced by Napoleon III. It may well be doubted whether outside Paris the change resulting from the *coup d'état* was anything like as great as an Englishman would suppose. The Parliament of Prussia was for more than five years not abolished but defied and defied with success by the Crown. If the parliamentary government of Germany or of Prussia were overthrown—a calamity I may add which is in the highest degree improbable—this would after all mean nothing but a return to a system of which many men now living can remember the existence. The truth is that the Parliament in Prussia, for example, so far from being the centre of Prussian public life is, so to speak, an institution imported from abroad which does not even as it is work very easily into the arrangements of a monarchical and a military state. There is no constitution in the world which is so strictly parliamentary as that of England.

D. The Modern Constitution of England is a *Democratic* Constitution

We may call a polity democratic which has two features.

The one is that power should finally reside in the numerical majority of the citizens. This no doubt is not as yet in strictness the case in England. One thing is however certain. Every change which has taken place during the last sixty years and every change proposed for adoption is democratic, i.e. tends to increase the authority given to the majority of the citizens.

The other is the sentiment or conviction which is essentially democratic that the action of the nation in legislation and otherwise ought to be controlled by the will of the majority. This is the substantial meaning of the old phrase 'the sovereignty of the people'. It is now a principle which admittedly rules the public life of England.

E. The Constitution is a *Unitarian* or *Unitary* Constitution

A unitarian or as it may be more conveniently called a unitary constitution is contrasted with a federal constitution.[4]

Under a unitary government the sovereign power clearly and visibly, so to speak, resides in some one body, e.g. the King, Parliament, or the like who is supreme throughout the whole of the country. All other authorities, whatever power they may possess, can claim nothing but delegated powers; they have no appearance of sovereignty and they are not in any sense part of the sovereign power.

Under a federal government the several States or cantons, by whatever name they are called, have generally been at one period independent or quasi-independent states[;] the very object of the federal bond is whilst forming them for some purposes into one state or country, to leave them a large amount of independent action, or as it is conveniently called semi-sovereignty. The relation of the States to the central government differs immensely in different federations. In this as in other respects, federalism has different forms which admit it is probabl[y] of almost infinite variation. Hence the federalism of the United States differs considerably from the federalism of Switzerland and each again differ from the federalism of Germany. Nor

---

[4] See *The Law of the Constitution*, ch. III, 'Parliamentary Sovereignty and Federalism'.

would it be impossible to construct a federal union differing in many respects from any existing confederacy. The one point in which every federal government differs from every unitary government is that wherever there is federalism you will find that certain localities or States, the union of which makes up the federation, have, as such, State rights whilst under a truly unitary government such as that of France, Italy, or the United Kingdom, there is no such thing known as State rights. To this we may add that the modes in which the independence or quasi-independence of the States under a federal form of government is secured are, as far as one can draw inferences from experience, two. The several States making up the confederacy may be bound together by nothing more than a perpetual alliance. They do not in reality acknowledge a common sovereign; there exists no power which can act directly on the citizens of the several States except the power, be it Prince or legislative assembly, which is supreme in that State. This seem to have been theoretically at any rate the condition of things in the united provinces under the German Empire, under the German Confederation between 1815 and 1866, and in the Swiss Confederacy up to 1848 except during the short period when there existed a unitary government, the Helvetic Republic, supported by France. A confederacy of this kind is a body of confederated States, it is not in reality a federal state.

The several States which intend to form a federal state may create a real sovereign power, be it an assembly or any other body, but the States are in effect themselves members of the sovereign body and hence possess means for protecting their State rights. To this we may add that where a true federal state is thus formed it will generally he found that under the constitution the different powers of legislation and government are carefully distributed so as to make it difficult for the central government which represents the nation to encroach on the reserved rights of the States or for the States to control in matters concerning the whole nation the action of the central or national government. The country in which the federal system has been carried out with the greatest elaboration is America. The United States exist in virtue of the Constitution or as we might almost call it the fundamental pact under which a sovereign power is so constituted that it shall at once represent the nation as a whole and the several States. Revolution or violence can change or overthrow any institutions whatever, but as long as the Constitution of the USA is respected it is impossible for the States to be deprived of any right given them by the Constitution unless at least three-fourths of the States assent thereto. Nor is it at all likely that while the Constitution remains really in force even the attempt to evade the rights of the States can be made unless a very large number of them wish these rights to be curtailed. The outward and visible sign of the acknowledged rights of the States is to the found in the constitution of the Senate which represents and represents equally every State great and small, and without the assent of the Senate a change in the Constitution is impossible. On this matter it is unnecessary at present to dwell. The point to be forced on the attention of students is that the English constitution knows nothing of federalism.

This is from one point of view a matter for surprise. The United Kingdom consists of three—if you include Wales one may even say of four—bodies which at one time constituted different countries. It might have been expected *a priori* that the union of these countries, should it ever take place, would assume a federal form. As a matter of fact nothing of the sort has happened. This is the more noteworthy because the people of England, Wales, Scotland, and Ireland have been by no means so completely fused into one undistinguishable body as the inhabitants of the different provinces, say, of France. The explanation of a singular phenomenon is probably to be found in the history of England. From the time of the Norman Conquest the central government was stronger in England than in almost any other European country. The Crown, as represented by the Courts, was supreme throughout the whole land. The power of the Crown was first encroached upon by, next shared with, and lastly transferred in effect to, Parliament. But the process by which Parliamentary authority grew up had no tendency whatever to alter the unitary character of the constitution. The very contests with the Crown led to union among every class of the people. The Houses of Parliament never relied upon local rights or the privileges of particular 'Estates'. In the very height of civil war they asserted quite as strenuously as the Crown the sovereignty of the nation. The first union with England was the complete legal fusion of Wales with the rest of the country under Henry VIII, but union took the form of fusion not of alliance. When at the beginning of the 18th century union with Scotland became an urgent necessity English statesmen and England generally had become thoroughly accustomed to the idea of an incorporative as contrasted with a federal union and in 1706 the English Commissioners for negotiating the terms in which the two kingdoms should be united absolutely refused to entertain any idea of constituting a federation.

> The English offered an article containing the fundamental principles of the treaty—one kingdom with a new name, one Parliament and a destination of the new Crown according to the Act of Succession. It was felt that on the adoption or rejection of this proposition the fate of the whole project depended.[5]

When nearly a century later the Act of Union with Ireland was carried, the Treaty of Union with Scotland was an authoritative precedent which there was neither the wish nor the intention to neglect. A large party in Ireland objected to the policy of Union but no one, I conceive, in 1800, whether he were a friend or an opponent of the Union, advocated federalism.

The constitution of the United Kingdom therefore, though formed by the combination under one polity of three countries politically and geographically distinct, bears no trace of a federal character. It is emphatically a unitary constitution.

---

[5] 8 Burton, p. 119.

2

Constitutionalism of the Commonwealth

Analysis*

A. General Character of Puritan Constitutionalism
   I. *Both a revival and a revolution*
   II. *Different types of Puritan constitutionalism*
B. Constitution of 1653
   I. *Revival*
      1. Protector (Instrument of Government (Arts 1–6, 24, 30)
      2. Council of State (Arts 2, 21, 23, 25, 26)
      3. Parliament
   II. *Revolution*
      1. Abolition of monarchy and House of Lords
      2. Written and rigid constitution (Arts 24, 35–39)
      3. Union with Ireland and Scotland (Arts 1, 9, and 10)
      4. Religious toleration (Arts 35–38)
      5. Standing army (Arts 27–29)
      6. Relation of executive to legislature
C. Comparison between Constitution of 1653 and Constitution of 1905[†]

(See Act Declaring England to be a Commonwealth (Gardiner, *Constitutional Documents*, p. 297);
Instrument of Government (Constitution of 1653), ibid. p. 314;
Agreement of the People, ibid. p. 270;
Masson, *Life of Milton*, iv, pp 10, 542;
Gardiner, *History of the Commonwealth*, vol. ii, ch. XXVIII;
Gneist, *History of English Constitution*, ii (English trans.), p. 257.)

---

* Its contents have been derived from a manuscript entitled 'The Constitution of 1653 (Instrument of Government)' and, in a later manuscript note, dated 10 May 1905, which, according to the attached lecture schedule, was the date of the lecture for which this was the Analysis. This Analysis is included here (and not the earlier Analysis attached to the lecture schedule headed 'Easter & Trinity Terms, 1897' and used to derive most of the other Analyses in Part I) because the remaining full lecture text was substantially developed later in 1897, partly reflected in this later Analysis. See p. 30, n., below.

† Later manuscript deletions and insertions so as to adapt this Analysis for use in 1908 (see p. 335 below) have been omitted here.

Constitutionalism of the Commonwealth[*]

The Puritan movement is at once a revival and a revolution.

It is an attempt to maintain a more or less imaginary past; it is also an attempt to carry out ideals which were realisable, if at all, only in the distant future.

This double character is traceable in every sphere of Puritan thought and action.

In the realm of theology Puritanism represents from one point of view a reactionary attempt to maintain a narrow and rigid form of Calvinism. The supremacy of Laud no doubt involved the oppression of ministers whom we should now call Low Churchmen, but the Liberal Anglicans, or even the Broad Churchmen of today would have felt the yoke of Laud lighter than the bondage which the divines at Westminster wished to impose upon the English people. Generosity and a sense of justice makes us sympathise with the clergymen who in 1662 were expelled from the Church of England. The Bishops of the Restoration do not compare favourably with their opponents at the Savoy Conference. Yet, as has been often remarked, if we take one by one the particular points on which the Anglican differed from the Puritan Divines we shall find that the views upheld by Anglicans far more nearly corresponded with the sentiments, the beliefs, and the practice of to-day than did the doctrines insisted upon by the fathers of English Nonconformity. One example may show my meaning. Sabbatarianism was upheld by Puritans of every school. Sabbatarianism is in effect rejected by modern Englishmen. King James would have approved, as surely as his opponents would have condemned, the mode in which respectable Englishmen of the 19th century keep their Sunday. Yet even in the sphere of theology Puritanism, from another point of view, represents, or rather is, a step towards freedom of thought and toleration. No doubt most of the so-called Puritans (under which name are included persons who differed widely from one another in their theological no less than in their political opinions) denounced toleration. Most of them would have restrained freedom of discussion within rigid limits. But Puritanism, even of the narrowest type, was an appeal from authority to reason, from the decrees of the Church to the dictates of the conscience, and the men who became the leaders of the Puritan revolution not only represented aspirations for religious freedom but also in fact carried out what for the age was a wide scheme of toleration.

Turn again to the foreign policy of Cromwell. Here we may rely upon the guidance of Mr. Gardiner, and he reveals to us just the same doubleness of aim which we have found in the sphere of theology. The Protector had a vague desire to place England at the head of a great Protestant alliance which had been rendered impossible by the result of the Thirty Years War, and still more by the ideas of which that result was the

---

[*] This single lecture text was developed from the texts for two earlier lectures, 'Constitutionalism of Commonwealth' and 'Characteristics of Puritan Constitutionalism' (both dated April 1897), from which pages were transferred. On the title page of the first of these earlier lectures, they were both recorded as having been rewritten in October 1897.

expression. He also aimed at that expansion of the English Empire which turned out to be in fact the path marked out for England by destiny.

Nothing interested more keenly the reformers of the Commonwealth than the amendment of the law of England and the removal of legal abuses. In many of their special reforms they anticipated improvements which have been at last adopted within quite recent times. Yet even as reformers of the law, they exhibit a singular mixture of conservatism and of innovation. They were prepared to change much, yet, after all, they were the ardent admirers of Coke, and must have held, as did Selden, that Equity was the substitution of the arbitrary fancies of each successive Chancellor for the fixed law of the land. One can dimly perceive that their ideal was the removal of many obvious abuses, and the purification, so to speak, of the common law, but that they failed, for the most part, to perceive that the development of all the complexities of modern life and of modern commerce made the kind of flexibility introduced by the Chancellors into the law of England an absolute necessity.

What is true of Puritanism in the field of theology, of foreign policy, and of law reform holds equally true in the sphere of constitutionalism. Here again we find the paradoxical combination of revival or reaction with innovation or revolution.

Nor is the paradox hard to explain. At the beginning of the century when James I ascended the throne, a change in the system of English government had become inevitable. The country was passing into a modern state. Military tenures, to take one example, needed abolition.[1] Systematic taxation was essential to the welfare of the state. The relation between Church and State and the limits of legal toleration required to be resettled. Either an extension of the administrative powers of the Crown or more frequent use of the legislative authority of Parliament could alone meet the wants of the nation. Then a closer union between England and Scotland was, as every man of insight saw, of vital importance. In truth the whole state of the world was changing. In most countries the power of the monarch was on the increase yet, though change of some kind was necessary, no one clearly perceived what the change should be or what were the means by which it should be carried out. The people did not trust the King, and the King did not trust the people. Innovations came, or appeared to come, from the side of the Crown. They were in some cases sanctioned or promoted by statesmen of great wisdom. Bacon, and in a different way, Strafford, were the representatives of a class of reformers who wished to increase the authority of the King in order to effect improvements in the government of the country. But the people distrusting the Crown saw in its increased power nothing but a revolutionary inroad on the rights of the nation and fully sympathised with lawyers like Coke, whom one hardly knows whether to term patriots defending established law and justice, or obstructive conservatives to whom all change, especially where it lessened their own authority, seemed pure evil. Hence Puritanism in the world of politics at any rate was in the first instance opposition to change. It was

---

[1] See Gardiner, *The Great Contract* and Digby, *History of Law of Real Property*, ch. IX. Note that they were in fact abolished by the Long Parliament in 1645, and by an Act of the Protectorate of 1646, and this policy of abolition was confirmed by 12 Car. II, c. 24.

a conservative effort to keep unaltered the constitution as it existed, or was supposed to have existed under Elizabeth. For this purpose maxims derived from the premature constitutionalism of the Lancastrian dynasty were revived and revival meant, as it always does, innovation. With the progress moreover of the contest between Charles I and the Houses of Parliament the extreme party, as will happen in revolutionary periods, came to the front. The general result was that a movement which had been conservative became revolutionary, and an effort to preserve the constitution resulted in the destruction of the monarchy to which the English people were as a body still loyal and in the attempt which for a time succeeded to establish a Commonwealth or Republic, the very name of which was unknown to, and disliked by, the vast majority of Englishmen. It is well, however, to note that the gradual change of opposition to arbitrary power into a revolutionary movement has been witnessed in other countries than in England, and in times far nearer to our own than the 17th century. In 1848 and 1849 the conflict between Hungary and Austria underwent a similar transformation. The original purpose of the Hungarians was to maintain or restore the ancient constitution of Hungary under their legitimate King who was also Emperor of Austria. Circumstances threw the leadership of the nation into the hands of Kossuth and his supporters who desired the complete national independence of Hungary, and proclaimed the deposition of the House of Hapsburg. Though the aid of Russia made the Austrian Emperor for a time successful yet within twenty years the old constitution of Hungary was restored by the statesmanship of Deák, and the Hungarians were reconciled to their King. It is clear enough that here, as in England during the 17th Century, we witness a movement which went beyond its mark. The Hungarians as a nation no more wished in 1849 to overthrow the monarchy or to found a Republic than the majority of Englishmen in 1649 desired the death of Charles I or the foundation of the Commonwealth.

The contradiction involved in the very essence of the Puritan movement and the false position of the men who throughout the Interregnum, as well before as after the beginning of the Protectorate, guided the Commonwealth must he constantly borne in mind by anyone who wishes to understand their constitutional ideas and the attempts which they made to carry these ideas into effect. It will be well first to consider what were the principles of government more or less consciously upheld by the men who abolished the monarchy, and then to criticise with care the Instrument of Government or, as we should now call it, the Constitution of 1653. It constitutes by far the most complete and in some respects the most characteristic record of Puritan constitutionalism.

A. Characteristics of Puritan Constitutionalism

Whoever examines the constitutional documents of the Commonwealth will find that their authors pursued different ideals which led to different constitutions and further that each form of Puritan constitutionalism bears a rough likeness to different schemes of parliamentary government which exist in the modern world.

For the sake of clearness we will examine, first, what are the characteristics which all forms of Puritan constitutionalism have in common and, secondly, what are the essential points in which they differ from each other.

I. *What all forms of Puritan constitutionalism have in common*

The common element of Puritan constitutions obviously contains the fundamental or essential ideas of the Puritan movement, in so far as its objects were political, or at any rate were connected with changes in political institutions.

1. A fixed or written constitution

If England has prospered under the oldest and most stable of customary constitutions England is also the country which first tried the experiment of a written or enacted constitution. We are now thoroughly used to the written constitutions of the Continent and of the USA; we find it hard therefore to realise that in 1654 [*sic*] a written constitution was an original invention, we might almost say a startling novelty. It was, however, an invention which commended itself to all the thinkers of the Commonwealth. Their experience of the danger to freedom must have led them to the conviction shared by many statesmen of later ages, that if liberty and the rights of men were to be protected they must be fortified by being embodied in a definite written document.

2. The new constitution must be what is now termed a rigid constitution. It must embody, that is to say, certain fixed principles which were to be held more or less sacred

This notion of fundamental laws together with its correlative of guaranteed rights is characteristic of the age. In the Constitution of 1654 [*sic*], in the Agreement of the People, in the Constitutional Bill which was meant to establish the supremacy of Parliament, and even the Humble Petition of 1657 which was clearly intended to lead to the establishment of a Cromwellian monarchy, an attempt is made to provide special securities for religious freedom, whilst in the Agreement of the People many other matters are treated as essential or fundamental. The idea, in short, which dictated the celebrated Declaration of the Rights of Man and has filled the constitutions of American States with enunciations of rights was prevalent in the England of the 17th century and hence too the inevitable result that the Puritan constitutions tended towards a kind of immutability utterly foreign to the flexible and indefinite constitution of the United Kingdom.[2]

3. A Parliament meeting at regular intervals

No Puritan statesman dreamt of establishing institutions of which an elective legislative body did not form a part and the attempts of the Stuarts to dispense with Parliaments impressed upon men the necessity for providing both for the habitual

---

[2] See Agreement, Art. 10; Instrument, Art. 24.

summoning of the legislature and for its right to continue sitting for a definite period when once summoned. Note however that few, if any, of our reformers meant the elective body to resemble the modern Parliament of England. No one intended that it should meet every year; its meetings were to be biennial or triennial. Men who had suffered under the rule of the Long Parliament felt that a parliament in constant session was only a less evil than a parliament which never sat at all.[3] The new legislative body or, as it was sometimes called, the Representative was intended to play something like the part assigned to an Elizabethan Parliament. It bore a closer resemblance to the American Congress, to the German Diet, or to the Swiss Federal Assembly than to the Imperial Parliament of the United Kingdom. It was to be a legislative body, but by no means a sovereign Parliament.

Most constitutionalists of the day felt also the necessity of Parliamentary reform. It was as manifest though not as pressing a need in the time of Cromwell as in the time of William IV. Nor was there apparently much doubt as to the lines which 'Reform', as it is now called, ought to follow. A redistribution of seats so as to place parliamentary representation in the hands of the flourishing and populous parts of the country, and perhaps the introduction of what may be called an improved form of franchise in the counties seem to have been accepted by all classes of reformers. It is curious to note that, whilst the Instrument of Government gave the right of election, at any rate in the counties, as it would seem wholly to landowners possessing land of the value of £200 which in modern days would apparently be equivalent to bestowing it upon persons who possessed land of the value of £600, the more democratic Agreement of the People proposed nothing like universal suffrage, but anticipated the arrangements of to-day by giving votes to every householder rated to the relief of the poor.[4]

4. Religious freedom or toleration

Every constitution of the Commonwealth embodies an attempt to secure some kind of religious toleration.[5]

This toleration was according to our views narrow and its limits were differently fixed by reformers of different types. On three points, however, they were all more or less agreed. Direct persecution ought to be forbidden; to use the words of the Instrument of Government 'to the public profession no one shall be compelled by penalties or otherwise'.[6] 'All persons', in the next place, 'who profess faith in God by Jesus Christ' are to be freely allowed the public exercise of their religion, and, lastly, this freedom is to be granted with considerable hesitation, if at all, to Papists or Prelatists, and is denied though in very vague terms to persons who under the profession of Christ hold forth or practise licentiousness. On the whole the result of Puritan toleration may be thus summed up: direct persecution or punishment on account of religious belief is absolutely abolished and this, be it noted, is no small step in

---

[3] Compare Agreement, Arts 3 and 6; Instrument, Arts 7 and 8; and Constitutional Bill, Arts 22–24.
[4] It rather looks as though the Constitution of 1654 left the parliamentary franchises of boroughs untouched. See however further as to this Constitution pp [48–50] *post*.
[5] Agreement, Art. 9; Instrument, Art. 37; Constitutional Bill, caps. 41, 42; Petition, Art. 11.
[6] Instrument, Art. 37; Agreement, Art. 9; Constitutional Bill, cap. 41.

advance. Orthodox Protestants, or rather orthodox Low Churchmen, enjoy complete religious freedom, but considerable though indefinite restrictions are placed on the religious liberty of Romanists or of Prelatists. Socinians or the wilder sectaries are vaguely menaced with something like restraint. How this kind of limited toleration would, if the Commonwealth had endured, have worked in practice, it is hard to say. It is, however, probable that whilst the National Church would have represented the beliefs of the vast body of religious Englishmen, no large body of Englishmen would have been exposed to molestation on account of their creed. If the Restoration had not intervened England would probably have become from the foundation of the Commonwealth the country where the mass of the people have both enjoyed religious liberty and practised toleration more fully than in any other European land.

5. Exclusion from political rights

Every constitution put into force or established under the Commonwealth contained wide electoral disqualifications. These disqualifying clauses betray the true weakness of the Revolutionists: men of the Revolution, all of them, whatever their differences, appealed to the support of the nation, but they all knew that the people of England were neither Puritans nor Republicans. Hence the Puritan leaders occupied a false position; they dared not trust the nation whose authority they theoretically acknowledged, but in practice set at naught. That Roman Catholics should be permanently excluded from political life was, in the England of the 17th century, a matter of slight consequence. What was important was the temporary exclusion from the field of politics of whole classes, such for example as all the Cavaliers who had taken up arms against the Parliament, as well as any Royalist who had conspired against the Commonwealth or the Protector.

The situation of democrats who cannot trust the people and want to found a Republic without Republicans lends itself to satire. But the difficulties which beset the founders of the Commonwealth are not without historical parallels. Whenever a democratic revolution has placed a revolutionary party in office its leaders have found themselves confronted by the necessity for establishing a national government without having obtained the allegiance of the whole, or of anything like the whole, of the nation. The Revolution of 1689 was national yet the Whigs found that they could not save the fruits of the Revolution without passing a Septennial Act, a step which was very like a *coup d'état* under legal forms. France sanctioned the French revolution yet the Convention dared not transfer its power to a freely chosen assembly, and in defiance of early democratic principle packed before hand the legislature which was to be its successor. The carefully framed Directorial Constitution was deliberately violated by at least two *coup d'états* which could be justified only by the knowledge of Republicans that any assembly which truly represented the nation would favour reaction. The *coup d'état* of the 18th of Brumaire was due immediately to the ambition of Napoleon, but it was sanctioned not only by the army, but also by some of the best and most patriotic of French citizens, because it checked reaction and, in spite of the people, saved the popular principles of 1789. In 1865 the triumph of the North was complete and the Southern States of America resumed their places in the federal system; but the national leaders of the Southern States were of necessity excluded for years from public life and the federal government which throughout the South nominally restored Republican freedom, supported State governments which were placed in power by the vote of the negroes and which were guided by Northern adventurers; the federal government that is to say was compelled to keep in power men who could not have retained office for a week if the support of the United States had been withdrawn. The difficulty which the statesmen of the Commonwealth were forced to meet was in short a difficulty which has been faced with success by the leaders of popular movements in England, in France, and in the United States. Towards the end of Cromwell's rule circumstances appeared to favour the Commonwealth and sagacious observers expected that it would secure the adherence of the English people. The reasons why this expectation proved false belong to the field not of law but of history. All that need here be noted is that Puritan constitutionalism in all its forms bore the mark of its weakness. It was the creed of revolutionary leaders who had not conciliated and therefore could not trust the people.

6. All the statesmen of the Commonwealth, whatever their differences of opinion, respected and meant to preserve the foundations of English society

They all, for example, with exceptions so rare that they need not he taken into account, respected the common law. They all wished to maintain the traditional habits, customs, or sentiments which governed the public life of England. We ought not to be misled by the execution of the King which was brought about far more by distrust of Charles Stuart than through hatred for monarchy, nor by the abolition of the House of Lords which though it no doubt gratified some speculative Republicans, cannot be taken as betraying any settled hatred for the Peerage. There are certainly few traces in the Puritan revolution of that desire to change the traditional institutions of the country from top to bottom which is the most patent note of the great French revolution. The English revolutionists of the 17th century would no doubt, had they finally triumphed, have destroyed many things which they intended to keep alive, just as the Whigs of 1689 who meant to change little more than succession to the Crown, introduced unawares into England freedom of the press, practical religious toleration, and ultimately parliamentary and constitutional government of the modern type. The French revolutionists left in fact alive a great deal which they meant to destroy. Since the publication of Tocqueville's *Ancien Régime* every intelligent student has known that in the departments of law, and especially in the administrative system, the spirit of the monarchy has in many striking ways survived the Revolution. But for all this the contrast between the English and the French revolutionists holds good. The one class respected and loved, the other class condemned and detested, the traditional institutions of their country. The judges who were about to act under the Commonwealth undertook to perform their duties on the terms that they should decide civil and criminal cases, in so far of course as was consistent with the abolition of the monarchy, in accordance with the law of England. Judges who had received commissions from the King held office under the Commonwealth, and judges who had discharged their duties during the Interregnum took commissions from Charles II. Some of the acts done and more of the aspirations entertained by English Republicans were revolutionary. But for all this the English Commonwealth was based on reverence for the history and traditions of England. Nothing is in reality more remarkable than the essential conservatism of Puritan revolutionists.

7. The Union of England with Scotland

One may number among the ideas common to all the Puritan leaders—one may almost say common to almost [all] the leading statesmen of England—the necessity for uniting England and Scotland into one state. The Union was in fact carried into effect under the Instrument of Government and, though it was dissolved on the restoration of the monarchy, was in reality though not in form one of the permanent results of the great rebellion. It is impossible to doubt that the fact of England and Scotland having formed one state for nearly ten years, and of both countries having prospered as a united commonwealth, told for a good deal in promoting the policy which some sixty years later created the United Kingdom of Great Britain.

II. Wherein the different forms of Puritan constitutionalism differ

The constitutionalists of the Commonwealth may be roughly divided into three classes.

First—the Democrats whose ideal of government is embodied in the Agreement of the People.

This Agreement gives a fair view of the ends aimed at by its authors. The name, however, of 'Democrats' may mislead modern readers. The men who drafted the Agreement were no enthusiasts for universal suffrage. They did not mean the control of the country to reside in the hands of the class whom John Bright called the 'residuum', or even of the multitude; this is shown by their careful exclusion of domestic servants from the possession of the parliamentary franchise. Their real wish was to trust the government of the country to the body of rate-paying householders. What is of even more consequence the Democrats of the Commonwealth utterly rejected the creed that the state, as representing the people, is absolutely supreme. They recognized large spheres of action as for example of things spiritual or evangelical from which the activity of the state ought to be sedulously excluded.[7] What was really democratic in the adherents to the Agreement was their determination to form a truly popular government, and a popular government at the head of which there should not be (to use the Cromwellian expression) 'one person'. They objected equally to a King and to a powerful President or Protector. Their peculiar ideas may be thus summed up:

(i) The constitution is to be parliamentary in the sense that it is to contain a legislative body consisting of one House elected by the independent, rate-paying householders. This Parliament is to meet biennially for a stated time

---

[7] See Agreement, Arts 8 and 9.

and apparently is to be *ipso facto* dissolved at the end of each session, though extraordinary Parliaments may be convoked by the Council, i.e. the executive during the periods which intervene between each regular biennial session.

(ii) The Council is to be elected by each biennial Parliament and to hold office till immediately after the meeting of the next regular Parliament. The Council, it would appear, might consist of members of the Parliament by which it was elected.

(iii) There is to be what we should now call a division of powers, in this sense: that no member of any Parliament is to be either receiver, treasurer or other officer during that employment, subject to the saving that a member of Parliament might be a member of the Council.

(iv) The really striking point in the constitution sketched out in the Agreement is the strict limitation on the constitutional powers both of the Parliament and of the government. The most original and the most fundamental idea which the Agreement contains is the absolute necessity for securing a wide sphere for individual freedom.

Legislation is not to concern itself with things spiritual or evangelical. The limits of religious toleration are to be extended so widely that even Papists or Prelatists would be allowed at any rate the private practice of their religion.[8] Parliament is, under no pretence, to take away the foundations of common right, liberty, and safety, contained in the Agreement, nor to level men's estates, destroy property, or to make all things common.[9] Nor—and this will be felt to be a most remarkable fact when we remember that the Agreement embodied the ideas entertained by the most democratic members of the army—is any one to be compelled to take part in war unless it be—at least so I read Article 8—in strictly defensive warfare for the protection of the country.

These fundamental principles are, it would almost seem, sanctioned by a constitutionally reserved right of insurrection for while it is provided that any one who by force of arms resists the orders of the next or any future Parliament shall become an outlaw and be punishable with death as a traitor to the nation, the duty of obedience is qualified by the words 'except in case where such Representative [Parliament] shall evidently render up or take away the foundations of common right, liberty, and safety contained in the Agreement'.

The constitution of which the Agreement contains a sketch is at once democratic and non-parliamentary, for its authors had no idea of constituting a sovereign Parliament. Their conceptions of government were clearly unsuited for the England of the 17th century. They are scarcely more suitable for the England of the 19th century with her Imperial Parliament, with her elaborate administrative system, with her huge army, and fleet, which are the necessary support and defence of the British Empire. Yet it can hardly be said that the ideas upheld by the Democrats of the

---

[8] See [Agreement,] Art. 9.
[9] See [Agreement,] Art. 8.

Commonwealth are in themselves visionary. Several of them are realised in different modern states though there is probably no one state where they are all carried into effect. In several respects the kind of government dreamt of by the adherents to the Agreement actually exists in States of the American Union. The modern constitution, however, which most nearly carries out the ideas of Puritan Democrats is the Constitution of modern Switzerland.

In Switzerland, as under the Agreement, the Council of State is elected by each successive Parliament and holds office till in due course another Parliament assembles. In Switzerland, as under the Agreement, the Parliament is a purely legislative body meeting for fixed periods. Under the Swiss Constitution, as under the Agreement, religious liberty and various forms of personal freedom are guaranteed. Nor is it idle to remark that in each American State, as also in Switzerland, all important legislative or constitutional changes are or may be referred to the people for their express sanction, whilst the advocates of the Agreement intended to submit their constitutional programme to the vote of the electors. They in effect anticipated, in idea at least, the modern referendum.

Secondly—the governmental or Cromwellian Constitutionalists.

The views of the reformers who in combination with Cromwell, or at any rate with his assent, derived the Constitution of 1653 are embodied in the Instrument of Government.

As I shall examine this Constitution with some care at a later part of this chapter, it will be sufficient here to point out its general character.

The Instrument of Government is in a sense based upon the Agreement of the People, but it is as compared with the Agreement what a Frenchman would call an 'authoritative' document. Its aim is not to carry out an ideal but to constitute an actual working arrangement. It proceeds from the men of the government and in every line of the Instrument we can trace a leaning towards authority and the desire to constitute a strong executive.

The leading features of the Constitution of 1653 are, first, a strong executive at the head of which stands the Protector who is appointed for life, secondly, a permanent Council of State which is not dependent for its existence on Parliament, thirdly, a legislative body or Parliament, which though endowed with very considerable powers of law making is intended to be a purely legislative body, and lastly a written and, as we should now say, 'rigid' constitution which should set definite bounds to the constitutional authority both of the executive and the legislature and should above all provide real guarantees for religious freedom or toleration.

It may be well to note what is often forgotten: that by 1653 reformers as well as ordinary people had learnt from experience that the tyranny or the intolerance of an elected assembly might be as oppressive as the despotism or bigotry of a King.

Thirdly—the Parliamentarians.

Among the supporters of the Commonwealth who sat in the first Parliament held under the Instrument of Government were a body of Parliamentarians. The views of these men are expressed in the Constitutional Bills which they drafted with a view to amending the Instrument of Government.

They were willing within certain limits to accept the Protectorate and the Constitution of 1653. Their aim, however, was to amend this Constitution so as to give it a more parliamentary character.

For the attainment of this object they put the following amendments into the form of Bills. They made the appointment of the Council dependent on the approval of Parliament and—what is a matter of equal importance—they made the Councillor's tenure of office dependent on the approval of each successive Parliament. In several definite respects they increased the authority of Parliament. To Parliament for instance, if sitting at the time of the Protector's death, they gave the right of regulating the way in which his successor should be elected, though, if Parliament were not sitting, they left the election in the hands of the Council. They transformed the whole scheme of government from a rigid into a flexible constitution. Ordinary legislation was, as under the Instrument, to be the work of Parliament alone, but amendments to the Constitution were to be made by Parliament subject to the Protector's right of veto.[10] The provisions for constitutional revision are, it is true, incomplete and obscure. One thing, however, is clear. The Parliamentary constitutionalists did not intend to make the provisions for the security of religious liberty in any sense fundamentals or, as we should now say, immutable articles of the Constitution. Bills which directly violated the elementary principle of religious toleration by imposing penalties on the refusal to conform to the profession of religion established by the Commonwealth were not to pass into law without the consent of the Protector.[11] But laws for the restraining of atheism, blasphemy, Popery, Prelacy, licentiousness, and profaneness, as well as laws for the punishment of persons who preached or publicly maintained doctrines contrary to the established religion, might, it is clear, in the view of the Parliamentarians, be enacted by Parliament without any necessity for the Protector's consent.

The parliamentary Constitutionalists of the Commonwealth or, as we may term them the Republican Parliamentarians, have received, and perhaps deserved, little sympathy from historians. Their Republicanism was as much opposed to the general sentiment of England as were the doctrines of the Democrats who drew up the Agreement of the People or of the more practical statesmen who framed with no small skill the Instrument of Government. Their desire for the virtual supremacy of an elective legislature was hardly less opposed to the popular wish for the restoration of the monarchy than to the democratic ideal of what we now call the sovereignty of the people. The Parliamentarians moreover were impracticable doctrinaires. They wished or professed the wish to maintain the Commonwealth yet they could not perceive that as the mass of Englishmen were not Republicans the one chance of avoiding a restoration lay in the maintenance of a strong Republican government, and that in Cromwell they had a ruler who was both capable of ruling and incapable of establishing a despotism. To weaken the government and establish at such a time the supremacy of Parliament was to throw away the one chance of maintaining the

---

[10] See [Constitutional Bill,] cap. 2 [sic].
[11] [Constitutional Bill,] caps. 42, 43.

Commonwealth, and no one could doubt that the whole aim of the Constitutional Bills was to make Parliament supreme and to render the executive dependent upon a parliamentary majority. Yet the Parliamentarians, in spite of all just criticism have one claim to respect. In 1654 they anticipated the course of English history. They aimed at establishing the three leading doctrines of modern English constitutionalism, *viz*, the abolition of the Royal veto, the full legislative sovereignty of Parliament, and the control by Parliament of the executive government. The fact moreover which cannot be denied that in their ideas of toleration the Parliamentarians fell far behind the aspirations of the Democrats and the practical tolerance of the Protector may betray intellectual narrowness or moral insensibility, but it certainly does not show a want of practical foresight. The people of England were not prepared for any wide declaration of religious toleration, and it is quite possible that the maintenance by the Parliamentarians of the theory of intolerance might in England have heralded in that kind of illogical but actual tolerance which in reality resulted from the Toleration Act—a statute which, though it relieved the mass of Englishmen from even the fear of persecution, does not contain a word which need alarm Tories who abhorred the very name of toleration.

B. The Instrument of Government, or the Constitution of 1653

The Constitution of 1653, which is contained in the Instrument of Government, was not a mere speculative scheme but became for a short time an actually established form of government. What indeed was its exact relation to the Humble Petition and Advice by which within four years it was modified, is a question which had the Commonwealth lasted might have greatly perplexed constitutionalists and judges. We may, however, assume that the Instrument of Government, though subsequently modified, continued in some sense or other to be the law of the land till the end of the Protectorate. In any case it is the best expression which we possess of the constitutional ideas entertained by the Puritan statesmen who after the execution of the King endeavoured to found an English Commonwealth. Like every other work of Puritanism it is at once a revival and a revolution,[12] and one way at any rate of understanding the Constitution of 1653 is to separate as far as it be possible the elements in which it was a revival of the past from the elements in which it was an anticipation of the future.

I. The revival

1. The position of the Protector

The Protectorate is in itself the nearest approach to the restoration of the kingship which was compatible with the existence of a Republic. The office indeed is

---

[12] See pp [30–2] *ante*.

elective, but the Protector—the title, be it noted, is known to English constitutional history—is appointed for life, and in the Protector's hands are placed all the powers which could rightly be exercised by a powerful English King, say, for example, Henry VIII. Writs run and every act of State is done in his name.[13] To him belongs the chief magistracy, the administration of the government,[14] and the appointment to all offices. He has the disposal of all the national forces by sea and land.[15] He retains, with certain exceptions, the right of pardon. He is ensured an income of £200,000, and a revenue for the support of a standing army of 10,000 horse and 20,000 foot. He is endowed with large estates in land. Like an English King he forms part of the legislature,[16] and has a real, though not final, veto on legislation. There is not a trace throughout the Constitution of 1653 of any idea whatever that the Protector shall become a constitutional ruler, i.e. a monarch possessed of large nominal prerogatives who in reality exercises all his functions in subordination to Parliament. The Protector is intended to be a real monarch of the same type as Henry V or Elizabeth. He bears no resemblance to a constitutional King or to a Prime Minister; if he is to be compared with any modern ruler we had best compare him with the Emperor of Germany.

But note that the Protection has under the Instrument, Article 27, what no English King had ever possessed, a fixed yearly revenue for the support of a standing army of 10,000 horse and 20,000 foot, and this income cannot be diminished without the consent both of the Protector and of the Parliament.

2. The Council of State

This body which existed in one form or another from the death of Charles I till the Restoration is, as we shall see in a moment, the most original creation of Puritan statesmanship. Yet the Council itself was a revival of and moulded upon the Privy Council of the monarchy. The government of the Lancastrians and even more truly of the Tudors was a government by councils. A good King paid heed, and was expected to pay heed, to the advice of good Councillors. The autocratic power of a ruler who did not take counsel with others was opposed to all English principles and traditions. To a constitutionalist of the 17th century the Council of State of the Commonwealth must have appeared little different from the Privy Council of the monarchy.

3. The Parliament

Under the Protectorate, as under the monarchy, the legislative body was a Parliament, but this assembly, though it bore the name and was intended to continue the traditions of the ancient Parliament, was in its form and in its character very different from the Parliaments consisting of the King, the House of Lords, and the House of Commons, which had for centuries been convened by every King or Queen of

---

[13] Instrument, Art. 3.
[14] Ibid, Art. 2.
[15] Ibid, Art. 5.
[16] Ibid, Arts 1, 22, and 30.

England. Hence the Cromwellian Parliament belongs in truth not to the conservative but to the revolutionary elements of the new Constitution.

In estimating, however, the conservative character of the Instrument of Government, we must constantly bear in mind that, speaking roughly, whatever in English political or social arrangements it did not either expressly or impliedly abolish, it kept alive. Judges, sheriffs, magistrates exercised their functions under the Commonwealth much as they had exercised them under the monarchy. The old statutes, in so far as they were not directly inconsistent with the new state of things, continued in force. The common law remained unchanged, the authority of Coke and of the men whom Coke revered was greater than ever.

II. *The revolution*

1. Absence of the hereditary monarchy and of the House of Lords

This is the feature in the new Constitution which has impressed itself upon popular memory and would by many persons be considered to constitute the vital distinction between the old monarchy and the new Protectorate. Yet in maintaining the abolition both of the Kingship and of the second Chamber the Instrument of Government did no more than give effect to the legislation of the Commonwealth; the Long Parliament or rather the fragment of the House of Commons which took upon itself to act as the Long Parliament passed on the 17th of March 1649 an Act abolishing the office of King and two days later an Act abolishing the House of Lords. But these changes lost a good deal of their effect under the Instrument of Government. The powers of the King were revived and even extended in the hands of the Protector. The first article provides that supreme legislative authority, or as we should now say 'sovereignty', should reside in 'one person' and in the people assembled in Parliament. The change again from the old bicameral Parliament to an elective legislature consisting of one House only was considerable, but though the House of Lords was abolished the Peerage was left untouched. Peers preserved their hereditary titles and the place occupied under the monarchy by the House of Lords was to a certain extent filled under the Protectorate by the Council. It was in practice part of the legislature; it in many cases prepared Bills and recommended to the Parliament subjects of legislation.[17] The Council moreover possessed the power of making in combination with the Protector temporary laws and ordinances.[18]

2. Written and rigid constitution

The originality of the Constitution of 1653 lies in its being a written and a rigid constitution.

It was the first written constitution which the modern world at any rate has seen. It was an ingenious and, more or less, successful attempt to state in a definite form and in precise articles the law which was to govern the different members of the sovereign

---

[17] See Inderwick, p. 13.
[18] See [Instrument,] Art. 30.

power or, in other words, the relation between the executive and the legislature. It created in effect three powers—the Protector, the Parliament, and the Council. Each of these w[as], it is true, a revival of institutions which had existed under the monarchy and, as already pointed out, the statesmen of the Protectorate meant to keep alive all the existing mechanism of English law and of English government, such for example as the Sheriffship, the Justice of the Peace, and the like. But the mere fact of the Constitution being reduced to a written form changed to a great extent the whole of its character.

The relation between the different authorities became thereby definitely fixed. The Constitution moreover itself became a rigid, we might almost say, an unchangeable Constitution.

The Constitution indeed of 1653 lasted for so short a time (since in 1657 it was modified in accordance with the Humble Petition and Advice and the Additional Petition and Advice) that the provisions thereof as to its own amendment never received any careful consideration and have certainly never been studied by constitutional lawyers. We may further assume that Cromwell disregarded and did not fully understand the nice questions of interpretation to which the Constitution if it had lasted for any considerable time must have given rise. To a student, however, of constitutional documents it will appear certain that the Instrument of Government must have been originally drafted by some constitutionalist of no mean ability who had carefully thought over the question whether and if so in what manner the Instrument of Government should be subject to amendment. One point alone is clear. The founders of the Constitution did not intend that its articles should be changed or repealed as easily as the section of an ordinary Act of Parliament.[19]

A reader's first impression will be that the Constitution was intended to be strictly rigid and that no power was to exist under the Constitution legally capable of changing it.[20]

There is nothing indeed in itself to surprise us in such intended immutability. The idea that a supreme legislature cannot be really supreme and at the same time be limited by the constitution or, in other words, that the Act of a sovereign Parliament cannot bind the action of future sovereign Parliaments is one which the world has been very slow to accept and which, though now familiar to jurists, has hardly received popular acceptance. If Coke or any lawyer of his generation had been asked whether Parliament could abolish the House of Lords or the monarchy he would we may suspect have given a doubtful or indignant answer to what he would have regarded as an impertinent inquiry and if he had condescended to reply would while refusing to place any precise limit on the authority of Parliament have pointed out that this refusal was a very different matter from pronouncing its lawful power absolutely illimitable. It may well be doubted whether a member of Parliament who under the Tudors or the Stuarts had suggested the introduction of a Bill for the establishment of a Republic would not have exposed himself to a trial for treason. It must be remembered

---

[19] See [ibid,] Arts 24, 35–37.
[20] See [ibid,] Arts 12, 24, 35–37.

moreover that till well past the end of the last century changes in the fundamental laws of the realm have been except in periods of something like revolutionary violence of rare occurrence. The Revolution of 1688 introduced, almost without the knowledge and one may almost say against the wish of its authors, essential changes into the constitutional balance of power. The Bill of Rights declared authoritatively that certain claims of the Crown were illegal, but the men who placed William on the throne did not mean to change or reform the law of the land. We may say without any great exaggeration that from 1688 down to about 1828, that is till a period within the memory of men now living, there was not, if we except the Acts of Union with Scotland and with Ireland, any great change introduced by statute into the fundamental laws of England. The language moreover of these Acts is most instructive. It is as certain as anything can be that some of their articles were intended by the statesmen who proposed and the Parliaments who passed the Acts of Union to be all but immutable. Nor can it fairly be said that this conception of an unchangeable constitution was a mere popular delusion. It not only influenced politicians but was shared by jurists. Blackstone lays down that 'any alteration in the constitution of either of those Churches [i.e. the Churches of England and of Scotland respectively] or in the liturgy of the Church of England [unless with the consent of the respective Churches collectively or representatively given] would be an infringement of these "fundamental and essential conditions" and greatly endanger the Union',[21] and Bentham though a severe enough critic of the Commentator certainly so far agreed with him as to maintain that the articles of the Act of Union could not be rightly changed without the express consent of the Scotch people.[22] Add to all this that foreign constitutionalists have again and again endeavoured to give to their work a sort of eternity whilst the founders of the United States have founded a constitution which though not unchangeable hardly in effect admits of change.

But though there is nothing absurd in the belief that the men who framed the Instrument of Government meant to establish a strictly rigid or immutable constitution yet a careful study of that document suggests a doubt whether its author was not too sagacious a man to believe in the absolute immutability of his work. If the Constitution of 1653 had stood the test of time the Courts of England would assuredly have been called upon to give judgment on the validity of any law alleged to be invalid because it violated the Constitution, and a Chief Justice performing in England the part played by Marshall in the United States might with plausibility have drawn a distinction between three classes of laws.

First class—Ordinary laws affecting no part of the Instrument of Government (or, as we should now say, of the Constitution); these could be passed by Parliament, even if the Protector refused his assent to them.[23]

Second class—Laws amending the Instrument of Government or Constitution, but not touching certain fundamental provisions mainly having reference to religious

---

[21] I Blackstone, p. 98.
[22] See *Fragment on Government*, ch. IV, s. 37, p. 224 (Montague's edn.).
[23] Instrument, Art. 24; Gardiner, p. 320.

freedom; these laws could apparently be passed with the assent of the Protector but not otherwise.[24]

Third class—Laws inconsistent with certain fundamental provisions of the Constitution (called conveniently fundamentals); these laws were to be null and void, i.e. could not be passed at all.

Probably under the same head laws inconsistent with sales e.g. of Crown lands made under the authority of Parliament, or laws affecting the public faith of the nation.[25]

As to each of these classes there are several matters deserving attention.

(i) As to ordinary laws. As to the position of such laws there is no doubt whatever; they are governed by Article 24:

> That all Bills agreed unto by the Parliament, shall be presented to the Lord Protector for his consent; and in case he shall not give his consent thereto within twenty days after they shall be presented to him, or give satisfaction to the Parliament within the time limited, that then, upon declaration of the Parliament that the Lord Protector hath not consented or given satisfaction, such Bills shall pass into and become laws, although he shall not give his consent thereunto; provided such Bills contain nothing in them contrary to the matters contained in these presents.[26]

Two things are clear:

(a) These laws could be passed by Parliament, which consisted of one House, without the consent of the Protector.

(b) The Protector could compel Parliament to reconsider any law to which he objected.

His relation to legislation bore a close resemblance to the position of the President of the existing[27] French Republic, and also to the position of the American President.[28] He was intended to possess in fact a sort of suspensive veto. A student cannot help wondering whether the authors of the Instrument had grasped the fact that a suspensive veto may be a much more powerful because a much more workable prerogative than an absolute veto, and persons interested in the working of constitutions may naturally amuse themselves with considering whether if the Commonwealth had lasted the suspensive veto of the Protector would have turned out as ineffective as the veto of the French President which has never been exercised at all, or as effective as the veto of the American President which has been constantly exercised, and indeed is one of the most real of his prerogatives. Were it worth while to occupy one's self seriously with so speculative an inquiry one may answer with some little confidence that the suspensive veto of the Protector would have turned out a reality. The whole tendency

---

[24] Ibid, Art. 24, proviso.
[25] Ibid, Art. 39.
[26] Ibid, Art. 24; Gardiner, pp 320, 321.
[27] Law of 16 July 1875, Art. 7.
[28] US Constitution, Art. 1, s. 7.

of the Constitution of 1653 was to constitute a strong executive. The Council formed something like a second Chamber; it was intended to be in reality a sort of official Senate, and as against the Parliament the veto would when sanctioned by the Council have been a real and exercisable power though under a Protector like Richard it might have become the prerogative of the Council rather than of the Protector.

(ii) As to laws amending the Constitution. On the view generally adopted by most historians and sanctioned by Mr. Gardiner all laws for amending the Constitution were void and therefore this second class of laws which I have enumerated did not exist.

Whether this be so or not depends from a legal point of view on the meaning of the proviso to Article 24. This proviso runs as follows:

> Provided such Bills contain nothing in them contrary to the matters contained in these presents.[29]

Now the construction ordinarily put on this proviso makes "such Bills" mean any Bills whatever, but if the words of the proviso be taken strictly, and as a law Court would I think construe them, 'such Bills' must mean Bills presented to the Protector and to which he has not given his assent and on this view all that the proviso enacts is that Bills which contain anything contrary to the Instrument, i.e. in modern phraseology, for the amendment of the Constitution, are not to become law if the Protector refuses his consent to them. But if this be so it would seem naturally, if not necessarily, to follow that they are to become law if the Protector gives his consent. In this view the sense of Article 24 may be thus given. All Bills passed by Parliament shall be presented to the Protector for his consent. If he consents thereto they become law whether they touch the Constitution or not. If he does not consent they become law after certain preliminaries without his consent, provided that they do not alter the Constitution.

This interpretation of Article 24 is confirmed by reference to Article 38, which provides in effect that laws restricting religious liberty as secured by the Constitution shall be utterly void; for, if Article 24 forbade any alteration in the Constitution, Article 38 is at any rate superfluous. It may of course have been inserted *ex abund[anti] cautela* and this I presume is the opinion of persons who hold that the Constitution was absolutely rigid, but the emphasis laid on the immutability of the articles ensuring religious freedom certainly looks as if the persons who drew up the Constitution did not consider it as a whole immutable. The construction in short for which I argue gives a full and intelligible effect both to Article 24 and to Article 38, and certainly involves no absurdity.

(iii) As to laws touching the fundamentals. It was certainly intended that no law should restrict the religious liberty guaranteed by Articles 35–37 of the Constitution.

---

[29] Instrument of Government, Art. 24; Gardiner, p. 321.

Article 38 enacts 'That all laws, statutes and ordinances, and clauses in any law, statute or ordinance to the contrary of the aforesaid liberty, shall be esteemed as null and void'.[30]

The Puritan constitutionalists, it will be observed, anticipated the system now prevailing in the United States and took the only effective means of securing that fundamental articles of the Constitution should be unchangeable, *viz.* by enacting that any laws inconsistent therewith should be null and void. We can hardly doubt the existence of a deliberate intention that the Courts should treat as void any law which restricted the religious liberty conferred by the Constitution.[31]

It is not, further, strictly correct to say that even Articles 35–37 are unchangeable; they cannot be constitutionally changed so as to restrict the liberty which they confer but it is not quite clear whether they might not be changed, so as to extend the sphere of religious freedom. This suggestion very likely is an over-refinement. Still it is noteworthy that there is nothing in the Constitution of 1653 which in so many words bars the path towards more complete religious toleration.

3. Incorporative Union of Scotland and Ireland

The most material of the revolutionary changes effected by the statesmen of 1653 was the Union, or rather the incorporation, of Scotland and Ireland with England.

This was one of those changes which did not really fall to the ground. The temporary Union of England and Scotland as one Commonwealth assuredly contributed to their permanent Union not much more than half a century later in the Kingdom of Great Britain, and it was the success of the Union with Scotland which led to the Union with Ireland.

Note further that the Union under the Commonwealth was in some respects based on a wider and wiser policy than the Union, at any rate as regards Ireland, carried out under the monarchy. The Protestants of the whole Commonwealth might see in the Union of the three countries the guarantee for Protestantism and for a large measure of religious liberty, and to men who desired the material prosperity of the state the Union under the Commonwealth must have soon presented itself, as it certainly did to Scotchmen, as benefiting commerce by establishing freedom of trade throughout the whole country. That the removal of the restrictions on trade did in the case of Ireland not coincide with the Union with England was a misfortune only less than the calamity of the Union not being bound up with Catholic Emancipation.

4. The reform of Parliament

'Parliamentary reform', that is to say remodelling of the franchise, the abolition of rotten boroughs, and the distribution of seats more or less in accordance with population formed part of the Constitution of 1653 and apparently excited less opposition and

---

[30] Instrument, Art. 38; Gardiner, p. 324.

[31] Contrast with this the view which is apparently received without doubt in France that no Court can treat any law as unconstitutional and that therefore the constitutional provisions, e.g. as to the mode in which the Constitution is to be amended, are morally binding on the French Parliament, but have no legal validity if the Parliament destroys them. See Esmein.

even less attention than would be looked for by students acquainted with the conflict over the great Reform Bill, which more nearly brought England to revolution or civil war than did any political contest which has taken place during the present century.[32]

The first impression of anyone who studies the reform of 1653 is that it anticipated and would have made superfluous the Reform Act of 1832. In one sense this impression may be correct for the defects of the Cromwellian Constitution must have turned out so different from the defects of the unreformed Parliament that the provisions of the Act of 1832 would have been inapplicable to it. But, if the matter be carefully examined, it will be found that the Cromwellian reform of Parliament has very little in common with the Whig Reform Act. The differences between the two are at least as marked as their likenesses.

The Reform Act of 1832 changed the basis of the parliamentary franchise, and changed it in a democratic direction; so also did the Instrument of Government. Yet the character of the change made was in each case extremely different. The Reform Act made the predominant class in the boroughs the £10 householders, and in the counties, whilst leaving votes to the 40-shilling freeholders, yet gave votes to leaseholders and copyholders of no very great wealth, and to tenant farmers who paid a rent of £50 a year. The county constituencies were after the first Reform Act less influential and less independent bodies than they had been when no one had a county vote who was not a freeholder. The Instrument of Government on the other hand entirely remodelled the system of county representation and gave votes in the counties to every person seised or possessed to his own use of any estate real or personal to the value of £200, or if we keep in view the comparative value of money, the Instrument made the county voters consist of persons each of whom possessed property worth about £1,000. They were all persons therefore who had a real stake in the country, and we may take it that not only day labourers but the smaller class of farmers were in the counties excluded from the position of electors. What was the qualification for a vote in a borough appears to be somewhat uncertain. It would seem on the whole probable that in the boroughs which retained members the electoral qualification was the same as it had been under the monarchy.[33]

The reformers of 1832 disfranchised a considerable number of rotten or nomination boroughs and also carried out a considerable redistribution of seats. But the number of boroughs disfranchised in 1832 was far less than the number of boroughs disfranchised in 1652 [sic], and what is of far more importance the distribution of seats under the Reform Act had an effect very different from the effect of the distribution of seats under the Instrument of Government.

After as before the Reform Act the boroughs, many of them very small boroughs, returned a far greater number of members than did the counties. Under the

---

[32] It is worth notice that the Parliament summoned by Richard Cromwell was elected by the old constituencies in England, though it contained members (elected I presume in accordance with the Instrument) from Scotland and Ireland.

[33] But no rule seems to have been laid down as to the persons who were to be electors in the new boroughs, such for example, as Manchester. I cannot but suspect that the £200 qualification (Art. 18) was intended to apply at any rate to the new boroughs.

Instrument of Government the county members very greatly exceeded in numbers the borough members. In England and Wales the counties returned 261 against 139 borough members. In other words the effect of the Instrument of Government was to shift completely the centre of Parliamentary power from the small boroughs to the counties and the large towns, and we have already noted that the electors in the counties were all of them men of at any rate moderate property. Had the Constitution of 1652 [sic] continued in force England would in the main have been governed by the small and independent landowners. The disfranchisement of nomination boroughs would have prevented the growth of the parliamentary interest which gave political power up to the time of the Reform Bill to the large landowners or the nobility, and the increased power of the counties, as well as the considerable property qualification required of the county electors, would have prevented the predominance of the city democracy which has been more or less the characteristic of the constitution since the Reform Act. We may add that the Cromwellian reform resembled rather the kind of reform approved of by Chatham and his son than the kind of reform carried through by Lord Grey; and it is probable that in the 17th as during the 18th century the true policy of reformers was to increase the influence of the independent voters in the counties, but it must he recollected that, though the Instrument of Government did admit some growing cities, such as Manchester, to parliamentary representation, yet that had the Constitution of 1652 [sic] endured it would by 1830 have required reform, though it might be reform of a different kind, almost as much as the unreformed Parliament of that date. It was the growth of the manufacturing towns, and the shifting of wealth, population, and power from the North of England to the South and from the country to the cities, which in 1832 would under the Instrument of Government, no less than under the old parliamentary system, have made a change in the plan of representation a necessity.

The Reform Act again slightly increased the number of members of Parliament and later Acts have followed this most unfortunate precedent. The Instrument of Government fixed the number of members for England at 400 and gave 30 to Scotland and Ireland respectively. There is no one probably outside the House of Commons who would not admit that even at this day it would be a great improvement could our House of 670 members be reduced to the Cromwellian House of 460 members. But this is one of the changes which every sensible man knows would be an improvement and which every sensible man also knows will never be carried into effect.

5. Standing army

The Protector had risen to power as a successful general; the army not only represented, but almost constituted, the party of the Independents. Nothing but armed force could for a time keep the Commonwealth in existence. The result naturally followed that it was the Commonwealth, or rather the Protectorate, which first made a standing army a regular part of our scheme of government. Here, as elsewhere, we come across the essential characteristic of the Constitution of 1653. It was a revival, it restored to the head of the state complete control of the armed forces; but it was still more of a revolution. Not the most powerful of the Tudors had ever commanded an army or a navy such as were placed under the control of Cromwell and no government of any later age has even been able to direct the armed forces of the state with that freedom from Parliamentary interference which the Constitution of 1654 [sic] ensured to the Protector. Besides a standing army and a permanent navy he was ensured a constant yearly revenue for their maintenance. The large armies which, after the Revolution of 1688, have been found necessary for the defence of England or of the British Empire have all been in strictness Parliamentary forces. Their existence and their pay has directly depended upon Mutiny Acts and upon Appropriation Acts. If Parliament were to cease sitting for a single year, not a regiment could be practically kept on foot without an obvious and distinct violation of the law of the land. The Cromwellian army which had forcibly dissolved one Parliament was an army of which the legal existence was independent of the will of Parliament. It was a force uncontrolled by Mutiny Acts or Appropriation Acts.[34]

6. Religious freedom

In 1653 religious freedom or toleration, as then understood, was made part of the law of the land.[35] To modern critics indeed the liberty granted appears in some respects to be a very narrow form of toleration.

It certainly did not secure the right of what we should call religious freedom to Papists, to persons who 'under the profession of Christ hold forth and practice [sic] licentiousness' (by which class are probably meant religious fanatics, the violence of whose acts or heretics, the extreme character of whose opinion, excited scandal) nor to Prelatists. Yet these restrictions on the principle of religious freedom, though they left in the hands of both the Parliament and the executive the means of exercising a good deal of persecution were, it may be conjectured, intended to have less effect than the reader might ascribe to them. Roman Catholics stood in no worse position under the Commonwealth than they occupied under the monarchy which had preceded it, and legally their position seems to have been as good as it was after the Revolution of 1688 down to the reign of George III. In the 17th century no government and not many governments even in the 19th century would tolerate religious practices which shocked the moral tone or theological or anti-theological doctrines which were deemed dangerous to the peace of society. It may be doubted whether at the present day the Mormons would consider that the government of the United States had carried out in respect to them the full principles of religious toleration and it is certain that the gentile inhabitants of Utah did not find that the Mormon theocracy recognised the principle that every man had a right to enjoy

---

[34] As will be apparent to anyone who under Mr. Gardiner's guidance follows the details of the constitutional conflict between the Protector and his own first Parliament convoked under the Instrument of Government, [we] will see that the essential point at issue between them was the control of the armed forces. Under the Instrument of Government the revenue for the support of the army was permanent; under the Constitutional Bills a portion at any rate of that revenue was granted only for five years. (Compare Instrument, Art. 27, with Constitutional Bills, caps. 45–49; see Gardiner, *Documents*, pp 322, 368, 369.)

[35] See Instrument, Arts 36, 38.

complete religious freedom. In Switzerland the practices, harmless as we deem them, of the Salvation Army have led them into conflict with the cantonal laws, and I venture greatly to doubt whether any religious sect which did not belong to the four authorised forms of worship recognised by French law would find that under the French Republic it was easy to carry on a religious propaganda. At the present day no Roman Catholic ecclesiastic, or member of a religious order, can lawfully exercise the rites or ceremonies of the Roman Catholic religion, except in some usual place of worship of the Roman Catholic religion, i.e. except in some regular Roman Catholic church or chapel. The Roman Catholic Archbishop of Westminster, that is to say, has neither in theory nor in practice the same amount of religious freedom as General Booth. Any Jesuit who comes into this realm is guilty of a misdemeanour and is on conviction liable to be banished from the UK for his natural life;[36] the publication of the denial of the truth of Christianity or of the existence of the Deity is still at common law a misdemeanour;[37] any person who having been brought up and educated as a Christian, that is to say any ordinary Englishman, who by writing, teaching, or advised speaking denies the truth of the Christian Religion or the Divine authority of the Old and New Testament, is guilty of a misdemeanour and upon conviction thereof is liable to penalties which amount to something like a deprivation of all civil rights. He becomes for example at once incapable of holding any office or employment, ecclesiastical, civil, or military, and on a second conviction becomes further incapable of maintaining any action or prosecution, of being a guardian, an executor, or administrator, or of receiving any legacy or gift.[38] These laws are, it will be said, practically obsolete and some of them have never been enforced. This remark is in part at any rate true, but the benefit of the same observation must probably be extended to the limitations placed under the Instrument of Government on complete religious freedom. It is, to say the least, extremely doubtful whether under Cromwell any religious persons who behaved themselves decently were practically liable to persecution. It is certain that there were persons who continued worshipping in accordance with the forms of the Church of England; if the term Prelatists be used in its strict sense it was at that time applicable to the majority of the English people and there is I believe no reason to suppose that ordinary churchmen suffered penalties for observing the rites of the English Church.

Allow, however, as much as one likes for the restrictions on religious freedom contained in the Instrument, its articles will yet be found to mark an immense advance towards toleration.

These steps forward were at any rate made and, as far as the Constitution could achieve it, were secured:

First—active persecution, that is compulsion to profess the national religion, was absolutely forbidden.

---

[36] Catholic Relief Act, 10 Geo. IV, c. 7. ss. 26, 28–30.
[37] See Stephen, *Crim. Dig.* ch. 29, Art. 161.
[38] 9 & 10 Will. III, c. 35 as altered by 53 Geo. III, c. 160; Stephen, *Crim. Dig.* Art. 163.

For the Instrument enacts 'that to the public profession held forth none should be compelled by penalties or otherwise, but that endeavours be used to win them by sound doctrine and the example of a good conversation'.[39]

Secondly—the mass of orthodox Protestants are not only secured from persecution, but are guaranteed by law the right to profess and exercise their own form of religion.

For Article 37 enacts 'that such as profess faith in God by Jesus Christ (though differing in judgment from the doctrine, worship, or discipline publicly held forth) shall not be restrained from, but shall be protected in, the profession of the faith and exercise of their religion; so as they abuse not this liberty to the civil injury of others and to the actual disturbance of the public peace on their parts: provided this liberty be not extended to Popery or Prelacy, nor to such as, under the profession of Christ, hold forth and practice [sic] licentiousness'.[40]

Thirdly—even the body of persons such as Roman Catholics excluded from this complete liberty whilst they lost the right to be protected in the exercise of their religion seem to have been secured against penalties for exercising it.

Fourthly—religious liberty is made the rule, restrictions on the exercise of religious liberty are made the exception.

Lastly—religious liberty within the limits already described is absolutely guaranteed as a part of the Constitution. Any law conflicting with it is to be esteemed null and void and one can hardly doubt that had the Constitution of 1654 [sic] endured English judges would have treated any law abridging the freedom of religion as unconstitutional and of no effect. Note too that whilst laws which abridged religious liberty were made void the Instrument does not apparently invalid[ate] laws which should extend the area of religious freedom.

Of the toleration guaranteed under the Instrument of Government thus much may assuredly be asserted. It was a far wider scheme of toleration than at that time existed in any European country and it was far in advance of the ideas entertained in the 17th century by the vast mass of the English people.

The opposition of parliamentary Constitutionalists, wh[ich] in Cromwell's first Parliament attempted to modify the Instrument, wished not to enlarge but to restrict its principles of toleration.[41]

7. Relation of executive and judicial body

If we look solely at the different parts of the Cromwellian Constitution, e.g. the Protectorate, the Council, the Parliament, we may well imagine that they were in the main little more than the restoration under new forms of the monarchy as it existed or rather as it was imagined to have existed in the time of Elizabeth, or under the most powerful of the Lancastrian Kings. But, if we look not at the different parts of the Constitution but at their relation to one another, we shall find that the Instrument of

---

[39] Instrument, Art. 26.
[40] Ibid, Art. 37. Gardiner, *Constitutional Documents*, p. 324.
[41] See Constitutional Bills, caps. 42–44, Gardiner, pp 367, 368.

Government contained an essentially new and very remarkable constitution utterly unlike the institutions to which Englishmen had been accustomed.

(i) The executive. The executive, to use a modern term, constituted by the Instrument of Government consisted of two parts—the Protector and the Council.

(a) The Protector
The Protector was a powerful English King but appointed only for life. His position and powers bear a certain resemblance to what would be the situation and the authority of an American President who should be elected for life and should also be the real, as he is the nominal, Commander-in-chief. Suppose General Grant to have held his office for a life long tenure; suppose further that with a view to guarding against threatening rebellion in the South the United States had after the War of Secession maintained a large standing army. The General's position would have borne a close resemblance to the position of Cromwell in 1653. The Protector was at the head of large standing forces. The Protector was the real head of the government and also was the real Commander-in-chief. The Protector further, like the President, had no legislative veto.[42] In this it might be supposed he possessed less power than any English King but curiously enough he, like the President, possessed a suspensive veto,[43] and though it is a little difficult to suppose that Puritan Constitutionalists foresaw the inevitable effect of this apparent diminution in the power of the ruler everyone now knows that a suspensive is in reality a more powerful instrument than an absolute veto. The one can and the other cannot be used.[44] Take further into consideration that the rigidity of the Constitution increased the Protector's authority. The one thing which is clear is that none of its articles could be changed without his assent and the very fact that ordinary laws, which did not affect any constitutional article could be passed, as Americans now say, over his head, made his assent to constitutional changes a reality and not a matter of form.

(b) The Council
The real check on the executive action of the Protector was the Council. This body, though in one sense a revival of the Privy Council, was in another a new institution. It was the old Privy Council appointed in a new way and endowed with distinct functions and powers.

The mode of appointment is intricate. As any Councillor vacates his office by death or otherwise Parliament is to nominate six persons out of whom the majority of the

---

[42] [Instrument,] Art. 24.
[43] Ibid.
[44] Oddly enough the particular form of suspensive veto bestowed upon the Protector closely resembles the veto, if so it can be called, possessed by the French President. In either case it is nothing more than a right to delay legislation and force the Parliament to reconsider their determination to pass a particular law. The practical effect of such a power must clearly depend greatly on the character of the man who is head of the state. No French President has sent back a law to the Chambers for reconsideration, but it is highly improbable that a Bill to which the Protector refused his assent would have often passed into law. He would probably, if the Constitution had lasted, have exercised at least as strong a check on legislation as has been exercised by any American President.

Council are to elect two from whom the Protector is to choose a Councillor. The Councillorship is apparently to be held for life and it is a body consisting of seven members of Parliament and six Councillors who alone can punish and, *semble*, alone can expel from office a member of the Council.

Such a Council, not to be less than 13 or more than 21, constituted a permanent body of advisers of whom neither the Protector nor Parliament could get rid. To many of the most essential acts of government their advice or even assent was made essential.[45] Lastly it is by the Council and not by Parliament nor by the people that each successive Protector is to be elected. It is hardly rash to predict that though the Council might under Cromwell be a merely subordinate part of the executive government it would, had the Constitution lasted, have become under a Protector of not more than ordinary reputation and abilities the most important body in the state. It is hardly fanciful to compare it with the American Senate which originally was hardly a larger body than the Cromwellian Council. The Senate is subject to constant though gradual change and it does not, like the President and the House of Representatives, derive its powers directly from the people. It has nothing to do with the election of the President and its right to intervene in executive matters is strictly limited and of a purely negative character. Yet owing to the eminence of the men who became Senators, owing originally to the smallness of its numbers and also owing to the permanence, so to speak, of its existence compared with the transitory character both of the President's tenure of office and of the duration of the House of Representatives the Senate undoubtedly was for a considerable period the most powerful of the political institutions of the United States. Now under the Constitution of 1653 the position of the Council was in almost every respect stronger than the position of the Senate under the Constitution of the United States. The Councillors like the Senators were necessarily men of experience and weight. The Council consisted of not more than 23 as the Senate at first consisted of not more than 26 members. The number of the Councillors was not liable to be increased though it might be diminished to 13. The Council had very considerable influence on the nomination of its members; they each held office for life and even for misconduct could hardly be dismissed unless with the assent of the Council. The Council sat constantly, and took a leading part in all business of importance. Parliament was not certain of being assembled more frequently than every third year and was liable to dissolution. The Protector, it is true, held his office for life, but each Protector was elected and the electors of the Protector were the Council. Every thing points to the conclusion that under the Constitution of 1653 the Council was intended to be or assuredly would in time have become the centre of the government and the most powerful body in the country.

(ii) The Parliament.[46] The supreme legislative authority of the Commonwealth resides 'in one person' and the people assembled in Parliament. These words are curious and mark a change in the position of the representative body. It is the

---

[45] See e.g. [Instrument,] Arts 4, 23, 30.
[46] See [Instrument,] Arts 6, 7, 8, 9–21.

elected assembly and not as under the monarchy the monarch and the Houses which constitutes the Parliament. The Commonwealth legislature represents the nation in theory far more completely than did any English Parliament down at any rate to 1832. It has a constitutional right to be summoned once in every third year and when summoned cannot constitutionally be adjourned, prorogued, or dissolved during five months[47] from the day of its meeting without the Parliament's own consent.[48] It may, except during periods specified, be dissolved by the Protector. The Parliament has, subject to one article of the Constitution, the exclusive right of passing or repealing laws and of imposing taxation, and its ordinary legislative power is not subject to the consent of the Protector.[49] To the Parliament further is given the right to nominate six persons from among whom the Council and lastly the Protector must choose a Councillor to fill up a vacancy in the Council.

A student's first impression is that a Parliament under the Protectorate possessed all and more than all the power wielded by the Parliaments of the monarch, and the Constitution certainly provided against the possibility of the government being lawfully carried on without Parliament assembling and sitting for the transaction of business at least once in every three years. Still anyone who considers the matter carefully will soon perceive that, assuming the terms of the Constitution to have been respected, a Parliament which sat under the Instrument of Government necessarily bore a character not so much inferior to as totally different from the character of any English Parliament which was convoked by the Tudors or by the Stuarts. The Commonwealth Parliament was a purely legislative body and even its legislative authority was curtailed in more than one direction. The Constitution was, to borrow American expressions, 'the supreme law of the land', and Parliament could not alter, or at any rate could not freely alter, the Constitution. Nor did Parliament possess exclusive power of legislation. Under Article 30 the Protector, with the consent of the Council, has power 'to make laws and ordinances for the peace and welfare of these nations where it shall be necessary which shall be binding and in force until order shall be taken in Parliament concerning the same'.[50] The chief limit, however, on the action of Parliament is that under the Constitution its authority has been limited by the power of two coordinate bodies. The Protector wields actual power never held by any English King. He has a large standing army and an assured revenue. The Council again, though it may be said to be indirectly appointed by Parliament, is nothing like a parliamentary government. Whether its members could sit in Parliament does not clearly appear; they assuredly could not be removed nor could they be punished even for misconduct by Parliament and, as already pointed out, the election to the

---

[47] If specially summoned the Parliament has a constitutional right to sit for three months and in case of war with any foreign state must be summoned forthwith.

[48] Parliament is to be summoned every third year, but the Instrument of Government does not apparently contain any provision, such as that contained in the Triennial or Septennial Acts, limiting the duration of a Parliament otherwise than by dissolution.

[49] See [Instrument,] Arts 6 and 24.

[50] This may have been a merely temporary provision to provide for legislation before the meeting of the first Parliament of the Protectorate.

Protectorate belongs to the Council. Under the Instrument of Government, in short, Parliament is a legislative body limited like the American Houses of Congress even in matters of legislation by the Constitution. It is further a legislative body which like the Diet of the modern German Empire is placed face to face with a tremendously strong executive over which the Parliament can exert no effective control. Suppose further, as might well be the case, that the Protectorate should fall into the hands of a weak man. The Parliament is again in this too like the German Diet (Reichstag) opposed by a Council more compact, more permanent, and more closely connected with the executive than the Parliament. The Council bears some likeness to the American Senate, but it also may, especially as regards the influence it would be likely to exert in a conflict with the Parliament, be compared to the German Council of States, or Bundesrath.

(iii) The judicial body. The Instrument of Government contains not one word as to the position of the judges, and no one could from the mere words of the Constitution infer that the position of the English judges was affected thereby and still less that the Constitution conferred upon them the duty or right of pronouncing upon the constitutionality of Acts of Parliament. Very nearly the same remark might be made with regard to the Constitution of the USA yet it is common knowledge that since the foundation of the Constitution the American judiciary have in fact pronounced upon the constitutionality of Acts of Congress and have treated them and do treat such Acts as void if they conflict with the provisions of the Federal Constitution.

And to any one who studies the Instrument of Government with care it will become almost certain that under the Instrument the position and authority of the English Courts would have undergone a complete change. The primary doctrine of English law is now and long has been that no Court could treat an Act of Parliament as void, and though there are expressions to be found used by Coke and others which imply that an Act of Parliament might under some cases be treated as of no effect and though it is certain that judicial interpretation has at times in practice nullified the effect of statutory enactments it would I believe be impossible to point to a case of authority in which the Courts have treated a statute as a nullity on the ground of its being unconstitutional, or indeed on any ground whatever. Now the Constitution of 1654 [sic] just because it is a rigid and a more or less written constitution invites, we may almost say necessitates, the intervention of the judges. There are several ways in which a law might he passed which violated the Constitution. It might be passed without the consent of the Protector and also without the 20 days having elapsed within which his consent was required; it might alter the Instrument of Government and be passed after 20 days without the consent of the Protector which alone could make such alteration valid. It might lastly be a law contrary to the religious liberty guaranteed by Articles 35–38.

The last case is the clearest. Such a law must be 'esteemed as null and void'. This in accordance with English legal conceptions clearly means that when the attention of the judges was in a given case called to the unconstitutional character of the law they must treat it as void or non-existing, but in order to achieve this end they clearly must consider whether a given law, e.g. a law punishing a Prelatist for attending a service of the Church of England, was or was not contrary to the religious liberty guaranteed by the Constitution. In other words the Courts must pronounce upon the constitutionality of an Act of Parliament. But the judges called upon to perform this function would occupy a position never before held by any English magistrate. The Instrument of Government no less therefore than the Constitution of the US inevitably tended to turn the English judiciary into the arbiters of the Constitution.

C. Comparison between the Constitution of 1653 and the Modern Constitution of England

Did the first Protectorate really resemble the modern constitutional monarchy of England?

A student's first impulse is to answer this question in the affirmative.

The constitutionalists of 1653, as represented by the Instrument of Government, were both innovators and democrats. They advanced in some respects very far towards the realisation of modern ideas. Under their hands Parliament became a regular and normal part of the Constitution. Parliament itself was reformed and reformed much upon the lines which were tardily followed in 1832 and since 1832. Under the Commonwealth was for the first time united every part of what now forms the United Kingdom and for the first time England was provided with a strong regular army and with a sufficient navy. Add to all this that in theory at least the doctrines of toleration were more distinctly recognised as a part of the law of the land than they have ever been recognised in England until quite modern times and, whatever may be said as to the restrictions placed upon the operation of this theory, no fair critic can doubt that had the Constitution of 1653 endured all orthodox Protestants would have enjoyed practical toleration and what many of them did not enjoy till more than a century after the Revolution of 1689 [sic], political equality. It must never be forgotten that in point of toleration Cromwell and his followers were far in advance of their age.

But a little reflection will make us feel that though the Constitution of the Protectorate was in theory at least a democratic constitution and in more respects than one carried out ideas which we now associate with freedom and progress yet the constitutionalism of 1653 was not only accidentally but essentially different from the English constitutionalism of 1897. It is of some importance to seize this fundamental dissimilarity. Had the Constitution of 1653 stood England might have been a perfectly free country and would have been a country possessing parliamentary institutions. But the Republican Constitution of England would have been something very different from the existing constitutional monarchy. The mere fact indeed that the Protectorate was under the Constitution of 1653 not hereditary is a comparatively small matter. The main importance of the office of Protector being elective lies in the weight thereby given to the Council as electors of each successive Protector.

The points which are really worth notice are these. The constitution of England was turned into a written and rigid constitution. A strong executive was erected armed with powers greater than have been ever held by any English King. In the Council was formed a body which might in all matters of administration have overbalanced the power of the legislature. It might very probably have become cooptive. Parliament, lastly, was transformed into a merely legislative body, it did not in reality appoint the executive nor did it retain the powers by which Parliament has indirectly gained a right to nominate, or at any rate to control the nomination of, the executive body. Cromwell and the men who drew up the Instrument of 1653 might be called in one sense democrats, though the term does not very happily describe them. They were not Parliamentarians: they wished to make Parliament a part but not the predominant part of the constitution: they, whether knowingly or not, created a Parliament with restricted powers which should legislate but should not govern. Their constitutionalism has some points of affinity with the constitutionalism of the United States. It has yet stronger points if likeness to the constitutionalism of Germany. It does not in its essential characteristics resemble the parliamentary constitutionalism of modern England. Paradoxical though the assertion sound, the Cromwellian ideal of government had a good deal more affinity to the ideal of Strafford or of Bismarck than it has to the ideal represented in the world of politics by Pitt, or Peel, or Gladstone, or in the world of literature by Hallam and Macaulay.

3

English Constitutionalism under George III

Analysis*

A. Outward Likeness to Modern Constitutionalism
    1. Forms similar
    2. Government parliamentary in full sense
    3. Government national
    4. Absence of arbitrary power

B. Differences from Modern Constitutionalism
    I. *Differences in **form** of constitution*
        1. Parliament a *British* Parliament
        2. Parliament a *Protestant* and (practically) a Church of England Parliament
        3. Parliament an *unreformed* Parliament
    II. *Differences in **working** of institutions*
        1. The influence of the Crown
        2. The influence of the aristocracy
        3. The position of the Cabinet
    III. *Differences in **spirit** of the constitution*
        1. Form of constitution practically unchangeable
        2. Constitution rested on predominance of certain classes
        3. Constitution neither in theory nor in practice democratic
        4. Executive supported by Crown had considerable independence
        5. Independence of Parliament
        6. Limited sphere of state's activity

(See generally Paley, *Moral Philosophy*, ii, bk. VI, cap. VII;
1 Lecky, *Democracy*, cap. II, especially pp 202–216, 253–313;
Lilly and Wallis, pp 1–33;
Boutmy, *Études de Droit Constitutionnel*.)

---

* Its contents have been derived from an undated manuscript entitled 'English Constitutionalism under George the Third (1785)' and attached to the lecture scheme headed 'Easter & Trinity Terms, 1897'. A later manuscript insertion (to the reading list) has been omitted.

English Constitutionalism under George III[*]

Whoever compares the constitutionalism of Queen Victoria with the constitutionalism of the Commonwealth feels himself, so to speak, in a strange country. The more he considers the matter the more he is struck with the essential differences between the political ideas of the Puritans and the political ideas of today. Cromwell, it is true, wished like every other Puritan statesman to establish the rule of law and of freedom. His constant endeavour was to rule not without, but with, a Parliament. He had no wish to be a despot. But he was utterly unfitted for the part of a constitutional King. He could far more easily have been an American President, such as Jackson or Lincoln, or a modern German Emperor, such as was William I, or such as aspires to be his grandson. His Council was utterly unlike a modern Cabinet; one is forced to compare it not with an English Ministry but with the American Senate, not indeed as the Senate now is, but such as it was designed to be by the founders of the United States. Parliament again, as constituted by the Instrument of Government, is in its whole character a very different thing from any Parliament which has sat in England since the Revolution of 1689. It consists of one House; it has for many purposes uncontrolled powers of legislation; it had little hold on the executive. The Commonwealth, it may be said, was a democracy, and so also is the constitutional monarchy of Victoria. This remark is true but misleading. The Commonwealth was always in fact a government supported by a mere fraction of the people, and the democracy on which, had it lasted, it must ultimately have rested, was a democracy of independent landowners and under the Instrument of Government a democracy of comparatively well-to-do landowners. The constitutional monarchy is now supported by the whole nation; the government is in reality democratic but the democracy by which it is upheld is in the main a democracy of townsfolk. The majority of the electors are tradesmen, artisans, and labourers. The truth is that, as already pointed out, our Puritan forefathers aimed at results such as freedom from arbitrary power, the establishment of civil liberty, and to a certain extent of religions toleration which their descendants have obtained. But the path by which these results were reached is not the path marked out by the Whigs of 1689 and followed out, in ways which the Whigs of 1689 never foresaw, by the liberals and reformers of later days. The ideas of the Commonwealth have either not been developed at all or have received their full development rather in the United States than in England. It were indeed an error to suppose that the great Rebellion left no permanent traces on the institutions of England, but it is true that the Interregnum constitutes a break in the development of the English constitution. The ideas, no less than the institutions, of the Commonwealth, though they constitute a premature attempt to realise some essentially modern and democratic conceptions, cannot he made to square with the modern conceptions of

---

[*] Undated manuscript. The full lecture text appears to have been written in 1897 because it treats the constitution of that year as the existing constitution at the time of writing (see, e.g., p. 62 below).

constitutional government. It is at bottom the differences between the constitutionalism of the 17th and the constitutionalism of the 19th century which impresses any one who takes in hand the comparative study of institutions.

A critic, on the other hand, who compares the constitution as it existed in the reign of George III, say in 1787, with the constitution as it now exists in 1897, is in danger of exaggerating the points of likeness and overlooking some important, though less marked, points of dissimilarity. In 1787 the forms of the constitution were much what they are at present. The King was strictly a constitutional monarch; there existed a regular Cabinet supported by the majority of the House of Commons and the Cabinet was under the leadership of an acknowledged Premier. Pitt was as much a Prime Minister and the head of the government (though neither he nor his contemporaries would have called the government Pitt's government) as Mr. Gladstone or Lord Salisbury. It was fully understood that the House of Commons was the predominant body in the state, and it had come to be acknowledged that a majority of the House could not long retain its power unless it were supported by a majority of the electorate. George III, though a man who passionately loved power, never affected to be in any sense above the law. He never ruled or conceived it possible to rule, without a Parliament; he never claimed to create a parliamentary borough; he never made use of the Royal veto; he was perfectly aware that he must always act through Ministers and that no Minister could long keep office who could not command the votes of the House of Commons. Both in form and in fact parliamentary government was established in England and the unbroken continuity of our constitutional development tempts a student to think that the constitutionalism of George III was in all material matters the constitutionalism of today. Yet anyone who looks a little below the surface will feel that here, as elsewhere, continuity is a totally different thing from identity and that, both in form and still more in spirit, the Georgian differed from the Victorian constitution. Our aim should be to make perfectly clear to ourselves what are the points of real similarly, or even identity, and also of important difference.

A. The Points of Likeness

The essential point of likeness, we might even say of identity, is that by 1787, and indeed from the accession of the Hanoverian dynasty, the monarchy had become in the strict sense both constitutional and parliamentary. This was the work of the Whigs; it resulted both from the Revolution of 1689 and from the maintenance on the throne of the House of Hanover. Till 1745 the possibility of another Restoration made it necessary for the Hanoverian Kings, though both of them by nature despotic enough, to respect the constitution and to maintain parliamentary government. By the time George III ascended the throne the authority of Parliament had been established past dispute. The constitutional government of George III differed greatly from the constitutional government of Victoria but it belonged at bottom to the same class of governments. Each [h]as fully acknowledged the rule of law; under each form of government Parliament, and above all the House of Commons, has become the must important body in the country.

It is worth while to work out this fundamental similarity a little more into detail and note the main features which the English constitution of 1787 has in common with the constitution of 1897.

Arbitrary power is quite unknown. Under George III the law of the land was in many respects harsh and severe. The frequency of capital punishment and of even more frequent condemnation to death for very slight offences, and the constant imprisonment of debtors, are two examples whereof scores might be found of the prevalence of a spirit of severity or of cruelty unknown to the present day; but though the law might be cruel every man was subject to the law and to the law alone and no man stood in danger of losing life, liberty, or property simply because he opposed the will of the King.

The annual meeting of Parliament, though not directly guaranteed by any law was as much part of the constitution as it is now. It had become, so to speak, a political law of nature, and all opposition between Crown and Parliament had come to an end. George III exerted, it is true, very considerable authority. By means of what was called influence he could when he chose influence the action of the House of Commons but he never in reality came into conflict with Parliament. On one celebrated occasion he systematically defied a parliamentary majority, but he ventured upon this course because he, or rather Pitt, had the sagacity to perceive that the House did not represent the electors and that a dissolution would produce a House of Commons ready to support the policy of the King.

In the earlier part of his career George had struggled against the growth of Cabinet government as we now understand it. He knew that he could act only through Ministers; he knew that his Ministers must command parliamentary support, but he contended for the right to exercise a very wide discretion in the choice of his servants. He wished probably not to have an acknowledged Premier and rather to act through Ministers, each of whom should be the head of a particular department, than through a collective Ministry or Cabinet. But before George III came to the throne the possibility of permanently resisting the possibility of Cabinet government had passed away, for the rule was established that the King was not present at the meetings of the Cabinet. By 1787 the King had, though perhaps he was hardly conscious of the fact, given up in substance, though not in form, the effort to oppose the growth of a parliamentary executive. A conflict of more than 20 years ended, as have so many constitutional conflicts in England, in a very singular compromise. The King defeated the political party which he most detested, and overthrew the government which had been forced upon him by an overwhelming parliamentary majority. He appointed a Premier of his own choice, but Pitt whom he chose was supported from the first not only by the King but by the nation. The temporary defeat of an artificial majority constituted by an unprincipled coalition of factions procured for the King a striking triumph, but the triumph was purchased by his admitting in effect the sovereignty of the nation.

By 1787, and indeed long before that date, the supremacy of the nation had in effect become an essential part of the constitution. George III made many mistakes, one or two of which inflicted incalculable damage on the country, and, as they were denounced by the most prudent statesmen and the ablest thinkers of the time, might have been avoided by a King of genius or enlightenment. But the plain truth is that George's worst errors were sanctioned, if not applauded, by his people. The policy of England was in the long run the policy approved by Englishmen.

> 'The present representation', says Paley, after dwelling on its obvious defects, 'is still in such a degree popular, or rather the representatives are so connected with the mass of the community by a society of interests and passions, that the will of the people, when it is determined, permanent, and general, almost always at length prevails.'[1]

B. The Points of Difference[2]

In spite of outward resemblances the Georgian constitution is distinguished from the modern constitution of England by differences in its form, in its working, in its spirit.

I. Differences in form

1. The Parliament of George III was in 1785 the Parliament of Great Britain and not the Parliament of the United Kingdom. It was a British, we might almost say an English, Parliament. It was not what our present Parliament is, an Anglo-Irish Parliament.

This point, though obvious, has great importance. Up till the beginning of this century not a single member from Ireland sat in the Parliament at Westminster. Strictly Irish affairs did not occupy Parliament after 1782 at all. The Scotch members moreover were only 45 in a House of Commons consisting of 548 members. To put the matter broadly a twelfth part only of the House was Scotch. The rest were wholly English. The Scotch members acted, we may be pretty sure, together. They had practically a decisive voice on purely Scotch affairs. The chief effect of their presence as regards English policy was to strengthen the administration of the day or rather the Crown. On all English matters, on all matters of general policy England was during the 18th century governed by Englishmen in accordance with English ideas.

2. The Parliament was strictly a Protestant Parliament and though not absolutely yet with very slight limitations a Church of England Parliament.

---

[1] *Moral Philosophy*, bk. VI, c. VII, p. 223.
[2] The best authority for the character of the Georgian constitution is Paley, *Moral Philosophy*, ii, bk. VI, c. VII. pp [blank] The book is the work of a man who looked at the constitution as it actually existed. He has seen it and described it far more truly than either Burke, who was led astray by his rhetoric and his imagination, [or] Blackstone, who though a writer of supreme literary gift, either mistook forms for realities or did not care to distinguish them. The importance of the book as a picture of the constitution is increased by the date of its publication. It appeared in 1785 (Nat. Dict. 'Paley', xliii, p. 103). At that moment the modern Cabinet system was firmly established under Pitt and men's views of the constitution were not yet biassed by either enthusiasm for, or detestation of, the French revolution.

No Roman Catholic could by any possibility occupy a seat either in the House of Commons or in the House of Lords and no Roman Catholic could vote at an election.[3] Roman Catholics in fact were excluded from the public life of England, and even had they been admitted to the franchise and to seats in Parliament they could up to 1800 have exercised no substantial influence on English public life. They were not in England practically persecuted or even disliked by the educated classes though Papists were, as witness the Gordon Riots of 1780, hateful to the mob. Their numbers were very small. The Catholic gentry represented a dying class, so to speak. There were no Irish constituencies to send to England Roman Catholic representatives, and there was, I conceive, no extensive Irish emigration to fill the large towns with Irish labourers or artisans, and if the Irish poor had already settled in England they would not for the most part have obtained votes. Growing towns, such as Birmingham or Manchester, were unrepresented and, though in one or two constituencies there existed a wide franchise approaching to universal suffrage, in most boroughs a resident working man, whether Irishman or Englishman, had no vote at all. The Parliament therefore was an English Parliament dominated by English Churchmen.

3. The Parliament was an unreformed Parliament.

The Parliamentary reforms introduced under the Commonwealth had historically no effect whatever. The old distribution of seats and the old franchises reappeared as a matter of course at the Restoration, and the protest of the House of Commons against the creation of a new parliamentary borough (Newark) by Charles II practically abolished the Royal prerogative of creating boroughs and made the gradual extension of the parliamentary franchise to the growing cities of the North impossible.[4]

Men are still living who remember, and at least one eminent man is living, who sat in the unreformed Parliament, yet Englishmen of today do not easily realise what the unreformed Parliament really was, or rather perhaps what it appeared to be. It looked at least like the strangest system of representation or misrepresentation under which a great nation ever enjoyed freedom and prosperity. It is easy enough, if you search the right books, to find queer stories about the rotten boroughs. One of them consisted it is said of nothing but a field enclosed in a landowner's domain. The two or it might be three electors met there to elect, at the landowner's direction, a member of Parliament. The true elector had marked the spot with a stone on which was inscribed '*Vox Populi Vox Dei*'. When the Reform Bill was brought forward the representation of Ludgershall delivered this speech in the House of Commons: 'I am the patron of Ludgershall. I am the elector of Ludgershall. I am the member for Ludgershall. As patron, as elector, and as member, I shall vote for the abolition of Ludgershall.' In Mr. Walpole's painstaking or, to use an old expression, painful *History of England*, may be found elaborately collected together examples of all the anomalies, which were so common that the word anomalies is hardly appropriate, existing under the parliamentary system before 1832.

---

[3] [Dicey inserted a footnote here but did not supply any text for the note.]
[4] The constitutional changes of the Commonwealth seem to have been absolutely forgotten. See Paley.

'The 45 Scotch members', he writes, 'were nominated by 35 persons. 354 members were returned on the recommendation of the Treasury, and 197 patrons. The Union with Ireland added 100 members to the roll of the House of Commons. But 51 of these were returned by 36 Peers and 20 by 19 Commoners. The Union had increased the roll of the House to 658, and 424 of the 658 members were returned either on the nomination or on the recommendation of 252 patrons.'[5]

But though there is no reason whatever to doubt the accuracy of Mr. Walpole's figures, the picture of a past state of things, drawn, it may be, by a censorious critic, never equals in value the calm representation of an unbiassed contemporary. The best and shortest account known to me of the unreformed House of Commons is given by Paley.

'There is nothing in the British constitution', he writes, 'so remarkable, as the irregularity of the popular representation. The House of Commons consists of five hundred and forty-eight members, of whom two hundred are elected by seven thousand constituents; so that a majority of these seven thousand, without any reasonable title to superior weight or influence in the state, may, under certain circumstances, decide a question against the opinion of as many millions. Or to place the same object in another point of view; if my estate be situated in one county of the kingdom, I possess the ten-thousandth part of a single representative; if in another, the thousandth; if in a particular district, I may be one in twenty who choose two representatives; if in a still more favoured spot, I may enjoy the right of appointing two myself. If I have been born, or dwell, or have served an apprenticeship in one town, I am represented in the national assembly by two deputies, in the choice of whom I exercise an actual and sensible share of power; if accident has thrown my birth, or habitation, or service into another town, I have no representative at all, nor more power or concern in the election of those who make the laws by which I am governed, than if I was a subject of the Grand Signior—and this partiality subsists without any pretence whatever of merit or of propriety, to justify the preference of one place to another. Or, thirdly, to describe the state of national representation as it exists, in reality, it may be affirmed, I believe, with truth, that about one half of the House of Commons obtain their seats in that assembly by the election of the people, the other half by purchase, or by the nomination of single proprietors of great estates.'[6]

So much for the difference in form between the constitution of 1787 and the constitution of 1897. The constitution of 1787 may be summed up in the character of its Parliament, and that Parliament was what our present Parliament is not[:] a substantially *English* Parliament, a *Protestant* Parliament, and, lastly, a Parliament specially representing the *property* [sic], and especially the land-holding classes.

II. Differences in the working of the constitution

1. The position of the Crown

(i) The formal prerogatives of Queen Victoria are pretty nearly the same as the formal prerogatives of George III, but the *position* of the Crown is very different today from its position when George III was King.

---

[5] 1 Walpole, p. 136.
[6] Paley, *Principles of Moral and Political Philosophy*, bk. VI, ch. VII, 12th edn, ii, pp 217, 218.

The King possessed great and often decisive power in the government of the state. On at least three great occasions the will of George III determined the policy of the country. This power arose partly from his character but it was due in the main to a more obvious and material cause. The Crown in 1787 controlled or influenced the House of Commons by means of what was then technically known as 'influence'[7] or, in other words, of patronage, and the power of thus directing the action of Parliament arose from the fact that the Crown had at its disposal a vast amount of patronage in the way of seats in Parliament, of lucrative places, of pensions, of titles, and the like. That the amount of this influence was large and that its effects were important was admitted by all men. The evils of influence were denounced by Burke in language which no one can forget in his speech on economical reform, whilst the possible or hypothetical good effects of influence are suggested by Paley in the most ingenious of paradoxes or apologies. But neither the assailants nor the defenders of Royal influence denied its existence.

But the two points which deserve our notice are, first, that influence in the sense in which it existed under George III does not exist under Victoria and, secondly, that influence produced several indirect but very important effects on the working of the Georgian constitution.

(ii) Influence no longer exists.

The government of course has places and titles at its disposal and their distribution by the Ministry of the day is a matter of great public importance, but the number of places which a Premier can freely give away are small; few of them are sinecures. He has no seats whatever by which he can at his own will introduce into or keep his followers in Parliament. Of pensions or sinecures to be given away at the will of the Crown or Ministry there are practically none. The gifts which a political leader can make to his partisans are in fact so small that they cannot by any possibility purchase a majority in the House of Commons, or even retain the allegiance of a wavering party.[8]

(iii) The existence of influence had several important results.

In the first place it manifestly increased the power and authority of the government. It counteracted the tendency which in modern political slang is called the swing of the pendulum. It prevented a Ministry from losing power simply because it had been for a long time in office and having of necessity fallen into mistakes and made foes found itself the object of increased hostility on the part of its opponents without having been able to retain what may be called the personal allegiance of its friends. In estimating the effect of influence in counteracting the effect of growing

---

[7] As to influence, see Paley, pp 224–231.

[8] Let no one however suppose that corruption is dead. It is an evil, which like sin itself, will never die. It is at least judging from experience, or from our knowledge of human nature, as likely to flourish under a democratic as under an aristocratic form of government. The American Congress is at least as [corrupt as], and the Legislature of New York far more corrupt than[,] ever was the worst House of Commons. It is further as easy to corrupt classes as individuals. All that is maintained in the text is that corruption in the present day cannot exist in the form of influence of the Crown. Paley and, no doubt, other acute observers perceived that reform of Parliament would mean the abolition of influence.

unpopularity we must remember that the Crown or the Ministry possessed a number of seats which were strictly at the disposal of the government, or had in effect the power to nominate a number of MPs. Under George III it was a distinct and a calculable advantage for a party to be in office during a general election. At the present day it has often been maintained that at a general election the party in opposition has a slight advantage over its opponents. Influence moreover very directly, at any rate in the case of a strong man like George III, increased the personal authority of the King. He was after all, in theory, the man who appointed to every public office; he was the great patron and George was determined that his patronage should be under his control. For a certain period he made himself in virtue of his influence the real head of the state. It was the King, and not Lord North, who from 1770 to 1782 guided the policy of the country. The calamities of the war with the Colonies made it impossible for the King to retain the power he had acquired, but thus much he finally established: that influence should be exercised either by the King or by a Minister whom he cordially supported. As long as George III maintained his throne and his sanity the Crown was a most important factor, if not the most important factor, in the working of the constitution. Two facts give us some measure of the power possessed by the Crown. In 1788 Pitt was the most popular of Premiers, yet every one expected that if the Prince of Wales became Regent, Pitt would be turned out of office and the Whigs placed in power. Whether the result would have followed may be doubtful, but it is certain that popular opinion attributed even to a Regent, and to a Regent whose moral character would have carried no weight, the power to determine who should be Prime Minister. There cannot be a doubt, again, that between 1801 and 1804 the country desired to put Pitt in power, yet Addington was kept in office and the members of Parliament prepared to follow Pitt in opposition to the government were apparently [few].

In the second place the existence of influence, combined no doubt with other circumstances, made politics in the last century a professional career.

If we want to have a notion of the change in this matter which has taken place in recent times, we should note two facts. The one is that the lower class of politicians, the Rigbys of the day, certainly made and intended to make a gain out of politics. Theodore Hook, who could be described as little better than a political satirist of a low type received a place—in Jamaica, it is true—of £2,000 a year. Pitt was admittedly in pecuniary matters the most disinterested of men, but Pitt, who is said to have had about £300 a year of his own, received for the greater part of his life an income of some £10,000 a year, and, as Warden of Walmer Castle, held what was equivalent to a good pension on retirement. Burke, again, was in some respects the noblest statesman of his time, yet Burke, who was the son of an Irish attorney[,] who at the early part of his career edited the *Annual Register* it is said for £100 a year, and who most nobly gave up for the sake of his political convictions the chances or certainty of holding gainful offices which fell to men who gained the favour of the Crown, did nevertheless in some form or other make a livelihood out of politics. He received £30,000 from Lord Rockingham, he purchased a landed estate, at the end of his life he received a handsome but well deserved pension from the Crown, and is said to have been at his death on the point of receiving a Peerage. These things are not of course mentioned as charges against men of extraordinary genius and of the highest integrity. They are referred to as showing that a century ago political life was a profession just as legal life is a profession at the present day. The blanks no doubt were in the field of politics, as now in the field of law, far more numerous than the prizes. Still the prizes were great and relatively more valuable than we now imagine. The mercantile millionaires of the 19th century were unknown and the gains of authors were trifling. Professional fees were, as measured by our standard, small. Politics in short was to those who ventured on the hazardous pursuit a profession like any other. It is a profession no longer. The politician who had made a fortune in politics does not exist or, if this statement be deemed exaggerated, it is certain that no sensible man goes into politics with the idea that he will make a fortune in Parliament. Hence the 18th century presents more than one example of a character which no longer exists, *viz.* the patriotic adventurer. The noblest of the class was Burke. We may call him an adventurer became he meant to make politics his profession and a profession which would support him. He entered so far into public life in the same spirit in which a man of high character, such as Roundell Palmer, goes to the Bar; he intends to succeed in an honourable career by the use of honourable means, and he does so. But he conceals neither from himself nor from others that he intends also that his professional career shall provide him with a competence, and it may be, with a fortune. We call Burke a patriot because he devoted his genius to the promotion of the public welfare, and throughout his life was ready to sacrifice his fortunes to his principles.

2. The position of the Peerage and House of Lords

From the accession, at any rate of George I, the House of Commons, and not the House of Lords, was the most important body in the state. But the weight of the Peerage in England has never depended on the constitutional powers of the House of Lords. It is far nearer the truth to say that the House derives its power from the Peerage than that the Peerage derives its authority from the powers of the House. The House of Lords itself had more weight in the time of George than at the present day. On one celebrated occasion at any rate the House in effect overthrew a Ministry supported by a large majority in the Commons, but this triumph was due not to the inherent powers of the House but to the energetic support of the King and of the electors. What is more to the purpose as showing the weight of the House itself is the fact that on the whole the House under the influence of Whig magnates was more favourable to toleration than was the House of Commons.[9] The true source of the power of the Peerage was that they were the chiefs of the class, namely the whole body of landowners who were then predominant in the state. As the century passed away the mercantile classes—a somewhat different thing from the manufacturing classes—increased in power, but Pitt, whether designedly or not, freely promoted men of wealth to Peerages and the House of Lords came to represent the mercantile no less than the landed interest. The Peers moreover made up for their want of authority in their own House

---

[9] [Dicey inserted a footnote here but did not supply any text for the note.]

by the influence they exercised over the House of Commons. To them in the main belonged the nomination boroughs. A glance through Oldfield's *Representative History* will easily explain the methods by which harmony was maintained between the Commons and the Lords and the power which up to the passing of the Reform Bill was exercised by the Peers.

3. Position of Cabinet

The Cabinets of George III were smaller than, some of them not being half the size of, a modern Cabinet. Pitt's first Cabinet, for example, consisted of seven members. It was for purposes of government a body which under a powerful Premier might make a compact and vigorous executive.

III. Differences in the spirit of the constitution*

Few things are more difficult of definition than the expression 'spirit of a constitution'. It has, to say the truth, at least two or three different meanings. It may mean for example the end or final cause for which a constitution, or law, or institutions generally exist or may be supposed to exist. This is apparently the sense in which the word 'spirit' is used by Montesquieu in *Ésprit des Lois*. It may, again, mean something very near to the working of a constitution, but the term refers rather to the way in which the persons of a given time look upon their institutions, the way in which they expect them to work or assume that they will work than to the actual working of the institutions themselves. The words I am going to use seem pedantic, yet they more nearly express my meaning than any others. The spirit of institutions is the subjective side of their working. When we say, for instance, that the spirit of English institutions is legal, or that the spirit of Prussian institutions is military, what we really mean is that Englishmen as a rule look at their institutions from a legal point of view, and expect that the law will be rigidly respected, and what has been termed the rule of law be maintained, whilst Prussians look upon their institutions from the point of view of soldiers, that military ideas are predominant amongst the government and the people, that they expect that the authority of the state shall be maintained and that the Constitution shall comply with the requirements of a well and justly governed army. It must, however, at once he admitted that the term 'spirit' is an extremely vague one, which conveys a notion as indefinite as it is important. It is certain to any one who with adequate knowledge meditates upon the matter that the spirit of Georgian constitutionalism was very different from the spirit of Victorian constitutionalism. My aim is to enumerate some of the points in which this difference of spirit is apparent.

1. The forms of the constitution were practically unchangeable

The theoretical sovereignty of Parliament was at least as well established in 1787 as in 1897. The classical passage for the definition or description of Parliamentary

---

* On Dicey's notion of a constitution's spirit, its relation to Montesquieu's notion of *l'esprit des lois*, and its functional similarity to notions of constitutional culture today, see Editor's Introduction, pp xxiii ff above.

sovereignty is to be found in Blackstone but for all this the sovereignty of Parliament was far less a reality in the 18th than it has become towards the end of the 19th century. No one expected that any government would propose or carry fundamental changes in the political institutions of England and the expectation was fully justified by historical facts. From 1689 to 1828 there was, if we except the Acts of Union with Scotland and Ireland, no fundamental change made by legal enactment in the constitution of the country. This tacit and almost unconscious conservatism is a marked feature of 18th century politics. The simple truth is that among the Englishmen who cared about politics at all there existed profound and, if you looked at the matter from a practical point of view, not unreasonable satisfaction with the national institutions. Political parties were divided as to the policy of the country not as to the maintenance of its institutions. The most conservative government of modern days proposes every year changes which a century ago would have startled the most energetic of Whig reformers.

2. The constitution rested on the predominance of certain classes

The constitution rested on the predominance of certain classes, the large landowners, the merchants, the independent freeholders, and the like. There was, in reality though not in name, something analogous to the body which used in France to be described as the 'legal country', or the limited body of citizens who, e.g. under Louis Philippe, alone exercised full political rights and were supposed to represent the sentiment and interests of the whole nation, and, let it be added, that in the England of George III the legal country to a far greater extent than one would suppose did really represent the nation, or at any rate as much of the nation as felt any effective interest in public affairs. This is the strong point of the intelligent conservatism, a totally different thing from Toryism, represented by Burke and Paley.

> 'Let us', writes Paley, in answer to the attacks made on the anomalies of the representative system, 'before we seek to obtain anything more, consider duly what we already have. We *have* a House of Commons composed of five hundred and forty eight members, in which number are found the most considerable landholders and merchants of the kingdom; the heads of the army, the navy, and the law; the occupiers of great offices in the state; together with many private individuals, eminent by their knowledge, eloquence, or activity. Now, if the country be not safe in such hands, in whose may it confide its interests? If such a number of such men be liable to the influence of corrupt motives, what assembly of men will be secure from the same danger? Does any new scheme of representation promise to collect together more wisdom, or to produce firmer integrity? In this view of the subject, and attending not to ideas of order and proportion (of which many minds are much enamoured), but to effects alone, we may discover just excuses for those parts of the present representation, which appear to a hasty observer most exceptional and absurd.'[10]

---

[10] Paley, *Principles of Moral and Political Philosophy*, bk. II, ch. VII, (12th edn), pp 220, 221.

3. The constitution was neither in theory nor in practice democratic

A constitution is in its principles democratic when it recognises the voice or the consent of the majority of the citizens as the only legitimate source of authority. In this sense the Federal Constitution of the United States, all the French Republican Constitutions, and also the French Imperial Constitutions constituted by Napoleon I or Napoleon III may be called democratic.

A constitution is in practice democratic when the policy of the state in all matters of importance, whether they be domestic or foreign, is determined by the wishes, or at any rate by the supposed wishes, of the majority of the citizens.

But neither in principle nor in fact was the will of the numerical majority of the people supreme under George III.

The whole system of parliamentary representation which reached the height of paradox or anomaly in the case of Scotland—where the representation of a country which contained two millions of inhabitants was confined to the *tenants of the Crown* in the several counties, to a corporation of *thirty-three* individuals in the City of Edinburgh, and to sixty-five delegates from the same number of self elected corporations of Royal burghs[11]—was a theoretical and practical denial of what is called the sovereignty of the people.

Nor is there any reason to suppose that the will of the majority of the inhabitants of Great Britain was in fact supreme. It is certain that the most popular Minister of his age—Chatham—was kept out of office in deference to the will of the King and also to the jealousy of the nobility. It is probable too that in some respects the actual government of the country was more 'liberal', to use a modern expression, than were the opinions or prejudices of the people. English sentiment disapproved of the favour shown by George III to the Scotch, though his partiality for Scotchmen cemented the Union between the two parts of Great Britain. Pitt's Free Trade policy was distinctly unpopular. His attempt to relieve the Catholics from political disabilities drove him from office. There is every reason to suppose that the followers of Lord George Gordon represented the predominant religious sentiment both of England and of Scotland. The governing classes were more tolerant and enlightened than the people.

But the constitution, though not democratic, was national. The paradox, though it remains rather a paradox than an established fact, that the unreformed Parliament represented the various classes in the nation more truly than could any representative assembly formed on a purely democratic model,[12] contains an element of truth. The nomination boroughs did in fact open a career to men of talent to whom since the abolition of close boroughs public life has been more or less closed, and a limited number of constituencies, such, for example, as Westminster, which contained more than 20,000 electors,[13] provided a means which hardly existed under the Reform Act of 1832 for giving expression to the sentiment or the prejudices of the mass of the people. The constitution, in short, did on the whole enable the classes who took an

---

[11] 6 Oldfield, p. 119.
[12] Compare Paley, p. 222.
[13] 4 Oldfield, p. 218.

interest in politics, and these may from a political point of view be fairly termed the nation, to make known, and in the long run enforce, their will. It was the gradual shifting of population, wealth, and power towards the North of England which, combined with other circumstances, made the old constitution cease to represent the nation and which thus caused the passing of the great Reform Act.

4. **The executive, by which for the present purpose must be understood the Cabinet, when fully supported by the Crown, possessed a kind of independence unknown to modern Ministries**

It was possible for the government to defy prevalent opinion. The contest with Wilkes, the suppression of the Gordon Riots, and of the movement of which it formed part, the execution of Dr. Dodd, the peace of 1761, we may even say, the concession of legislative independence to Ireland in 1782, all bear witness in different ways to the freedom with which the executive could act. In some of these cases the government was, in the opinion of most modern critics, in the wrong, whilst in others it was in the right, but my immediate point is not that the executive was wiser or more foolish than the people, but that the executive was more or less independent. It has been already pointed out that the Crown and the Ministry, which generally, it must be remarked, was connected with and commanded therefore the influence of certain noble families, had means for guiding and controlling the action of the House of Commons. They were not nearly so liable, as have been some Cabinets of later times, to be thrown out of office by loss of popularity in the House.

5. **Parliament itself possessed a large amount of independence**

The true Whig theory, as represented by Burke, is that Parliament was no merely representative assembly, but was the sovereign. This is of course the theory of English law. It is, as has been often pointed out, the only logical vindication for the passing of the Septennial Act. But in the 18th century the theory of Parliamentary sovereignty corresponded much more nearly than it does at present with political facts. Within certain limits hard to be defined, but which were very real, Parliament, that is the King, Lords, and Commons, did really and habitually exercise supreme power. Frequent or unexpected dissolutions were all but unknown and, though a dissolution might no doubt change the balance of parties, it did not, as it does now, make the seat of every MP unsafe. Dissolution or no dissolution the patrons of the nomination boroughs retained their power, and their nominees retained their seats, whatever were the changes in public opinion.

6. **Limit to the sphere of the state's activity**

We should always remember that men are after all ruled by their opinions or beliefs, though their opinions are generally determined by their interests or their supposed interests. Now both the working and the spirit of the constitution [were] in periods with which we are dealing essentially influenced by an opinion, we might almost say habit, which for good and bad has more or less passed away or at any rate temporarily has ceased to exert its former power. This opinion was in effect that the state was called upon to protect men's personal safety, freedom, and property, but ought to act within a very limited sphere. No doubt the theory of *laissez faire* was in the time of George III not formulated either by statesmen or by the public and there were large portions of English social life which represented, so to speak, survivals of other opinions. The Established Church, the Poor Law, the legislative protection of different interests all depended for their existence or justification on the opinion that the state ought to intervene in many things beyond the protection of person and property. But the habit of the governing classes was to leave things alone. There was little of legislative reform or legislative innovation. To put the matter at the very lowest, the legislative and administrative powers of the state were not used to effect changes. Whole departments of government, such for example as the Education Office, as the Local Government Board, as the Police, are of modern creation. They all bear witness to a revolution of ideas. Inactivity was the characteristic of the English government under George III. This inactivity favoured the growth of abuses, it favoured also the development of individual freedom.

4

American Constitutionalism

Analysis*

A. How far American Constitutionalism Based on English Ideas
   I. *The rule of law*
   II. *The form of constitution*
B. Essential Differences between American Constitutionalism and English Constitutionalism
   I. *Constitution the supreme law of the land*
   II. *Non-parliamentary executive*
       1. President
       2. Governor of State
   III. *Legislature a law-making body and a subordinate law making body*
   IV. *The judiciary*
   V. *Popular legislation—the Constitutional Convention*
C. Comparison between American and English Constitutionalism
   I. *Unlikeness to modern English constitutionalism*
   II. *Likeness to constitutionalism of the Commonwealth*

(See Constitution of the United States;
Constitution of State of California, 1 Bryce, 3rd edn, p. 111;
  As to *national* government, 1 Bryce, pp 15–400;
  As to *State* government, 1 Bryce, pp 411–650;
  As to Constitutional Conventions, 1 Bryce, p. 667.
NB American Constitutionalism not considered here in its federal aspect.)

---

* Its contents have been derived from an undated manuscript attached to the lecture scheme headed 'Easter & Trinity Terms, 1897'.

American Constitutionalism[*]

Introduction

American institutions may be regarded from two different points of view.

The United States may, on the one hand, be regarded as the type of fully developed federal government. This is not the point of view from which they are considered in this lecture.

The Constitution either of the United States, on the other hand, [or] of any of the separate States, such e.g. as Massachusetts, may be looked at as a form of Republican government. This is the point of view from which I shall try in this lecture to regard the institutions of America. My aim is not at this moment to compare the federal government of America with the unitary government of England, but, omitting as far as possible all reference to the federal tie which binds together the States of the Union, to compare the constitutionalism of Republican America, as it is exhibited in the institutions either of the United States or of the separate States, with the modern monarchical constitution of England.

It will be well then to consider three points: first, the extent to which American constitutionalism is based on English ideas; secondly, what are the essential differences between American constitutionalism and modern English constitutionalism; and, thirdly, what are the points in which the constitutionalism of the United States bears a certain resemblance to the constitutionalism of the Commonwealth.

A. How far American Constitutionalism is Based on English Ideas

American constitutionalism is primarily and mainly based upon English ideas.

This statement is nothing but the assertion in an abstract form of an undeniable historical fact.

The Constitutions and the laws of the thirteen Colonies at the time when they separated from England were English and neither the Declaration of Independence (1776) nor the final separation in 1783 effected any material change in the law or the institutions of the States. The common law of England and the statute law of England enacted before 1776 in so far as applicable to the Colonies remained after the Declaration of Independence, as to a great extent it remains today, the law of each of the thirteen States. The Colonial Constitutions, except in so far as they were necessarily modified by the separation from England, remained in force, and in matter of fact the Constitutions of several of the States were not changed till years after the Declaration

---

[*] The manuscript was dated May 1897 in a later manuscript note added to its title page.

of Independence. Rhode Island, for example, was till 1842 governed by the Charter of 1653,[1] and where new Constitutions were formed they probably did not to any great extent change the existing system of government for the men who carried through the American revolution were not only men of English descent but in the strictest sense of the word Englishmen. Till 1776 they had been subjects, and in many cases perfectly loyal subjects, of the British Crown. In one respect at any rate they resembled the Whigs of 1689; they were the least revolutionary of revolutionists. There was nothing, it should be noted, in the conflict with England to make the founders of the Republic hostile to English institutions. The middle of the 18th century was a period when the pride of Englishmen in English institutions was intensely strong. England stood before the world as preeminently the Free State. On the Continent despotism was triumphant. Every state which was powerful was according to English notions despotically governed and the few countries such as Switzerland or Holland which maintained a show of freedom were obviously weak or were declining from their former greatness. In England alone strength was combined with liberty. The English people were free and the English state was powerful. At the close of Pitt's administration [in] 1761 England was not only powerful but victorious, and nowhere was greater exultation felt than in the American Colonies which had seen and taken part in the expulsion of French power from Canada. The fall of Quebec announced to the world that the freedom of England, not the despotism of France, was to control the destinies of America, and, be it remembered, that all Englishmen then attributed the prosperity of England to the English constitution. There cannot be a doubt that this belief was shared by the English colonists. The contest with England may have excited the detestation of George III or even hostility to England herself, though as a matter of fact a good deal of loyalty to England survived the acknowledgement of American Independence, but there was nothing in the American revolution to shake the belief of Americans in the substantial excellence of the English constitution. The complaint of the colonists was not that the principles of the constitution were bad but that in their case the principles of the constitution had been violated. Their struggle with the English Parliament to vindicate the principle that there ought to be no taxation without representation did not even suggest the idea that parliamentary government, as it existed in England, was not in itself the best form of government. There is no reason to suppose that Washington might not have termed himself, as did George III, 'a revolution Whig'. They both believed in the principles on which the Whigs justified the Revolution of 1689 though they disagreed as to their application. Blackstone's *Commentaries* had a circulation which for that time was immense in America. Kent has left on record the profound effect produced on his mind by reading when a young man the work of the great Commentator. Montesquieu, who was held to have penetrated more deeply into the mysteries of the English constitution than any other thinker, was admired by Burke as much as by the authors of *The Federalist*. It was absolutely impossible that the English constitution should not at the very moment of separation from England have seemed to every American to be the model of a free government. Note too that with the

---

[1] [Dicey inserted a footnote here but did not supply any text for the note.]

common law the English colonists had brought to the New World all those conceptions of individual freedom and of the proper relation of the government to private citizens which have found expression in the constitution of England.

The statement that American constitutionalism is based on English ideas must be taken subject to certain qualifications.

English colonists could carry with them from England only those laws, institutions, or conceptions which are compatible with colonial life and in New England at any rate the colonists were in the main men who had imbibed the political and the religious principles of the Puritans. Hence, to put the matter broadly, the American colonists and the[ir] descendants dropped more or less completely the so called feudal elements of the English social system.[2]

Americans looked at the English constitution through the eyes, so to speak, of Montesquieu, and believed with many Englishmen that its most essential principle was the separation of powers.[3]

The necessity, lastly, for substituting a written and rigid for an unwritten and flexible constitution worked a far greater change in the nature of the constitution itself than American constitutionalists probably realised.

I. *The rule of law*

The feature which establishes under great apparent differences an essential similarity between English and American constitutionalism is that the inhabitants of both countries share the reverence for what I have elsewhere called the rule of law.[4] Neither in England nor in the United States is there any tolerance of arbitrary power; in neither country is the executive and its agents armed with special rights or authority as representing the state; in neither country does there exist anything equivalent to the *droit administratif* of France and of other Continental states.[5] In both countries the private rights of citizens to personal liberty and the like are in reality rather the foundation than the result of the constitution.

---

[2] On the whole English law has been less changed by its being carried to America than one would *a priori* have expected. The land law of the USA, though it has been modified so as to suit the needs of Americans, e.g. by the abolition of primogeniture (see 4 Kent, *Comm.*, p. 385), is based upon the law of England (see 4 Kent, *Comm.*).

[3] [Dicey inserted a footnote here but did not supply any text for the note.]

[4] See Dicey, *Law of the Constitution*, chs IV–XII and especially ch. IV.

[5] This has been recently disputed (see 1 Goodnow, *Comparative Administrative Law*, pp 6, 7) but without reason. No doubt in all civilized countries there must exist rules of law for the organization of government offices and for regulating the conduct of state officials, though of such special rules there are fewer in England than one might perhaps expect to find. But by administrative law, or *droit administratif,* is not really meant merely laws affecting the conduct of officials, but a body of law which governs the relations and responsibility of the state and its officials towards individuals, under which law in France at any rate is included the existence of a body of official Courts (*tribunaux administratifs*) for the determination of questions involving the conduct of officials as agents of the state. Note too that in France it is the official Courts which determine the jurisdiction of the ordinary Courts of the land, whilst in England it is the ordinary Courts which determine the limits of their own jurisdiction. That *droit administratif,* in the French sense of the term, is unknown to England or America, is one of Tocqueville's profoundest observations (compare de Tocqueville, p. 66), and is fully borne out by Hauriou, pp 170, 174.

II. *The form of the Constitution*

That the form of the Constitution of the United States, and indeed of American Constitutions generally, is borrowed from England is too patent to require careful demonstration.

The President not only recalls the English King, but is in reality an official who was intended to possess in substance the powers exercised under the English constitution by George III. The Senate recalls the House of Lords; the House of Representatives has the rights of the House of Commons.

Nor does the difference between the Constitution of the United States and the constitution of England as it existed in 1786 depend upon the existence under the Constitution of the Union of a wide suffrage. It is true that at the present moment universal suffrage does I believe exist in every American State, but there is nothing in the Constitution of the United States to necessitate the giving a vote to all the citizens of every State. As a matter of fact universal suffrage did not exist in all the thirteen Colonies when they separated from England, and there is nothing in the articles of the Constitution forbidding any State from limiting the number of citizens entitled to electoral rights. If for example the people of New York should amend their Constitution so as to confine the right of voting to householders the amendment would in no way violate any article of the Constitution of the United States.[6] If we are to look for the differences between American constitutionalism and the constitutionalism of England, we must examine something more than the mere form of an American Constitution and we must constantly bear in mind the influence exerted in the last century by Montesquieu's[ft] doctrine that the maintenance of liberty depended on the separation of powers. This doctrine as understood by the American and English followers of Montesquieu meant that the executive, the legislative, and the judicial power should each fill a distinctly marked province of their own upon which neither of the other powers should in any way encroach. It was believed moreover both by Montesquieu and his disciples not only that this dogma, thus interpreted, embodied a profound political truth but also that it was actually put into practice in the English constitution and further that adherence to the principle of the separation of powers had preserved the liberties of England. It is not at this moment my purpose to examine what was the amount of truth contained in Montesquieu's political theory. All that we need here note is that it commanded the absolute assent of every political thinker engaged in constructing the Constitution of the United States and further that the inconsistency of Montesquieu's teaching with the actual working of the English constitution was less visible towards the end of the 18th than it is at the close of the 19th century. In any case American statesmen made the most consistent attempt to carry out Montesquieu's ideas and to this attempt may be traced not all indeed but many of the features in which the Constitutions of America differ fundamentally from that of England.

---

[6] See Arts 1, and 2.

[ft] This page should be altered so as to insert a sketch of Montesquieu's doctrine of separation of powers. [Later unnumbered manuscript footnote.]

B. Essential Differences between American and English Constitutionalism

I. *The Constitution the supreme law of the land*

If the executive, the legislature, and the judiciary are to be each kept within their separate province it is plain that there must be constituted some power superior to any one of them. This power is in the United States the Constitution. No doubt the necessity for making a constitution which should be superior to all other powers arose as regards the Union in part at any rate from the necessity for a federal compact which should prevent the States from encroaching on the rights of the nation and the nation from encroaching on the rights of the States. But this supremacy of the Constitution belongs not only to the Constitution of the United States but also to the Constitution of each separate State. The Constitution of the United States is of course supreme throughout the whole Union but, subject always to the Constitution of the United States, the Constitution of any particular State is in that State the supreme law. Thus in New York any law passed by the New York legislature which is inconsistent with any article of the Constitution of New York is void. So any law passed by the Legislature of Massachusetts which violates the Constitution of Massachusetts is void, or in other words is no law at all. It is of consequence that we should realise this supremacy of the State Constitution in any given State no less than the supremacy of the US Constitution throughout the whole United States. It is absolutely essential to the maintenance of the separation of powers. Hence:

II. *Non-parliamentary executive*

I have already pointed out that one of the most essential features of our modern English constitution is that the executive is a parliamentary executive placed and kept in power by the will of Parliament or rather of the House of Commons. Throughout the length and breadth of the American Republic a parliamentary executive is unknown.

1. The President

The President is, as you all know, not elected by Congress but by the citizens of the United States. He holds his office by the will of the people, not by the will of Congress, and Congress has neither the right nor the power to dismiss him. But, more than this, the President during his tenure of office has very wide powers. He is Commander-in-chief of the army and navy; he has in his gift, subject to some offices with the advice of the Senate, a large number of appointments. He, acting with the Senate, has the right to make treaties. He can exercise a decisive influence over the whole executive government of the country and, further, he has in effect the right to veto any Bill passed by Congress, and a Bill so vetoed cannot be passed over his head, as the expression goes, except by a vote of two-thirds of both Houses of Congress, and this power of exercising a suspensive, which may well become a final, veto, is no obsolete power but has constantly been exercised. The plain truth is that the President is an authority coordinate with Congress, and he has powers which used by a strong man, or by a man who at a grave crisis is supported by the country, enable him to balance, or even overbalance, the authority of Congress. Such check as is placed upon him proceeds partly from the short time for which he holds office, from a desire for re-election, and from the necessity in certain cases of obtaining the assent of the Senate to his action.

I have not spoken, you will observe, of the President's Cabinet. A body popularly called by that name exists; it means the political heads of the great Departments of the government, but these officials or ministers who are appointed by the President, are not a Cabinet in the English sense of the term; they are not members of Congress, they are not necessarily party leaders; they do not form a collective body; they are simply the heads of certain Departments;[7] and they are heads of Departments who owe their posts to and depend for their tenure of office [on] the will of the President. They are just such a Cabinet or Ministry as George III would have constituted if he could, that is a set of officials who were at the head of separate Departments, but who depended for their position on his choice and not on the support of Parliament. The President in short is the executive, and the President is in no way dependent upon Congress.

2. The Governor of State

What is true of the President is true of the Governor of each State. The powers, whatever they be, vested in him are powers which he can exercise independently of the State legislature. As a matter of fact he is sometimes a man put into office in order that he may check the vagaries of a legislative body which excites distrust. I have heard it said of President Cleveland, whether with truth I know not, that the reputation which he acquired as Governor of New York was due to the freedom with which he vetoed Bills passed by the Legislature of New York.

It is true that in ordinary times the power of a President or a Governor may be small, but such power as he possesses, e.g. the power of vetoing bills, is independent of the legislative body. He loses, it is true, (from not being a member of the legislature) the sort of influence possessed by an English Premier, but he is also saved not only from the danger of dismissal by the legislature, but from the indirect encroachment on the exercise of his functions which makes an English Cabinet intensely sensitive to the wishes of the House of Commons. A State Governor, again, has in many cases no control as to the appointment to subordinate offices, but note that the officials whom he does not appoint are appointed not by the legislature, but by the people. A President, on the other hand, and in a less degree a Governor, have a source of authority unknown to any parliamentary executive. They represent the nation as truly as the legislature, perhaps more truly. Hence, for example the power of a President or Governor to make actual use of his veto. Hence too the result that at a great national crisis a President may exert supreme authority. It has been well said by Mr. Bryce that Abraham Lincoln was more powerful than had been any single Englishman since the time of Oliver Cromwell.

---

[7] 1 Bryce, c. IX.

III. *The legislature is a law-making body, and a subordinate law-making body*

Every legislature throughout the United States is primarily a law-making body; it is not a body which can appoint or dismiss the executive.

Every legislature throughout the United States is again a subordinate law-making body.

Congress can make laws only on the definite topics, 18 in number, as to which it is allowed to legislate under a Constitution of the United States.

Every State legislature, again, is of course subject to the Constitution of the United States and can make no laws which violate any article of that Constitution. Thus the assembly of Massachusetts cannot pass any law which impairs the obligation of contracts;[8] it could not, for example, pass a law resembling the various Irish Land Acts which have been enacted since 1869.

The State legislature is bound by the Constitution of the State. The Constitution indeed of a particular State, e.g. New York, might without violating the Constitution of the United States vest in the New York legislating body all the authority of the State, including the right to amend the Constitution. But no State Constitution has done this, no State Constitution has given to its legislature even that kind of 'subordinate sovereignty' which is possessed by the Parliament of Victoria. The Parliament which meets at Melbourne is except in matters of Imperial concern, in all matters in short which merely concern Victoria, almost as supreme a legislature as is the Imperial Parliament and possesses powers which are not possessed by any American legislative body. Nor does the matter end here. It might be expected that the State legislatures would as time went on widen the scope of their powers just as have the Imperial Parliament and the colonial Parliaments scattered throughout the British Empire. Nothing of the kind has happened. In every American State the Constitution has been constantly remodelled, but speaking broadly each amendment of the Constitution has added to the articles of the Constitution or, what we shall find is in effect the same thing, has limited the area of the legislature's authority. Thus lots of subjects which are not in any sense in their nature constitutional have in different States been excluded from the competence of the legislature, that is articles have been inserted in the Constitution prohibiting the legislature from passing any law on certain enumerated subjects.

The most important classes of prohibited laws are—

Statutes inconsistent with democratic principles, as for example, granting titles of nobility, favouring one religious denomination, creating a property qualification for suffrage or office.

Statutes against public policy, e.g. tolerating lotteries, impairing the obligation of contracts, incorporating or permitting the incorporation of banks, or the holding by a State of bank stock.

Statutes special or local in their application, a very large and increasing category, the fulness and minuteness of which in many Constitutions show that the mischiefs

---

[8] United States Constitution, Art. 1, s. 10.

arising from improvident or corrupt special legislation must have become alarming. The lists of prohibited subjects in the Constitutions of Missouri of 1875, Montana and North Dakota of 1889, Mississippi of 1890 are the most complete I have found.

Statutes increasing the State debt beyond a certain limited amount, or permitting a local authority to increase its debt beyond a prescribed amount, the amount being usually fixed in proportion to the valuation of taxable property within the area administered by the local authority.[9]

The plain truth is that distrust of legislative action is the fundamental characteristic of modern American constitutionalism.

And, as already implied if not absolutely stated, no American State legislature can of its own authority change the State Constitution.

The restrictions on the action of legislative bodies are supported by two other institutions which have been developed or created in America.

IV. *The position of the judiciary*[10]

It is the function of American as of English Courts to determine the cases which come before them for decision, and this is in the United States as in England in strictness their sole function.

Yet American judges do in fact fulfil in the United States a duty which does not fall upon English judges, at any rate with regard to cases decided under the law of England.

Let us see how this happens, and for the sake of clearness put aside for the moment all reference to the Constitution of the United States and consider what are the duties of say a Pennsylvanian judge sitting at Philadelphia and deciding a case which clearly depends for its decision upon Pennsylvanian law. In the first place he has to decide as a judge what is the effect of the acts of the party according to the law of Pennsylvania; whether, for example, a given contract is valid according to Pennsylvanian law. Let us suppose that it is a wagering contract and that the Court is called upon by the counsel for the defendant to treat the agreement as invalid on the ground that some Act of the Pennsylvanian legislature makes void all agreements by way of wagering. The primary question for the decision of the judge clearly is whether the contract is a wagering contract and whether there be a Pennsylvanian statute making it void. So far he has to act exactly as an English judge would act were he called upon to determine the validity of a contract alleged to be a wagering contract, and therefore void within the Gaming Act, 1892. In each case the judge or Court has, the facts being ascertained, to determine whether the terms of an Act against wagers apply so as to make the contract void. The Philadelphian judge and the English judge alike have to interpret a statute.

---

[9] 1 Bryce, c. X4, pp 490, 491.
[10] Compare Dicey, *Law of the Constitution* (5th edn), pp 87–89, and 166–172, with 2 Bryce, *American Commonwealth*, 3rd edn, cap. XXIII, 'The Courts and the Constitution', especially pp 249–260.

Supposing that the English judge holds that the Gaming Act, 1892, applies[11] he treats the contract as void and his whole duty is fulfilled. With the Philadelphian judge it is, or may be, otherwise. He may see with perfect clearness that the Pennsylvanian Act applies to the case, and that the very object of the enactment is to invalidate the sort of contract on which the plaintiff is suing. But it may be objected by the defendant that though the Act passed by the Pennsylvanian legislature does undoubtedly make wagering contracts void yet that this Act does for some reason or another violate the Pennsylvanian Constitution and therefore is of no authority as being itself void. The American judge must then compare the articles of the Constitution with the enactment, and if he discovers that the Act against wagering is unconstitutional must treat the statute as void, or in other words, as non-existent. This is exactly what no English judge is ever called upon to do with regard to an Act of Parliament, because no Act of Parliament can be unconstitutional or, to put the same thing in other words, an American judge may be called upon to treat a Philadelphian statute as void because it is one which under the Constitution the Philadelphian legislature has no authority to pass, whilst the power of the Imperial Parliament being constitutionally unlimited, no judge can pronounce any Act of Parliament unconstitutional or void.

The difference between a Philadelphian judge and an English judge is that the Philadelphian judge may be called upon to determine for the purpose of deciding a particular case whether the Philadelphian statute violates the Constitution of Pennsylvania, but no English judge can be called upon to determine whether an Act of Parliament violates the English constitution.

It is necessary to understand exactly the duty discharged by an American judge when determining whether a given law is or is not unconstitutional, for his action is often described in two ways each of which contain an element of truth but each of which may easily be misunderstood.

An American judge, it is often said, 'declares void or annuls acts which are unconstitutional'.

This is in so far true that a judge does in deciding a particular case treat as having no effect or being void a law passed e.g. by the Pennsylvanian legislature in contravention of the Pennsylvanian Constitution, but no judge in any part in any Court of any State throughout the Union, or of the United States itself, ever annuls a law or declares it to be void. All that he does do is that for the purpose of a particular case in which A is plaintiff and X defendant he treats the law as having no effect. Nor let anyone suppose that the difference between annulling a law and treating it for the purpose of a particular case as void is a mere verbal distinction. There is this among other differences. The same Court in another case, or another Court in a similar case, may possibly consider the Act constitutional and valid which has by one judge been treated as unconstitutional and invalid. The Supreme Court of the United States, for instance, has more than once changed its views as to the constitutionality of Acts of Congress. In any event an American judge is never called upon in strictness to annul an Act of any legislature; he is simply a judge and never exercises any other but judicial functions.

---

[11] See *Carney v. Plimmer* 1897, 1 QB (CA) 634.

An American judge again, it is sometimes said, never does anything but 'interpret the law'.

This sort of statement is put forward by writers who well understand the nature of American institutions and wish to guard their readers against the error that in the United States a Court or a judge may he called upon to pronounce a law unconstitutional and annul it in the same sense in which under some of the Imperial Constitutions of France the Senate had the right, which I believe was hardly ever or never exercised, of annulling or abrogating laws which violated the Constitution.

But though it is a far less serious error to say that an American judge never does anything but interpret a law than to allege that he annuls a law, still the statement that, e.g., a Pennsylvanian Court never does anything but interpret the law of Pennsylvania is, if not absolutely erroneous, certainly misleading and cannot be vindicated except by an undue extension of the meaning of 'interpretation'.

When, to recur to my example, a Philadelphian judge has before him a wagering contract alleged to be made void by a Pennsylvanian Act against wagers he, in the first place, considers the meaning of and in strictness interprets the Pennsylvanian statute and makes up his mind whether it is or is not intended to make void a given contract. He holds that such is its effect. He is then asked to treat the enactment as void as being unconstitutional. In order to be sure to make up his mind on this point he must consider or interpret the effect of the Constitution, but if he finds that the Pennsylvanian Gaming Act is unconstitutional he in no way interprets the Act. Its meaning he has already determined; he does not go through the fiction that it cannot be unconstitutional and therefore means something else than it appears to mean. What he may say is the meaning of the Act is clear but it is unconstitutional; he does not interpret the Act, he treats it as void; he does not assume that the Pennsylvanian legislature kept within the Constitution, he lays down in effect that the Pennsylvanian legislature has exceeded its constitutional powers, and that the Act passed by the legislature is therefore *ultra vires* and void.

I have purposely confined myself to the case of a State Court dealing with a State law, but of course exactly the same principle applies to a law passed by Congress. Such a law, as also a State law, may be in contravention of an article of the US Constitution and every Court throughout the United States be it a State court or a Federal Court treats as invalid or void any law by whomsoever passed which violates the Constitution of the United States.

V. Legislation by People—the Constitutional Convention[12]

No American legislature can of its own authority change the Constitution. It may and occasionally does pass an Act amending the Constitution in which it is provided that the amendments shall not come into force until they are submitted to and approved of by the people, i.e. by a majority of the citizens voting.

---

[12] 1 Bryce, *American Commonwealth*, 3rd edn, p. 667.

The normal way of amending the Constitution is by means of a thoroughly American institution, namely:

The Constitutional Convention

Such a Convention is a representative body called together temporarily and for the special purpose of drafting a new or amended Constitution to be submitted to the people for their approval.

The Convention is not a legislature. It is not its function to enact any law; its function is simply to prepare a Constitution which is to be enacted by the vote of the sovereign people. It is, as Mr. Bryce expresses the matter, 'an advisory body, which prepares a draft of a new Constitution and submits it to the people for their acceptance or rejection'. Its powers even of proposing change may be limited by the statute under which the people elect it.[13]

A Convention therefore differs from the ordinary State legislature. It is not a legislative body at all and on the other hand it can propose changes in the Constitution which the ordinary legislature, as already pointed out, cannot change at all.

A Convention therefore has no resemblance to the English Parliament: it is not a legislative body, it has nothing to do with the government or administration of the State; its meeting does not in any way affect the ordinary transaction of affairs; it is in no way a sovereign body.

A Convention, again, is unlike the Constituent Assemblies which from time to time have assembled in France. A Constituent Assembly is, it is true, an elective assembly brought together to draw up a new Constitution and it is an elective assembly such as was the National Assembly of '48, or the National Assembly of 1871, convened for this particular purpose, but a Constituent Assembly is a body in which is for the time vested the sovereignty of the nation. It is in fact a sovereign Parliament convoked indeed to draw up and enact a Constitution, but convoked also to pass ordinary laws and to control the administration of the state.

The distinction between a Constituent Assembly and a Constitutional Convention ought to be particularly noted, because at one time even in the United States they were more or less identified and it was supposed that a Convention once brought together to amend the Constitution became, *ipso facto*, the supreme body in the State with enacting as well as deliberative powers.

The proposals of a Convention, according to the prevailing constitutional notions of the United States, do not come into force unless and until they are accepted by the people, and as a matter of fact the whole or a part of the amendments proposed by a Convention have been frequently rejected by the people.

The Constitutional Convention therefore is at bottom a form of popular as contrasted with Parliamentary legislation, but it is the very best form of law-making by the people. It is a system which presents so many advantages that it may now be considered the best known arrangement for introducing constitutional changes. Its advantages are briefly these:[14]

---

[13] Ibid.
[14] See 1 Bryce, pp 668, 669.

(i) a Convention being chosen for the sole purpose of drafting a Constitution is not necessarily elected on party lines or in obedience to party considerations and can hardly be used for corrupt purposes;

(ii) a Convention may contain men of eminence, judges, and the like, who would not or could not take part in ordinary political affairs;

(iii) a Convention gives its whole mind to the one purpose of Constitution-making;

(iv) a Convention is not like a Constituent Assembly distracted by the party considerations or even the national dangers of the moment;

(v) a Convention whose proposals must if they come into force receive the sanction of the people cannot carry measures opposed to popular opinion.[15]

For our purpose what should specially be noted is that the powers of an American legislature are limited by the Constitution and that the limitations placed upon the legislature are upheld:

(i) by the authority of the Courts;
(ii) by a system of Constitutional Conventions.

American constitutionalism then agrees with modern English constitutionalism in their being both based on the reign of law and in the fact that the outward form of American Constitutions is suggested by the constitution of England. American constitutionalism differs from modern English constitutionalism in the following points:

(i) the Constitution is the supreme law of the State;

(ii) the American executive is a non-parliamentary executive;

(iii) the American legislature is a subordinate law-making body limited at once by the authority of the Courts and by the legislative action of the people.

It is worth noting that the features in which American constitutionalism differs from English constitutionalism are the characteristics in which it has an affinity to the constitutionalism of the Commonwealth.

Under the Instrument of Government and under the Agreement of the People, as in every American State, the Constitution is the supreme law of the land.

Under the Instrument of Government as under every American Constitution the executive is a non-parliamentary executive.

Under the Instrument of Government, as under the American Constitution, the legislature body is a subordinate law-making body.

---

[15] The Constitutional Convention is so much more used and better understood in the United States than in any other country that it may fairly be considered as an American invention, and indeed the first Convention was that which drafted the Constitution of the United States. The Directorial Constitution, however, of 1795 contains under the head Revision of the Constitution, Arts 336–350, provisions for changing the Constitution by an 'Assembly of Revision' or, in other words, a Convention which has no other function than the proposal of amendments in the Constitution, and these are not to come into force until accepted by the people.

The Agreement of the People anticipates in theory the American practice that amendments of the Constitution should be ratified by the vote of the people.

No Constitution of the Commonwealth states *totidem verbis* that the judges must treat as void laws which violate the Constitution; neither for that matter does any American Constitution. If the Constitution of 1653 had stood, it is not a very bold assumption that English Courts would have followed the course subsequently adopted by American Courts, and treated unconstitutional enactments as void. Chief Justice Hale might well have anticipated the work and the fame of Chief Justice Marshall.

5

French Constitutionalism

Analysis*

A. Relation between French History and French Constitutionalism
    I. *The Crown*
    II. *The States General*
    III. *The Parliaments*

B. General Ideas Governing French Constitutionalism
    I. *The nature of a constitution*
    II. *The Sovereignty of the people*
        1. Nothing between the state and individual citizens
        2. Universal suffrage
        3. Constitution cannot be changed by ordinary legislature
    III. *Separation of powers*
    IV. *Authority of executive*

C. Existing Constitution
    I. *Universal suffrage*
    II. *Absence of judicial control*
    III. *Executive*
    IV. *Parliamentary government*

D. Comparison between French Constitution and English Constitution
    1. In both parliamentary government
    2. In French Constitution no direct connection with historical development
    3. In France basis of Constitution is will of individual citizens
    4. In France the sphere of the judges is wholly non-political
    5. In France attempt has been made to form a non-parliamentary executive, but has failed

(See Lowell, *Governments and Parties in Continental Europe*, i, chs I and II;
Boutmy, *Studies in Constitutional Law* (trans.), pp 141–175;
Plouard, *Les Constitutions Françaises*, especially Constitution of 1791 (p. 14) and Constitution of 1875 (p. 279);
Borgeaud, *Établissement et Revision des Constitutions*, bk. II, pp 249–307;
1 Chéruel, *Institutions Moeurs et Coutumes de la France*, arts 'Constitution' and 'États Généraux', and 2 Chéruel, art. 'Parlement';
1 Stephen, *Lectures on the History of France*, Lectures X–XII, p. 343 and following.)

---

* Its contents have been derived from an undated manuscript attached to the lecture scheme headed 'Easter & Trinity Terms, 1897'. Later manuscript deletions and insertions (to the reading list) have been omitted.

French Constitutionalism[*]

A. The Relation between French History and French Constitutionalism

The Constitution of the existing French Republic is not an 'historical constitution' in the sense in which this term is applicable to all the main political institutions of England. This at first sight seems so obvious a matter as to be hardly worth mentioning. Anyone who chooses to look at the proper books, as for example Mr. Lowell's most excellent *Governments and Parties in Continental Europe*, can easily ascertain the precise date, or rather the precise dates, at which the present French Constitution was framed. It is to be found in a limited number of Constitutional or Organic laws passed between 25 February 1875 and 17 March 1889 (both inclusive). By the most friendly and liberal interpretation of which the facts are capable it is impossible to carry the existence, I will not say of the existing Republican institutions, but even of the present French Republic, further back than 4 September 1870. It cannot from any point of view be considered to have lived longer than 26 years, yet, and this is a curious point for observation, it has already lived longer than any polity formed in France since 6 May 1789 when the last States General met at Versailles. Nor is it only the shortness of the Republic's existence which prevents us from calling the French Constitution an historical one. Neither the executive nor the legislative, nor the judicial bodies of modern France, can trace their descent up to ancient institutions. The French President is not the political heir of Louis XIV. Paradoxical though the assertion sound, he has far less connection with the monarchy of the Bourbons than had the Protector with the kingship of the Stuarts. The modern Parliament is not the offspring of the States General; the Senate has nothing to do with the ancient nobility of France, the Chamber of Deputies does not in any special sense represent the *Tiers État*. The Courts of modern France have no resemblance to the *Parlements* of the *ancien régime*. If there exist in modern days any assemblies which bear a slight resemblance to the French 'Parliaments' these assemblies are to be found not in France but in the Channel Islands.

It is indeed the Great Revolution which has broken the historical development of French institutions. There is a sense, and a very true sense, in which the law itself of France dates from 1789. The institutions, it is true, of the *ancien régime* emerged in many cases from the revolutionary storm, in effect, untouched though under new names and under altered forms; the Council of State, for example, the centralised administration of the *Intendants* under the modern name of *Préfets*, and the like, belong to the *ancien régime*. But all the actual institutions of France, even those which in reality descend from the past, are governed by new 'authorities', using that

---

[*] The manuscript was dated 13 May 1897 in a later manuscript note.

word in its legal not in its political sense. The old authorities (*anciens textes*), such as the Royal ordinances, the decrees (*arrêts*) of the Council of State, the decrees of the *Parlements*, have been abolished. Revolutionary legislation has recast all the legal institutions of the country. Legal authorities, for example, such as Royal ordinances, for which nothing new has been substituted, have lost their value, because they belonged to a state of things which the Revolution has condemned. The consequence is that, subject to very limited exceptions, French law takes no account of authorities of an earlier date than 5 May 1789.[1] An English lawyer will realise what this change means if he imagines to himself what would be the condition of things in England if the general principles of the law were reduced to a short code, and a statute were at the same time passed absolutely depriving of all judicial authority and forbidding reference to any Act or case of an earlier date than, say, 1890.[2] Nor in constitutional matters is there anything like unbroken continuity since 1789. The various polities which have succeeded one another in France cannot by any stretch of imagination whatever be derived one from the other. The present Republic in no sense descends from the Constitution framed by the first National Assembly. The Republican Constitutions of France cannot be derived from the Royal or the Imperial Constitutions. More than this the Republican Constitutions themselves are not historically connected together. The Republic of 1848 was not historically linked to the Directorial Constitution of 1795 and though the Republic of 1848 was destroyed by an act of illegal violence even those who proclaimed the Republic in 1870 did not dream they were reviving the Constitution destroyed in 1852.

At first sight therefore it might well he thought that the institutions of modern France have no links which connect them with the pre-revolutionary history of the country and therefore can hardly be called in any sense historical except indeed in the sense in which everything which exists must have a cause for its existence, and therefore a history. No idea, however, could really be more unfounded. The Revolutionists of the last century intended to make a clean sweep of the past and to start France afresh on a new career of freedom. But they failed in their design. Tocqueville, Taine, and others have demonstrated the essential connection between the ideas of the *ancien régime* and the institutions of modern France. It must always be remembered that a political constitution may be changed without any substantial alteration in the law and in the habits of the country. English history itself bears witness to this fact. The Instrument of Government substituted a united Commonwealth for the old Kingdom of England, but it left for the most part the laws of England and the habits of Englishmen all but untouched. The revolutions which France has undergone or welcomed during more than a century give rise to a false idea that France is a country of change. It is in reality the country of a conservative people. One reason why political revolutions have been frequent is that they have not involved any great change

---

[1] Hauriou, pp 35, 36.
[2] Contrast the theory of English law that no statute ever becomes obsolete and the authority possessed at the present day by the writings, e.g., of Coke. See, e.g., *Pinnel's Case*, 1602, 5 Rep. 117a; *Foakes v. Beer*, 1884, 9 App. Cas. 605; *Calvin's Case*, 1608, 7 Rep. 5a; *De Geer v. Stone*, 1882, 22 Ch. D. 243; *Pigot's Case*, 1614, 11 Rep. 27a; *Suffell v. Bank of England*, 1882, 9 QBD (CA) 555.

in the civil institutions or ordinary life of Frenchmen. The constitutional changes no doubt have been great, but even in the sphere of constitutional law we may discover, if we look for it, a good deal of conservatism. There are, at least, three institutions of the *ancien régime* which have in one way or another, though sometimes by way of repulsion rather than attraction, greatly affected modern French constitutionalism, not so much because the institutions themselves have survived, as because they have impressed certain permanent ideas or habits upon Frenchmen. These three institutions are the Crown, the States General, the *Parlements*.

I. The Crown

The ancient monarchy has been destroyed and it is not perhaps likely that a monarchy of any kind can be restored in France. But the Bourbon kingship has in several respects left permanent traces on French institutions though they are not nearly so marked as the influence of Napoleon.

The ideas of the monarchy survive, first, in the practical impossibility of framing for France any scheme of government in which there is not one man, whether Emperor or President, who is in name at least the head of and the representative of the state, [secondly,] in the large powers left to the executive in the way, *inter alia*, of legislation though of a subordinate kind, [thirdly,] in the principle that acts of State are beyond the jurisdiction of the Courts and, [lastly,] above all, in a centralised administration, subject to administrative law to be interpreted in the last resort by administrative or official Courts; and here perhaps it should be added that the administrative system of France, while it differs from anything known to England by its authoritative and centralised character, differs apparently from the administrative system of Prussia because it is an administration carried on by civilians in a civil spirit and not an administration modelled on the principles of an army. The *ancien régime* was, as compared with the government of England, a despotism, and it involved the existence of a large standing army used for purposes of aggression on other states, but, as contrasted with other governments of Europe and especially with the Prussian monarchy, the *ancien régime* was a system of government by civilians, and this predominance of the civil element and of civil ideas has, in spite of the Empire, still on the whole been maintained in France. Throughout all her revolutions France has avoided *pronunciamentos*. *Coup d'états* themselves have been carried through under the semblance at least of civil authority.

II. The States General[3]

No assembly even faintly resembling the States General has ever been convened in France since 1789, nor could such an assembly representing as it did the different 'estates' of the clergy, the nobility, and the commons be easily got together in any of the great countries of modern Europe, yet it is maintainable at least that to the

---

[3] For the Constitution of the States General see 1 Stephen, pp 343–348.

existence of the States General are in part attributable several ideas which have from time to time reappeared under the different forms of French constitutionalism.

The notion, in the first place, which has constantly prevailed in France that the proper way of altering a Constitution is to convene a body which shall specially represent the authority of the nation and being endowed for the moment with the national sovereignty shall more or less supersede all other authorities, certainly harmonises very well with the character of the old States General. When they had the power to do so, the States General claimed to be something very like what would now be called a Constituent Assembly, that is to say a body in which was temporarily lodged the national sovereignty,[4] and it is clear that the action of the National Assembly under Louis XVI impressed upon if it did not suggest to Frenchmen that a special Constituent Assembly was the proper organ for all changes in the Constitution.

Universal suffrage, in the second place, though it has been a permanent part of French institutions only since 1848, i.e. for nearly fifty years, can hardly be called a novelty. It is hard to follow the intricate scheme of election under which the different orders were represented in the States General, but it certainly looks as if the representation, at any rate of the *Tiers État,* depended at bottom upon something like universal suffrage though the individual citizens did not elect their representatives directly, but indirectly by electing the electors.

III. *The Parliaments*

The French Parliaments have not only been abolished but have, so to speak, vanished. Could they by any freak of reactionary antiquarianism be revived in modern France they would be so utterly out of keeping with all the ideas of today that they could scarcely be kept nominally alive for a year.

The *Parlements* were, as every one knows, utterly unlike our Parliament. They were in reality Courts of law but tribunals in which the magistracy who succeeded to their places by purchase possessed an independence unknown to most of the bodies existing under the French monarchy. They were also tribunals which, in a manner though to modern students [that] is very puzzling, combined their regular judicial duties with more or less irregular or extraordinary political functions. Their decrees (*arrêts*) had a certain legislative character, and the doctrine that ordinances of the Crown had no validity until registered by the Parliaments, combined with the claim of the Parliaments to oppose registration until it was actually ordered by the King in person, enabled these tribunals, when supported by public opinion, to put a check upon the authority of the Crown.

The existence of the *Parlements* has had two effects on modern France.

It has perpetuated the tradition of the high character and the personal independence of the magistracy.

But the main effect of the action of the *Parlements* has been by way of repulsion. The strange mingling of judicial with political functions acted badly. The independence of

[4] Note, for example, the claims and the action of the States General in the 14th century, 1 Stephen, pp 363–374.

the *Parlements* might be admired by foreign critics such as Burke but to the French reformers of the 18th century they appeared to be the strongholds of intolerance and of irrational conservatism. It is pretty clear that experience of the *Parlements* was one of the causes which suggested to Montesquieu the doctrine of the separation of powers. It is certain that to Voltaire they seemed antiquated corporations which obstructed the reforms to be looked for from intelligent and benevolent despotism. Their right to control legislation was utterly opposed to all the principles of the men of the Revolution. Hence Frenchmen have adopted to the full the dogma of the separation of powers so interpreted as to forbid the intervention of the Courts in any matter of State. American critics of French institutions think it strange that under a written constitution which should be the law of the land, French judges neither exercise nor claim the right to pronounce a law void on the ground of its being unconstitutional. To an Englishman it seems even more strange that on most matters in which state officials are guilty as such of illegal acts the persons aggrieved must seek a remedy not in the ordinary law Courts but before administrative tribunals, and that, when disputes arise as to the limits of civil and administrative jurisdiction, it is an administrative body and not the civil Courts by which these limits are fixed. But here, if anywhere, we can see clearly the influence of the past. It is the injudicious use of usurped political power by the *Parlements* which has led to the exclusion of modern French judges from the decision of any legal question which can be described as political or as affecting the rights of the state.

B. General Ideas Governing French Constitutionalism

The founders of the various constitutions which France has tried and discarded during little more than a century have been governed in the main by four ideas.

I. The nature of a constitution

'By the constitution of a country', writes Paley, 'is meant so much of its law, as relates to the designation and form of the legislature; the rights and functions of the several parts of the legislative body; the construction, office, and jurisdiction of courts of justice. The constitution is one principal division, section, or title, of the code of public laws; distinguished from the rest only by the superior importance of the subject of which it treats.'[5]

Paley's language does not afford a very accurate definition of a constitution, but it most happily describes the meaning which Englishmen attached to the term when they speak of the English constitution. They mean simply that part of the law of the land which deals with certain topics and especially the relation to one another of the different members of the sovereign power, *viz.* the King and the Houses of Parliament, and which defines the powers of the bodies, e.g. the Courts and the like, through which the sovereign mainly acts.

---

[5] Paley, bk. VI, ch. VII, p. 190 (12th edn).

'The type', writes Monsieur Boutmy, 'of a French Constitution is an imperative law promulgated by the nation calling up the hierarchy of political powers out of chaos and organizing them.'[6]

These words sound to an Englishman a little strange, but it is worth while to put them side by side with Paley's matter of fact statement and consider what they really mean. They imply or involve the notion that the constitution of a country is something very different from the ordinary law of the land. It is a body of principles laid down by the sovereign which in France is now always conceived of as the nation, determining what are the political powers in the state, what is the authority of the executive, the legislature, and the like, and what [are] the rights of the citizens. If we want to understand the French conception of a constitution we shall find it far less in the institutions of the existing Republic which in its form at any rate is to a certain extent the result of historical accidents, but in the earlier French Constitutions, such as the Monarchical Constitution of 1791, the Directorial Constitution of 1795, the various Imperial Constitutions, or the Republican Constitution of 1848. In all of these typical products of French genius we shall find attempts to draw up a complete constitution forming something like a work of art representing or professing to represent the will of the nation, and creating the different authorities, such as the legislature, [executive, and] judicial bodies and which represent the state[,] and at the same time defining or laying down the rights of the citizens. The will of the nation, acting through an assembly endowed with special authority or ratifying a constitutional law by a national vote, creates the Constitution. The Constitution as the expression of the nation's will is superior to and is the direct source of all the powers conferred, for example, on local bodies.

II. *The sovereignty of the people*

This conception of the Constitution as the direct expression of the national will is connected with the expression of the idea which is generally summed up under the term the sovereignty of the people. This expression may of course mean no more than the doctrine now admitted in every civilized European state that government exists or ought to exist for the benefit of the whole nation and is a tyranny or not morally legitimate unless it commands the support of the nation. But as applied to France it means something more than this. It means that the numerical majority of the citizens are or ought to be the sovereign power in every country and that their will expressed by the majority is the only legitimate source of authority.

Hence three results:

1. French constitutionalists hardly admit the existence of any intermediate authority or power between the state and the individual citizens

In England there have always been bodies which whether technically corporations or not may be generally described as corporate in so far as they have exerted and still

---

[6] *Studies in Constitutional Law*, p. 154.

exert great and independent authority, such for example as the Crown, the Parliament, the body of the Peerage, the Church, the Universities, the old City Corporations, the boroughs, and other corporations. In France since the Revolution at any rate the institutions of the state, such for example as the Departments or the different corporate bodies, have been or have been considered simply as the creation of the state. One noticeable sign of this is that, whereas in English history bodies destroyed by a revolutionary movement have reasserted their powers under changed circumstances, bodies which, such as representative assemblies which have once been destroyed by a revolution or a *coup d'état*, have never reappeared. No one has ever felt they have a life or authority of their own. Note for example, by way of contrast the way in which the Long Parliament of Charles I reasserted after the fall of the Protectorate the claim of its still existing members to be the legitimate Parliament of England. Note again the pedantry with which the whole period of the Commonwealth or the Interregnum was, so to speak, blotted out of English history. It would be difficult to find real parallels to this in the history of modern France. The monarchy of Louis Philippe fell by a riot; the Provisional Government was at once acknowledged; a reaction soon set in, but the wildest reactionists never maintained that the Chamber of Peers or the Chamber of Deputies which legally represented France on the morning of 24 July 1848, or the Orléanist dynasty itself were still the lawful government of France and had a constitutional right to exercise authority. The Republic of 1848 was in no sense a revival of the earlier Republican regimes. Napoleon III imitated to the best of his power the Imperial institutions of his uncle. The Empire had been approved by the nation and had been destroyed by foreign invaders, yet Napoleon III, through he imitated, did not restore, the Empire. The Republic of 1848 was destroyed by a *coup d'état* which all the foes of the Empire denounced as an act of lawless treachery, but the men who nineteen years after the *coup d'état* overthrew the Empire never treated the Republic of 1848 as still the legitimate government of the country. The state and the individual citizens stand under typical French Constitutions face to face with one another.

2. French constitutionalism naturally leads to universal suffrage[*]

The right of voting for the members of the legislature has under various French Constitutions been more or less limited. If, however, the Constitution derives its moral authority from its expressing the will of the citizens, the result, as a matter of logic, almost necessarily follows that every citizen should be empowered to express his will or, in other words, that every citizen should be a voter.

This sentiment has been recognised even under the most autocratic of the Imperial Constitutions. The direct appeal to the people through a plebiscite was a formal tribute to the sovereignty of the people or the will of the majority.

---

[*] For detailed elaboration, see 'Why Universal Suffrage Suits France', app. VII below.

3. **As the Constitution expresses the final will of the nation and the ordinary legislature exists only by virtue of the Constitution and, so to speak, as agents of the people it seems to Frenchmen to follow that the Constitution can legitimately be changed only by the direct and immediate expression of the will of the people**

Hitherto at any rate France has never completely acquiesced in Parliamentary sovereignty, that is in the complete transference to the ordinary legislature of the full authority of the nation.

Hence the idea prevails that no constitutional change is morally legitimate unless either it be made by a 'Constituent Assembly' such as were the National Assembly of the great Revolution, the Convention, the National Assembly of 1848, i.e. a legislative body elected to change the Constitution and endowed for the time with the sovereign powers of the nation, or it be ratified by the direct vote of the people, such as were the plebiscites under the 1st and 2nd Empires, and it would seem that French political theorists incline to carry the matter somewhat further than this and hold that the moral validity of a constitutional change depends on its ratification by a popular vote, nor can it be doubted that the mode in which the 'Charter' of 1830[7] was enacted deprived the Orléanist monarchy in the eyes of many Frenchmen of the moral authority belonging to a government existing *de jure* as well as *de facto*.[8]

This view of national sovereignty is not it would seem peculiar to Republicans or to men of extreme opinions.

Tocqueville seems to have doubted whether the Orléanist Constitution provided any legitimate means for its own amendment. Hélie who represents Imperialism seems to hold illegitimate for want of popular ratification both the Monarchical Constitution of 1830 and the Republican Constitution of 1848. Borgeaud, a moderate Republican, maintains that the Constitutional laws of 1875 cannot be rightly changed unless the amendment be submitted to a popular vote for ratification,[9] and this dogma is maintained by him in face of Article 8 which provides for the change of the Constitution by a vote of the two Houses sitting together as a National Assembly, in the face of the fact that the Constitution has actually been so changed, and in spite of the admission that the principle for which he contends cannot be shown to have been established as a recognised principle of French law.[10]

III. *Separation of powers*

Article 16 of the celebrated Declaration of the Rights of Man declares that a society in which the separation of powers is not established has no constitution.[11]

This doctrine is drawn directly from Montesquieu;[12] it is manifestly ambiguous and has in fact been interpreted in different ways. In England it has been more or less accepted in words at least by writers like Blackstone who came under Montesquieu's

---

[7] Plouard, p. 201; Hélie, ch. VI, pp 285–296.
[8] What is [sic] the Art. 75 of the Charter referred to by Hélie, p. 994.
[9] See Borgeaud, ch. VIII, (trans.) pp 248–257.
[10] Borgeaud probably relies on the Declaration of the Rights of Man, Art. 6.
[11] Plouard, p. 16.
[12] [Dicey inserted a footnote but did not supply any text for the note.]

influence. With them, however, the doctrine of the separation of powers means little more than what we should call the independence of the judges which is really the common-sense principle that a magistrate in exercising his judicial functions should neither be interfered with by the influence of the government nor take into consideration the political effects of his judicial decisions. In the United States again the Constitution of which was drawn up by men who fully meant to carry out the teaching of Montesquieu, the 'separation of powers' means that the executive, the legislature, and the judiciary are each to fill a distinctly separate sphere and being all subject to the Constitution are none of them to interfere with each other's province and especially that it is the duty of the judges to treat as null any legislative act which is inconsistent with the Constitution. In France the separation of powers means that the ordinary judges whilst independent and not liable to be interfered with in the exercise of purely judicial functions, i.e. in determining questions of private right or of criminal law, are to keep strictly within their own province. They are not to interfere with questions of State; they are not to determine questions involving a state official's liability for acts done in his official character; they are not to treat as null enactments of the legislature even though they may contravene the terms of the Constitution. This conception of the separation of powers whilst respecting the independence limits the authority of French judges. It originates partly, as already pointed out, in a reaction against the intervention of the *Parlements* in political matters and partly in a sense of the authority of the executive as representing the state.

IV. Authority of the executive[13]

Occasionally and so to speak spasmodically, attempts have been made in France to limit the power of an executive supposed, whether rightly or wrongly, to be hostile to public liberties. But on the whole under every form of government, whether monarchical, Republican, or Imperial, the permanent tendency of French opinion, as evidenced by French history, has been to vest wide powers in the hands of the executive body and to give special protection to the officers of the state at any rate when acting in their official capacity.[14] The executive for instance has still considerable legislative powers. It is at the head of a huge administrative body who on many points are responsible for their action not to the ordinary Courts of law but to administrative Courts. In a very large number of cases the sanction of the government is required under French law for acts for which no governmental licence would be necessary in England or America. To say this is not to say that France is ruled despotically, but it does amount to the statement which is strictly true that in France the powers of the executive are very wide. Nor does the present Republican government tend to diminish the discretionary powers of the executive; its tendency, in contradiction it must be added with the general course of French constitutional history, is to subordinate the use of these powers to the will of Parliament.

---

[13] Compare Hauriou, pp 1–63, especially pp 29–33 and pp 46–63.
[14] See 1 Lowell, pp 53 ff.

C. The Existing Constitution of France

The present Republican Constitution of France is a very singular polity. It has compared with other French Constitutions two salient peculiarities.

It has attained its majority, it has lasted for more than 21 years, which is more than can be said for any constitution which has existed since the great Revolution.

It is, in the next place, hardly what Frenchmen would call a constitution at all. It consists of a limited number of Constitutional laws organizing the chief powers of the state, and passed at different dates in 1875 by the National Assembly, convoked in 1871 in consequence of the invasion of France by the Germans and the taking of Paris.

To these Constitutional laws should be added certain organic laws which do not in strictness form part of the Constitution as they can be changed in the ordinary way of legislation, but they deal with what may be called constitutional subjects. Such for example is the law on the election of Deputies o[f] 30 November 1875.[15]

The explanation of the anomaly that the French Republic can hardly be said to be endowed with the kind of constitution which in one form or another has existed under every succeeding French government since the Revolution of 1789 is that the majority of the National Assembly undoubtedly wished to restore a monarchy under the House of Bourbon or of Orléans and at first intended to erect merely temporary institutions which should facilitate a monarchical restoration. Constitutional laws passed from time to time sufficed for this object. Under the stress of circumstances and the weight of public opinion the Assembly was induced or compelled to establish the Republic. The Republicans, however, naturally wished to bring the rule of the Assembly to an end whilst the Monarchists still hoped that a monarchical restoration might be possible whilst Marshal M'Mahon remained President. Each party in fact intended to change the Constitution; each party were compelled to accept it for the moment as it stood. In spite, however, of its fragmentary character, the present Constitution, with one exception which I shall emphasise later, to a great extent represents the permanent constitutional ideas of Frenchmen.

I. *Universal suffrage*

Universal suffrage, or in other words the right of every male citizen who has attained his majority to be an elector, is the foundation of the Constitution.

Universal suffrage indeed is likely to be in future one of the really immutable foundations of French institutions. It is in harmony with French ideas; it exists in neighbouring countries, such as Germany and Switzerland. It was indeed introduced though not for the first time by something little better than an accident in 1848, but it has held its ground. It may have been corrupted, it may have been tampered with, but it has never been abolished during the last 49 years. An attempt was made by the reactionists of 1850 to restrict its operation and it was this attempt which gave a certain pretext or justification for the *coup d'état* of 2 December 1851.

---

[15] Hélie, p. 1431.

II. Absence of judicial control

The Constitution of France can in accordance with its provisions be changed only in a particular way, it cannot be altered in the general course of legislation. It is abundantly plain, however, that the Assembly with, or perhaps even without, the sanction of the President might violate the Constitution either by changing the Constitution without following the forms provided by it for the carrying of Constitutional amendments or, what is more likely, by passing laws inconsistent with the terms or the meaning of the spirit of the Constitution. It is morally certain that no French Court will treat any law as null. The Courts respect the separation of powers as that term is understood in France.

III. Executive

The present, like other French Constitutions, leaves very wide powers in the hands of the executive. The power of appointment, the power of subordinate legislation, the independence of officials when acting as such, of the ordinary Courts [sic], still belong to the executive.

The President has a suspensive though not an absolute veto on legislation though this suspensive power is never apparently used.

The President can, lastly, with the consent of the Senate, dissolve the Chamber of Deputies, but this power has never been put into force, except on one celebrated occasion by Marshal M'Mahon. Still it cannot be denied that the power exists and may became very important.

IV. Parliamentary government

For the first time in French history there exists a really parliamentary government. The two Houses—the Senate and the Chamber of Deputies—and the latter is the more powerful—are in reality the supreme authority (subject of course to the electors) in the state. This is the really important change introduced under the Third Republic.

The present Parliament, or, to use the French term, the Chambers, is a sovereign body.

The Parliament has in reality full powers of legislation; it can pass any ordinary law in the ordinary way. The President can it is true require the Chambers to reconsider a law before it is finally promulgated, but it may then, to use an American expression, be passed over his head. The two Chambers further can, when sitting together as a National Assembly or Congress, change the Constitution itself.

The executive again is in reality a strictly parliamentary executive; the Ministry, it may be said, are appointed by the President. This is true, but the President appoints and dismisses his Ministers in accordance with the wishes of the Assembly or rather of the Chamber of Deputies; and observe that the modern French Parliament is hardly subject to any of the constitutional checks by which French elective bodies were restrained at other times. There is no King like Louis Philippe to exercise an independent and often decisive authority in choosing a Ministry or in determining the policy of the country. There is no Emperor claiming to be the chief authority in the state; there is no President who like Louis Napoleon being elected by a popular vote can claim an authority co-ordinate with or superior to the authority of Parliament. The President, it is true, and the Ministers as his servants possess large powers; but the Ministers are appointed or removed at the wish of the Parliament and the President is elected by it. He indeed holds his office for seven years certain. This is the theory of the Constitution but already theory has been changed by practice. It has been proved that the Parliament can, in the last resort, dismiss the President or, in other words, compel him to resign, and in any case he looks to the favour of Parliament for his reelection. In practice too it is hardly possible for the Assembly to be dissolved. The result is this: the Senate is a permanent body each of whose members holds his seat for nine years, the Senate itself being renewed by thirds every three years.

Nor is the National Assembly under some of the restraints which limit the authority of representative bodies in many other countries. It is not nearly so liable to dissolution as is an English Parliament. Gambetta at the height of his popularity retired from office because he was not supported by the Chambers and had no available means of appealing from them to the country. It is not restrained as is the American Congress by a practically immutable constitution. It is not restrained by the power of the Courts to declare a law unconstitutional and void. The real restraints on its action are the existence of a very strong permanent bureaucracy and the absence of any of that traditional authority with which the history of England has invested the British Parliament. To which we may add that any disposition toward large changes is checked by the innate conservatism of the French people. France is a country of revolutions, but since the Great Revolution constitutional changes however violent have affected very slightly the ordinary law of France. There are probably a greater number of institutions in France than in England which no government would venture to touch.

D. Comparison between French and English Constitutionalism

The French Republic and the English monarchy belong in the main to the same type of government.

The essential resemblance between the two lies in the fact that in each country we have at the present moment a strictly *parliamentary government.*

The National Assembly, like the English Parliament, is a sovereign legislature. It can constitutionally (if it act with due formality) change the Constitution, as well as alter or repeal ordinary laws. Nor will any judge question the validity of any law enacted by the Assembly and duly promulgated.[16]

---

[16] [Dicey inserted a footnote but did not supply any text for the note.]

The executive is in France no less than in England a strictly parliamentary executive and in both countries, oddly enough, this undeniable fact is more or less concealed by the forms of the Constitution. In England the Cabinet, though really appointed by Parliament, consists of the Crown's servants who in theory hold their offices at the pleasure of, as they are appointed by, the Queen. In France the President was intended to hold office when once appointed independently of the will of the Assembly. It was intended to form what may be called a semi-parliamentary executive. This intention has been frustrated by the course of events. The President has three times been compelled to resign, i.e. dismissed from office, by the Assembly. To judge from the past he does exercise, and is likely to exercise, less weight in the appointment of the Ministry or in determining the policy of the country than Queen Victoria or some other constitutional monarchs.

French constitutionalism does present, on the other hand, some marked points of difference from English constitutionalism.

1. The present French Constitution has no direct connection with the historical development of French institutions.
2. In France the basis of the Constitution is much more clearly than in England the will of the majority of the citizens.
3. In France the judges fill a sphere which is wholly non-political.
4. In France the power of the executive is at the present moment subject to parliamentary control because Ministers depend for their existence on the support of the Assembly. But the powers of the executive are very great and of quite a different kind from the authority possessed by the Crown and its servants in England, and in spite of the present supremacy of the French Parliament an observer, who notes the defects of the parliamentary regime and what slight roots it has struck in the history of France, may doubt whether French constitutionalism will ultimately be embodied in the form of Parliamentary sovereignty.

It is, however, worth notice that from one point of view the constitutions of England and of France tend towards increased resemblance. The English constitution becomes as time goes on more of a written constitution than it was a century ago. A smaller part of it depends upon custom, a greater part of it takes the form of actual law. The influence moreover of large corporate bodies has decidedly decreased. As one generation passes away after another the spirit of the constitution becomes more and more democratic, and the one final authority becomes the voice of the country expressed by the majority of the citizens. The sphere too of government tends to increase and if England has not yet anything like what Frenchmen would call an official hierarchy it is certain that we already possess a huge body of officials utterly unlike anything which existed say in 1760 when George III ascended the throne. In all these matters and others the English system of government approaches towards the constitutionalism of France, but French constitutionalism on its side also begins to bear a resemblance to the constitution of England. The present French Republic has no ancient historical pedigree, but it is the growth of something like historical accidents. It is embodied not in a formal Constitution but in two or three laws; its whole working depends on institutions of which no mention is to be found in the Constitutional laws, and, as already pointed out, under this Constitution which has grown rather than been made an elective assembly or Parliament has in effect become the sovereign power.

Appendix to Chapter 5[*]

Droit Administratif and Constitution of Year VIII, Article 75

(Hauriou, pp 171–174)
Officials are protected (*garantie des fonctionnaires*) in two ways.

1. (i) The state, and not the official, is responsible for damage arising from the *thing itself done* under the orders or the authority of the state, even though the act be in itself illegal (*faute de service*) and for *slight* errors committed by the official in carrying out the act done in the service of the state.

    In such a case the remedy, if any, of the person aggrieved is a proceeding for indemnity against the state.

    (ii) The official is personally responsible for damage which arises from his own wrongful action (*fait personnel*) in carrying out the orders of the state, which may be either [sic] a distinct wrong (*délit caractérisé*).

    This distinction for non-liability for the act (*faute de service*) and liability for the *fait personnel* may (*semble*) be thus stated:

    (iii) An official who carries out rightly the orders of his proper superior is protected from any liability even though the thing ordered is, or involves, a breach of law, e.g. trespass; and the same thing holds good even though damage may arise not from the order itself but from slight errors in carrying out the order.

    (iv) An official who, in carrying out the order of a superior, commits a wrong not necessarily involved in the order, e.g. a trespass, or who causes damage by carrying out the order with gross negligence, is personally liable, and the state (*semble*) is not liable.

2. The ordinary Courts have no jurisdiction as regards a *faute de service*, and they have jurisdiction where the wrong complained of is a *fait personnel*. But the decision whether the action of an official complained of is to be brought under the one class or to the other belongs not to the ordinary Courts but to the *Tribunal des Conflits*.

---

[*] Its contents have been derived from the attachment (dated 5 May 1897) to the lecture manuscript. It was listed as its appendix on the second page (headed 'Old forms of Mss Lectures') of the four-page manuscript, entitled 'Comparative Study of the Constitution: List of Papers etc', that has been used here to derive the contents of Part I. See Editor's Introduction, p. xviii above.

On this matter two systems have prevailed.

(i) Under Article 75 of Constitution of Year VIII

The Agents of the Government . . . cannot be proceeded against for acts relating to their official functions unless proceedings be sanctioned by a decision of the Council of State; i.e. if such sanction be given the proceedings take place before the ordinary courts [i.e. the ordinary courts have jurisdiction].

> Whilst this Article was in force the Council of State decided whether the act complained of was a *fait personnel* or an *acte de service* and sanctioned proceedings only if the act were a *fait personnel*, i.e. the Council of State determined before any proceedings were taken whether the ordinary Courts had or had not jurisdiction.

(ii) Since repeal of Article 75, 19 December 1870.[17]

> This repeal removed [the] necessity for preliminary sanction by [the] Council of State, and since the repeal proceedings can be taken against an official in the ordinary Courts which have *primâ facie* jurisdiction to entertain them, the question then arose, have they also jurisdiction to determine whether a particular act is in its character a *fait personnel* or a *faute de service*. After variation in judgments, it has been finally decided that, when the question is raised (by the proper official) what is the character of the act, its character is to be determined, not by the ordinary Courts, but by the *Tribunal des Conflits*.
>
> It is therefore the official Court which fixes the limits of jurisdiction.

NB It would seem that whilst Article 75 applied strictly only to agents of the government the principle now established applies to all officials and from one point of view the protection of officials has thus been rather extended than limited by the repeal of Article 75.

---

[17] Repealed by Government of Defence, *semble*, ratified by the National Assembly [*sic*].

6

Prussian Constitutionalism

Analysis*

Introduction
    1. Constitutionalism of Prussia is in fundamentals constitutionalism of Germany
    2. Prussia at once a military and a progressive state
    3. The Constitution a concession of Crown
    4. Hence Prussian constitutionalism an experiment in military constitutionalism

A. Fundamental Principles of Prussian Constitutional Law
    I. *The King the true head and governor of the country*
        1. The King the true head of the executive
        2. The King has independently of Parliament considerable legislative powers
    II. *Statutes are made by the Prussian Parliament and by the Prussian Parliament alone*
        1. Parliament, which consists, not only in name but in reality, of the King and the two Houses, has real legislative authority
        2. Parliament is a mere legislature and does not appoint the Ministry
    III. *The powers vested in any person or body (e.g. the Houses of Parliament) under the Constitution cannot constitutionally be exercised in such a way as to change the position and authority of the person or body in whom they are vested*
    Illustration. The constitutional conflict of 1862–1866

B. Comparison between Constitutional Government in England and in Prussia
    I. *Likeness*
        1. Outward forms similar
        2. In each country the constitution is a reality
    II. *Unlikeness*
        1. In England the Crown is not, whilst in Prussia it is, the predominant power in the state

---

* Its contents have been derived from an undated manuscript attached to the lecture scheme dated Oct.–Dec. 1897 in a later manuscript note. This Analysis is included here (and not the earlier Analysis attached to the lecture scheme headed 'Easter & Trinity Terms, 1897' and used to derive most of the other Analyses in Part I) because the full lecture text below was substantially altered and this Analysis more closely resembles the text as altered.

2. In England Parliament is not only a legislative body, but also the creator of the real executive. In Prussia the Parliament is merely a legislature
3. The English constitutionalism of the Tudors or of Cromwell has a closer resemblance to Prussian constitutionalism than modern English constitutionalism
4. Essential difference: the non-military character of the English, and the military character of the Prussian, state

(See J. H. Robinson, *Constitution of Prussia*;
1 Lowell, ch. VI, pp 286–333;
Schulze, 2 Marquardsen, *Prussia*;
1 Morley, *Life of Cobden*, p. 130.)

Prussian Constitutionalism[*]

Prussian constitutionalism deserves separate and attentive study.

The principles of public law which prevail in Prussia govern the Constitution of the German Empire, in so far of course as the Empire can be looked at apart from its federal character, and these principle are far more easily studied as developed in a single state than when they are mixed up with all the complicated compromises which are inherent in a federal form of government. German constitutionalism in short is best explained by examining with some care the nature and working of the Constitution of Prussia.

Prussia again, is not only the most powerful of the states included in the Empire, but is also the centre of the Imperial system. Every Prussian King is, as King of Prussia, German Emperor, and his Imperial authority depends upon his power as ruler of the Prussian Kingdom.

The aim of German patriotism has been for more than 50 years the political union of the German people. The endeavour to achieve unity has taken different forms. At times it has been thought that it might be achieved under the guidance of Austria. In 1848 Liberals hoped that unity might result from the triumph of democratic ideas. The policy of Austrian supremacy and of unitary democracy both failed. The political consolidation of Germany was at last achieved by the military success of Prussia. This was [established by what was][†] called the policy of 'blood and iron' and will be for ever connected with the name of Bismarck. The predominance of Prussia as the strongest and best governed of military states having ensured the political unity of Germany, Prussian ideas lie at the foundation of the Imperial Federation which was created by the victories, is supported by the renown, and protected by the arms[‡] of the Prussian army.

What, then, are at bottom these Prussian ideas?

They are the conceptions of good government which naturally result from the history of Prussia. And the peculiarity of this history is that Prussia has for generations been at once a military and a progressive state which owes its creation and existence to the military capacity and to the administrative ability of its rulers. It sometimes happens in the lives of nations as of men that an accidental combination of circumstances is typical of their whole career. Such an event in the annals of Prussia is the friendship between Frederick the Great and Voltaire. You see in it the singular combination of military genius devoted in some respects to carrying out the ideas of a benevolent and intelligent despotism. Voltaire, it is true, was no worshipper of

---

[*] The manuscript's title page was dated 15 May 1897, but the text was substantially altered presumably after that date. The text as altered is published here. For Dicey, it remained work in progress, evident, for example, in the following, later, unnumbered manuscript note at the foot of one of the pages dealing with the King as the true head of the Prussian executive: '*NB* To investigate further the nature of the Prussian administration'.

[†] Words surmised from context, rough deletion, and an illegible later manuscript substitution.

[‡] Illegible and seemingly abbreviated later manuscript substitution of 'arms' possibly with 'claims'.

prowess in war, and Frederick assuredly was something very different from a philosopher on the throne, yet in some respects the ideas of the two men run together. They both shared the eighteenth-century enthusiasm for enlightenment; they both condemned anything which savoured of superstition or priestcraft; they both wished to promote intellectual progress and religious toleration; they both were revolutionists. No man, to be sure, was further removed from a democrat than Frederick, but Voltaire himself neither had nor pretended to have any sympathy with democracy. Ignorance, stupidity, and intolerance were no more respectable in his eyes when found in a crowd than when found in a King, and he held that crowds were more likely to be the dupes of priestcraft than monarchs. The reforms which Voltaire desired were reforms which could be carried out by a King, and were in effect carried out by the enlightened despots of the eighteenth century. Neither the King nor the philosopher objected to the use of despotic power and they both wished it to be used for the spread of enlightenment. In spite of the personal quarrel which divided them the policy of Frederick was from one point of view the policy of Voltaire. In Frederick, and in many of his successors, you find combined the determination to organise the state on a military basis and yet to use its powers for purposes of good and intelligent administration. This combination has made Prussia the natural leader of Germany and, at a time when her Kings were still absolute, had made her system of government one which excited the keen admiration of reformers who valued good administration above what is termed political freedom. Consider for example these expressions of Richard Cobden, contained in a letter written from Berlin in 1838:

> I very much suspect that at present, for the great mass of the people, Prussia possesses the best government in Europe. I would gladly give up my taste for talking polities to secure such a state of things in England. Had our people such a simple and economical government, so deeply imbued with justice to all, and aiming so constantly to elevate mentally and morally its population, how much better would it be for the twelve or fifteen millions in the British Empire, who, while they possess no electoral rights, are yet persuaded they are freemen, and who are mystified into the notion that they are not political bondsmen, by that great juggle of the 'English Constitution'—a thing of monopolies, and Church-craft, and sinecures, armorial hocus-pocus, primogeniture, and pageantry! The Government of Prussia is the mildest phrase in which absolutism ever presented itself. The King, a good and just man, has, by pursuing a systematic course of popular education, shattered the sceptre of despotism even in his own hand, and has for ever prevented his successors from gathering up the fragments... You have sometimes wondered what becomes of the thousands of learned men who continually pass from the German universities, whilst so few enter upon mercantile pursuits. Such men hold all the official and Government appointments; and they do not require £1,000 a year to be respectable or respected in Prussia. Habits of ostentatious expenditure are not respectable there. The King dines at two, rides in a plain carriage, without soldiers or attendants, and dresses in a kind of soldier's relief cap. The plays begin at six and close at nine, and all the world goes to bed at ten or eleven.[1]

---

[1] *Life of Richard Cobden*, i, pp 130, 131 (Sep. 11, 1838).

Ten years later the government which had excited the unbounded admiration of the English Radical was for a moment nearly overthrown by the popular desire for the parliamentary institutions which Cobden did not value highly and by the passion for national unity which he did not value at all. The strength of the Prussian army and the fundamental soundness of the Prussian administration enabled the King of Prussia to weather the revolutionary storm. He was compelled, however, to make some concessions to popular sentiment. After dissolving a democratic constituent assembly he granted a constitution to his subjects. It embodied indeed in its terms many provisions dear to German Democrats, but it came into existence not by the will of the people, but by the grace of the Crown. It conferred upon Prussians a real and substantial voice in legislation, but subject to this concession it left untouched the absolute authority of the King. The Crown retained, to use English expressions, the whole of the Royal prerogative, except in so far as it was expressly limited by the Constitution. The Constitution would, it is true, never have existed but for the force of a democratic movement, and some of its articles were drawn up by revolutionists who designed to reduce the power of the Crown to nothing, but the Constitution was also the grant of an absolute King who intended to preserve as much as possible of his Royal prerogative. Such an instrument is certain to contain, as the Prussian Constitution does contain, many inconsistencies, but its general drift, as interpreted by German jurists, and what is of far more consequence, by the force of events, is clear. The King remains since 1850, as he did up to 1850, the real and effective head of the state. He is an absolute monarch who is head of an efficient administration and Commander-in-chief of a powerful army. In one direction only is the exercise of his Royal authority substantially limited. Legislation can be normally exercised only by Parliament, but of the Prussian Parliament the King is, like an English King, a part, and he is what an English monarch at the present day is not, a real not to say a predominant member of the legislature. In Prussia then is being tried the experiment which to Englishmen, through forgetfulness of their own past history, seems a strange one, of combining a real legislature or Parliament with a powerful monarchical government, supported by a large army and a highly efficient administration. Whether the attempt can ultimately succeed may be open to doubt. Two considerations, however, make this endeavour to create a form of military constitutionalism possible, and may ultimately make it successful. The very existence of Prussia with which is now bound up the existence of the German Empire necessitates the maintenance of a huge army under the guidance of an autocratic King; whatever else a Parliament achieve, it cannot perform the part of Commander-in-chief. The Prussian army again under the system of general service is the Prussian people. Hence ideas of discipline and obedience are instilled into the minds of civilians whilst it is difficult to suppose that the army can in the long run be used for any purpose which does not receive at any rate the tacit sanction of the nation.

If we are to understand a system which might be termed a scheme of military constitutionalism, our best course is first to examine the fundamental principles of Prussian public law and then compare the constitutionalism of Prussia with the constitutionalism of modern England.

A. Fundamental Principles of Prussian Public Law

These principles may be brought under three heads.

I. The King of Prussia is the true head and governor of the country. **He is, if one may describe a peculiar position in terms which sound paradoxical, an absolute monarch who has agreed to a restriction of his powers in one direction alone, namely in the direction of legislation.**

This principle contains the fundamental characteristic of the Prussian monarchy which distinguishes it from the constitutional monarchy of modern England.

The King is, in reality, what Queen Victoria is only in name, the actual ruler of the country. German writers indeed often lay down that he holds in his hands the undivided power of the state. Such expressions may it is true be easily misunderstood and convey to Englishmen the impression, which is certainly false, that the Prussian monarch is a despot in the sense in which this term can be applied to the Czar or the Sultan. This is far from being the case. The King is no more likely to overthrow the Constitution, to defy the law, or arbitrarily to displace the judges, than is the English Queen. The truth which German writers mean to convey is that within the limits of the Constitution which are very wide, and subject to the definite laws of the land, the King of Prussia governs his country and can govern it in accordance to a great extent with his own will. It is the possibility of enforcing one's own wish or decisions, even though opposed to the desire of other men, which constitutes power, and power is the characteristic of any man who, under whatever name, is a true ruler. It belongs for example to an American President such as Lincoln, when supported by the nation. It belongs to an English Prime Minister who can rely on being followed by Parliament or by the electors. It belonged to Pitt as it has belonged to Gladstone. It belongs to the King of Prussia, and of course there is this difference between the power of a President or Minister and the authority of a King. The force exercisable by a President, and still more by an England Premier, depends directly and immediately upon opinion. The popularity which gave can of course when it fails him or shifts to his opponents take away his power. A German King derives his force directly and immediately not from public opinion but from his position and from the moral certainty that he will be obeyed by the civil administration and by the army. No doubt a King and especially a King the exercise of whose authority is on one side limited by the Constitution must consult public opinion. It is quite conceivable that the King of Prussia might go so directly in his policy against the convictions of his subjects that his own authority might be shaken. This is true of Frederick William as it was true in England of Henry VIII and Queen Elizabeth. It is, however, none the less true of a Prussian King, as it was true of a Tudor sovereign, that his authority must be regarded as indefinite if not strictly unlimited, and as accruing to him simply in virtue of the Crown.

How wide and effective is the authority of the Prussian King will be best seen by an examination into some of the definite powers which he can exercise both in theory and in fact.

1. **The King is the true head of the executive or, rather, is the only holder of the executive power and is entitled to exercise all the various functions which in the nature of things belong to the executive of a civilized country**

The King is therefore the real Commander-in-chief.

His position as *generalissimo* is in no sense a fiction. He is the head of the army and has in matter of fact gone through a strict military training. All Prussians moreover are bound to military service, as indeed are now all Germans. Hence the Prussian King is Commander-in-chief not only of the Prussian army but also as Emperor of the whole German army. To express the same thing in other words all Prussian and all German citizens are either in fact or are liable to be soldiers of the Prussian King and German Emperor.[2]

The King again is head of the whole Prussian civil service and has the appointment to all the posts in the civil service.[3]

The officials are entirely and solely dependent upon the monarch who is the supreme director of the administrative system for their rank and pay.[4] And be it noted that civil servants in Prussia have a position totally different from that of civil servants in England; they are really a class, they might almost he called a civil army with rights, privileges, and duties of their own. They like French officials are in many respects subject to administrative law (*droit administratif*) administered by administrative Courts, and are more separate from the mass of citizens who are not in the employment of the government than are French civil servants. The difference between the French and the Prussian administration would seem to be this: even when the French monarchy was absolute the civil service was in its character essentially civilian and in sympathy with the civil life of France, but, on the other hand, the French government officials were not, and are not, a scientifically trained class. The Prussian civil service, on the other hand, seems always to have resembled and even now to resemble an army. The persons admitted to it all receive special training. The officials have as it were an independent status of their own in something like the sense in which the clergy and the army have a special status in England; they are more or less protected from arbitrary dismissal and in that sense probably more independent than in France, but they are a disciplined *corps* [and], subject to laws which do not affect ordinary citizens, they are certain to be a pre-eminently governmental body. Of this body, as already stated, the King is the head.

The King has the real appointment of the Ministry.

They are it is true nominally responsible and this responsibility has the effect as in England of protecting the King from any legal liability for his acts.[5] But it has not

---

[2] See as to the army the Prussian Constitution Arts 34, 35, 46. Compare the Imperial Constitution, Art. 57.
[3] Constitution, Art. 47.
[4] Robinson, p. 36, note 2.
[5] Constitution, Art. 44.

the other effects which the doctrine of ministerial responsibility has in England. The Ministers cannot be made criminally responsible for their acts[6] since, though they are constitutionally liable to impeachment, yet the law which was to regulate all details 'as to matters of responsibility procedure and punishment'[7] has never been passed, nor are they subject to the kind of political or parliamentary responsibility which in England makes a Ministry dependent on the will of the House of Commons. They are not placed in office nor can they be removed from office by a Parliamentary vote. The truth is that in Prussia there does not exist a Ministry or Cabinet in the sense in which those words are used in England. The Ministers are each heads of departments appointed by and holding their places at the pleasure of the Crown. Ministerial responsibility is responsibility not to Parliament but to the King.

Ministers moreover, as well as the officials appointed to represent them, e.g. under-secretaries, have access to each House of Parliament and must at all times be heard on their request, but need not be members of Parliament.

The Prussian doctrine as to the position of Ministers has been declared in a rescript issued by the German Emperor and King of Prussia in 1882.

> The right of the King to conduct the government and policy of Prussia according to his own direction is limited by the constitution (of January 31, 1850) but not abolished. The government acts (documentary) of the King require the counter-signature of a minister, and as was also the case before the constitution was issued, have to be represented by the King's ministers; but they nevertheless remain government acts of the King, from whose decisions they result, and who thereby constitutionally expresses his will and pleasure. It is therefore not admissible, and leads to obscuration of the constitutional rights of the King, when their exercise is so spoken of as if they emanated from the ministers for the time being responsible for them, and not from the King himself. The constitution of Prussia is the expression of the monarchical tradition of this country, whose development is based on the living and actual relations of the King to the people. These relations, moreover, do not admit of being transferred to the ministers appointed by the King, for they attach to the person of the King. Their preservation, too, is a political necessity for Prussia. It is, therefore, my will that both in Prussia and in the legislative bodies of the empire (*Reich*) there may be no doubt left as to my own constitutional right and that of my successors personally to conduct the policy of my government; and that the theory shall always be rejected that the (doctrine of the) inviolability of the person of the King, which has always existed in Prussia, and is enunciated by Article 43 of the constitution, or the necessity of a responsible counter-signature of my government acts, deprives them of the character of royal and independent decisions. It is the duty of my ministers to support my constitutional rights by protecting them from doubt and obscuration, and I expect the same from all state officials (*Beamten*) who have taken the official oath to me. I am far from wishing to impair the freedom of elections, but in the case of those officials who are entrusted with the execution of my government acts, and may, therefore, in conforming with the disciplinary law forfeit their situations, the duty solemnly undertaken by their oath of service also applies to the representation by them of the policy of my government during election times. The faithful performance

---

[6] Compare Art. 61.
[7] Ibid.

of this duty I shall thankfully acknowledge, and I expect from all officials that, in view of their oath of allegiance, they will refrain from all agitation against my government even during elections.

Berlin, January 4, 1882. Wilhelm von Bismarck. To the Ministry of State.[8]

The King has hereditary revenues or hereditary civil list which is not as in England fixed at the beginning of each reign.[9]

2. The Crown possesses, independently of Parliament, very considerable legislative powers

The Crown, it is true, cannot, under the Constitution, of its own authority make laws, or, to use English expressions, pass Acts or statutes; but the Crown can, and does, issue ordinances which have in many respects the force of law.

Such Royal ordinances are of four kinds:

(i) temporary ordinances which remain in force until disapproved of by the Chambers or Houses of Parliament; these are in reality temporary laws;

(ii) ordinances with regard to the duties and rights of state officials (civil servants); such ordinances are laws as regards the class to which they apply and their validity is independent of any parliamentary sanction;

(iii) ordinances made to carry out or give effect to a law or, as we should say, Act of Parliament; these are ordinances which carry out into detail the principle laid down in a Parliamentary enactment;

(iv) ordinances issued under the authority of an Act; these correspond with Orders in Council or rules made under or in accordance with the provisions of an Act of Parliament.[10]

The Crown, it will be observed, has under its ordinance-making power nearly as much legislative authority as was possessed in England by Henry VIII or by Cromwell. Henry was empowered by statute to issue proclamations which had the force of law and the Protector could under the Instrument of Government[11] make ordinances which had the effect of law until disapproved of by Parliament. To appreciate at any rate the extent of the Prussian King's right to legislate under the form of ordinances we must note that under the Constitution ordinances, no less than Acts of Parliament, are *ipso facto* binding when published in the form prescribed by law, and that the examination into the validity of properly promulgated Royal ordinances belongs

---

[8] Robinson, p. 35, note 3.
[9] 'The civil list, which is granted not for the life of the monarch as in England, but in perpetuity, is absolutely at his disposal, and out of it he is expected to provide for all the members of the royal family; and in this connection it is worth while to observe, as an illustration of the relation of the imperial office to the royal one, that the Emperor as such has no civil list, and that there is no imperial household, with its chamberlain, its marshal, and so forth, all these high dignitaries being officers of the Prussian Court.'

1 Lowell, p. 288.

[10] 1 Dupriez, pp 437–9.
[11] See p. [56] *ante*.

solely to the Chambers and is not within the competence of the judges or other governmental authorities.[12] In other words an ordinance is a law until pronounced invalid by Parliament.

Whoever attempts to appreciate the authority of a Prussian King must bear in mind that the prerogatives of the Crown are in Prussia indefinite and cannot be arrived at by making a list of the definite powers possessed by the King. Those enumerated in Title 3 of the Constitution are only a partial catalogue of the prerogatives which remain vested in the Crown after the granting of the Constitution. The King was an absolute monarch till the Constitution in 1850 came into force and he still possesses every right of sovereignty of which he did not then expressly divest himself. In strictness indeed the Constitution does not deprive the Crown of any prerogative whatever. Every transaction carried out by or on behalf of the state takes place in the name of the King. He is, as it is sometimes expressed, the personified power of the state. The exercise of his authority is in certain definite respects now limited or controlled and it is the main function of the Constitution to define the limitations and the method of control. They all come within the second principle of Prussian constitutionalism.

II. *Statutes are made by the Prussian Parliament and by the Prussian Parliament alone*

To use the words of the Prussian Constitution:

> The legislative power shall be exercised in common by the King and the two Chambers.
>
> Every law shall require the assent of the King and of the two chambers.
>
> Money bills and the budgets shall first be laid before the second chamber; the budgets shall either be accepted or rejected as a whole by the first chamber.[13]

This Article undoubtedly introduced a great change into the system of Prussian government. The most important change, it has been said, we might perhaps say the only change, which the establishment of the Constitution in Prussia produced was the admission of the people to a participation in legislation.[14]

An English critic, however, must be on his guard against exaggerating the results ensuing from the introduction of something which looks like a parliamentary legislature into Prussia.

The Prussian Diet is not by any means the equivalent to the English Parliament. It is in truth a strictly and solely legislative body. The Houses can make laws, or rather take part in the making of laws, but they exert no control over the policy or the action of the executive and though regular laws, or as we should say statutes, must in Prussia as in England take the form of Parliamentary enactments, yet Parliamentary legislation

---

[12] Constitution, Art. 106.
[13] Constitution, Tit. V, Art. 62.
[14] See Robinson, p. 17.

is itself in Prussia controlled or directed by the King and his Ministers. Any member may introduce a Bill, but all the Bills which actually pass are introduced by the government. The right of the Crown to refuse assent to a Bill or in popular language to veto it is a real and not a nominal right, the existence of which no one contests. If there has been hitherto little necessity for the use of the veto it certainly would, if need were, be put into force. The obligation again of a law depends upon its being duly published and the Constitution contains no means for compelling its publication by the Crown. The assent of the House of Lords moreover is required for the passing of any Act and the Crown could in most cases induce the upper House to refuse its assent. Nor must we forget that the King possesses an acknowledged power to legislate in many instances by ordinances. The great matter, however, is that the Ministers of the Crown are not appointed nor can they be removed by the Houses of Parliament. They are the servants of the Crown; they need not be members of Parliament, they have an absolute right to address either House at their pleasure. Nor does an annual Mutiny Act, or any Act of the kind, give the Prussian Diet indirect control over the army. The Constitution in effect gives the Prussian Diet the right to participate in regular legislation and therefore bestows on the Diet and on the Prussian people through their representatives, a genuine veto on legislation of which the nation does not approve. But the powers of the Diet are purely legislative and, even in the matter of legislation, have in fact rather a negative than a positive character. The Chambers, and especially the lower Chamber, might make use of rights such as the right to grant taxes, which have been found of immense importance in England. But here we touch upon a third principle which though not stated in any article of the Constitution appears to be in fact recognised and affects the whole working of Prussian institutions.

III. The powers vested in any person or body, e.g. the Houses of Parliament, under the Constitution cannot constitutionally be exercised in such a way as to change the position and authority of the person or body in whom they are vested

This principle sounds in itself not an unreasonable one. Even in England it is as regards many of our institutions in substance recognised. We are all tacitly agreed that the Crown ought not to exercise its veto or the House of Lords its power of rejecting Bills, for the purpose of extending its authority or becoming supreme in the state, and a principle which to a certain extent has obtained recognition under an unwritten and conventional constitution which itself is the result and the record of contests between the House of Commons and the Crown must almost inevitably be received as sound in a country governed by a written constitution which has been the free grant of a despotic monarch and has been given by him to his people within the memory of men now living. It is certainly a very bold assumption that a King who concedes to an elected body or Parliament the right to fix the amount of the yearly budget virtually concedes and intended to concede to Parliament the right to use the power of the purse so as to make itself supreme throughout the state. In England we have been accustomed almost from time immemorial to the historical extension of the influence of the House of Commons to the free use of its right to grant or refuse taxes. We find it hard therefore to believe that this use of the taxing power may in Prussia be *bonâ fide* looked upon both by statesmen and by jurists as illegitimate and unconstitutional and a simple abuse. It is true to be sure that Liberals and Democrats hope that the powers granted to the people under the Constitution of 1850 might be used so as to introduce into the country the English Cabinet system and a supremacy of the House of Commons. But the Constitution was not the work of the Liberals and it is certain that the Crown always contested the legitimacy of this use of the authority vested in the Diet. The Constitution was to be the law of the land, but the Constitution, on the view of it taken by the Crown, could be changed by law and by law only. Neither one House of Parliament nor both of them could any more than the King himself use the powers which they acquired or retained under the Constitution to subvert it, and on this view the attempt to introduce the English system of government by refusing to grant taxes would be as unconstitutional as would be an attempt by the King to legislate by means of perpetual ordinances without the co-operation of the Diet. Hence arose:

The constitutional conflict of 1862–1866*

The nature of this conflict has never been properly understood in England yet the essential facts are few and the principle at stake may be easily grasped by anyone who looks at the dispute unblinded by English precedents. The King reorganised and greatly strengthened the army. The Liberals who commanded a decided majority in the representative Chamber or the House of Commons did not trust the policy of the Crown and failed to perceive the necessity from a German nationalist point of view of strengthening the army. They therefore refused to settle a budget or, as we should say in England, to grant the supplies and by this means tried to compel the Crown to give up the scheme of military reorganisation. Bismarck as Minister, supported by the King, denied the right of the Commons thus to control the government [and] maintained the duty of the House [was] to grant the proper supplies and the legal validity of the existing budget until supplies for the year were granted in the proper way. Maintaining these views Bismarck in effect governed for five years in defiance of Parliament. The Royal scheme of reorganisation was kept on foot and developed, and the army was thus constituted which vanquished Austria in 1866. Prussian victories used for the purpose of consolidating Germany gave power and popularity to the government and reconciled it with the Liberals. An Act of Indemnity was passed and the Crown in substance triumphed in what nominally might be called a drawn battle.

---

* Early in the conflict, in the summer of 1862, Dicey actually visited Germany with James Bryce and other friends from Oxford: R. S. Rait, *Memorials of Albert Venn Dicey, being chiefly Letters and Diaries* (London: Macmillan, 1925), 35 ff. In the journal he kept of his visit, he commented that 'Prussian politics occupy all my interest. This curiosity lies chiefly in the light they throw on constitutional theories': ibid. 43. From his reading of the German papers and pamphlets, he took the view that the 'essence of the conflict between the "Lower House" and the Ministry (one may probably say the Crown) lies in the question whether Parliament shall or shall not be the ruling power in the State': ibid. 44. Dicey's visit to Germany seems to have been a formative experience in his understanding of the distinction between a parliamentary executive and a non-parliamentary executive and of its importance. See generally Editor's Introduction, pp xxxii ff above.

The principle on which I have already insisted was thereby established that Parliament could not use the power of the purse so as to make itself in effect supreme or in other words so as to introduce into Prussia the Parliamentary sovereignty and the parliamentary executive which are the characteristics of English constitutionalism.

An English critic is at first inclined to look, as most English liberals in 1862 did look, upon Bismarck's policy as the overthrow of the Prussian Parliament and the violation of the Prussian Constitution, but an observer *ab extra* who tries to regard the contest with perfect impartiality will feel that Bismarck's position was if not sound yet at any rate far more defensible than it at first sight appears.

The letter of the Prussian Constitution, or rather of one or two of its articles, clearly favours the doctrine maintained by the Liberals of 1862.[15] Nor can it be denied that the Opposition in their attempt to established the supreme authority of Parliament could rely on a whole line of precedents drawn from English history. The latter consideration, however, decides nothing for the main point at issue was whether the Crown, when granting the Constitution of 1850, established or intended to establish a constitutional government like that of England.

But there is also a strong case in favour of Bismarck's position.

Even under the *letter* of the Constitution he could plead some justification, since Article 109 which belongs to its general, and not to its temporary, provisions enacts that 'existing taxes and dues and all provisions of existing statute books single laws and ordinances which do not contravene the present constitution shall remain in force unless altered by law.' It is therefore at any rate arguable as a proposition of law that the budget already fixed remained in force until a new financial arrangement was legally established under Articles 62 and 100.

As regards the *spirit* of the Constitution his position was even stronger. No doubt some of its articles were dictated or suggested by parliamentarians or democrats, but its provisions taken as a whole do not read as if they were intended to introduce the English Parliamentary system. It is all but incredible that a constitution granted by an absolute monarch during a period of reaction against a democratic movement which had ended more or less in failure was intended to make the Houses of Parliament in reality sovereign.

As a matter of general policy the King and Bismarck were clearly in the right. There is probably not a man in Germany who now disputes that the reorganisation of the Prussian army laid the foundation of German political unity. Constitutional conflicts are at bottom contests decided by policy and power rather than by argument or law. The triumphs of 1866 and 1870 have determined, not it may be to the advantage of the world, that German unity should be established by the armed forces of Germany and that the Constitution of Prussia should be construed in the sense put upon it not by the Liberals but by the Crown and by Bismarck.[16]

---

[15] See Arts 62, 99, 100.

[16] The political incapacity of the German Liberals who being ardent supporters of national unity opposed the reorganisation of the army by which alone that unity was won may be paralleled with the political incapacity of the Republicans of the Commonwealth who, by their opposition to Cromwell, prevented the establishment under the Instrument of Government of a Republican Commonwealth.

Why, it may be asked by English critics, was not the constitutional conflict determined by some judicial decision?

To this natural inquiry there are at least two answers.

Constitutional conflicts are, it has been well said, questions rather of power than of law. Except in communities very peculiarly constituted, such for example as the United States of America, disputes which go to the very foundation of the Constitution cannot even nominally be settled by the judgment of any tribunal and in the American Republic itself the opposed claims of State rights and of national sovereignty were settled at last by the force not of legal argument but of the sword. When England was on the verge of revolution the timidity, the prudence, or the patriotism of the judges made them most unwilling to adjudicate upon the case between the King and the Houses of Parliament. Some attempts, however, it is said were made by a Prussian Hampden to raise before the Courts the question whether he was bound to pay taxes not imposed by Parliament. These endeavours came to nothing. Nor could anyone expect them to be successful who realised what is the position of the judiciary in Prussia, or indeed in any Continental country. The Prussian judges are a highly respected and independent body of magistrates who though appointed by the Crown hold office during good behaviour but for all this they have not the political importance either of the American judiciary or of the English Bench; they cannot pronounce judgment upon the validity either of an Act of Parliament or of a Royal ordinance. They cannot therefore be as in America in any sense the protectors of the Constitution. The existence again of administrative law and of administrative Courts makes it impossible for a Prussian judge to exercise that control over the action of the executive which since the Revolution of 1689 has been exerted by English tribunals. Nor is there any reason to suppose that the judges of Prussia, could constitutional questions be brought before them, would take up an attitude of opposition to the Crown or the government. In Germany, as in other Continental countries, judges are not appointed from among advocates or barristers. Their career has not brought them into contact with Parliament or parliamentary parties. A Prussian judge is an official who has entered the judicial side of the Civil Service. He has been trained at once as a judge and as a civil servant. His personal independence is secure but he has risen as have other servants of the government by due discharge of official duties which in his case have been magisterial. For promotion he has looked to the Crown, and from the Crown must come any further promotion which is open to him. Training and interest alike have imbued Prussian judges with the convictions and the habits of highly educated civil servants. There is nothing in their position or in their turn of mind which is likely to bias them against that interpretation of the Constitution which favours the power of the Crown. It is most improbable that a Bench of officials would refuse, as a French writer would say, to 'support authority', and let it be remembered that even the English Courts in *Bates's Case* and in the *Case of Ship Money* gave judgment in favour of the Crown. Nor, in spite of the ideas which have grown up amongst us, owing to the triumph of Parliament is there reason to suppose that decisions which Whig historians condemn were given by men who violated their oaths or who meant to misinterpret the law. The attitude at any rate of the

Prussian Courts proves that the judges are not prepared or able to support doctrines of English constitutionalism.

B. Comparison between Constitutional Government in England and in Prussia

There exist a considerable number of apparent resemblances between the constitutional monarchy of England and the constitutional monarchy of Prussia.

The resemblances of form are such as to strike even a casual observer.

In Prussia, as in England, there is an hereditary monarchy and a House of Lords containing Peers (some of whom possess hereditary seats) appointed by the Crown. In Prussia as in England laws are made, or as we should say Acts are passed, by the combined action of the King and of the Houses of Parliament. In Prussia as in England Parliament has power to change the Constitution and the House of Commons has the sole power of granting supplies. In both countries the Crown is represented in Parliament by Ministers. In both countries you can find a body of independent judges who are men of high character and hold their offices during good behaviour.

There are again many maxims inserted in the Constitution of Prussia which re-echo the principles of freedom which have for generations been acknowledged in England. All Prussians are equal before the law;[17] personal freedom is guaranteed;[18] a man's *domicil* is inviolable, in other words 'his house is his castle';[19] punishments are not to be inflicted except according to law;[20] property is inviolable. 'It shall,' runs Article 9, 'only be taken or interfered with from considerations of public weal, and then only in a manner to be prescribed by law, and in return for a compensation to be previously determined. Even in urgent cases a preliminary valuation and compensation shall be made.' Freedom of religious confession, of association in religious societies, and of the common exercise of religion in private and public, is guaranteed. The enjoyment of civil and political rights is not to be dependent upon religious belief.[21] Science and its teachings are free.[22] Every Prussian is entitled to express his opinion freely by word, writing, print, or pictorial representation. Censorship of the press may not be introduced, and no other restrictions on the freedom of the press shall be imposed except by law.[23] The right of petition belongs to all Prussians.[24]

These and other well worn maxims of English constitutional law, such for example as the provision of Article 44, 'the King's Ministers shall be responsible: all official acts of the King shall require for their validity the counter signature of a Minister,

---

[17] Constitution, Art. 4.
[18] Ibid. Art. 5.
[19] Ibid. Art. 6.
[20] Ibid. Art. 8.
[21] Ibid. Art. 12, and compare Arts 14, 30, and 31.
[22] Ibid. Art. 20.
[23] Ibid. Art. 27.
[24] Ibid. Art. 32.

who shall thereby assume the responsibility for them, are recognised, no less in Prussia than in the United Kingdom, and a first glance at the language of the Prussian Constitution makes a student wonder wherein it is that the constitutional law of Prussia differs essentially from the constitutional law of England.

The answer is given by a consideration of the three fundamental principles which, as already provided out, lie at the basis of Prussian public law. They show us that constitutional government as practised in Prussia is essentially different from constitutional government as it exists in modern England. It is hardly an exaggeration to say that whatever is real in the one is fictitious in the other.

In Prussia the King in not an absolute monarch, but he is the true head of the government and possesses at least as much power as falls in England to the share of a Prime Minister backed by a large parliamentary majority. In England the Crown exercises no doubt a good deal of authority, but this authority, though a good deal greater than is generally believed, is tacit and indirect and never on any occasion comes into conflict with the declared and avowed wish of Parliament or of the leaders whom Parliament supports. In Prussia ministerial responsibility means the responsibility of the Ministry to the Crown, whilst in England it means the responsibility of Ministers to Parliament, and the Ministers are the true servants of the Crown by whom they are appointed and by whom they are kept in power. They are not the servants of, for they are neither appointed nor dismissed by, Parliament. Parliament again is in Prussia a really law-making body, but Parliament's functions are purely legislative and even in matters of legislation the Prussian Parliament is led and controlled by the Crown and the Crown's servants.[25] The Constitution, lastly, in Prussia, though changeable by Parliament, is in a very true sense the law of the land. It is in effect the security, from one point of view, of the Royal prerogatives. It leaves to the Crown considerable authority even in matters of legislation and presents to the King all the powers of an absolute ruler which are not, in so many words, taken from him. It forbids to Parliament the use of Parliamentary powers so as to change its constitutional position. Hence the Constitution, as now interpreted, prevents the gradual development of Parliamentary supremacy. At the bottom of all these differences of constitutional law lies one great fact. Prussia is a military state built up by the military prowess of its monarchs and owing its greatness and its existence to the maintenance of its armed power which in its turn depends on the obedience of a national army and a highly trained administrative body to the King. It is the military necessities of Prussia which have given its peculiar character to Prussian constitutionalism just as it has been the possibility of dispensing with a large armed force and the commercial prosperity of England which has impressed its special character upon English constitutional history. As long as the strength of the monarchy was necessary to the prosperity or to the protection of England, the Crown played a real and substantial part in the government of the country, and

---

[25] Add to this that the power of the Imperial Diet to pass laws for the whole of the Empire lessens the authority of the Prussian legislature.

Prussian constitutionalism, different as it is from the modern system of government in England, constantly recalls English constitutionalism as it existed in the time of the Tudors, or even so late as the reign of Anne.

It is of course the natural assumption of Englishmen that as the Prussian people have already acquired a legislative Parliament which possesses the right to grant taxes, and as there is no reason to suppose that the King can overthrow the Constitution, or wishes to do so, the Parliament will, as in England, gradually acquire supremacy. That this may possibly be the outcome of Prussian constitutional history is possible but there are several circumstances which make it doubtful whether the precedents of England, of France, or of Belgium will be followed. To her Kings Prussia owes her existence. The revolution which has united Germany has so far from lessened that it has greatly increased the prestige of the Hohenzollerns. They stand now in the sort of position which was occupied by Henry VIII after carrying through the Reformation, or which would have been occupied by the French Bourbons had they after 1789 headed the popular movement and established the civil equality with which is associated the name of Napoleon. The Prussian Kings moreover stand at the head of a military and civil administration which is thoroughly national and which is necessary for the power, if not for the very existence, of Prussia. What is of even more consequence there is nothing in the ancient or modern history of the country to attach Prussians to the Parliament. If therefore the Prussian Kings have the sagacity to pursue a policy which on the whole commends itself to the nation, there does not appear to be any very clear reason why a constitutional regime in which a military monarch coexists with a legislative Parliament, should not continue for an indefinite period. In England the Houses of Parliament form the centre of the fabric of the state. Everything which exists, the Crown, the administration, and the army, have been for generations in effect appendages, so to speak, of the Parliament. In Prussia it is far otherwise. Prussian constitutionalism may be compared to a building of which the Houses of Parliament form an ornamental façade; but the façade masks and conceals a series of government offices and a huge barrack. Under the military system of Prussia it is the national army under the national King and not the national Parliament which gives to the Constitution its essential character.

7

Party Government

Analysis*

Introduction
    1. Distinction between party and party government
    2. Inconsistent feelings with regard to party system

A.   Meaning of Party System
    (See *Present Discontents*, Works of Burke, i, 1871 ed., pp 375–381.)
    1. Two bodies of men or parties bound together among themselves, and opposed to each other by adherence to definite principles and policies
    2. Each party under leadership of well known parliamentary leaders who, whether as Government or Opposition, are prepared to enforce their own principles and resist the principles of their opponents

B.   Apparent Advantages of Party System
    I. *Check upon individual selfishness*
    II. *Exposure and hindrance of errors committed by Government*
    III. *Administration of affairs by men of known capacity*

C.   Inherent Defects of Party System
    I. *Measures cannot be considered on merits*
    II. *Waste of capacity*
    III. *Exaggeration of differences*
    IV. *Policy of Government spoilt by influence of Opposition*

D.   Conditions Necessary for the Party System
    I. *Loyalty to constitution*
    II. *Existence of real differences of principle*
    III. *General interest of nation in politics*
    (IV. *Existence of only two parties* (?))

E.   Evils from Failure of Conditions

F.   Mitigation of Evils of Party System
    I. *Party system not the essence of parliamentary government*
    II. *Mitigations*
        1. Separation from party system of judicial and administrative bodies
        2. Politics not made a lucrative profession
        3. Questions of policy kept as far as possible outside party system

---

* So that this Analysis approximates to the remaining full lecture text, which is the product of substantial alteration, its contents have been derived from two manuscripts. The Introduction and A–E have been derived from a manuscript on which it was recorded as the lecture on 5 May 1899. The contents of F and G and the reading list have been derived from an undated manuscript attached to the lecture scheme headed 'Easter and Trinity Term[s], 1905'. For the full Analysis used in 1905, see that used in 1908, which is almost identical (see p. 340 below).

G.   Explanation of Inconsistent Views with regard to Party System

(See Lowell, *Governments and Parties*, i, pp 69–108;
Bodley, *France*, ii, pp 75, 76, 163–165, 297–306;
Ostrogorski, *Democracy and Organization of Political Parties*.)

Party Government[*]

Introduction

Everyone is influenced by inconsistent feelings with regard to government by party.

On the one hand we are prone, in England at least, to assume that party government is an essential characteristic of popular, or at any rate of parliamentary, government, and publicists often attribute the real or alleged failure of parliamentary government in France, or in Italy, to the absence of defined parties, the lack whereof makes it impossible to establish true party government as it exists in England.[1]

It is even asserted that the party system is probably the strongest purifying agent in parliamentary government under extended suffrage.[2] This assertion indeed sounds an extravagant paradox to anyone who reflects on the condition of affairs at New York. Yet we all perceive that in some way or other there is a close connexion between the party system and parliamentary government as it has existed in England for about two centuries, and further that certain definite evils arise when parties break up into groups each representing different interests or different ideas.

On the other hand, no one can help feeling that there is a sense in which government by party is an evil, even though it be a necessary evil. Most persons are at times haunted by the desire for a condition of feeling under which 'none are for a faction and all are for the state'. There is something irrational in the supposition that for the promotion of good government it is essentially necessary that there should be a constant conflict between the men in office and the men out of office or that, as Maine has somewhere put it, the sixteen ablest men in Parliament should be employed to carry on the administration of the country's affairs, and the sixteen next ablest men in Parliament should be employed in hindering them in the administration of the country's affairs. Nor is it possible for any student to disguise from himself that the party system is a comparatively new phenomenon, and that countries have been and are well governed in which that system does not in reality exist; consider for instance Cobden's eulogy of Prussian administration in 1835, and the prosperity of modern Switzerland where party government of the English type has not been developed.

The problem before us is how to reconcile this apparent contradiction in men's feelings as to government by party.

---

[1] See 2 Bodley, *France*, pp 76, 163–5, 297, 301; 1 Lowell, *Government and Parties*, pp 69, 70, 72.
[2] 2 Bodley, p. 297.

---

[*] The manuscript's first page was dated July 1898, but the lecture text was altered substantially, presumably after that date. The lecture as altered is published here. See also Dicey's earlier 'Memorandum on English Party System of Government', app. I below; Editor's Introduction, p. xxx f. above. This 'Party Government' lecture and the following 'Parliamentarism' lecture were on the interface of Dicey's two schemes of lectures. The same or similar lectures were also part of the scheme of Dicey's lectures on *The Comparative Study of Constitutions* at the Lowell Institute in Boston. See Editor's Introduction, pp xi ff, xviii, especially p. xii, n., above. See generally R. S. Rait, *Memorials of Albert Venn Dicey, being chiefly Letters and Diaries* (London: Macmillan, 1925), ch. 10, especially 160 f.

My purpose is to see if this reconciliation can be achieved by examining, *first*, what is meant by the party system; *secondly*, what, if you take that system at its best, are its merits and defects; *thirdly*, what are the conditions under which it can work for good; *fourthly*, what are the evils which the absence of these conditions produces; and, *fifthly*, to what extent the party system can be dispensed with under a parliamentary constitution.

A. Meaning of the Party System

Those who write about the party system have in view the form of party government which has existed, or is assumed to have existed, in England at any rate for the last hundred years.

In England during this period there have existed two main parties whom for the sake of convenience one may call Tories and Whigs or Conservatives and Liberals, who have been, or have supposed themselves to be, influenced by different principles of government and have been represented in Parliament by the Government or the Opposition as the case might be. Each of these have constituted distinct parliamentary parties under the leadership of known parliamentary leaders: whose object it was to enforce as far as possible their own policy and to oppose the policy of their opponents. The leaders moreover of each party have been prepared to conduct the government of the country when called upon to do so by the Crown which was itself guided in its choice of servants more or less directly by the wishes of the House of Commons. The Tories for example when in power conducted the administration of public affairs, including in that term all important parliamentary legislation, in accordance with Tory principles. The Whigs if in opposition made it their main effort to turn the Tories out of power and if they failed in this to introduce into the conduct of affairs as much of Whig principles as they could enforce upon their political opponents. The result of course has been that on a change of government there ensued or was supposed to ensue a change of principles. The place of each party was reversed: the Tories, e.g. (in 1830) passing from the party of the Government into the place of the Opposition, and the Whigs becoming the Ministry of the day or, in other words, the Government.

B. Apparent Advantages of System

The different ways in which the system [described above] facilitates the action of parliamentary government have often been dwelt upon and are pretty obvious.

The existence throughout the country and in Parliament of two organised bodies each linked together by common principles and each prepared to support their leaders when in office is a guarantee against the kind of anarchy into which parties [may fall]; whether in or out of Parliament, [parties] break up when they are not held together by strict discipline. The influence of the party exerted through its leaders may thus be a check upon the selfishness or treachery of individuals. In estimating the merits and demerits of connections based on partisanship it must be remembered that men may fall below, as they may rise above, loyalty to their associates.

If you examine, for example, the career of the class of adventurer of whom Wedderburn was in the last century a fair type, you see clearly enough that it required all the power of party discipline, in which one must include the natural sympathies inspired by comradeship, to prevent unscrupulous politicians from turning public life into a mere game for the promotion of their own interests. Burke's arguments in favour of Party at bottom amount to this: that in the earlier years of George III nothing but honourable adherence to party connections would enable average politicians to act in accordance with principle. The charge against George, and in a measure against Pitt, was that their attempt to break up Party resulted in leading politicians to forsake their principles for their interests.

The party system, in the next place, put the administration in the hands of well known leaders, who whatever their defects, must have been able to produce an impression upon Parliament, and especially upon the House of Commons. At lowest they were men possessed of talents which rendered them distinguished in an assembly which contained many of the wisest, the most capable, and the most influential men in England. They were persons qualified to be leaders of men. Under the party system bad men might be in power. It was hardly possible that office should long be held by nonentities. If you take the English Cabinets which have held office since George III came to the throne you will find that they contained members of considerably more than average ability.

The existence further of two parties each of whose leaders were prepared to take office had two good results. There were never lacking a body of persons by whom the government might be carried on; and the Government was checked and prevented from committing errors by the criticism of the Opposition, and the censures of the Opposition were moderated by the knowledge that the censors might at any moment be called upon to undertake the responsibility of carrying on the government.[3]

If, lastly, you may assume that, as no doubt was often the case, Tories and Whigs really advocated essentially different principles it then follows that the party system is or may be based upon fundamental differences of conviction and that the maintenance of party connections was in reality a means of keeping the conduct of average men in harmony with their conscientious beliefs.

---

[3] The security against bad government afforded by the criticism of an Opposition may be greatly exaggerated. Just because an Opposition must be *ex officio* censors deprives their criticism of weight. A more serious defect not sufficiently noted is that the feelings or interests of the Government and the Opposition may often coincide, and that, when this is so, the supposed security against bad government ceases. The High Churchmanship of Lord Salisbury and of Mr. Gladstone has, combined with other causes, given undue weight for the last 30 years to the High Church party. An Opposition again which may itself come into office is almost as unwilling as the Government to do anything which may check the freedom of a Ministry as to appointments and therefore does very little in the way of criticising jobbery.

So much at any rate may be granted to the advocates of the party system that in more ways than one it facilitates the regular and beneficial action of parliamentary government.

Note, however, that even in England [the] theory of the party system [was] never perfectly carried out in fact. Considerable disagreements of principle exist among members of the same party, e.g. as to the 'Catholic' question, 1820–1829, [and m]easures [have been] carried by [the] party which has opposed them, e.g. Catholic Relief, 1829, [and] Repeal of Corn Laws, 1845.

C. Inherent Demerits of Party System

These are clearly seen, if we take the system in England at about its best, [in] 1832–1845.

I. It makes impossible consideration of measures on merits

Peel was [the] best administrator of his age, and no one can doubt that many of the subordinate Whig reforms which he or his followers delayed, e.g. [the] institution of County Courts, would have been promoted by himself if in office.

II. An Opposition, which cannot carry out its own policy, maims and renders abortive the policy of the Government

This is illustrated by the political history of 1832–1841. Most persons would now grant that the Irish policy of the Whigs was on the whole sound. Everyone would concede that if it were to be tried it ought to have been tried fairly. Yet the history of the Opposition as to the Irish Church, as to Irish Municipal government, as to collection of tithes in Ireland, as to the relation between the government and O'Connell, is nothing but an account of successful attempts to delay and embarrass a policy which the Opposition could not reverse. To sum the matter up shortly Peel was the ablest parliamentary leader of his time. His administrative capacity and the circumstance that he twice carried through popular reforms have given him the reputation of a reformer, yet, under the influence of the party system, his substantial work as a leader was to delay reforms till they became all but useless.

III. The party system involves a waste of capacity

Peel and his immediate followers were the best administrators in England. The public lost the use of their administrative powers because the Whigs, who were poor administrators, pursued on the whole the policy approved by the nation, whilst Peel advocated, or was supposed to advocate, a policy opposed to that of the Whigs.

IV. *The party system leads to an exaggeration of the points on which the whole of one party, e.g. the Tories, are supposed to agree and to be opposed to the whole of their opponents, e.g. the Whigs*

It is to say the least very dubious whether between 1832 and 1845 the differences[,] which divided the Conservative leaders from the Whig leaders, were most of them very serious[;] could they irrespective of the party system have been formed into a Board or Cabinet for carrying on the business of the nation, such as is the Swiss Council, it is quite conceivable that Peel, Lyndhurst, and the Duke of Wellington might have acted harmoniously together with Melbourne, Lord John Russell, and Macaulay.

Hence, further, not only political leaders but the whole of a party come to think that the party to which they belong is made up of good men and that the party to which they are opposed is made up of bad men, whence partisans come to hold that their own party, especially if it has been long in office, has a moral right to be in power, and that there is something shocking to the national conscience in a transfer of authority from a party which has long held sway to their opponents. This was the feeling of the Whigs in 1760; it was the feeling of the Tories in 1829, it became the feeling of the Liberals in 1886. What makes this state of sentiment the more dangerous is that it is often based on a certain amount of fact. It will be found, if you look at English history, that from time to time the morality of the nation has in truth been in the main represented by a given political party. Thus in 1783 and for at least thirty or forty years longer, the men who most deserved national confidence and respect did in fact belong to the Tories, and though it is more difficult to speak with certainty of later times it is maintainable that on the whole, from, say, 1845–1865, the moral force of the country belonged to the Liberals, including in that term Whigs, Peelites, and Radicals. But though this shifting of moral respectability from one party to another is a noticeable fact, it still is true that the party system intensifies the tendency of politicians and their followers to look upon their own side as the party of the good, and upon the opposite side as a faction of bad men, whence, among other evils, results the sort of political hypocrisy which leads men of sense and merit to overlook or palliate the decline in moral principle of a party which they have at one time held, perhaps rightly, to represent public virtue.

The patent evils, in short, of the party system, even at its best, are that it prevents men from considering measures on their own merits, that it produces that kind of vicious compromise by which an Opposition maims a policy which it cannot resist, that it involves a waste of political capacity, that it exaggerates the differences which divide one party from another, and [that it] promotes the idea which is often false, and at best only partially true, that one party in the state has a monopoly of public virtue.

These, be it noted, are not so much the corruptions of government by party, as understood in England, but rather its inherent faults, and these faults have, even where the party system under the guidance of men such as Sir Robert Peel, Lord Althorpe, or Lord John Russell, assumed its best form, worked great evil to England.

Let us for a moment, however, lay aside the defects of the party system, and assuming that on the whole they are overbalanced by its merits, examine:–

D. The Conditions Necessary for the Beneficial Action of the Party System

These conditions are, speaking broadly, four.

1st condition—all parties in the state must be loyal to the constitution

Government by party, in the English sense of the terms, can hardly exist or at any rate cannot produce its best results if any considerable body of citizens are disloyal to the constitution, and are prepared to overthrow it by force or intrigue, or even are so completely hostile to it that they will take no part in administering the government of the country, and do not wish to promote the proper working of its institutions.

This state of things is an absolutely essential condition for the proper working of the party system and this for an obvious reason. If in a given country a large number of persons are revolutionists or reactionists prepared if necessary to change the constitution, it is impossible that they or their leaders should be admitted to power, for the moment they came into office they would use the authority of the state not for carrying on the administration of affairs but for carrying out a revolution. To take an extreme case, it was absolutely impossible under the Commonwealth or the Protectorate to put the government in the hands of Cavaliers or even of moderate Presbyterians since it was certain that they would use power to effect a restoration, and in passing one may note that the real reason why the Puritan revolution failed is that the revolutionary government, even when in the hands of Cromwell, did not command the loyal adherence of large portions of the nation. So again up till 1760 it was practically impossible to bring the Tory party, though probably it represented the majority of the nation, into office, and the Septennial Act was in truth a pacific *coup d'état* by which the Whigs guarded against the chance that what we should now call the swing of the pendulum, or in other words the regular operation of the party system, should give a parliamentary majority to Tories who would destroy the revolution settlement. Exactly the same difficulty beset the governments who, after the first violence of the first French revolution was passed, tried to establish something like orderly freedom. They had introduced the party system and yet could not trust its operation since it might at any moment place in office reactionists who would overthrow the Constitution. The *coup d'état* of 13 Vendémiaire (5 Aug. 1795) as also of 18 Fructidor (4 Sept. 1797) were both caused or justified by the necessity for asserting the triumph of a party which might lead to the overthrow of the Republic. It were easy to give other examples of the obvious fact that disloyalty to the constitution on the part of a large party in a given country makes the regular operation of the party system impossible. It is worth note, however, that the proper action of Party is inconsistent not only with active disloyalty or conspiracy, but also with the negative disloyalty which takes the form of abstention from political life. Republican government in France suffers from the attitude of the Legitimists or reactionists; the constitutional monarchy of Italy rests on an unsound foundation because all genuine Catholics, that is all Italians who in political matters are guided by the Pope, abstain from taking part in parliamentary elections. The reason again why the system of obstruction organised by Mr. Parnell intensely alarmed English statesmen is that it made patent the existence of a disciplined party which was morally disloyal to the constitution. Even if we put aside every question as to the connection between the Parnellite opposition and Fenians or dynamiters, this at any rate must be admitted. The aim of Parnellite obstruction was to frustrate the conduct of business in Parliament. It was disloyalty using for its ends not arms but parliamentary forms. Like other forms of rebellion it may have had its justification. On that point I say nothing, all I maintain is that it struck at the root of the party system.

It will be granted that substantial loyalty to the constitution, on the part at any rate of that portion of the citizens who take a real part in public life, is an essential condition for the proper working of the party system. What Englishmen, and I think Americans, fail to note is the rarity with which this condition is fulfilled. It is only during a very short portion of the modern history of England that it has existed in Great Britain. It does not exist at the present moment in France, in Italy, or [in] Spain. It does not exist in the Austrian Empire. Whether it exist in the German Empire may be doubtful. There are only two Continental countries where we can confidently say that loyalty to the constitution flourishes. These countries are Belgium and Switzerland. The Belgian system we may add is about the most satisfactory reproduction of the English constitution and of the English party system to be found in Europe. Switzerland is the most successful of European democracies but in Switzerland, though we find one of the conditions requisite for the party system, thoroughly fulfilled government by party is unknown.

2nd condition—the distinction between the two parties in the state must depend upon real differences of principle

There exists on the face of things a great difficulty in ensuring the combined existence of our first and our second condition. In other words, the party system implies that a nation should not be divided by differences of political creed which can be described on the one side as loyalty and on the other side as disloyalty to the constitution, but that the nation is divided by differences of principle sufficiently marked to form the basis of real parties. What is needed, in short, is a very singular state of opinion which may be described as one of agreement as to fundamentals, combined with disagreement as to matters of importance which are not fundamentals. If one may borrow ecclesiastical terms and apply them to political life, one may say that the party system requires at once the absence of scism and the presence both of orthodoxy and of heterodoxy.

Let, however, this primary difficulty of combining fundamental agreement with really important disagreement be dismissed from consideration. Yet when this is done it will still be found that the necessity for basing party organisation on true differences of opinion of itself makes the maintenance of party government a matter by no means easy to achieve.

Differences of principle which at one time were real may from the course of events or the turn of opinion come to an end. Up till 1745 England was more or less divided into Whigs who supported and Tories who disapproved of the Revolution settlement. The rebellion of that year terminated all real chance of a Jacobite restoration. On the accession of George III fifteen years later, men found to their surprise that Jacobitism was dead, and that the substantial difference which had divided them was at an end. For more than a century the political world of Europe has been divided under different names and in different forms into promoters and the opponents of democracy. We are just beginning to perceive that the spread of democratic principles is rendering this basis of division unmeaning. This does not mean that men are agreed on the solution of all or even of the most important of political problems. What it does mean is that the old lines of division are out of date. In Switzerland, for example, and the United States, and with some qualifications one might add in England, the distinction between democrats and anti-democrats has little real import. The old foundations of party division are obsolete and for the moment the existence therefore of parties based on principles is almost an impossibility.

The same result follows from a different cause.

Where a large number of citizens are disloyal to the constitution and either conspire against it or refuse to take any part in public life, the 'loyalists', who of course in a Republic would be Republicans, as under a constitutional monarchy they would be constitutionalists, are compelled to act together and to exclude the 'disloyalists', (if one may use such a term) from office. This it may be noted is at the present moment the state of things in France and in Italy, just as it was the political condition of Great Britain between the accession of the Hanoverian dynasty, 1714, [and] the accession of George III, 1760. Hence followed two consequences. There is no real party system, the men in power inevitably belong to one only of the two great political divisions in the country, e.g. in the case of modern France to the Republicans. But in the next place there is certain to spring up a sort of false party system, i.e. mere struggles for office between the different divisions or groups of the predominant party. This is one explanation of the constant changes of French Cabinets. One unknown Ministry succeeds another, equally unknown, just because there is no real difference between the Opposition and the Government. They are of necessity fractions of the Republican party. Exactly the same phenomenon, though it showed itself in a different form, was seen in England during a great part of the 18th Century. Hence a:

3rd condition—parties must not be kept together mainly by personal interest

The legitimate party system depends upon the existence of real divisions of political opinion. From the moment that the main tie which binds parties together is personal interest, under which term one ought perhaps to include mere personal partisanship, the true foundation of party government is undermined. Yet when for any reason whatever the other requirements of the party system do not exist, it is almost certain that the attempt will be made to keep parties together by motives of self-interest which in the last resort amount to corruption. The downright bribery of Walpole, the lavish expenditure which kept together the King's Friends, the 'austere corruption' of Guizot, all at bottom arose from the same cause. They were all attempts to keep together parties by appeals to private interest.[4]

4th condition—there must if possible exist only two important parties

It is not indeed necessary for the fulfilment of this condition that these parties should not themselves be divided into smaller groups, but it is necessary that they should be groups strictly within each of the parties and that the difference dividing any group from the rest of the party to which it belongs should be felt by the members of such group to be less important than the difference dividing the two parties.

The party system as a means of parliamentary government cannot work to any good effect if Parliament itself is divided into small groups or bodies each of which works for its own end with little regard to the ends aimed at by the whole party to which it professedly belongs. This is so obvious and is nowadays so constantly noted that the point is hardly worth working out. But it is well to observe that the breaking of parties into groups may arise from one of two different causes.

It may be due to fanaticism, that is excessive and disproportionate zeal for the attainment of some special end, e.g. Free Trade, Temperance, Anti-vaccination, and the like. If a body of politicians are willing to support any party whatever which will favour the particular cause, be it good or bad, which such politicians wish to succeed, then, as far as they are concerned, the party system is at an end. If twenty members of Parliament are induced by the promise of a Protective tariff, of Free Trade, or of a Local Option Act, to support a given party, whatever be its other principles, then the party system is, as far as these twenty members are concerned, at an end. Their motives may be excellent, but their action enables one of two parties which *ex hypothesi* does not fairly command a majority to gain office.[5]

The breaking up into groups may, on the other hand, be due to self-interest. If, to take an extreme case, twenty members of Parliament were willing to sell their votes to either of the great parties for place or pay, these members would as far as lay in them break up the party system.

Look at the matter which way you will, the rise of separate groups or factions pursuing their own ends without regard to the principles of the party to which they ally themselves is fatal to any beneficial system of party government.

---

[4] Walpole's bribery was the most respectable, as it was the most successful, form of corruption. It could more or less be defended by, as it owed its success to, the consideration that Walpole and the best of his supporters though they secured power by dubious means yet were a real party bound together by common principles and pursuing a legitimate end, *viz.* the maintenance of the Hanoverian succession on which ultimately depended the maintenance of English liberty.

[5] This statement must be taken subject to one limitation; a particular measure, e.g. the Reform Bill of 1832, may involve so many general questions of policy as to form the basis of a new division into two parties. In this case the supporters of such a measure may readjust, instead of destroying, the party system.

5th condition—the nation must take a real interest in politics

This perhaps ought to have been put forward as the primary and most essential condition for the proper working of party government. Popular government, and certainly parliamentary government, will never work well—it will scarcely work at all—in a country where men are not really interested in politics. If the electors have no real care as to the political conduct of their representatives it is absolutely certain that Parliament will be governed by factions kept together by self-interest and intrigue.

The statement that the nation must be interested in politics requires, however, some explanation. For our present purpose it is not necessary that the whole of a nation should be politicians. The party government existed and in some respects worked well in England between 1714 and 1832, yet whilst Parliament was unreformed large classes had nothing to do with the government of the country and presumably took little interest in it. The same thing was more or less true of large bodies of the people between 1832 and 1884. But what is really meant by the assertion that the nation must be interested in politics is that the portion of a state which holds political power, the 'legal country', to adopt a French expression, should be interested. The best feature in English public life has been the constant interest of the electors in political questions. Faction, though more reviled, is far less dangerous, than indifference.[6]

E. Evils from Failure of Conditions

The party system has at its best defects which have been already noted but in addition to these there flow from party government several distinct evils which may be fairly attributed to the failure of the conditions on which the good working of the party system depends.

These evils may take different forms. They may be the obvious sacrifice of public interest to party spirit—the tendency to create questions or, to use the popular expression, cries, which may cause the kind of division in opinion needed for the existence of parties,[7] or actual corruption or bribery. But all these evils may be summed up under one head. Whenever they exist they mean that parties are degenerating into factions, that is to say that they have become, or are becoming, bodies of men not bound together by community of principles but either by self-interest or by the feeling of partisanship.

---

[6] Contrast the small interest taken in politics by the French electorate. A practical moral suggested by our fifth condition is the peril of extending political rights to classes devoid of political interest.

[7] No sensible man can doubt that again and again political controversies have been raised in England mainly for the sake of keeping a party together. One reason why Parliamentary reform excited legitimate alarm, in the minds of many men who were not strong Tories, was the perception that changes in the constitution would henceforth be advocated for the sake of keeping a party together.

F. How Far can the Party System be Dispensed with and what are its Mitigations?

It is perfectly plain that the party system, as it has existed for the last 150 years or so in England, is not a necessary part of parliamentary government. In England it has been in existence (historically speaking) for only a short time, that is for not more than a century and a half, and even during this period it has not been fully developed. Till 1832 the crowd exerted great influence independently of Party. At times moreover, e.g. from 1800 to 1820, the Opposition was generally so feeble in numbers and weight that the party system, as now understood, existed rather in name than in reality, and in comparatively recent times, e.g. between 1860 and 1865, the party in office has been in fact supported by a large number of nominal opponents so that the Government possessed in reality rather a national than a party support. Switzerland, again, which is the most successful of modern democracies, possesses parliamentary government without the support of the party system.

Party government, in short, though in many countries an all but inseparable accident is not an essential property of parliamentary government. Still in England at least the party system is so well established that its continuance must be taken for granted, and the part of wisdom is not to plan its abolition but to consider what are, or may be, its mitigations.

These are some of the most obvious.

1. The judicial[8] and administrative bodies of the country should be kept as far as possible beyond the sphere of Party

This has in fact been to a great extent achieved both in England and in Belgium, where alone the party system has worked satisfactorily. In both countries partisans may be made judges but the judges are not partisans.

In both countries the Civil Service has taken no part in politics, and at the present day appointments to the Civil Service are in England at least little, if at all, dependent upon political favour. Civil servants moreover, though for the most part legally dismissible, in practice hold their offices by a tenure nearly as certain as that of the

---

[8] The appointment of judges from among the leading members of a particular party is an evil mainly because it militates against the promotion to the Bench of the best lawyers on account of legal merit[.] [T]hough the appointment of law officers to judicial places is an advantage since it results in the Bench being filled by the real leaders of the Bar [and] though the appointment of e.g. Conservatives as judges by a Conservative Chancellor is [only] a slight evil, since a judge appointed by Tories need not become a Tory judge[,] [n]othing can be imagined more noxious than the appointment of judges as partisans, i.e. as representatives of a party on the Bench. The idea has been broached and acted upon that the magistrates of a county ought to represent in certain proportions the political parties which exist there. The idea, if true, applies logically to every Court in the Kingdom. It is, however, totally false, and those who wish the deterioration of the party system should oppose every suggestion for the representation of parties on the Bench. One of the leading errors of the day is the misapplication of the doctrine of representation; in the discharge of official duties the primary thing to look to is not representative character but capacity, and, as regards judicial functions, capacity includes an independence of Party[,] which is inconsistent with the representation of a party.

judges. The independence of the Civil Service has been one main though unnoticed cause of the success of party government in England.[9]

It were further well to consider whether some of the Cabinet offices might not be held by men who were independent of Party. The questions which come before a Lord Chancellor, either as a judge or as a Minister of Justice, have generally but slight connection with party differences, and the nation would gain could a lawyer who discharged well the duties of the Chancellor hold office in Cabinets of different political colours. The same thing may perhaps be said about the Minister for Foreign Affairs. But here we touch upon a different point.

2. Large questions of general policy should whenever possible be so determined that they may be placed outside the realm of Party

Some examples will show my meaning. When Peel accepted the results of the Reform Bill, he placed the changes introduced by the measure of 1832 beyond discussion. Between 1800 and 1886 the Union with Ireland was supported by each party in the state. As far as Great Britain was concerned Repeal was not a party question. So again for the last 50 years Free Trade has been the settled policy of England. It has been placed outside the realm of Party. A main object of patriotic statesmanship should be to increase the number of matters which could not become the subject of party difference. On all the main points of national concern there ought in short to be a traditional policy to which each party in the state should adhere. It is certainly not past hope that the time may arrive when the number of closed questions may be so great that the party system may work, and work well, within a limited area.

G. What then is the Explanation of the Contradiction which is to be found in most People's Feelings with regard to the Party System?

The answer is this: the conditions necessary for the beneficial working of the party system are also the requirements under which alone popular government can flourish. Thus loyalty to the constitution, an active interest in public affairs among the mass of the citizens, the management of national business by leading men of marked talent and of high character, and the like, are all conditions required for the satisfactory working of the party system, and they are also the necessary requirements of popular government. The party system therefore when at its best is a sign, though it is not a cause, of the good health of the state. And Englishmen at any rate attribute to Party itself benefits which really flow not from partisanship but from the circum-

---

[9] Note that where the long predominance of one party in power has filled the leading places in the Civil Service with men in the main belonging to one party there have occasionally been signs that the party system has not worked well. One may suspect that the administrative failures of the Whigs between 1832 and 1845 were in part due to want of zealous support by Tory officials. Nor is it certain that in 1852, or perhaps later, Disraeli and his colleagues did not suffer some inconvenience from the political bias of the permanent civil servants.

stances which make political partisanship innocuous. Hence the idea that the party system is itself beneficial.

The moment, however, that the conditions of healthy party contests or, in other words, the conditions required for the healthiness of popular government cease to exist, it becomes obvious to everyone that Party, which is then called the spirit of faction, is the destruction, not the salvation, of the Commonwealth. Men then begin to deprecate party spirit and condemn the party system.

If this be the true answer to the question before us it leads to an important result. Patriotic statesmanship need take no trouble to maintain the party system where it is established, and still less to create it where it is unknown. Their [sic] whole effort should be devoted to maintaining or nurturing the requirements of good popular government. It may happen that under certain circumstances the maintenance of these requirements may for a time give rise to party government. It is equally possible that under other circumstances the maintenance of these requirements may destroy the party system. The diffusion for example of loyalty to Republican institutions throughout the whole French people might it is possible in France give birth to *bonâ fide* party government, but it might also inaugurate a system like that of Switzerland, or even resembling that of Prussia[,] which ensured freedom and popular government without invoking the aid of parties. It is always to be borne in mind that Burke, who was the most systematic defender of the party system, himself towards the end of his life destroyed the party organizations of his day. As in most of Burke's conduct we have here an apparent inconsistency arising from passionate adherence to one consistent principle. Burke's eulogy of Party meant that in his judgment the morality of public life could in 1766 be maintained only by the loyal adherence of honest men to their Party principles. His appeal to the Old Whigs and their consequent union with the Tories meant that in 1794 the break-up of the party system was necessary for the maintenance of public morality and of loyalty to the constitution. In 1766 and in 1794 Burke, assuming that his view of the facts was correct, defended the conditions of sound popular government.

8

Parliamentarism

Analysis*

A. Parliamentarism
   I. *Meaning of term*
      1. General discredit and inefficiency of government by Parliament
      2. Complaints from all quarters: England (obstruction); Austria (parliamentary civil war); France (weakening of national government); Italy (corruption)
      NB Complaints not new, e.g. Carlyle, Dickens, Disraeli, Cobden, Maine
   II. *General causes of Parliament's discredit*
      1. Predominant form of government always open to censure
      2. Parliamentary government is government in public. Hence loss of dignity. Contrast unreformed Parliament.
      3. Parliamentary government suitable for system of *laissez faire*, but not suitable for effective administration
      4. Real merit, *viz*, discussion, not appreciated by uneducated and of less importance than in other times
   III. *Special charges against Parliaments*
      1. Faction, i.e., predominance of cliques and of selfish interests
      2. Obstruction and deficiency in useful legislation
      3. Failure to represent national will (Switzerland)
      4. Localism and corruption of localities (France)
      5. Degradation of public life, e.g. France, Italy, USA, English Colonies (?)
      6. Administration weakened and executive and judiciary controlled by parliamentary considerations
B. Remedies for Parliamentarism
   I. *Extension of local self government*
      1. Ambiguity of term
      2. Confusion fostered by Tocqueville
      3. Demands extraordinary amount of public spirit
   II. *Proportional representation*
      1. Its meaning
      2. Its alleged merits
      3. Several popular objections untenable
      4. Criticism

---

* Its contents have been derived from two successive undated manuscripts both of which were attached in a sequence of Analyses the very first of which was dated 25 July 1898. The first manuscript was entitled 'Parliamentarism'; the second, 'Remedies for Parliamentarism'. The titles of these two Analyses have here been made into the main headings of a single composite Analysis. The two manuscript Analyses seem originally to have been for two separate lectures, from which the single, full lecture text below was developed. No reading list was provided.

  (i) Proportionate representation not *in itself* desirable
  (ii) Increases division into groups
  (iii) Favours tyranny of minorities and coalitions founded at best on mutual aid of groups with regard to their respective crotchets

III. *Referendum*
 1. Recommendations
  (i) Diminishes influence of parties
  (ii) Separates measures from persons
  (iii) Increases honesty of political conduct
  (iv) Asserts supremacy of nation
 2. Objections
  (i) Essentially conservative. See Maine, *Popular Government*
  (ii) Diminishes moral influence as well as power of Parliament
  (iii) Perhaps decreases a representative sense of responsibility
  NB Whether advantages or objections predominate depends on circumstances of given country. Contrast Switzerland, USA, France, and England.

Parliamentarism[*]

Introduction

'Parliamentarism' is a new name for a newly discovered political disease; it means the increasing inefficiency and consequent discredit of parliamentary government. The outward sign, so to speak, of the malady is the predominance of parliamentary factions and the decline in the character of parliamentary leaders. But the complaint takes different forms in different countries. In England it appears as 'obstruction' whereby a reckless minority, or a combination of minorities, may make Parliamentary legislation impossible and hamper the executive energy of the government. Hence, as it is alleged, the House of Commons has lost at once dignity and power. In France Parliamentarism means the undue predominance of parliamentary groups or factions whose sinister interests lower the character of politicians, substitute intrigue for policy, forbid useful legislation, and shake the great institutions of the country such, for example, as the grand administrative system created by Napoleon, or the honoured magistracy whose traditional independence dates back to a period prior to the great Revolution. In Italy, we are told, all the signs of the disease are seen in its worst form. The Parliament is a centre of intrigue and it is alleged of corruption. Transitory Ministries are made up of men of low intellectual and moral character. The taxation becomes heavier and heavier, the misery of the country increases, and no man or party dares to carry or propose the reforms necessary to save the country from ruin. Statesmanship has vanished from the land of Cavour, and enthusiasm and public spirit, from the land of Mazzini, of Garibaldi, of D'Azeglio, and [of] Ricasoli. The age of constitutional freedom has produced a moral degradation which was not created by the foreign despotism of Austria, or the priestly tyranny of the Bourbons. Nor can I suppose that traces of this political disease may not be found even in the New World. I have never heard it asserted that of recent years the character or the influence of either House of Congress has risen. A student at any rate who observes that each successive new Constitution in any American State is longer and more minute than its predecessors will suspect at any rate that there exists a widespread desire to limit more and more closely the powers of elective legislatures. Nor does the absence of complaints as to Parliamentarism in a state such as the German Empire

---

[*] The manuscript's first page was dated 30 August 1898, but the remaining lecture text is the product, in part, of substantial alteration that seems to have been mainly after that date. This 'Parliamentarism' lecture and the previous 'Party Government' lecture were on the interface of Dicey's two schemes of lectures. The same or similar lectures were also part of the scheme of Dicey's lectures on *The Comparative Study of Constitutions* at the Lowell Institute in Boston. See Editor's Introduction, pp xi ff, xviii, especially p. xii, n., above. An earlier draft 'Parliamentarism' lecture is also available in the Dicey Papers. It was dated 27 August 1898, and its structure and headings are similar to the structure and general headings of the composite lecture Analysis above. It was recorded, on its first page, as being a first draft in a later manuscript note and has therefore been treated as superseded by the lecture text published here.

tell for much; the absence of Parliamentary vices is accounted for by the limitations on Parliamentary power.

Half a century ago few were the observers who suspected the existence of defects alleged now to be inherent in the parliamentary system; its universal adoption has revealed its supposed flaws. In 1848 every reformer or revolutionist throughout the Continent wished to establish or extend the authority of Parliaments. In that year were published the first volumes of Macaulay's *History*. They sold by thousands and expressed [with] accuracy the political creed of the time. The practical and experienced thinkers of England believed fully in the benefits to the derived from parliamentary constitutionalism, [and] the differences between different forms of what may be called the Parliamentary faith, were, as we now see, of minor significance. Republicans believed that a representative assembly should be based on universal suffrage and that the powers of a King were inconsistent with the supremacy of a Chamber representing the people. English Whigs believed that a constitutional monarchy was the best form of parliamentary government and that an hereditary King was preferable to an elective President. But neither Whigs nor Radicals, monarchical constitutionalists, or revolutionary Republicans doubted that at any rate for nations which had attained a certain stage in civilization the path of progress led to the adoption of the parliamentary system. The sceptics, if any, who disavowed this orthodox faith were either ultra conservatives such as Bismarck, or paradox mongers, such as Carlyle. Today men are beginning to dispute as to the very fundamentals of the Parliamentary creed. The denunciations of Parliamentarism are in reality attacks on the whole scheme of representative government. This new phase of opinion well deserves examination. My purpose is to consider three questions. First, why has parliamentary government fallen into discredit; secondly, how far are the complaints against parliamentary government, or in other words how far is the charge of Parliamentarism, justifiable; thirdly, what, if any, are the remedies for Parliamentarism?

A. Why has Parliamentary Government Fallen into Discredit?

The decline in the reputation of representative government is due in part to general causes which certainly do not prove that the rule of Parliaments has turned out a failure.

The very fact that parliamentary constitutionalism exists everywhere diminishes the popularity of Parliaments. There never has been a time when men did not complain and with justice of the shortcomings of their rulers. Whilst the world was ruled by Kings and their Ministers every evil which afflicted any country was ascribed to the faults of the monarch or his servants. Now that every civilized nation is governed by a Parliament the legislative body becomes the mark of the attacks which have at all times been directed against the government.

The parliamentary system means government by public discussion, but the very publicity which indirectly benefits a nation because it exposes and corrects abuses is fatal to the dignity of the government. No Parliament has ever exhibited, or can ever exhibit, greater want of wisdom than did Louis XIV. But no elective assembly has ever displayed the dignity of a King or has earned the veneration which surrounded the *Grand Monarque*. Discussion and debate involves wrangling, delay, and the appearance of inefficiency. People admire great strokes of state; they will never admire the bit-by-bit policy of concession and compromise which mars the effectiveness of Parliamentary legislation. We have heard much of the benefits conferred upon a country by a free press. Some of them are real; but the freedom of the press and the presence of reporters robs deliberate assemblies of their impressiveness. In the last century the House of Commons objected to the reporting of its debates. The instinctive dread of publicity was not wholly unsound. The secrecy which at one time concealed from public view the weaknesses of the House of Commons still shrouds in mystery the debates or dissensions of the Cabinet. Common sense suggests that a government which talks and acts in the sight and the hearing of the whole world will with difficulty maintain the respect of the public.

A Parliament, again, is a first-rate instrument for making known public grievances and under favourable circumstances for removing them. It is a very bad instrument for carrying out constructive legislation. The fame of the Parliament of England was created in one age by the vigour with which the House of Commons maintained the law of the land against the attacks of the Crown. It was kept alive in a later age by the continuous energy with which the English Parliament removed patent abuses. Conservative resistance to arbitrary power and the maintenance or the extension of a system of *laissez faire* are tasks within the capacity of an intelligent assembly and have on the whole been well performed by the Parliament of England. But for constructive legislation which shall use the powers of the state for the benefit of the people, or for the creation of an effective administrative system, an elective assembly has no natural aptitude. Now for the last 50 years at least, public opinion in England at least, we may even say throughout the civilized world, has demanded constructive legislation and the improvement of administrative machinery. The English Parliament has been therefore set to do work for which it is not properly fitted. No wonder that its bungling has excited derision. It is worth notice that in England the complaints of parliamentary government came at first from rhetoricians such as Carlyle, who exalted vigorous administrators at the expense of parliamentary orators and party leaders, or who, like Cobden, were men of an essentially administrative genius. Even in 1835 he scoffed at the British constitution, and believed that for the common people the ideal of government was to be found in the Prussian bureaucracy.

Then again the credit, not only of the parliamentary system but of all forms of popular government, has been diminished in a way which is little noticed by the spread of general education and the increase of ordinary intelligence. Popular government and especially parliamentary government means government by majorities, but the condition which gives moral impressiveness to a necessary though essentially awkward political arrangement is the feeling that the majority which passes a law or maintains a policy does virtually as we say represent the whole body of the nation[,] or in other words that[,] when the majority of the electors e.g. of England gives a decision[,] its judgment approaches very near to the expression of national unanimity and at some periods and under certain circumstances the voice of the majority is in substance the voice of the nation. Unless historians deceive us we may believe that this was so when on the 6th May 1789 the States General assembled at Paris; France we may say with truth desired a fundamental change in her institutions. So again we may assume that in 1832 the demand for Parliamentary reform was in England, though opposed by a minority (whose numbers were probably larger than we suppose), the demand of the nation. A similar remark applies to the votes which in Italy decreed the unity of the nation or to the acts more striking than any votes which in 1870 demonstrated the determination of Germany to resist and avenge the attacks of France. But we now know what the democrats of a century ago certainly did not know that a popular or parliamentary majority constantly represents nothing more than a slight balance of national opinion. We have no real voice of the nation, because intelligence and education have produced their natural result and produced differences of opinion. But where there is disagreement even virtual unanimity is impossible. Parliamentary majorities therefore have lost much of their moral weight and loss of moral weight means loss of power and authority.

Parliamentary government, therefore, because it rests upon public discussion, because it is ill suited for the carrying out of constructive legislation or for effective administration, and because we now know that the voice of the majority in or even out of Parliament constantly expresses rather a slight balance of public opinion than the deliberate will of the nation, has lost prestige and become exposed to criticism which easily turns into censure.

B. How Far is the Charge of Parliamentarism Justifiable?

The charges brought against the parliamentary form of government, in so far as they are due to the very general causes which I have enumerated, hardly justify the charge of Parliamentarism, but it must fairly be admitted that during the last 50 or 60 years the parliamentary system has betrayed at least two special flaws which were hardly perceived by the thinkers or politicians of the last generation.

I. Development of groups

The first of these is that the legislative bodies of all countries tend to break up into groups or factions, the existence of which makes the effective working of the parliamentary system difficult or impossible. This is a matter to which I have already called attention when examining the nature of parliamentary government. All that need now be said is that most, if not all, the evil consequences implied in the term Parliamentarism have their immediate cause in the existence of groups or factions which whether they be bound together by ties of self-interest or by common fanaticism have this in common: that they place the objects for whose attainment the group is formed above the maintenance of good government or of the general policy which most conduces to the interest of the nation[;] and we may fairly say that the existence of parliamentary groups is in many countries at least the immediate though not the original cause of the evils laid to the charge of parliamentary government.

To the baneful influence of groups or factions are immediately though hardly in the last resort due most of the grosser defects attributed to parliamentary government. To this source may be ascribed in England the decline of Parliamentary efficiency and of Parliamentary dignity. In France [to it may be ascribed] the feebleness of successive Cabinets, the intellectual and moral insignificance of French political leaders, and the enfeeblement if not the corruption of the whole administrative and judicial system[;] and in Italy [to it,] the combined feebleness, expensiveness, and corruption which makes even wise men wonder whether the country is not paying too high a price for the benefits of constitutional government.

II. Misrepresentation of the nation's will

The second and the least suspected defect of the parliamentary system is that a fairly elected Parliament may nevertheless fail to represent the wishes of the nation.

The assumption was made till recent times by every democrat and to a great extent admitted by persons who were not democrats that a fairly and properly elected Parliament must on all important matters represent the will of its electors. Even reformers or revolutionists who advocated a wide extension of the suffrage did, not so much dispute that members of an elective legislature who we may for simplicity's sake call members of Parliament represented the wishes of their constituents, as assert that the electoral bodies were so constituted as not fairly to represent the nation. Hence followed the conclusion on the part of democrats that members of Parliament fairly elected by universal suffrage would, assuming that the elections had been really free and subject neither to intimidation nor to corruption, in the main represent the wishes of the nation or at any rate of the majority. Now this assumption, reasonable enough as it seems in itself, and true as it must be within certain limits, is at any rate far less universally true than was supposed by the thinkers and the statesmen of the last generation. This is a point on which the experience of Switzerland is invaluable. The referendum, whatever its defects, does enable us to see how far the legislation of elected representatives corresponds with the wishes of the representatives by whom they were elected. The great experiment of referring laws to the arbitrament of the electors has at any rate produced this result. It has shown that the supposed correspondence between the wishes of the elector and the elected may often be a mere fiction. This too, remember, does not in Switzerland arise from any form of corruption. It does not arise from any special vice on the part of the Swiss representatives. The Swiss electors have constantly rejected legislation passed by their Parliament and have elected again as members of Parliament the very men whose laws they disapproved. Nor is this phenomenon really peculiar to Switzerland. I am speaking to an audience on this matter much better informed than myself, but it will not I fancy be disputed that in many States of the Union constitutional amendments framed by a fairly elected Constitutional Convention have been rejected by the people.

C. What are the Remedies for Parliamentarism?

Whoever attempts an answer to this question must never lose sight of one general consideration. It is this: the Parliaments of different countries exhibit defects which, because they have a certain general similarity, are attributed to the parliamentary system and may be summed up under the term Parliamentarism; but in matter of fact the defects of representative government in different countries are often essentially different in kind and are due to dissimilar causes; it is therefore idle to suppose that they all admit of any one cure. The condition of Italy, for example, differs fundamentally from the state of things in England and the true cure for the Parliamentary diseases of the one country differs therefore from the remedy for the Parliamentary maladies of the other. What Italy mainly needs is the introduction of sound and rational finance and the suppression of increasing corruption; the worst evils which can be imputed to the parliamentary system of England are a decline in the dignity of Parliament and an increasing want of backbone or independence in our public men. Hence the drastic measures of reform which may be needed at Rome would be quite out of place at Westminster.

Bearing this reflection in mind, let us examine two remedies for the defects of the parliamentary system which have obtained credit and which have in some countries been actually put into practice. The one is known as proportional representation, the other as the referendum.

I. Proportional representation

The fundamental principle of the system known as 'Proportional Representation' is that the political opinions prevailing in a country ought, as far as possible, to be represented in its Legislative Assembly, or Parliament, in the proportion in which they exist throughout the country, or, to put the same thing in a more concrete shape, that all the opinions existing in a constituency which returns representatives to the legislature, e.g. in Boston or New York, should be proportionally represented in the Senate and Assembly of either country.

The advocates of this system maintain, and I conceive with undeniable truth, that their fundamental principle is violated in every country, and certainly in England. They also maintain, and as it appears with great plausibility, that arrangements can be devised by which the opinions either of a country or of a given constituency may be represented in the legislature in at any rate a near approach to the proportion in which they exist in such country or constituency.

Oddly enough it so happens that it is round these subordinate contentions that the battle for and against proportional representation has mainly raged. This I conceive is strange because on the issues here joined there appears to be little ground for rational dispute. No one can doubt that in a given constituency which, as is often the case in England, returns only one member, the political views of, it may be, nearly half of the voters are not represented. No one again I think can dispute that there may very well be in the English House of Commons a Conservative or a Liberal majority larger than would exist if the whole electorate of England could be assembled together and, like the Athenian Assembly, vote in person. Nor in spite of the ingenious criticisms suggested by opponents is it easy to believe that human ingenuity may not invent electoral machinery which will give in a representative assembly something like proportionate representation to the opinions which exist throughout the country.

The essential question is, whether the fundamental principle of proportional representation be sound. Is it or is it not desirable, that opinions be represented in Parliament in the proportion in which they exist throughout the country?

To this single inquiry I shall direct your attention and for the sake of simplicity I shall discuss it with a view to the English House of Commons though the principles of discussion apply more or less to all representative legislatures.[1]

The apparent strength of the case in favour of proportional representation is obvious. A 'representative' assembly ought to 'represent', but under the present system the opinions, either of a constituency or of the whole country, are 'misrepresented' rather than represented if they do not reappear in their proper proportion in the House of Commons. If, to take a simple instance, there are in Oxford about 4,000 Conservatives as against 3,500 Liberals the one Conservative member who sits for the town assuredly does not represent the opinion of Oxford. That every opinion entertained by any section of the people should have fair weight given to it in the House of Commons is of the essence of representative government, but under the present system opinions entertained by minorities scattered throughout the country may in the House obtain either inadequate attention or no attention at all. The public discussion of unpopular or unsound theories is an essential part of national education, but in an assembly where all opinions are not fairly represented you cannot be sure that any opinion will receive adequate discussion. Proportional representation is, in short, needed to ensure adequate representation, freedom of discussion, and the national education which is ensured by public debate.

Yet the replies to a case which is apparently very strong will be found to deserve the gravest consideration; they all turn on the consideration that the real object, the real matter to be kept in mind in constituting a Parliament, is not the carrying out of any abstract theory, but the constituting of a body fit to perform the functions at once legislative and governmental for the sake of which the British Parliament at any rate exists.

---

[1] The issue may be thus summarised. The case for proportional representation rests on three propositions:

(i) Political opinions are not represented in the House of Commons or in any English constituency in the proportion in which they exist in the country or in a given constituency. This proposition is undeniably true.

(ii) Machinery has been or may be invented by which opinions may be represented in the House of Commons more nearly in the proportion in which they exist throughout the United Kingdom. This proposition again is almost certainly true. It is no confutation of it to say that no scheme of proportional representation is absolutely perfect.

(iii) It is expedient that the opinions of the country or the opinions of a given constituency be represented in the House of Commons in the proportion in which they exist in such country or constituency. The truth of this proposition is the point at issue.

The replies to the advocates of proportional representation may take two lines.

First—It may, for the sake of argument, be conceded that proportional representation would be desirable, were it not that the means for its attainment involve evils greater than the benefits which could be expected from the suggested reform.

This is in fact the line taken by Bagehot.[2] His criticisms apply directly only to one particular form of proportional representation, but indirectly they attack the whole system. Any elaborate and artificial scheme, he in effect urges, for the election of members of Parliament in fact requires for its working careful management and management in electoral matters means the supremacy of managers or wire-pullers. A constituency for example is called upon at a moment of political excitement, such as has been caused by the conflict about Home Rule in England, to elect members of Parliament. The very essence of any scheme of proportional representation is to give the freest scope to individual choice, in other words to render it very uncertain how the election will go, but Unionists and Home Rulers alike are determined if possible to gain a victory. Some system of voting will have to be arranged so as to prevent waste of party power, but the arrangement of this system means nothing less than management and the supremacy of managers. I know that this will be disputed, but anyone who has kept his eyes open and has observed what electors and elections are will assent to the conclusion that the apparent freedom of individuals under an elaborate system of election means an increase of party management and the increased power of managers.

Secondly—Proportional representation, it may be urged, is in itself undesirable.

Its advocates are the slaves of the word 'representation'. The House of Commons is not a discussion forum. It is in reality part of the government of the country. Legislation itself is action as may be seen at once when the House is called upon to pass a so-called Coercion Act, to suspend the Habeas Corpus Acts, or the like. But the House not only legislates it appoints and within certain limits controls the executive. The true question to be considered is whether its vigour would or would not be increased by the proportionate representation of opinion. No one can hesitate to answer this question in the negative. A government with a small or a fluctuating majority is a weak government, but division of opinions involves the existence of small and fluctuating majorities. From the moment you recognise that a legislative body is to a great extent a governing body the case for accurate representation of opinions falls to the ground. Under our present system at any rate it would be simple madness to constitute a Cabinet in which you have a proportionate representation of every political party. Such a Cabinet could not govern.

Opinions, it is said, ought to be represented. If it be meant that every opinion which is entertained by a large number of electors should obtain a hearing, this assertion is roughly true. But it does not follow that for the purpose of being heard in the House of Commons an opinion should obtain proportionate representation. Let us suppose that a tenth of the British electors are anti-vaccinationists. On the theory of proportional representation there ought to be nearly 70 anti-vaccinationists seated

---

[2] Bagehot, *English Constitution*, pp 150–157.

in the House of Commons, but for the purpose of discussion, that is for stating the fallacies or arguments of anti-vaccinationists, 10 members are as good as 70.

But the attempt to represent opinions is of itself an error. The comparison between an assembly of the whole English nation and a House of Commons in which the different opinions of the English people are proportionately represented is fallacious. There is this vital difference. The representatives of an opinion or a 'cause' will tend to put the interest of their cause above every other consideration. A man who simply holds an opinion will constantly subordinate it to his other beliefs or convictions. Sixty anti-vaccinationists elected as anti-vaccinationists would it is morally certain hold that their one duty was to promote the repeal of the vaccination laws. But a man or body of men not so elected might well enough on the subject say of Home Rule set aside their convictions about vaccination and vote as Unionists or Home Rulers. Add to this that, politics being what they are, the temptation to the representatives of different and even incongruous opinions to coalesce together for the promotion of the objects to which they were each devoted would be almost irresistible. Imagine a House of Commons in which special opinions were proportionately represented: there would be say 60 anti-vaccinationists, 100 anti-vivisectionists, 100 Disestablishment men, 100 Fair Traders, and the like. We know what would happen. The more genuine the belief of each section in its particular cause the more certain their coalition. It is quite conceivable that in a House meant to represent opinions measures would constantly be carried which were opposed to the judgment of the vast majority of the nation: and this might be the case even though the members of each group acted with perfect honesty, but it were vain to assume that fanaticism would not often join hands with egotism or self-interest. The disease of modern Parliaments is the formation of groups who place their own objects above the general interest of the nation. But the representation of opinions is nothing less than the artificial creation of groups. If the matter be explored to the bottom the fallacy of proportional representation lies in the idea that a legislative body such as the House of Commons exists primarily for the sake of discussion or for the formation of opinion. It is not a debating club; it is not a school; it is part of the government, and the decisive, even exaggerated, authority of majorities is a necessary condition for giving to a representative assembly the force needed for governmental action. Whatever be the merits of proportional representation, it offers no cure for Parliamentarism.

II. *The referendum*

The essence of the referendum—an institution, I may add, which exists, in reality though not in name, in the United States no less than in Switzerland, is that the passing of important laws and especially of laws touching the constitution needs the sanction of the electors. It places the electorate in the position once occupied in England by the Crown; it is the nation's veto.

The recommendations to this system may be thus summarised.

It establishes the only conservative check on legislation which is clearly in harmony with those democratic principles which in the modern world form the moral bases of government.

It calls upon the mass of the people to pronounce just that kind of judgment of which alone they are in reality capable. It never has been and, whatever be the spread of education, it never will be the case that the mass of a nation can devise good legislation or pass judgment upon its details, but it is the case in a well ordered community that men of average education and capacity can form an opinion for or against an extensive change in the constitution or even the adoption of a new policy by the nation. This distinction between knowing how to do a particular thing which is the function of an expert and pronouncing whether a particular thing shall be done which is often the proper duty of a man with no special training is elementary and holds good both in public and in private life. The electors it will be said would be guided by their wishes. This is partially true and is an inherent defect of popular government, but as regards legislation it is constantly necessary to take into account the feelings of the people. The referendum is a conservative, and may become an obstructive, arrangement. But one can mention many laws which either ought never to have been passed or ought never to have been repealed. The maxim 'more haste, worse speed' has a very wide application.

The referendum has one supreme merit. It cuts at the root of parliamentary intrigue; it enables the people to override the machinations of politicians; it impresses upon every member of the state the principle that party systems are merely means for the promotion of good government, and that behind and above parties lies the will of the nation.

The nation's veto is open, however, to objections which are not without force.

It is in the strictest sense a conservative institution, for it places an obstacle in the way of change. Whether, therefore, it is likely to produce good effects depends at bottom upon the condition of a given country. There are undoubtedly lands in which the obstacles to progress which must involve change are far too great. Maine is right in pointing out that in certain stages of English history the referendum could have produced nothing but harm. Its existence in the 17th or 18th century might have retarded by 50 years the progress of religious liberty. But this does not prove that there may not be countries where the constitution has ceased to supply a protection against inconsiderate or sudden change. It is at least maintainable that this is so in modern England.

The referendum again, it may be said, is at best useless, since a fairly constituted and fairly elected Parliament must represent the wishes of the nation. The answer to this objection is that modern experience shows that the assumption on which it rests is unfounded. The Swiss Republic is a democracy. The Swiss people are fairly represented. The Swiss Parliament is as respected and respectable a body as any representative assembly, yet it has constantly happened that laws passed by the Swiss Parliament have been rejected by the Swiss people, and what is more surprising the electors who have rejected a law passed by their representatives have after this reelected as representatives the men whose legislation they have vetoed. In itself there is nothing inconsistent in this conduct. A sensible gentleman may refuse on a particular point to take the advice of his solicitor, [and] he may rightly continue to employ a good man of business though he has refused in one instance to follow his counsel. It is the weakness of parliamentary constitutionalism as it exists in England, France, or Italy to foster the absurd notion that the nation cannot make use of a Minister's ability and character unless the nation is on every occasion prepared to follow his advice. However this may be, experience certainly negatives the assumption that a properly constituted and freely elected legislature will invariably represent the wishes of the electors.

The veto of the people in this resembling the veto of the Crown must, it is said, diminish the importance of Parliament. The assertion is true but to any critic who is alive to the evils of Parliamentarism such an objection must sound irrelevant. That the referendum diminishes the importance of Parliament and limits the sphere of parliamentary intrigue must to such a critic seem its great recommendation.

The advocates of a national veto are sometimes met by the assertion that it will lessen the independence of members of Parliament; many a man will vote for a measure which he does not approve in the hope or the expectation that it will be rejected by the people. Such a man, it is supposed, may argue that, though holding himself e.g. that vaccination ought to be enforced, it is right to give the people an opportunity of passing judgment on the question whether the vaccination of infants shall be enforced by the law of the land. This objection has some real force. There is little doubt that the referendum would to some slight degree diminish an MP's sense of personal responsibility for the vote he gives in respect of any matter which will be submitted to the electors for their approval. But if the referendum diminishes, from one side, a representative's sense of responsibility for his vote, it may, on the other side, increase his independence and his honesty. A representative who now votes for any law is almost constrained to pretend that he himself thinks the law expedient. Hence the wearisome and demoralising efforts on the part of parliamentary politicians to make it appear that actions really dictated by the fear of offending electors and losing seats are the legitimate result of principles which condemn the policy of the legislation which an MP supports. Under the system of the popular veto an MP will be able to take up a different and far more honest position. He may vote against a measure and give his reasons for disapproving of it, but, when once it has been submitted to and sanctioned by the electors, not only may he give up opposition, but he may frankly accept and carry out a policy which, though he does not think it a wise policy, has received the sanction of the nation. When a man acts under the orders of another, there is nothing ignominious or dishonest in his carrying out a course of action which he himself thinks imprudent. No one blames a Permanent Under-Secretary of State for zealously executing the orders now of a Conservative and now of a Radical Minister. No one supposes that a solicitor cannot honestly draft a will or a settlement because he thinks its provisions unwise or imprudent. It is the pretence that a statesman approves of a policy which in his heart he condemns, that entails disgrace. Under the system of the referendum there would be no need for pretence. In England at least it might go very far towards introducing among parliamentary leaders an honesty and outspokenness which does not always characterise even the most eminent of our statesmen.

Conclusion

Whoever has seriously reflected on the lessons suggested by the comparative study of constitutions must hesitate greatly before he presses on the public any mechanical change (such for example as the introduction of proportional representation or the referendum) as a panacea for the evils of popular government. More or less mechanical changes may, it is true, occasionally cure or mitigate diseases which themselves flow from vicious constitutional arrangements. It is easy for example to perceive that the obvious reform of reducing the number of the English House of Commons, though it is a change which will certainly never be carried out, would raise the character of our Parliamentary life. It is clear again that the rule, forbidding a Minister of the English Crown to address the House of Parliament of which he is not a member, is foolish and impolitic, and that its abrogation would be beneficial. A stranger may venture to assert that the United States suffer greatly from the rule or habit which makes it impossible for a Senator or a member of Congress to represent any State or District in which he does not live. It is not too much to say that the existence of such a custom would have been fatal in England to the amendment of the law, or the reform of the constitution, and that any American party who should succeed in breaking down an irrational habit would render a great benefit to the country, but, when all this is granted, the reflection must haunt the mind of every thoughtful man that constitutional changes or constitutions themselves can work but a limited effect. The best result of a well constructed constitution is to set free the forces of the nation and above all to give free scope in the sphere of public life to what is at best [sic] in the morality of the country. Do the institutions of a country really bring the strength and virtue of the country into the service of the state? If they do this the institutions are, whatever be their form, good. If they do not they are, however artfully contrived, bad. But no institutions can create strength which does not exist. The plain truth is that the working of constitutions depends at bottom upon the character of the citizens among whom they exist. Almost any institutions may work with success where you have good men and good citizens. Holland flourished during the 17th century though the Dutch Constitution was not a model which anyone would follow. But no constitution will give prosperity to a nation which does not contain in its ranks large bodies of men marked by good sense, by zeal for justice, and by public spirit.

9

General Conclusions

Analysis[*]

A. The Extent to which Prosperity of Country Dependent upon Constitution
 1. Difference of opinion between last and present century
 2. Constitution cannot give strength which does not exist, but may aid national development
 3. Defective constitution impediment to national development
 Holy Roman Empire; Swiss Confederacy; American colonies under Articles of Confederation
 (Fiske, *Critical Period of American History*, ch. IV)

B. Apparent Similarity and Essential Difference between Different Modern Constitutions
 I. *Similarity*
 1. Form
 2. Democratic basis
 3. Substitution of written for conventional constitutions
 II. *Difference*
 1. Constitutions with parliamentary executive, and
 2. Constitutions with non-parliamentary executive

C. Different Types of Constitutionalism
 1. Parliamentary constitutionalism
 2. Democratic constitutionalism
 3. Monarchical constitutionalism

D. Difficulties of Modern Constitutionalism
 1. In some countries want of support from whole of nation
 2. In all decline in authority of representative assemblies

E. Any Institution may become Embodiment of Nation
 1. Parliament in England
 2. Executive and administration in France
 3. Reigning family in Prussia
 4. Church in Scotland
 (Compare on this point Scotch Parliament and Irish Parliament)

---

[*] Its contents have been derived from a manuscript recorded, in a later manuscript note, to be for a lecture on 17 May 1897 and attached to the lecture scheme headed 'Easter and Trinity Terms, 1897', which has been the source of most of the Analyses above.

General Conclusions*

To anyone who studies political institutions from a comparative point of view two leading questions will sooner or later present themselves.

First Question—To what extent does the prosperity of a country in reality depend upon its constitution?

On no point are the differences between the prevalent sentiment or opinion of the eighteenth century and the prevalent sentiment or opinion of the nineteenth century more markedly different than on the reply which ought to be given to this inquiry.

It is hardly an exaggeration to say that at any rate during the latter half of the eighteenth century everyone who thought about politics at all believed that a country's political constitution determined its fortunes. What the constitution of a country ought to be, whether an ideal polity was to be discovered really suited for all civilized lands, whether in constructing a constitution it was best to be guided by considerations based on abstract reasoning or by considerations resting upon history, whether we ought to frame institutions in accordance with the natural rights of man, or whether the wise course was to measure the value of every law by constant reference to the principles of utility, were matters on which individuals and schools disagreed, but men of all politics and of all schools[,] Tories, Whigs, Republicans, or Revolutionists, thinkers so different as Rousseau, Montesquieu, Burke, and Bentham, all, it may be taken, really agreed in the doctrine that the character and fate of nations were more or less moulded by their political institutions. Montesquieu's assertion that the wonderful system of government existing among the English was discovered in the forests of Germany, and that the English constitution alone had for its direct object the preservation of political liberty, Rousseau's declaration that 'man is born free but is everywhere in chains', Burke's religious not to say superstitious reverence for all the mysteries or paradoxes contained in the constitution of England, Bentham's enthusiasm for legislation based on the principle of utility, all rest on the one common assumption of the supreme importance to be attributed to political institutions. Nor did this feeling, in England at least, cease to prevail with the end of the last century. The Whigs of 1832 were not fanatics yet their fervent belief in the Reform Bill and the blessings which it was to bring upon England is hardly comprehensible to the men of today. We are startled when we find a man such as Lord Cockburn burst into unexpected thanks to Heaven because the Whigs were in power and when we read of a woman such as Mrs. Fletcher that it was some consolation

---

* The manuscript's first page was dated 17 May 1897 in a later manuscript note. The lecture text was altered, in places, either before or after that date. Dicey's broad institutional focus in his comparative constitutional lectures was qualified by the institutional scepticism he expressed in this concluding lecture. See Editor's Introduction, pp xxvi ff, xxx ff, xxxiv f. above.

even to a mother when grieving over the death of a son that he had lived just long enough to see the dawn of Parliamentary reform for Scotland. Even in the pages of Tocqueville though he belongs in date wholly to the nineteenth century, we still can trace the latent conviction that institutions determine the character of nations at least as much as the character of nations creates their institutions.

Since the earlier part of this century public opinion has undergone a change. The sentiment to which Carlyle's writings have given the best known expression in England, that constitutions are matters of small consequence, has become gradually prevalent. Into the causes of this change there is no need here to enter; they are various, such for example as the influence of historical study, the weight exerted if not by the ideas yet by the phrases of physical science, and the smallness or the apparent smallness of the direct advantage conferred on the masses by political improvements. No doubt the old belief in the importance of institutions has not vanished; it has rather taken a new form. The innovators of today are more bent on the achievement of social than of constitutional revolutions, but the faith and the power of legislation to transform or renovate society is neither more nor less rational on the part of a Socialist than a Republican. But however this may be the fact is undeniable that we attribute far less direct importance than did our fathers or grandfathers to a nation's constitution.

To say that opinion on a given subject has varied is not at all the same thing as proving that a recent or prevailing belief is more near the truth than the creed which it has superseded, and it is well to consider carefully how far, despite changes of opinion, a state's prosperity does or does not depend upon its political institutions.

The answer to this question, as far as it can be given at all, may be summed up in two statements.

A good constitution assuredly cannot give to a nation, which is after all nothing but a name for a large number of men occupying a common territory and more or less linked together by connections of blood and history, virtues which the individual citizens do not possess.

The institutions of the United States and of other countries have great merits, but they assuredly will not give to uncivilized or half-civilized people the virtues of Englishmen or of American citizens. The idea, for example, that the Federation of the United States can be transplanted to Spanish South America and there create a nation as powerful and orderly as the United States is an absurdity. The notion that the English constitution which is the product of very peculiar historical conditions would suit every country of civilized Europe is one of those delusions which is not ridiculous only because it has possessed the minds and guided the policy of statesmen otherwise entitled to deep respect. Nor is it the case that a constitution which in itself may have great merits is merely harmless when introduced into countries the inhabitants where of are not fit for it. Such a constitution may when so introduced work infinite evil. The imitations for example of the so-called free institutions of the United States which have been attempted in South America have retarded the progress towards civilization which the population of that country might otherwise have made. Popular government can never exist in reality in countries where order and obedience to law which are the foundations of civilized society have not as yet been established, and the attempt to found popular government may well only prolong periods of anarchy or of despotism. Thus much we may safely assert. The constitution of a state is never the source of its strength. Wherever you find a good constitution that works well there you may be certain that there exists a people many of whom are endowed with high civic virtues.

A bad constitution, on the other hand, may impede or arrest the development of a state or nation.

The merit of political arrangements will be found in the main to consist in their giving free play to the strong and healthy parts of the social organism or, what will be found to be nearly the same thing, in their placing power in the hands of the vigorous and therefore the powerful portion of a community. Now that bad institutions, by which I mean either institutions which were originally or have become by degrees unsuitable for the development of a given society, may greatly hinder its prosperity is a fact almost past dispute. The long weakness of Germany and the incapacity of the German people for resisting the inroads of foreigners cannot be attributed to any special vice of the German people, or to any inherent incapacity for political organization. The Holy Roman Empire was for centuries a bar to the progress of Germany. Its existence was enough to prevent the growth of national unity, yet the Emperors were not strong enough to establish for effective purposes their own supremacy. The weakness of the Empire meant the power of the nobility. Of course the defects may always be referred back to antecedent conditions. Still the fact remains that the constitution, first, of the German Empire and, then, of the Confederation stood in the way of German unity and German prosperity. One may fairly say that, at any rate since the fall of Napoleon, the efforts of Germans have been directed towards the creation of a constitution which should consolidate instead of dispers[e] the forces of the nation and that the attainment of this end, though still incomplete, has shown that a suitable constitution may almost at once develop the strength of a state. Nowhere are the effects of bad and of good constitutional arrangements more plainly visible than in the history of Switzerland. The Swiss are a nation who have ever since the rise of the Confederacy proved that the population of Switzerland possessed in a very high degree the faculties which tend towards national greatness. Their martial prowess has been at all times the admiration of Europe. The Swiss Republics small as they are in size have diffused political training throughout the people. It is a noteworthy fact that no Swiss canton or Swiss city has ever suffered from a tyrant, yet the defective institutions of Switzerland prevented the country from obtaining when at the height of its military repute the substantial results of victory. The Reformation, by the introduction of religious differences, arrested the progress towards unity, but the permanence of the divisions which divided the country and made Switzerland at one time all but the dependent of France were assuredly fostered by the Constitution which prevented the existence of anything like a strong central power. For a century or more the Swiss have consciously desired national unity, yet their institutions made it all but impossible to give effect to the will of the nation. The short-lived Helvetic unitary Republic, the form of federation imposed by Napoleon, the lax federal bond established after the fall of the French Empire, did not meet the real wants of the Swiss people. The *Sonderbund* war all but split the state in pieces. The vigour and rapidity with which secession was suppressed gave the Swiss people the means of forming a constitution suited for their needs. The federal government of 1848 has, unlike most of the political experiments of that year, been a permanent success. The ease with which it has from time to time been modified reveals the strength of its foundations, and prosperity has followed the creation of a good constitution. There are many things in the condition of Switzerland, such for example as the differences of race, of religion, and of language, which suggest the impossibility of maintaining the unity, the independence, and the prosperity of the country. Yet for now all but fifty years Switzerland has exhibited all the outward signs of a united and progressive community. This, it may be said, is due to the virtues of the people, and, as already pointed out, it is certainly true that institutions cannot supply the qualities by which alone any people can make even good institutions work with tolerable success. But there is no reason to think that the Swiss, say of 1815 or of 1846, were in any way inferior to the Swiss of today. If we ask what was the circumstance which for 40 years rendered Switzerland a weak state distracted by discords ending in civil war we must answer—the defects of the Swiss Constitution. If we ask why it is that for 50 years Switzerland has been the home of liberty, order, and progress, we must answer that the immediate cause is the possession by Switzerland of a good constitution.

If, however, we look for the most signal instance of the evils which a bad and the blessings which a good political constitution may at times confer upon a people we ought to study the history of the American Colonies during the period which elapsed between the acknowledgment of their independence and the creation of the United States. This has well been termed the critical period of American history. The colonists in their contest with England, and their descendants since the time when the Constitution of the United States was accepted by the Colonies, have shown, as indeed anyone would have anticipated, that Englishmen settled on the American Continent had inherited all the political capacity of the nation to which they belonged. Yet during the six years or so which immediately followed on the termination of the War of Independence intelligent observers of the course of events may well have doubted whether separation from England was not about to prove the ruin of the Colonies which had asserted their independence. They drifted, as the expression goes, towards anarchy.[1] Their national credit sunk to nothing; their powerlessness was visible even to the pirates of Tripoli. The Barbary States not only defied the independent Colonies but demanded from them blackmail. Congress had no means of enforcing the laws or resolutions which it passed. New York and New Jersey carried on a war of protective tariffs. There were armed outbreaks in the Green Mountains; there was insurrection in Massachusetts. It became in fact a question whether the Colonies were to be thirteen hostile states or one united nation. The answer to it was given by the foundation of the

---

[1] See especially Fiske, *Critical Period of American History*, pp 134–186.

United States. Note that the Constitution was introduced with great difficulty and that from the very first the existence of negro slavery and the essential differences between the civilization of New England which was essentially democratic and the civilization of the Southern States which was essentially oligarchical made the working of the new Constitution difficult. Yet the new Constitution saved the country. It gave to the thirteen States unity, peace, and power. Note too that there was nothing changed in the character of the people. If we look at the state as a mere aggregate of individuals we must admit that the men who formed citizens of the United States were exactly the same persons as the men who under the Articles of the Confederation had been citizens of the separate state. No doubt the feelings which produced the Constitution, or in other words the gradual predominance of national sentiment, may be termed, if you like it, the ultimate cause of the prosperity of the Union. But it was the Constitution of the United States which made it possible for the sentiment of nationality to produce its proper effect and also in turn fostered and increased the feelings to which the Constitution owed its birth. As the ill conceived arrangements instituted by the Articles of Confederation all but brought about the ruin, so the Constitution of the United States was the proximate cause of the prosperity of the American people. The admiration of American for their institutions has excited the amusement of more than one satirist, but this admiration had its ground in the well founded belief that the Constitution of the United States had in fact secured the prosperity of the nation.

A constitution is, as has often been said, the vestment of a nation. A suit of armour will not change a weakling into a warrior, but the strength of a giant may be rendered useless by a strait waistcoat.

Second Question—What general conclusions is it possible to draw from a comparison of different polities?

There are three or four such conclusions which appear to be true and to possess a certain importance.

I. All modern constitutions possess a certain similarity

They all include a Parliament consisting wholly or in part of an elected House or Chamber. They mostly though not invariably more or less imitate the forms of English constitutionalism. You find in them an executive whether a King or President who more or less occupies the position of a constitutional King. You also find in general two Houses, consisting of an upper or select Chamber which under whatever name it passes is intended to fulfil some of the functions of the House of Lords, and a lower or more democratic House which, as it directly represents the people, resembles the English House of Commons. To this House generally belongs the sole right of initiative as regards the granting of taxes. In most countries further where parliamentary government exists it will be found that the magistrates possess what is ordinarily called judicial independence. Almost invariably in theory the judges exercise their judicial functions free from the control or the interference of the executive. The government moreover and the legislature in theory at any rate abstain in most countries from the exercise of judicial duties. The doctrine of the separation of powers has, taken in one sense, been pretty nearly accepted by the civilized world.

Modern constitutions again resemble one another in resting upon a democratic basis. In some shape or other the majority of the citizens generally obtain representation and, what is a matter of more consequence, the feeling prevails or tends to prevail among the people of most civilized countries that the numerical majority of the citizens have a right to rule. No sane man believes that majorities are always right just as no sane man has ever believed that a King was always wise and good. But the mass of men, throughout the civilized states of Europe as also throughout the United States of America, feel that the voice of the people, that is of the majority, is the source of legitimate authority. A faith in the divine right of the majority has substituted itself for a faith in the divine right of Kings.

It is further obvious that on the whole written or enacted constitutions are gradually superseding unwritten or conventional constitutions. The reasons for this change are complex. One cause has not received the attention which it deserves. The progress of democracy accompanied by an extension of the suffrage means the transference of power from a limited class to the whole or something like the whole of a large nation. But this transfer is of itself unfavourable to the maintenance of mere constitutional understandings. As long as the powers of the state were either vested in or practically exercised by a small body of citizens, as for example in the vague body of persons who in England would be called the gentry, the citizens who ruled the state were in fact influenced by the same notions of fairness and expediency, of the right way of conducting business, and the like. It was therefore easy and natural for them to act on tacit agreements which everyone conformed to almost as a matter of course. Strict community of feeling will often make formal compacts or laws unnecessary. But when political power becomes vested in and is more or less exercised by the whole people, it follows that different classes who do not share exactly the same notions of fairness or political expediency take part in public life and do not in many respects understand one another[.] [W]hen once this state of things exist[,] understandings or tacit conventions are difficult to form and still more difficult to maintain. It is a necessity that matters, which were regulated by common feelings or habits, should now be governed by definite agreements, fixed rules, or laws. Then too it must be remembered that a constitution grounded on tacit understandings is necessarily the work of time. A new constitution must be a written constitution, and an unwritten constitution which for one reason or another has ceased to work easily must give way to a new or written constitution. Constitutions such as those of England or of Hungary were once common; they are now pretty nearly the only unwritten constitutions to be found in Europe.

II. Modern parliamentary governments exhibit under all their apparent similarity marked and essential differences

An observer may note at least three types of constitutionalism, which may conveniently though not perhaps with strict accuracy be termed parliamentary constitutionalism, democratic constitutionalism, and monarchical constitutionalism.

(These three types however, though essentially different, tend to shade off into one another and one may easily find countries as to which one may fairly doubt whether they are governed on the parliamentary, the democratic, or the monarchical system.)

The essence of parliamentary constitutionalism is this: the Parliament is while it exists the sovereign power in the state. Where the party system is completely carried out the whole authority of the nation is for the time transferred to the representative body, and the Parliament, however it be constituted, is for the time able in theory to do any act which the nation might do. Hence the Parliament is, to use foreign terms, a constituent assembly authorised if need be to change the constitution. It is also the body which really and in substance appoints the executive. For our present purpose it is not necessary or desirable to define with any precision the nature of sovereignty, or to consider the minor limitations by which, even in countries where parliamentary constitutionalism exists, the actual power of the Parliament and especially of the most democratic part thereof may be limited. All we need note is that there are countries, such as England, France, Belgium, or Italy where under very different forms the Houses of Parliament and especially the most democratic Chamber thereof are whilst they exist the chief power in the State. As we are talking only of parliamentary governments, it of course will be understood that behind the Houses of Parliament stand the electors or in popular language, the people, and that therefore the constitutional omnipotence ascribed e.g. to the English Houses of Parliament, and especially to the House of Commons, is subject in practice to great limitations. All that is meant is that both theoretically and practically the Parliaments of the countries we have mentioned do exercise the authority of the state and exercise it not only in legislation but even more in the appointment and dismissal of the real executive.

The essential feature of democratic constitutionalism is that under the constitution the mass of the citizens or the electors remain in effect the supreme and sovereign power. The Parliament or legislature admittedly does not possess anything like the full authority of the state. It is not a sovereign body. It is both in theory and in fact the agent of the people and an agent acting under limited authority. It has neither unlimited power of legislation nor has it anything like full control of the executive. Democratic constitutionalism may itself take very different forms. The democracy of Switzerland exercises its authority in methods which in many respects are not the same as the means by which the democracy of the United States retains power in its own hands. The parliamentary institutions, if we may call them so, of Switzerland have grown up in a country which has never historically known parliamentary government as it exists in England. The parliamentary institutions of the United States have been inherited by the American people from their English forefathers, yet under all the dissimilarities, some of which are very great, it will be found that neither in Switzerland nor in America do the people ever mean to vest full authority in any Parliament or legislature. No legislature throughout the Union has unlimited power of legislation. As time passes the checks placed on the legislative authority of the State legislatures become more and more narrow. Neither the President nor the Governor of any State is elected by a legislative body. This is the reason why everyone almost instinctively avoids giving either to the Houses of Congress or to the Houses of Assembly of New York or Massachusetts the name of Parliaments. What is true of the United States is true in essence of Switzerland. In the European even more markedly than in the American Republic the people take the task of law-making into their own hands. The democracy neither of America nor of Switzerland favours the supremacy of Parliament.

The essence of monarchical constitutionalism is that large powers, especially as regards matters of administration, are vested in a monarch or single and generally hereditary ruler who does not derive his authority from the legislative body or Parliament. In a country such as Prussia where this kind of constitutionalism exists, the monarch, it is true, is not absolute for in respect of legislation he must act in combination with some kind of parliamentary assembly; but he is in truth the chief of the state. His prerogatives are in reality a check upon the authority of Parliament. The monarchical form of parliamentary government exists at the present day chiefly if not exclusively in countries where a King or Prince, who was at one time an absolute ruler, has either voluntarily or under the pressure of circumstances granted to his people representative institutions. But it is quite possible that the kind of polity with which we are now occupied may exist without an hereditary monarch. The English Protectorate, the French Consulate, the condition of things in France which existed after the *coup d'état* of the 2nd December and before the Proclamation of the Second Empire, to which we may perhaps even add the Second French Republic during the Presidency of Louis Napoleon, all afford examples of constitutions which, though they contained a representative legislative assembly or Parliament, also gave great powers to a single ruler who was not an hereditary monarch. These instances no doubt all belong to times of revolution, but it is by no means inconceivable that, even under a well organised Commonwealth and still more under a monarchy the head of which had at one time been an absolute King, the monarchical type of constitutionalism should have as much permanence as belongs to any kind of political institution.

No doubt the three forms of constitutionalism here described tend at times to blend one with the other. It is, however, worth notice that there is in reality a closer affinity between democratic and monarchical constitutionalism than between either of them and the fully developed parliamentary system. Whether the people as in America or in Switzerland directly limit the functions of representative assemblies, or, as in Prussia and in France during the existence of the Napoleonic Empire treat one man whether you call him King, President, or Emperor, as the true representative of the nation, parliamentary constitutionalism as understood in modern England cannot exist. True parliamentary sovereignty is inconsistent with the political predominance of one man who does not owe his position to parliamentary support.

III. Parliamentary government, we might almost say constitutional government, labours at the present day under difficulties which are great and novel

In no civilized country is there at the moment indeed any reason to suppose that the representative assembly will be overthrown. The perils of parliamentary government do not spring, as they have arisen at former times, from the imminence of revolution or of a *coup d'état*.

The true danger is that the moral authority of representative bodies should vanish. The immediate causes of this peril are different in different countries. In some lands, such as France and Italy, the constitution has failed to enlist anything like the support of the whole nation. Italy affords a most striking example of my meaning. The political unity of the country is due to Kings and statesmen whose whole fame depends on the creation or maintenance of constitutional government, but the body of 'active citizens' (to use a French expression), that is of citizens who enjoy full political rights, is in Italy small. This would not of itself be of paramount importance. It may well happen, as was the case in England up to 1832, we might almost say up to 1884, that a limited body of electors fairly represented the will of the country. But in Italy this notoriously is not so. Genuine Catholics, who are really guided by the commands of the Pope, do not exercise their political rights as electors, and it may reasonably be believed that any extension of the franchise would add greatly to the number of ardent Catholics among the electorate. And the same thing, though of course in a much slighter degree, holds good of France[:] as long as convinced Catholics and strenuous conservatives do not take their share in political contests, it is impossible to say that the Italian constitutional monarchy or the French Republic can count on the assured support of the nation[;] and, on the other hand, if in France or in Italy the genuine Catholics once exert the influence to which they are entitled by their numbers and position, it may be doubted whether the Republic or the House of Savoy will stand. The perils, however, to popular government which are of necessity incidental to the establishment of liberal or democratic institutions by means of a revolution have been overcome at other times in other countries, and may, it is possible, pass away. The more subtle cause of the weakness which at this moment infects popular governments is the spread of the political disease known abroad as 'Parliamentarism'. This is at bottom nothing less than the growing distrust of or contempt for representative institutions. That this sentiment is widespread can hardly be questioned by any candid observer. The awe and dignity which used to surround Parliaments has, even in England, greatly decreased; in other countries it has all but vanished. No one really supposes that in France or Italy the representative bodies are greatly trusted or greatly admired. In Switzerland there is possibly no conscious contempt for the Federal Assembly, but the whole course of events since 1848 shows that the Swiss people are bent upon limiting the powers of their representatives. This tendency to distrust the very men in which the country, since it elects them, is supposed to place confidence is nowhere so patent as in the United States. The extreme rigidity of the national constitution, which hardly admits of change without something like a revolution, has barred attempts to curtail the powers of Congress. Nor would it be possible to limit Congressional authority without strengthening State rights at the expense of the national government, and this is a course of action which as long as the memory of Secession lasts will never be sanctioned by the most powerful States of the Union. If anyone wants to see how strongly the current of popular feeling runs against anything like Parliamentary supremacy, he should note the way in which each change in the Constitution of any State—and such changes are frequent—means the restriction of the authority of the legislature. Into the cause of this low estimate of Parliaments it is not necessary here to enter. The one thing to note is that genuinely representative assemblies fairly elected by the votes of the citizens may yet cease to represent the wishes, and still more to embody the spirit, of the nation. But here we come across the most weighty of the thoughts suggested by the comparative study of constitutions.

IV. *Any institution whatever may become the embodiment of a nation*

Admirers of popular government generally assume that a Parliament or other body elected for the very purpose of representing the people must be a truer representative of the people's ideas, wishes, or prejudices than any other body or person. This assumption is one which a student of English history is certain to accept as unquestionably true. The annals of our country consist of a series of constitutional conflicts and record the gradual progress of Parliament, and especially of the House of Commons, towards sovereignty, and the strength of the lower House clearly lies in its having more truly than either the Crown, the nobility, or the Church represented the nation; yet the assumption that either an elected assembly, or any one person or institution is certain to embody the spirit of the nation is contradicted by some of the most obvious facts of history. True it is that with us in the long run and at most times the Houses of Parliament have commanded the support of Englishmen, and be it noted that the Houses have never been more powerful than at periods when they did not, technically speaking, represent the people with any accuracy. The unreformed House of Commons misrepresented the electors, but the unreformed House of Commons of 1797 was the embodiment of the nation and from some points of view a more powerful and more independent body than the reformed House of 1897.[2] The House of Commons moreover though it has in general reflected the national will has not invariably been the truest representative of the nation. A slight acquaintance with the

---

[2] A person or an association is powerful in so far as it can enforce its own will against the will of others. During the last century the House of Commons could make a treaty which, like that with France in 1761, was profoundly unpopular, could prevent Wilkes, though supported by the electors of Middlesex, from taking his seat, could keep Chatham, the most popular Minister of the day, out of office, and, to look at the House from a more favourable point of view, could carry through legislation too tolerant for the taste of the electors. Many Tories looked it is said with favour or indifference upon the Reform Bill because an unreformed Parliament had admitted Roman Catholics to equal rights in the face of popular prejudice in favour of their exclusion. Could the reformed Parliament of today act with the same independence of public opinion? If not, the modern Parliament is in reality less powerful than the Parliament of the last century.

history of the Tudors shows that under Henry VIII and Elizabeth the Crown, rather than the Parliament, gave effect to the will of the country. We marvel at the adulation offered by men of eminence to monarchs who were in many respects far less worthy of respect than the subjects by whom they were adored, and we assume too rashly that inordinate eulogy was the same thing as insincere flattery and proves that countries and statesmen were servile hypocrites. The truth appears to be that not politicians or men hungering for office alone, but men worthy of the highest respect and of marked independence, worshipped the Crown as representing the dignity of the nation and as the main security for order and prosperity. The weakness of James, the stupidity and mendacity of Charles I, the worthlessness of Charles II, and the blind obstinacy of his brother, were at last sufficient, but not more than sufficient, to break down the belief in the divine right of Kings. It was only after the Revolution of 1689 that slowly and by degrees the loyalty of the people was transferred from the Crown to the Parliament, and that the House of Commons finally became the representative or embodiment of the nation.

Whatever may be said about the extent to which Parliament has always in England been the true centre of English public life, the history of foreign countries lends no countenance to the idea that it is in a representative assembly that the spirit of a nation must necessarily find its home.

The annals of France are the record of the steps by which provinces that originally hardly formed one country were at last under the monarchy consolidated into the Kingdom of France. The King, the Court, the centralised administration or, in one word, the Crown is seen, as time goes on, to be the embodiment of the nation's wishes. The States General, the nobles, the Protestants, the Parliaments, the Church, any person in short or institution whose resistance to the Crown menaces the unity of the country are compelled to give way to the King. The great Revolution itself though it destroyed the kingship was, paradoxical though the assertion sound, not in reality a movement directed against the Royal authority. If the Crown had become the leader of the people in suppressing the privileges or the rights of the nobility Louis XVI might have been as great and as popular as was Louis XIV at the height of his power. As a matter of fact Louis XVI commanded at the beginning of the Revolution great popularity at any rate in the provinces. It was the dislike to the *ancien régime* with its privileges and inequalities which roused the people against the King who appeared as the friend of the nobles. Neither his virtues nor his weaknesses enabled him to play the part of despotic reformer though in performing it he would have commanded the applause of France. This assertion rests on no idle speculation as to what might have been; its truth is suggested by the policy of such a statesman as Mirabeau, but rests for its establishment on the triumph both of the Jacobins and of Napoleon who rose originally as a Jacobin and had studied with assiduity in the school of Robespierre. The horrors of the Reign of Terror were endured and its heroes kept in power because the Jacobins re-erected a centralised despotism and destroyed opponents who were thought to menace the unity of France. Napoleon restored the monarchy in a new and stronger form and made Imperialism the guarantee for social equality and national power. At no time, unless it be at the opening of the States General in

1789 or for the short period immediately preceding and following the Revolution of July, has a Parliament of any kind commanded the enthusiasm of France, and if cool observers doubt the stability of the existing Republic their fears for its permanence are excited by the thought that for the first time in French history representative assemblies and assemblies not calculated by the character of their members to kindle any fervent admiration among the French people have become the real government of France. Can true parliamentary government exist in a country which is without any true parliamentary history?

In Prussia again you have parliamentary government of a special kind, but no one can suppose for a moment that an assembly which has existed for not quite 50 years can in Prussia transfer to itself the loyalty which has become attached to the Prussian monarchy. For good or bad the reigning family of Prussia has created the country. The excellences or defects of the Prussian administration, the power and the weakness of the State, the victories of Frederick, the rout at Jena, the triumphs of 1870, are all connected with the character of successive Prussian Kings. When, as already pointed out,[3] a conflict arose between the Crown and Parliament, or rather between the Crown and the House of Representatives, it became clear, first, that in statesmanlike foresight the King and his Ministers surpassed the parliamentary leaders, and, next, that it was the King and not the Parliament who could in the last resort command the allegiance of the Prussians. Whether the fact be one to be regretted or not, it remains the undoubted fact that on the whole the reigning family of Prussia have hitherto been the embodiment of the Prussian state.

No country exemplifies the principle on which I am now insisting more clearly and in a more curious form than does Scotland.

It might naturally have been expected that in Scotland either the King, as in France, or the Parliament, as in England, would have become the centre of Scotch loyalty. The peculiar course of Scotch history frustrated this natural expectation. The Crown never attained that undisputed supremacy which enabled the French Kings at once to secure the unity and independence of the nation and at the same time to suppress the power and the tyranny of the nobles. It were hardly an exaggeration to say that in Scotland the Crown and the nobility were each strong enough to prevent the other from becoming supreme whilst neither Crown nor nobility were strong enough to establish that rule of law and order which was required by the nation. This perhaps was the cause of the phenomenon, for which no one but a person deeply versed in Scotch history could adequately account, that the Parliament never played anything like the part which was played by the Parliaments of the Southern Kingdom. The institution of the Lords of the Articles, which may be described as a committee much under the control of the Crown to which the legislative powers of Parliament were confided, shows how little as against the King was ultimately the authority of Parliament, yet the people of Scotland found for themselves a really representative body. From the time of the Reformation the Church and the Church Assemblies were the true Scotch Parliament. During the whole of the contests with the Stuarts the Church

---

[3] See ch. [6, pp 116 ff] *ante*.

and its Assemblies are the centre of popular resistance. The Union with England was not really popular in Scotland; could the Treaty of Union have been submitted to a plebiscite or a referendum, it is probable, if not certain, that it never would have been carried into effect. Sir Walter Scott tells us in one of his letters that he himself remembered old persons who looked upon the Union with England as the ruin of Scotland and that, had he lived in 1707, he would have resisted to the death a measure which, when living not quite a century later, he counted a blessing to his country. To understand this resistance to a policy of far-sighted expediency, we must remember that during the eighteen years which elapsed between the Revolution of 1689 and the Act of Union of 1707 the Scotch Parliament had become a more conspicuous and more powerful body than at any other period of its existence. Had the consolidation of Great Britain been deferred for 50 years longer, the Parliament of Scotland might well have become the symbol and standard of Scotch independence and Scotch nationality. If on the other hand we wish to see why it was that Scotchmen after all at any rate tacitly assented to the destruction of the Scotch Parliament, we must remember that the true Parliament of Scotland was the Church Assembly. The Revolution was the final victory of the Church over its oppressors. The Union with England was a guarantee against a restoration. If it was the death of the Parliament which had never commanded the loyalty of the nation, it gave security to the Church and secured the authority of the Church Assembly which was the real representative Parliament of the Scotch people. In the resistance to the Stuarts and in the final Union with England the Scotch Church proves itself the representative of the Scotch people.

Whoever wishes to draw its true moral from the parliamentary history of Scotland should compare the career of the Scotch and of the Irish Parliament.

In many respects a worse framed representative assembly than the Parliament of Ireland could hardly be conceived. Its constitution was to a great extent an artificial constitution; the Parliament was marked by and exaggerated all the faults to be found in the unreformed Parliament of England and suffered in addition to these from special vices of its own. Except for 18 years of its existence it had never at the time of the Union been a really independent body. Its government of the country from 1782 to 1800, under what is known as Grattan's Constitution, has been the object both of indiscriminating eulogy and of indiscriminating attack. Grant that both praise and blame are exaggerated, still no one can deny that Irish Parliamentary independence led up to one of the most savage of rebellions which suggested if it did not justify the destruction of the Parliament. Its most zealous admirers were the most vehement asserters of the necessity for its radical reform, and whatever be the view taken of the Act of Union and the transactions which led up to it, they are the condemnation of the Parliament. Suppose that, as often alleged, the independence of Ireland was sold by her Parliament in return for gross bribes in money or in titles. Then no further proof is needed of the vileness and corruption of the body which for private pelf bartered away the independence of the country. Suppose, on the other hand, what is certainly the more charitable and probably the truer view, that though many members of Parliament were corrupted many or the majority of the men who voted for the Union believed that the separate parliamentary government of Ireland had ended in failure and that the safety of the country could only be ensured by Union with Great Britain. The case then stands thus: the Parliament of Ireland had impressed upon those who knew it best the conviction that its existence was a calamity to the country. Note too that the Parliament did not represent the mass of the people. Not a single Roman Catholic could sit in either of the Houses, and not two years before the end of the century the Parliament had supported by Acts of Indemnity all the most violent and cruel of the means used in suppressing the Rebellion of '98 or, in other words, the insurrection of Papists against Protestant supremacy. Under these circumstances it would be natural to suppose that the Irish Parliament would have represented Irish sentiment at least as little as the Parliament of Scotland represented the sentiment of the Scotch people. But this natural expectation is entirely disappointed; we are met by one of the strangest of historical paradoxes though like every paradox of history it is of course explainable. Irish patriotism, looking back at an era utterly unlike our own, ascribed, it may be conjectured, to Grattan's Constitution merits and glories which it never possessed. One thing, however, is certain. The Irish Parliament did in spite of all its defects become the embodiment of Irish sentiment. It was, though it technically represented only one part of the nation, in its faults and in its virtues national. It was moreover, with the possible exception of Trinity College, Dublin, the only institution in the country which could claim to represent the whole people. Though no Catholic sat in it, Catholics had since 1791 voted for members of Parliament and, what is of far more consequence, educated Catholics at any rate were proud of the Parliamentary glories of Ireland. It was through the Parliament[,] guided by parliamentary leaders, backed no doubt by armed volunteers[,] that Ireland had[,] within the memory of the men who were asked to ratify the Treaty of Union, achieved what was called independence. No Church could claim to represent the whole nation[;] it was in the Parliament that were embodied the aspirations, the wishes, or the romance of the country. If we ask for a full explanation of the fact that the Union with Scotland has been crowned with a success which has not followed the Union with Ireland we must of course pursue investigations which would lead us far beyond the comparative study of constitutions, but among the immediate causes of the comparative failure of the hopes based upon the Union between Great Britain and Ireland one at least may be noted by constitutionalists. The Scotch Parliament had not, whilst the Irish Parliament had become at the time of its abolition, the embodiment or the emblem of the nation, and the history of Scotland and of Ireland alike proves that almost any institution may become the home, so to speak, of the national spirit.

PART II

THE COMPARATIVE STUDY OF CONSTITUTIONS

Introduction
Nature of Comparative Study of Constitutions

Analysis[*]

A. Meaning of Comparative Study
 1. Elucidation of constitutional arrangements or questions by *comparison* of constitutions or institutions
 2. Distinction between historical and comparative method. Historical method involves comparison, but comparative method does not involve history, e.g. account of English constitution from e.g. reign of Queen Elizabeth to Victoria indirectly involved comparison. But comparison of constitution under Elizabeth, under Cromwell, and under Victoria, or of Presidential Constitution of USA with monarchical constitution of England, does not involve history.

B. Merits of Comparative Study
 I. *Brings into light unnoticed aspects of institutions*
 II. *Frees us from dominion of assumptions derived from constitutional history to which we are mainly accustomed*
 Examples
 —the idea of the essential connection between right to tax and right to legislate or that taxation involves representation
 —the idea that a real legislature must also control executive
 —the idea that a representative assembly has a constitutional right to use its powers for the attainment of supremacy
 —the idea that the ordinary judges of the land can pass judgment upon every kind of legal question
 —the idea that an elective legislature must of necessity be the embodiment of the national will
 All these ideas are fostered by English and many of them by American history or habits; but are shown to be erroneous by even a cursory comparison with constitutions of other countries, e.g. English Commonwealth, French Republic, German Empire.

---

[*] Its contents have been derived from a manuscript dated 25 July 1898 on its first page. It was placed first in an attached bundle of manuscripts on the back of the last of which was written 'Scheme for Lectures at Lowell Institute'. It is the only Analysis of a separate Introduction available in the Dicey Papers that was evidently used for *The Comparative Study of Constitutions* course. Elsewhere, the course seems to have begun with the 'Historical Constitutions and Non-Historical Constitutions' lecture.

III. *Gives new modes of dividing or grouping constitutions*
   1. Constitutions where there is a parliamentary executive and constitutions where there is a non-parliamentary executive

   NB This is one of the most important and least noted [distinctions]

   Notice three points
   (i) Under this criterion group together English monarchy, most constitutional monarchies, and French Republic (parliamentary executives) and, on the other hand, all American constitutions, German Empire, Prussian Constitution, English Commonwealth, and Second French Republic (non-parliamentary executives).
   (ii) Cabinet government and Presidential government only two specimens of different species
   (iii) Attempts to combine advantages of parliamentary and non-parliamentary executives, e.g. French Directorial Constitution and Swiss Federal Constitution
   2. Direct democratic government and indirect or parliamentary democratic government

1

Historical Constitutions and Non-Historical Constitutions

Analysis*

Introduction
What [is] meant by historical constitution
    1. What [it] does not mean
    2. What it does mean, *viz* combination of three† ideas
        (i)   Immemorial *origin*
        (ii) Unbroken *continuity*
        (iii) Connection with country['s] *history*

A.   Comparison in regard to these Ideas between English and other Constitutions
B.   Likeness as to Historical Character between Roman Constitution and English Constitution
C.   Merits and Demerits of Historical Constitutions
    I. *Merits*
      1. Constitution made to meet actual want
      2. Presumption that constitution suited for country
    II. *Demerits*
      1. Institutions become mere survivals
      2. Adaptations may be mere adaptations
      3. A state of things comes into existence which no one intended to produce

(See Freeman, *Growth of the English Constitution*;
Pelham, *Roman History*;
Warde Fowler, *City State*.)

---

* Its contents have been derived from a manuscript dated 1 May 1900 and attached to the lecture schedule headed 'Easter & Trinity Terms 1900'.
† In the full lecture text, four (not three) characteristics—antiquity, continuity, spontaneity, and originality—were attributed to historical constitutions. See p. 182, n., below.

Historical Constitutions and Non-Historical Constitutions*

To the constitutions of certain countries and notably to the constitutions of England and of Rome, we apply the term 'historical' or express very much the same idea by saying that they were 'not made but grew', and we contrast such historical constitutions with polities such for example as the 16 constitutions that have enjoyed a transitory existence in France since 1789. These we say, whatever their other merits, are not historical, and every one used to think[ing] about institutions perceives that the distinction made is a real one and that there is a sense in which the constitution of England or of Rome is historical, whilst many or most of the existing polities, as for instance the Constitutions of the USA, of France, or of the German Empire, are not historical. Yet though the distinction is real there is some difficulty in determining exactly wherein it consists.

There are several meanings of the term 'historical', or of expressions equivalent to it, which cannot be used as distinguishing one constitution from another since they are applicable to all constitutions alike.

When we say that the constitution of England is historical we certainly do not mean that it has a history. This assertion is perfectly true, but it applies to all things in the world, be they great or small. It is true of the universe, the history of which is the object of geological investigation. It is equally true of the last divorce case which has occupied the Probate Division of the High Court. It is obviously true of all human institutions; the present French Republic has existed for not quite thirty years yet it has a history and a very curious history indeed; for there is nothing stranger or at first sight more paradoxical, and yet more completely explainable, than the course of events by which the French National Assembly of 1871, which consisting as it did for the most part of conservatives or reactionists, who hoped and intended to restore the Bourbon dynasty, was led to found a democratic Republic which whatever its defects has already lasted longer than any form of government which has been tried in France since the opening of the great Revolution.

We do not again mean, when we call a constitution historical, merely that it is intimately connected with the growth of a particular people.

This assuredly is true if not of all yet certainly of most polities. The French Republic may, compared with the English Kingdom, be termed a creation of yesterday; a glance at the annals of France is sufficient to assure a student that monarchy, rather than democratic Republicanism, has generally been the form of government which the French people have found to be in harmony with their habits and wishes. Yet, though the present Republic was born within the memory of many persons now

---

* The manuscript's title page was dated 26 May 1900, but the lecture text was the product, in places, of alteration that was presumably mainly after that date. On Dicey's characterization of historical constitutions, see Editor's Introduction, pp xliii ff above.

living, though Republicanism does not appear, at first sight at any rate, to be the form of government which best harmonises with the history of France, still if we look below appearances to realities we soon discover that French Republicanism stands in the closest connection with the past development of the French nation. There is scarcely an institution of modern France and, what is more important, there is hardly an idea which governs Frenchmen in the conduct of public affairs, that has not its roots in the past and often in the very distant past. The position of the French judiciary, the pre-eminently French conception of administrative law, the relation of the French Ministers to the French Assembly, above all the acceptance by the nation of universal suffrage as the basis of their institutions, and a score of other matters which will occur to my readers, are explainable only by the whole course of the history of the French people. This general truth cannot be worked out here in detail, yet it is well to direct special attention to the acceptance by Frenchmen of universal suffrage; for there are few occurrences which better illustrate the principle that institutions which appear on a superficial view to originate in accident owe their permanent existence to deep-seated historical causes. On 24 February 1848, the Chamber of Deputies, which under the Orléanist Monarchy was supposed to represent France, was elected by a very limited body of Frenchmen. We may say with substantial truth that under the French Charter of 1830 the right to vote for members of Parliament, or as it is popularly termed the parliamentary franchise, was more narrowly restricted than in England under the Reform Act, or as a foreigner might have said under the Constitution of 1832. We may indeed doubt whether even the unreformed Parliament of George III did not represent the English people more truly than did the modern Orléanist Parliament of Louis Philippe.

On 24 February 1848 Louis Philippe's reign was brought to an end by a riot at Paris. The Provisional Government immediately proclaimed universal suffrage. A main reason for this immense change was that it had been long advocated by a leading member of the Government—one Ledru-Rolin, a politician never much known out of France and whose name is now all but forgotten in France. Another reason no doubt was that the men installed in office by the mob of Paris knew that their followers expected democratic changes and believed that universal suffrage suited the condition of the country. This belief has turned out well founded. Since 1848 a Republic has in France succeeded the Monarchy, been in its turn superseded by an Empire, and again has become the recognized form of government. Yet neither Republicans nor Imperialists, nor the reactionary assembly which desired to restore the monarchy, have ventured upon openly attacking universal suffrage. The reason of this becomes clear to any one who considers the history of France. Ever since the commencement of the great Revolution all Frenchmen have acknowledged, in theory at any rate, the supremacy of the nation. The different institutions, such for example as the monarchy, or the ancient *Parlements* which possessed an independent authority of their own, have vanished. The basis on which alone according to French ideas supreme authority or power can rightly rest is the will of the nation expressed by the votes of the whole body of male citizens; in other words no authority seems to ordinary Frenchmen absolutely legitimate but the authority of universal suffrage.[1] This sentiment is so strong that many Frenchmen deny the moral right of any assembly whatever, even though elected by the votes of all French citizens, to change finally the articles of the Constitution. Such change, it is argued, ought to be sanctioned by a popular vote. This theory, it is true, seems to most Englishmen inconsistent with the terms of the existing French Constitution, but it is advocated by men who are loyal to the Republic and who maintain that their doctrine is not only consistent with, but implied by, the Constitutional laws. However this may be, the one thing which is certain is that universal suffrage though established by an accident maintains its existence because it is in conformity with the political ideas of Frenchmen, and that these ideas are in their turn the fruit of French history.

Nor is it in France alone that new institutions are closely connected with past history. The constitutional government of Prussia dates back only to 1850. It looks like a copy of the English constitution, and there is not the remotest doubt that its forms were really borrowed from England; but the things which give Prussian constitutionalism all its peculiar character and colour, such as the authority of the Crown, the influence of the army, the power and independence of the bureaucracy, the restriction of the Parliament to merely legislative functions, and the like, are all due to the very peculiar and special history of Prussia.

The German Empire came into existence in 1871. It is a federal government of a most curious, not to say anomalous, description. It is not a revival of the Holy Roman Empire; it is not a development of the feeble Confederation which fell to pieces in 1876. It is in one sense an original creation, yet the very existence of the Empire, the peculiarities of its federation, everything we might almost say which is really important in the existing constitutional fabric, represents the surviving influence of some historical fact. The German Empire would be absolutely incomprehensible to one who knew nothing of the annals of Germany. The form of government then, which has not existed for more than thirty years, may in one sense of the word 'historical' be ranked amongst the most historical of political institutions.

What then do we really mean when we call, e.g. the constitution of England, in a very special sense historical?

The answer is that under this expression, or others analogous to it, we combine more or less unconsciously at least four different though closely interconnected ideas.

We mean to assert, for instance, of the English constitution that it exhibits four characteristics some of which at any rate are not easily to be discovered in the constitutions of other countries. These qualities may be conveniently designated by the terms—'antiquity'—'continuity'—'spontaneity'—and 'originality'.

My purpose in this chapter is, first, to institute a comparison in respect of these qualities between the historical constitution of England and the non-historical constitutions, whether monarchies or commonwealths, of other countries and, in the course of this comparison, to explain the exact meaning of terms which certainly

---

[1] Boutmy.

need explanation, and, secondly, to consider what may be the gain or the loss to a country of possessing political institutions which are truly historical as being rather the undesigned outcome of its history than the product of deliberate design or statesmanlike foresight.

A. Comparison between Historical Constitution of England and Non-Historical Constitutions

I. Antiquity

The immemorial origin of the English constitution is the characteristic which at once arrests the attention of even a casual observer. Our political institutions, whether we[2] take them as a whole or look at them separately, are for the most part of indefinite antiquity. They are not only ancient. More than this they cannot in reality be assigned to any one definite date. Of each of the 16 constitutions of France we may say it originated or came into force on such a year and even on such a day. Thus we have the Constitution of 1791, of 1795, of the Year VIII (1800), of the year 1875, which we may add was promulgated on 28 February 1875. This too holds good not only of the French forms of government which have succeeded one another since 1789, but even of the ancient States General. This body, time-honoured though it was, will be found to be almost as much assignable to a definite date as the Constitution, say, of the Year VIII. The States General were as truly created in 1302 by Philippe le Bel as the Constitution of the Year VIII was created in 1800 by Buonaparte. Nor is it French constitutions alone which date from a particular year. The Constitutions of Italy and of Switzerland came into being in 1848, the Constitution of Prussia in 1855, the Constitution of the German Empire in 1871, indeed it would be all but impossible to point to any foreign polity either in the New or in the Old World[3] the origin of which cannot be referred to a definite year. But this manifestly does not hold good of the constitution of England.

No historian would dream of asserting that in such and such a year our constitution was created. Even at a time when tercentenaries and the like are in fashion nobody imagines that we can on a given year appropriately commemorate the birth of English freedom and what is true of the whole constitution is also true of most of our institutions. There was a time indeed when people fancied that to the best of our Kings might be referred the most popular of our institutions and that Alfred was the inventor of trial by jury. We all have now learned that the jury system like Parliament itself has been slowly developed and has not been ordained by any one legislator at any one definite date.

Here, however, we pass from the characteristic of immemorial antiquity to the more important quality of unbroken continuity.

---

[2] Paley 1, p. 192.
[3] Unless it be the constitution of Hungary.

II. Unbroken continuity

The English constitution is much more than ancient, it is the result of development or growth which has never been interrupted. This is what we mean by continuity. We see that this is so if we try to begin our constitutional history at any one given point. The moment we make the attempt we find that the choice of a beginning is arbitrary and therefore unsatisfactory, and this for the simple reason that the constitution as it has existed at any one moment can hardly be explained or made intelligible without going back to some earlier date. Suppose, for example, a writer begins his account of modern England at the beginning of the nineteenth century. The date is not a badly chosen one; it has more than the recommendation of falling in with our chronological system and of thus coinciding with the commencement of a definite century. For 1801 marks the beginning of the United Kingdom of Great Britain and Ireland. The date nevertheless chosen by our imagined historian turns out to be little better than an arbitrary one. It is absolutely impossible to explain the political arrangements of 1800 without going back a good deal further. They are nothing more than the continuation and development of the English constitution as it was finally fixed by the Revolution of 1688. Can we then date the constitutional monarchy from the Glorious Revolution? The experiment seems hopeful but it at once breaks down. The statesmen of 1688 did unknowingly carry through a revolution but to their own minds the revolution appeared to be a restoration. The dethronement of James II, which the Whig orthodoxy termed an abdication, was treated by its authors as a return to those fundamental laws of the lawful monarchy which had been violated by a Papist and a despot. The Bill of Rights was not the claim of any new rights of man but the reassertion of the immemorial privileges of Englishmen. Reformers could maintain, and within certain limits could maintain with truth, that the constitution preserved and reinvigorated by the Revolution of 1688 was nothing but the constitution which was restored in 1660. The difficulty presented by the breachless continuity of the political history of England meets us in short at whatever point of English annals we choose to make a beginning. The constitution under Charles II is in one sense the same as the constitution as it excited at the accession of James I, the position of the first of the Stuarts cannot be understood without understanding the constitutional position of the last of the Tudors. Henry VIII, though a despot, inherited, in theory, only the rights and powers of the Kings from whom he descended; carry the monarchy back even to the Conquest, and you find to your astonishment that William himself claimed to be the legitimate successor of Edward the Confessor. At every step you find change, but at none—with one possible exception—do you find arrested development, and the English constitutional historian is at last compelled to begin his inquiries with the earliest known stage in the history not of England but of the English people, and to confess that the practical absurdity of Montesquieu's dogma, that his artificial constitution of England with all its supposed checks and balances and separation of powers was invented in the forests of Germany, has at least this justification: that the primitive conceptions of our German and barbarous ancestors contain the germs from which were developed the elaborate fabric of English constitutionalism. What is true of the whole constitution is also true of each of its parts. Take, as an illustration, the House of Lords. The assembly which exists in 1900 is essentially different from the *Magnum Concilium* of 1066, but if you are to explain the form and powers of the existing House of Peers you must go back step by step to the Great Council of the Norman Kings, nor must you stop with the Norman Conquest. The inquirer is inevitably led back to a period earlier than the age of William the Conqueror and finds himself embarked in inquiries as to the *Witenagemót*. The House of Lords, in short, is essentially connected with and the real descendant of earlier assemblies in a way in which the French National Assembly of today is not connected with nor descended from, we will not say, the States General, but the Parliaments of Louis Philippe or even the National Assembly of the Second Republic.

In truth this unbroken continuity is the characteristic which more than any other distinguishes the constitution of England from not only the transitory governments of France but also from constitutions which looked at from other points of view might make out a claim to be historical.

The Swiss Federal Republic, for example, is, as truly as can be any commonwealth, the outgrowth and the natural result of Swiss history. In its present form indeed it has existed for hardly more than half a century and may look to a superficial observer like a mere miniature copy of the gigantic federal government created by the founders of the United States. But whoever looks a little below the surface will soon perceive that the Swiss polity is of native growth. The position of the Federal Assembly, the subordination of its legislative power to the popular referendum, the peculiar combination of judicial with executive authority, is hardly to be found in any other country than Switzerland. Above all the attributes and authority of an executive, which, though elected by the Federal Parliament, bears as little resemblance to an English Cabinet as to the Presidential government of the United States, prove the original and essentially Swiss character of the Swiss Commonwealth. The unity moreover of the Confederation, though in its present form the result of statesmanship as recent as it was masterly, is merely the attainment of an end pursued for centuries by each generation of Swiss patriots. No philosophic student feels surprise that Switzerland should at last have attained to national unity under the suitable form of a federal government. He is astonished only that a goal towards which Swiss history seems to point from the beginning should have been reached only after centuries of effort and that its attainment should have been delayed so long by divisions which to the men of today seem as unnatural as they were certainly calamitous. To whatever criticism, in short, the institutions of Switzerland are open, no competent judge can deny that they are the natural outcome of the annals of Switzerland and in full harmony with the character of the Swiss. Yet, for all this, Swiss constitutionalism lacks the quality of continuity. The Federal Assembly which sits at Bern is no modification of the old Diet. The Council of States or Senate does not descend from any second Chamber known to the 13 cantons. Here, as elsewhere, the French Revolution has broken the thread of national development. The French Directory, when they imposed upon the unwilling Swiss centralised institutions modelled on the newest French fashion, may have unwittingly confered a lasting benefit upon Switzerland, for they wiped out inequalities which divided class from class, canton from canton, city from country, and they thus facilitated the ultimate unity of the Swiss people. But the revolutionists and invaders of France assuredly did not preserve what neither they nor their disciples valued, the continuity of Swiss national development. The centralised government introduced by the Directory and the decentralised federation constituted by Napoleon's Act of Mediation broke the outward links which connected Switzerland with her past. The reaction of 1814 could not in reality restore the old state of things. When the patriots of 1848 gave their country real unity, they created a constitution suited indeed for the requirements of Switzerland but which formed a new work of statecraft which could not by any fiction be linked with the earlier forms of Swiss government.

What has been said of Switzerland applies in principle to the modern German Empire. Imperial federalism is the result of German history. The tradition of the Holy Roman Empire mingling with the popular enthusiasm for a powerful and united Germany not only stimulated the desire for unity but it determined the form in which German unity should be realised. Yet, though the German Empire would never have taken its present shape but for the influence of the past, it were idle to contend that the present Empire is the development of the Holy Roman Empire which was dissolved in 1806. The formal dissolution of the old Empire and the existence first of the Federation of the Rhine, and next of the German Confederation, broke the line of German constitutional development. The present Empire was not only in name, but in fact, created in 1871. It cannot from the nature of things give to German institutions that continuity of which English constitutionalism affords an almost perfect example.

The use of the words 'almost perfect' is intentional. At one point, and at one point only, the continuous chain of English constitutionalism is broken. The Interregnum—1649–1660—introduced an undeniable breach which was likely at one time to be much more than a temporary interruption. If the Constitution of 1654 [sic] embodied in the Instrument of Government, or the Protectorate in any of its forms, had become a lasting form of government, the constitution of today would have dated from Oliver's accession to power. Historians no doubt would have shown that the Commonwealth founded in the middle of the seventeenth century derived many of its characteristics from the older monarchy just as historians now trace out the close connection between the Constitution of the United States and the institutions of the 13 English Colonies, or between the Federal Republic of Switzerland and the ancient Confederacy of the 13 Cantons, but the most enthusiastic believers in historical continuity could, if England had remained a commonwealth, no more have identified the Protectorate with the old monarchy than they can now claim for the French Republic of 1875 an unbroken descent from the monarchy of Louis XVI. The temporary breach in the growth of the English constitution was repaired by the Restoration, and has been hidden out of sight under the fiction that in 1649 Charles II immediately succeeded Charles I. This substitution of theory for fact is astonishing in its boldness, but even more astonishing for its practical success. It blotted out from popular tradition the very memory of the Interregnum. Recent interest in the great Rebellion, and especially in Cromwell, conceals from us the extent to which Englishmen, from the moment of the Restoration down to a period within the recollection of persons now living, contrived to forget the fall of the monarchy and treated the Republic and the Protectorate as nothing better than names for a period of revolutionary violence which had no essential connection with the preservation of England's liberties. This process of ignoring the past began long before the restoration of Charles II. When the Rump was reassembled by Monk a tactless official referred to the 'dissolution' by Cromwell. Upon him was poured forth all the indignation of the resuscitated Long Parliament. For the Parliament in the eyes of its members had been unlawfully dispersed, but had never been legally 'dissolved'. It had existed during the seven years of triumphant lawlessness, and when in 1660 anarchy came to an end it remained the one lawful authority in the state.[4] Nor was this a new theory put forward by reactionists in the madness of a party triumph. When Cromwell told the Council of State on 20 April 1653, that the functions of the Council had come to an end and that they must take notice that the Parliament was dissolved, 'Sir, replied John Bradshaw, 'we have heard what you did at the House this morning, and before many hours all England will hear it; but you are mistaken to think that the Parliament is dissolved; for no power under heaven can dissolve them but themselves: therefore take you notice of that.'[5]

'And Bradshaw,' to cite the words of the most recent among the biographers of Cromwell, 'was right. The ideal of constitutional government which the Long Parliament represented would prove stronger in the end than Cromwell's redcoats.'[6]

The Protector was among the most successful of English generals and the most powerful of English rulers. He was succeeded as quietly by his son as was James I by Charles I, yet after the Restoration there remained no Cromwellians; there was no political party who claimed to represent the traditions of the Commonwealth.

James II and his son were expelled, but there was nothing which the Whigs of the Revolution more sedulously avoided than any connection whatever with Cromwell or the statesmen of the Rebellion. When in 1689 Ludlow ventured to return from exile, the last surviving general of the Commonwealth found that, instead of being generated as a patriot, he was cursed as a regicide. The Whigs of the eighteenth century gloried in the Revolution of 1689, they passed a moral Act of Oblivion over the Rebellion of 1641. In Ireland one might have expected that Cromwell would have remained the hero of the Protestants, but in fact Orangemen have gloried in the name not of the great English general but of the Dutch William of Orange. The Radicals who begun to exert influence towards the latter part of the last century were of many schools. Some of them were dreamers who wished to restore our ancient Saxon constitution; others demanded for Englishmen the natural rights of man. A third, and ultimately far more powerful, body were zealots for reform carried out in accordance with the principles of utilitarianism. But there did not exist, and there never

---

[4] See I Pepys's Diary.
[5] Firth, *Cromwell*, p. 324 (Heroes of the Nation series).
[6] Ibid.

has existed since the Restoration, any political party, however violent, which aimed at restoring the Republican Constitution of 1653. Its very existence seems to have passed out of general memory. Paley writes 'there never was a date or point of time in our history, when the government of England was to be set up anew and when it was referred to any single person, or assembly, or committee, to frame a charter for the future government of the country; or when a constitution, so prepared and digested, was by common consent received and established. In the time of the Civil Wars, or rather between the death of Charles I and the restoration of his son, many such projects were published, but none were carried into execution.'[7]

Every word of this statement, if it be read in its natural sense, is untrue. There exists a definite point of time, namely 1653, when the government of England was to be set up anew. There was formed at that date a known committee to whom it was referred to frame a charter or constitution for the future government of the country. A constitution, namely the Instrument of Government, was in fact so prepared and digested and this constitution was not only published but was actually carried into execution and Parliaments were convoked under it. If we suppose that Paley was ignorant of these facts then we have a patent proof that a very able and well instructed writer was, 131 years after the Restoration (i.e. after a period shorter than the time which now separates us from the accession of George III), totally ignorant of the history of the Protectorate. If, on the other hand, we suppose that Paley's language is to be read in a non-natural sense and to be qualified by the implied assertion that during the Interregnum no constitution was received and established 'by common consent', then we must assume that a moralist of marked honesty accustomed to the use of plain language felt that even 130 years after the Restoration it was hardly decent to treat a Cromwellian constitution as having had a recognised existence. Whichever be the alternative we adopt, we may safely assume that, in Paley's time, the political experiments of the Commonwealth had fallen completely out of general recollection. Nearly 50 years later than the date at which Paley published his *Moral Philosophy*, all England was passionately excited by the demand for Parliamentary reform. The best and most telling arguments for and against the abolition of rotten boroughs and the extension of the parliamentary franchise were put forward by the ablest speakers and these arguments are still on record. It will be found that they contain little, if any, reference whatever to the sweeping reform of Parliament carried out under the Constitution of 1653. From whatever point of view an inquirer looks at the matter he is led to one and the same conclusion. The events of the Interregnum fell sooner than one could have thought possible into oblivion. The breach in the continuity of our constitutional history was, so to speak, filled up by popular sentiment. When lawyers proclaimed that Charles II ascended the throne on the death of his father, they propounded a patent absurdity which was not felt to be absurd because it corresponded with national feeling, and also was an imaginative representation, if one may use the expression, of an important fact, namely that essentially and at bottom the fundamental institutions of England remained for the most part unaffected by

---

[7] 2 Paley, *Moral Philosophy*, p. 192.

the Rebellion and the Interregnum. The line of historical continuity, though for a moment interrupted, was not permanently broken. The constitutional government of Victoria, though essentially different, is really evolved from the constitutional government of Elizabeth and is not a modification of the Cromwellian Protectorate.

In the matter of continuity France affords an instructive contrast with England. French lawyers or statesmen, influenced no doubt by the English precedent, have tried to conceal breaches in constitutional development by the use of legal fictions. The title of Louis XVIII is a record of one such experiment, the title of Napoleon III is the record of another. In each case the attempt was a failure. No Frenchman has ever for a moment forgotten the Revolution, the Convention, or the Napoleonic Empire; no French citizen has ever felt that the Second Empire created by the *coup d'état* of 1851 was the restoration of the Constitution of the Year VIII. Facts in these cases were too obviously and palpably at variance with legal fictions. The France of the Restoration was not the France of the *ancien régime*; the France of 1851 was nothing like the France of 1800.

Had the Frenchmen of the nineteenth century been as anxious as were Englishmen of the seventeenth century to blot a period of revolution out of the national tradition, they would have found it impossible to carry out their wish. But in truth the desire for continuity which has exerted such a prodigious influence in England has always, at any rate since the beginning of the first Revolution, been lacking in France. When Louis XVIII was restored to the throne he took indeed a title which implied the reign of Louis XVII, and tacitly asserted the claim of the restored dynasty to reign in virtue of descent from the ancient Kings of France, but not the least effort was made to link the restored monarchy with what an English lawyer would have considered the legally existing constitution of France, namely the Constitution of 1791 created by the National Assembly and assented to by Louis XVI. When again Louis Napoleon was proclaimed Napoleon III he intimated by his title that the Empire was the one form of government which had duly received the sanction of the French nation. He moreover to the best of his ability imitated Napoleonic titles and court pageantry; the new Empire was in many respects modelled on the Imperial system of the first Napoleon. But for all this, Napoleon III never professed to restore the constitution as it had existed under Napoleon I. The Constitution of the Second Empire dated after all from 1852; it did not date from 1810 or from 1815. The Republic again of 1848 was not supposed even by the most ardent Republicans to represent or stand in connection with the last Republic of France which was overthrown by Bonaparte. The Republic of 1848 perished by an act of legal violence which even Imperialists confessed to be technically a crime. Twenty-two years later the Empire was in its turn overthrown and Republican freedom was re-established, but no Frenchman, either in 1870 or 1875, dreamed of treating the Republic as identified with, or the successor to, the Republic of 1848. In modern France they have revolutions; they have no real restorations. A restoration in the strict sense of that word is an effort to relink the present with the past. Such an effort is natural to a people who like the people of England or of ancient Rome are imbued with legalism and who import into their political arrangements that love of precedent and acquiescence in fictions which is proper to the law courts. It is utterly unnatural to a people such as the French, who are much more influenced by logical than by legal conceptions, and who do not value institutions on account of their traditional antiquity.

This point is worth notice, because it points to a conclusion which is generally overlooked. The continuity of a nation's development depends on the existence of two different conditions. The one condition is, if one may adopt the language of philosophy, objective and depends upon the existence of favourable external circumstances, such for example as the absence of those violent interruptions in a nation's life which are caused by domestic revolution or foreign invasion. Thus the peaceful and gradual evolution of the English constitution is due in great part, on the one hand, to the early date at which England obtained a strong government which maintained internal order and, on the other hand, to her insular position which made the foreign invasions difficult if not absolutely impossible. The other condition is subjective and consists in the existence among a people of a legal turn of mind and a love for forms and precedents. This disposition which is as conspicuous in the annals of Rome as in the annals of England may, if looked at from its bad side, be called formalism, but, looked at from its good side, may be described as a rational dislike to break with the past. The continuity therefore of a constitution depends, at bottom, as much upon national character as upon external events.

This uninterrupted growth of a country's institutions is nearly related to and may indeed almost be identified with the characteristic of spontaneity.

III. *Spontaneity**

By no one has the spontaneity or undesigned creation of the British constitution been better described than by Paley.

> 'Most of those', he writes, 'who treat of the British constitution, consider it as a scheme of government formally planned and contrived by our ancestors, in some era of our national history, and as set up in pursuance of such regular plan and design...Now this appears to me an erroneous conception of the subject. No such plan was ever formed...The constitution of England, like that of most countries in Europe, hath grown out of occasion and emergency; from the fluctuating policy of different ages; from the contentions, successes, interests, and opportunities of different orders and parties of men in the community. It resembles one of those old mansions, which instead of being built all at once, after a regular plan, and according to the rules of architecture at present established, has been reared in different ages of the art, has been altered from time to time, and has been continually receiving additions and repairs suited to the taste, fortune, or conveniency of its successive proprietors. In such a building we look in vain for the elegance and proportion, for the just order and correspondence of parts, which we expect in a modern edifice; and which

---

* 'Spontaneity' was absent from this lecture's Analysis dated 1 May 1900 (p. 171 above). The third heading was 'Undesigned creation' in the original manuscript for the full lecture text but was deleted and replaced with 'Spontaneity'. Dicey therefore appears to have developed the idea of spontaneity specifically for his comparative constitutional lectures. See Editor's Introduction, pp cliv f. above.

external symmetry, after all, contributes much more perhaps to the amusement of the beholder, than the accommodation of the inhabitant.'[8]

This passage exactly describes the characteristic which I have called spontaneity. Paley, it will be observed, attributes this quality to the constitutions of most countries in Europe whilst it has been treated by me as one of the special notes of an historical constitution. The apparent contradiction is explained by the date at which Paley wrote. His *Principles of Moral and Political Philosophy* was first published in 1785, i.e four years before the meeting of the French States General. At that moment such constitutions as existed in Europe were historical, and their disappearance is due to the French revolution. Paley's statement therefore was perfectly accurate at the period when he wrote. Its limitation to European countries is probably intended to exclude the then existing federation of the countries which a few years later formed the United States. Paley too, it is worth observing, does not for a moment deny that political institutions are in all cases the work of men and owe their origin and their whole existence to human will:[9] he knows as well as any thinker that constitutions in every stage of their existence are made what they are by human agency. What he does insist upon, and with reason, is that the British constitution taken as a whole was not created at any given moment in accordance with any deliberate plan, design, or principle. It is as a whole the undesigned result of spontaneous efforts suggested at different moments, by the varying circumstances of each time [in] which efforts had for their object to meet some immediate requirement or to attain some immediate result. To follow out Paley's own metaphor, which since he wrote has lost all its freshness by endless repetition, the constitution is a mansion which has been altered from time to time to meet the immediate wants or fancies of its proprietors. Each particular change may be compared, e.g., to the addition of a new drawing room, or the pulling down of an old tower, which has of course been the result of human volition and design, but the mansion itself has not been erected on any one plan. The constitutional fabric has not, as a whole, been created in accordance with any one scheme and may therefore be termed in a sense the product of historical accidents.

From the spontaneity of the English constitution arises in great measure its peculiar characteristic of originality.

IV. Originality

By the word 'originality' as here used is meant simply the absence of imitation. Our form of government is what it is owing almost exclusively to the history of the people of England. It is not to any great extent modelled upon the institutions of any foreign kingdom or commonwealth. It is hardly possible to make the same assertion about any existing monarchy or republic. The truth is that the constitutions of every civilized nation are at the present day all of them copies, though often poor copies, of the British constitution. There are few countries, for example, in which you

---

[8] 2 Paley, pp 192–4.
[9] See Mill, *Representative Government*, p. 4.

will not find that the legislature consists of two Houses. This arrangement has some real advantages no less than some real defects and the makers or critics of constitutions generally defend it on grounds of expediency, and thus suggest that its adoption throughout the civilized world is due to its inherent merits. But this suggestion is founded on an erroneous conception of the circumstances which really lead the people of a country to the adoption of particular institutions. Nowhere is human nature less inventive than in the field of politics. In this sphere the tendency towards imitation is supreme. The true reason why the bicameral system prevails is that it forms part of the constitution of England, and England has been the most successful, and therefore the most imitated, of free states. If, as seemed possible at one part of the seventeenth century, Sweden had become the leading free state of Europe, it is probable that the Swedish Constitution with its four Chambers would have been deemed the model to be copied by reformers of all countries and [is] certain that eminent thinkers would have demonstrated on *a priori* philosophical grounds the indubitable superiority of the quatri-cameral system; the prosperity of the Dutch Republic had, it may be suspected, a good deal to do with the desire of Puritan statesmen to establish an English Republican Commonwealth.[10]

Antiquity, then, continuity, spontaneity, and originality are the most characteristic features of our English form of government. They are a critic may object only different aspects of one and the same fact, namely that English institutions are home-made and have grown with the growth of the English people. This statement is perfectly true but, so far from being an objection to, is in reality the strongest proof of, the doctrine propounded throughout this chapter that these qualities, by whatever name they be described, are the essential features of an historic constitution.

The soundness of this doctrine is confirmed by the consideration that each of our four characteristics reappears in the one famous constitution which can be called historical in the same sense as the constitution of England. Roman institutions were, as long as they can be called in any sense Roman, historic. The historian of Rome cannot assign and does not try to assign any definite date for the creation of the Roman constitution. Its foundations are assuredly older than the expulsion of Tarquin; they must he carried back to the very origin of the city. The beginnings of Roman freedom and of Roman law are hidden amid the darkness and uncertainty of early tradition. Here then you have in the clearest form the characteristic of immemorial antiquity. The continuity again of Roman constitutionalism is indisputable. The revolution, such as it was, which expelled the Kings introduced some change in the form of a government but made little alteration in its essential nature. The transition from the free state to the Empire was no doubt in one sense a great revolution, yet looked at from another point of view it was little more than the natural development of tendencies which had been working for centuries. The whole policy of Augustus was an attempt to minimise in appearance at least the transition from the

---

[10] If Macaulay is to be trusted, the success of Holland did as a matter of fact suggest to Sir William Temple the introduction into England of at least one Dutch institution. So, when Louis XIV was the most powerful sovereign of the Continent, every smaller state imitated to the best of its ability the splendid despotism of the Great King.

Republic to the Empire. All the powers he exercised were powers held by Republican magistrates and which he exercised as filling their offices, and they were conferred upon him by the vote of the Senate and the people.

> He was given the 'consular' *imperium* for ten years, with the government of certain specified provinces. He was, moreover, declared commander-in-chief of all the forces of the state, and granted the exclusive right of levying troops, of making war and peace, and of concluding treaties. This authority abroad, an authority wider than that given to Pompey in 67–66 BC, he was to exercise as consul; and he would consequently be also the chief magistrate of the state at home, with precedence over all other magistrates in Rome or in the provinces. Finally, in recognition of his pre-eminent services, he was authorised by decree of the senate to assume the cognomen of Augustus.[11]

This was a transaction which admitted and was intended to admit of different interpretations. According to the official version of things there had been a restoration of the Republic. The affair was so described by Augustus himself and by the courtly writers of his time. 13 January 27 BC, the day on which the settlement was completed, was marked in the Calendar as the day on which the Republic was restored, and on coins Augustus was honoured as the champion of the freedom of the Roman people.[12] True it is that for the general public the essence of the matter lay in the recognition by law of the supremacy of Caesar, and in the establishment not of a Republic but of a personal government, yet the language of courtly adulation was neither ironical nor wholly insincere. It expressed under legal fictions the sense of and the desire for historic continuity. Step by step, it is true, the Empire changed its character but at no stage in its development, at any rate while it remained Roman, was there a conscious breach with the past. Nor did the institutions of Rome fall the least behind those of England in the quality I have termed spontaneity: they all, to use the terms of Paley, grew 'out of occasion and emergency', and the whole constitution was not set up in pursuance of any regular plan or design. Nor was the mark of originality lacking. There must have been similarities of which we have now little or no knowledge between the government of Rome and the governments of other Italian states as long as independent states existed in Italy. But no one doubts that Roman constitutionalism and Roman law are the natural outgrowth of Roman civilization.

The most formidable objection to the contrast made in this chapter between historical and non-historical constitutions is that the distinction is one of degree rather than of kind. In one sense this criticism is sound. Many constitutions have to a certain extent an historic character; they have some of the qualities which mark the modern monarchy of England and the ancient Republic of Rome. It will, however, be found that owing mainly, though not entirely, to the great French revolution few, if any, existing constitutions are in the full and complete sense historical; and, what is more important, differences in degree may in political matters amount to differences of

---

[11] Pelham, *Roman History*, p. 368.
[12] Ibid. p. 369.

kind. No man accustomed to analyse political conceptions can doubt that there is an essential difference between the constitution of England and the commonwealths or monarchies to be found at the present moment in other civilized countries, and this difference is at any rate conveniently described by the statement that the English constitution is historical in a sense in which the constitution, e.g. of monarchical Italy or of Republican France or of federal Switzerland, are not historical. What may be the best word by which to describe this distinction is a matter of minor consequence; the important thing is to understand the true nature of a far-reaching difference.

B. The Merits and Defects of an Historical Constitution

A certain school of reasoners regard a form of government as a sort of spontaneous product and political science as a branch (so to speak) of natural history. According to them, forms of government are not a matter of choice. We must take them, in the main, as we find them. Governments cannot be constructed by premeditated design. They are not made, but grow. Our business with them, as with the other facts of the universe, is to acquaint ourselves with their natural properties, and adapt ourselves to them. The fundamental political institutions of a people are considered by this school as a sort of organic growth from the nature and life of that people: a product of their habits, instincts, and unconscious wants and desires, scarcely at all of their deliberate purposes. Their will has had no part in the matter but that of meeting the necessities of the moment by the contrivances of the moment, which contrivances, if in sufficient conformity to the national feelings and character, commonly last, and by successive aggregation constitute a polity, suited to the people who possess it, but which it would be vain to attempt to superinduce upon any people whose nature and circumstances had not spontaneously evolved it.[13]

Those who accept the doctrine thus described by Mill naturally consider historic institutions as forming the only kind of constitution which is worthy of respect, and as naturally proceed to clothe the object of their admiration with mysterious and indefinite merits; and indeed appear sometimes to conclude not only that an historic form of government has certain peculiar virtues, but, what is a very different matter, that any institution, be it a law, a church, a monarchy, or a commonwealth, is proved to be beneficial when once it is shown to be historic. Yet to any man who looks at the matter without prejudice it must be apparent that the advantages to a country of possessing a form of government which has been constructed bit by bit, and has grown up so to speak of itself, admit of analysis, and it must be added, may easily be overrated. Here, as in other cases, we must be particularly on our guard against confusing effects with causes. It is true, within certain limits, that a country whose customs, laws, or institutions are the products of its history is likely to compare favourably with a country on which has been imposed or which has deliberately adopted a new and foreign form of government. But that this is so arises much less from the fact that

---

[13] Mill, *Representative Government*, pp 2 and 3.

an historic constitution confers a great benefit on any people than from the quite different fact that institutions which are the growth of ages can exist only in countries which have enjoyed certain peculiar advantages, such for example as freedom from foreign invasion or from internal revolution. It is not, to take a concrete example, the English constitution which has made England strong, independent, and prosperous, but the English constitution which is the result of the independence and the vigour of the people of England. But, when we have got rid of the fallacy which makes the permanence of a form of government the cause rather than the sign of a people's well-being, we should fall into an opposite error if we denied the advantages really presented by forms of government which are historical.

Political arrangements, in the first place, which have been framed to meet an actual want are likely to achieve their immediate object, and having endured have probably met the actual requirements of the time. This is a great deal more than can be said of the scores of paper constitutions which have been designed by theorists and put into force by statesmen during the last 110 years.

There is, in the second place, a very strong presumption that a monarchy or a commonwealth which is the growth of national character is suitable for the nation by whom it has been created.

A form of government, in the last place, which has long existed among any people has, we may *primâ facie* presume, conciliated their good will and loyalty. How great is the gain to a country of the prevalence among its citizens of loyalty that is of willing and spontaneous obedience to their government can be estimated at its proper worth only by noting the difficulty with which such loyalty is created and the almost irreparable evil which flows from its absence. The Protectorate was, judged by any fair standard, a good form of government. Cromwell it is now universally acknowledged was not in intention a despot. He wished to establish and tried to establish the supremacy of law and of justice. He was the most enlightened ruler of his day. In his conception of religious freedom he was far ahead of his contemporaries. Yet the Protectorate and the Protector's domestic policy ended in complete failure. The reason was that the Protectorate never gained the loyal adherence of the nation. The enthusiastic welcome of Charles II looks now like an exhibition of national folly. But the generation who hailed the Restoration with frantic delight had some justification for the madness of the moment. The triumphant return of the King was also the victory of the Parliament. A bad King and an ill balanced constitution which evoked the loyalty of the people was better in the long run for the nation than a patriotic ruler and a reformed Parliament which had never obtained the true sanction of national approval. The Whigs of 1688 had learned one lesson from the Rebellion and the Restoration. They strove to the very best of their power to give revolution itself a conservative character and to preserve for parliamentary government the loyalty which had attached itself to the really monarchical rule of the Tudors and the Stuarts. It is possible that if Anne had left descendants the experiment might have entirely succeeded. The accession of a German dynasty, to whom English was a foreign language, made loyalty to the revolutionary settlement all but impossible, and for 40 years exposed England to that risk of violent reaction which for now more than a century has kept France from enjoying that settled form of national government which can alone ensure the existence at once of order and of freedom. The simple truth is that since the death of Louis XVI no constitution has in France commanded anything like the complete loyalty of the nation. The great Napoleon did for a time become the willingly accepted ruler of the whole French people. It is just conceivable that, had he remained successful to the end of his career, he might have established in France a form of monarchy which commanded as ardent a feeling of loyalty as did the monarchy of Louis XIV, but the disasters which marked the last years of the First Empire, combined with the crimes, mistakes, and calamities of the Second Empire, have to all appearance destroyed the magic of the Napoleonic tradition, and no one, whatever his political sympathies, believes that either the Orléanist dynasty or the Republic can claim the loyal adherence of the majority of the mass of French citizens. The true founder of the last Republic described it as the form of government which the least divides Frenchmen. The statement was true when it was made and may be true still, but it is the admission that neither the Republic nor any other form of government gives complete moral unity to France.

But though it may justly be presumed that a form of government which is the result of something like a natural course of evolution meets the needs of the time, conforms to the national character of the country where it has grown up, and has gained the loyal attachment of the people subject to it, yet this is after all nothing more than a presumption, and like all presumptions may be found to be at variance with facts.

Adaptations, though suggested by the circumstances of the moment, are often misadaptations; institutions may survive the causes which gave rise to and justified their existence, and the course of history may well produce a state of things which no statesman or patriot would consciously have brought about and produce not loyalty but bitter hostility to a political system which is in the strictest sense historic.

Take, for example, the *ancien régime* as it was known to Frenchmen just before the meeting of the States General. It was in the strictest sense the result of the long train of events which make up the history of France. The absolutism of the King, the privileges of the nobility, the exclusive authority of the Church were each and all due to historical causes. They were each, as Taine and other writers have carefully shown, not only the natural, but the justifiable, consequences of the steps by which France had developed into a great nation. This is so emphatically true that a writer who tries to narrate and account for the drama of the Revolution is constantly perplexed by the question what is the point in French history at which he ought to begin his narrative. Wherever he makes a commencement he finds it difficult not to go back to some earlier period in order to account for the state of things from which he has to start. The French monarchy, in this point alone resembling the constitutional monarchy of England, had grown up bit by bit, and every part of the French form of government will be found to be a contrivance meant to meet the requirements of some particular time. But the *ancien régime*, whether you look at it as a whole or examine it in detail, had years before 1789 survived the causes which brought it into existence. The overwhelming power of the Crown which at one time was necessary to secure the unity of the nation was at the outbreak of the Revolution opposed to the rising feeling in favour of liberty, and did not even secure the efficient administration of national affairs. The privileges of the nobles were historically explainable but they were in fact oppressive and odious to the people. The Parliaments could claim as truly as could any institution in any country to be the growth of history. They had played a great part: they had put some check upon the despotism of the Crown, they had supported the independence of the magistracy, and they had, as is natural with judicial bodies, fostered that sense of continuity and that respect for legality which, as has been already pointed out, is lacking in modern France. An Englishman might have expected the Parliaments to be the most popular of French institutions. As a matter of fact they were more detested than most of the historic survivals of which France was then full. Their real merits were overlooked, their defects were patent. Reformers and revolutionists alike desired and carried out the complete and final abolition of the historic Parliaments. Modern thinkers labour to prove that the *ancien régime* had great merits of its own. All their efforts are made futile by the dictum of the wisest among the critics of ancient France. When I find, says Tocqueville, in effect, that the *ancien régime* was universally detested I conclude that it was detestable.[14] Yet, and this is the point which for our present purpose ought to be constantly kept in mind, the *ancien régime* is nothing but a short name for a mass of historic institutions. Add to this that what is true of the condition of France before the beginning of the Revolution is true, speaking broadly, of the greater part of Continental Europe. In Germany, for example, and in Switzerland, no less than in France, historic institutions had ceased to harmonise with the requirements of the time. The Holy Roman Empire was a simple obstacle to progress; it forbid the union of Germany and the reform of German governments. In Switzerland, which was accounted one of the free states of Europe, there was more political oppression and far greater social and political inequality than in France. The cities of Bern and Zürich oppressed the country districts of the cantons which they governed. The oligarchy which ruled in Bern itself was detested by the majority even of Bernese citizens. A student who dreams of Switzerland as the land of liberty is astonished to find that during the eighteenth century the government of Bern was exposed to constant conspiracies, and that the annals of Geneva are filled with contests between different classes of citizens which form a sort of prelude to the great revolutionary contests at Paris. The simple truth is that Continental Europe then suffered under historic institutions some of which had never conferred true benefit on the countries where they existed, and all of which had become out of date and were either useless or harmful survivals of other ages.

Even in countries which have gained most by the gradual and unconscious evolution of their institutions it is easy enough to find examples of the special defect to which historic constitutions are liable, namely the tendency to produce, by degrees and in consequence of an almost unconscious effort to meet the requirements of

---

[14] [Dicey inserted a footnote here but did not supply any text for the note.]

each particular time, a condition of things which everyone more or less condemns and which never could have been the result of deliberate design.

The history of Rome, for example, exhibits no more characteristic institution than the Tribunate. It was originally a natural and probably an effective device for the protection of the plebeians at a time when patricians and plebeians formed something nearly approaching to two opposed and hostile orders which were with difficulty united in one state. But a Roman historian may well doubt whether the Tribunate, which long survived the reasons for its creation, was not in the latter ages of the Republic simply a source of confusion and a means of revolution. Look again at the unreformed Parliament of England: it had great merits, but long before 1832 the system of close boroughs and the plan of representation, if plan it can be called, under which Cornwall had some thirty and Manchester and Birmingham had no representatives, had become indefensible. Historic causes had produced a state of things which casuists might defend, but which obvious common-sense condemned, and, oddly enough, the reformers who abolished abuses which were intolerable were themselves influenced by that preference for bit-by-bit reform which is pre-eminently characteristic of English constitutionalists. While they more or less abolished rotten boroughs, they took no pains to preserve the advantages such as they were which the existence of these boroughs had presented and for the sake of temporary convenience they committed the error of increasing instead of diminishing the numbers of the House of Commons. It were easy to find other examples of the evils which have flowed from the system of constantly repairing the fabric of the constitution in the way which best suited the immediate exigencies of the moment. But enough illustrations have been given to show that the historical character of a constitution is no absolute guarantee for its essential merit. There is another side to Paley's well worn metaphor. We have no right to assume that because an edifice has been built up in different ages and without any regular plan that it will be more fitted for the accommodation of its inhabitants than a building in which we find both elegance and proportion and internal no less than external symmetry.

Before, however, we pass away from the comparison between an historic and a non-historic constitution, it is worth while pointing out that the dispute as to the respective merits or defects of each is not likely to be ever finally adjusted. It is in reality only one form of an interminable controversy between two different views of life and philosophy. Thinkers[, on the one hand,] who in one form or another believe that men ought whether in morals or in politics to place their trust in instinct, in tuition, or generally in feeling, will inevitably and as a rule feel that historic institutions of all kinds, whether they be laws, or creeds, or churches, or constitutions, have a special and overwhelming claim upon our trust and admiration, since they are all the product of, or at any rate in conformity with, instinct, sentiment, or feeling. Thinkers, on the other hand, [who place men's trust]* in the reasoning powers of man, who believe that in politics as in every other sphere mankind ought to be guided by foresight and thought rather than by unconscious instinct or moral sentiment, will

---

* Changed from 'whose place in men's trust' in the manuscript.

inevitably tend to rate high institutions which are the result of deliberate design and foresight. To them, an historical institution seems as likely as not to be a time-honoured abuse and may at any rate be called upon to justify its existence by affording proof of its expediency, whilst a constitution deliberately framed by men acting in accordance with the ideas of utility is recommended to such thinkers by the very fact that it results from at least the effort to act in accordance with the dictates of reason.

2

Ancient Constitutionalism and Modern Constitutionalism

Analysis*

Introduction
How far are the ideas of ancient (classical) constitutionalism applicable to modern times? (See Arnold, *Thucydides*, App. I)

A.   Points of Apparent Likeness
       I.   *Political phraseology borrowed from classical authors*
       II.   *Real analogy between parties of classical times and parties of modern times*
       III. *Certain periods of classical history have an analogy to the condition of modern Europe*

B.   Points of Essential Difference
       I.   *Ancient constitutionalism based on city-state*
       II.   *Representative government unknown*
       III. *Ancient constitutionalism based on slavery*
       IV. *Non-existence of Church*
       V.   *Non-existence of feudalism*
       VI. *Absence until rise of Roman Empire of an administrative system*

C.   Results of Comparison
       I.   *Differences essential and comparison between ancient and modern constitutionalism suggests only analogies*
       II.   *In certain European countries, e.g. in mediaeval Italy and in Switzerland, conditions of ancient constitutionalism have to a certain extent reappeared*
       III. *Political speculation in the modern world has been influenced by ancient or classical constitutionalism*
       IV. *Modern constitutionalism as it gets rid of feudal ideas approaches towards classical constitutionalism*

(See Freeman, *Growth of the English Constitution*;
Pelham, *Roman History*;
Warde Fowler, *City State*; and as to feudalism, add
1 Pollock and Maitland, bk. I, ch. III, pp 66–73; bk. II, ch. I, s. 6, pp 296–307;
1 *Life of Arnold*, 5th edn, p. 255;
'Feudalism' 9 *Encyc. Brit.*, p. 120.)

---

* Its contents have been derived from a manuscript dated 2 May 1900 and attached to the lecture schedule headed 'Easter & Trinity Terms 1900'.

Ancient Constitutionalism and Modern Constitutionalism[*]

Introduction

'There is in fact an ancient and a modern period in the history of every people; the ancient differing [from], and the modern in many essential points agreeing with that in which we now live. Thus the largest portion of that history which we commonly call ancient is practically modern, as it describes society in a stage analogous to that in which it now is; while, on the other hand, much of what is called modern history is practically ancient, as it relates to a state of things which has passed away. Thucydides and Xenophon, the orators of Athens, and the philosophers, speak a wisdom more applicable to us politically than the wisdom of even our own countrymen who lived in the Middle Ages; and their position, both intellectual and political, more nearly resembled our own.'[1]

This passage from Dr. Arnold's notes on Thucydides expresses his deliberate, and often repeated, conviction that the annals of ancient states and especially the constitutional annals of Greece and of Rome illustrate the so-called 'modern' history of France or of England far better than the earlier records of each of these countries, and that modern England has more in common with the Athens of Thucydides or the Rome of Cicero than with the England of Alfred the Great;[2] whence it follows that the Peloponnesian War or the contest between Pompey and Caesar may throw far more light on the revolutionary movements of the nineteenth century than can be obtained from the conflict between the Popes and the Emperors or the hundred years of war between France and England; and this doctrine has been implicitly accepted by writers several of whom have little in common with Arnold: Mitford, Niebuhr, Thirlwall, Grote, and Mommsen, indeed all the most eminent among the authors who during the nineteenth century have tried to tell the tale of Greek or of Roman greatness have been influenced, not to say biassed, by their overpowering sense of the affinity between the political or social movements of their own day and the conflicts which marked the progress and even more the fall of Grecian and of Roman freedom. It is sufficient to note the existence of a feeling which assuredly rests on a sound foundation of truth.

This consciousness, however, of the close connection between ancient and modern history is balanced in the mind of every intelligent student by the sense that we

---

[1] Arnold, *Thucydides*, vol. 1, p. 522.
[2] Cf. Jones I, X. [partially illegible, interlinear, later manuscript note.]

---

[*] The manuscript's first page was dated 29 March 1900 and its second page was dated 18 April 1900 (presumably the date work resumed after an interrupted start), but the lecture text is the product, in places, of what was probably mainly subsequent alteration.

are aliens from the ancient world and removed from [the] civilization—greatly as we may admire it—of Greece and of Rome, not only by lapse of time but by an essential though indefinite change in the way of looking at life and society.

How far, then, are the lessons of ancient constitutionalism really applicable, as Arnold, Freeman, Maine, and others have held, to the political problems which have occupied the attention and perplexed the intelligence of modern Europe?

He who would obtain any thing like an answer to this inquiry must compare in outline the constitutionalism of the ancient with the constitutionalism of the modern world and examine, first, the points of real likeness, secondly, the points of essential difference, and, lastly, the results attainable by weighing the similarities against the no less marked dissimilarities.

A. Points of Apparent Likeness

These may be brought broadly under the following heads.

I. The very conception of a 'state', that is of an organized political body in which the rights and powers and duties of citizens are definitely defined, the conception of politics itself, are derived by us from Greece and Rome.

In the East we find despots, empires, cities, but except in places where the influence of Greece is apparent, as for example in the Greek cities of Ionia, we do not find states or constitutions. This does not necessarily mean that personal freedom or, still more, what one may call family freedom had no existence in Eastern countries. It would obviously be ridiculous to speak of the Jews at any period of their national existence as a nation of slaves. Nor can anyone believe that, however despotic may have been the rule of the Great King, the Persians at the time when they stood forth as the foremost nation of the ancient world were a body of bondsmen. But it is equally true that from no country in the East do we derive the idea of political rights. Eastern government has in general been at its best an expansion of 'paternal' government in the strict rather than in the metaphorical sense of the word 'paternal'. The King or the Sultan has been the father of his people; he has governed in accordance not with ideas of law, of rights, or of privilege, but in accordance with custom, with the dictates of religion, and with the prevailing notions of fairness. Consider the celebrated judgment of Solomon. It is clearly recorded as an example of the procedure befitting the wisest and most just of monarchs; it represents an idea of justice which we are told by travellers still commends itself to the people of the East. It has its natural place in the annals of an oriental country. Nothing of the kind will be found in the traditions of Rome or of Greece. It is foreign to the idea which led to the government of the state by an assembly of its citizens, and which at Rome first amended and codified customary law in the enactments of the Twelve Tables, and finally created the whole body of Roman jurisprudence. Individual rights, it is true, and personal freedom were protected in Judea better we may conjecture than in any other Eastern country. But Jewish law was the outcome of theological beliefs rather than of political ideas and the legislation no less than the religion of the Jews was developed not by praetors or jurists but by prophets and priests. The plain truth is that in the Jewish mind law was never separated from religion, and the political parties existing in Judea at the commencement of the Christian era, though sometimes compared to the factions of the classical world, were divided by theological rather than by political differences; the very desire for national independence took the form of religious hopes or aspirations. No doubt the very fact that the law was a body of theological dogmas and of moral precepts, no less than a legal code, has more than once in later ages encouraged the attempt to make it the basis of secular legislation. But the endeavour has always failed and was doomed to failure. It is the distinct separation between law and religion which has made it possible for the jurisprudence of Rome to become the foundation in many modern countries of the law of the land. It is the want of this separation which has thwarted the attempt to build up any modern system of law on the basis of the Jewish law, and if Judea has contributed little to the law she has contributed nothing to the political institutions of modern states, except in so far as ecclesiastical conceptions derived originally from Hebrew sources have extended or perplexed the political ideas of the modern world.[3]

Our current political phraseology bears witness to the closeness of our connection with ancient constitutionalism. Many of the terms we use are directly borrowed from Greece or Rome whilst others are mere renderings of Latin or Greek equivalents: 'politics', 'polity', 'society', 'constitution', 'legislation', 'monarchy', 'aristocracy', 'oligarchy', 'democracy', 'citizens', 'civilization', 'empire', and the like, are a few of the most obvious examples of our borrowings from the language of the ancient world. To these we may add the words 'judicial jurisdiction', and indeed the vast majority of the terms of art connected with the administration of justice.[4] These words, and a score more which could be collected together without any difficulty, are all derived from some Greek or Latin word, and every one of them is the sign for an idea with which we could not dispense.

Even where a constitutional or political expression is not derived from a classical source, you may often find its equivalent in Greek or Latin authors. Thus, to take one example, the word 'sovereignty', which so constantly recurs in modern works on jurisprudence and around which there has accumulated such a mass of disquisition and controversy as might fill volumes, is not to be found in classical writers. But the idea of the power which under whatever name is supreme under every constitution is to be found in Aristotle's *Politics*,[5] and, though there are notions, such for example as that of 'representative government', which cannot properly be translated into the language of Plato, of Aristotle, or of Cicero, and this for the

---

[3] But for one strange exception it might apparently be asserted with substantial truth that no Eastern race has developed a constitution. The exception is afforded by the Carthaginians but our imperfect acquaintance with their history precludes us from the explanation of their exceptional development.

[4] It may be doubted whether any one of these expressions occurs, at any rate in the sense in which they are here used, in the English version of the Old Testament. It is worth while noting this as a proof that our political conceptions are not derived from Jewish sources.

[5] Compare Holland's *Jurisprudence* (8th edn) p. 44.

very obvious reason that the idea itself was unknown to them, it is assuredly true that a good classical scholar could without difficulty reproduce in Greek or Latin a great deal of the political disquisitions which have been written during the last two centuries. The language in short no less than the ideas of modern public life may be described as an inheritance handed down to us from the classical ages.

II. The states of the classical world reached during the course of their existence a stage of social development which closely resembles the conditions of modern life.

Athens in the days of Pericles, or Rome in the time of Cicero, were civilized countries in the sense in which we may call modern England or modern France civilized and in the sense in which we cannot apply the word to the England say of Alfred the Great.

But this statement itself, while it summarises the point of likeness with which we are concerned, itself needs further explanation. Why is it that to certain societies we confidently ascribe the attribute of civilization, even though it be corrupt civilization, whilst to other societies which nevertheless may be marked by high virtues and even by potential greatness we with equal confidence deny the characteristic of civilization?

The explanation appears to be that, according at any rate to the ideas now prevalent, every civilized society possesses certain traits in common.

A society which can be termed civilized must have become in the strict sense a state or social organism. It is no mere agglomeration of families or clans.

A civilized society, again, must have passed beyond the stage of progress during which men are occupied wholly or principally in what may strictly be called the struggle for existence, that is the effort to ward off destruction either by savage animals or by human foes, and at the same time to obtain the means of supporting life and of averting famine. Victory in the fight for life is the foundation on which rests all hope of progress, but whilst the battle is going on a race can hardly be said to have attained civilization.[6]

A civilized society, further, must have achieved something more than an escape from the mere struggle for physical existence. It must have acquired the arts and knowledge which contribute to the ease and comfort of life. Many of its members must be able to enjoy the pleasures of existence. You can hardly conceive of a civilized

---

[6] This remark must not be applied to a body of civilized men, such for example as the Pilgrim Fathers, who, having emigrated [sic] to an unknown country peopled only by savages, are compelled for a time to devote all their efforts to the preservation of life, but such men are civilized because they have in their original homes belonged to countries the inhabitants of which had long passed out of the stage of barbarism, and it is worth remark that the long continuance of a struggle for bare existence destroys civilization. The break-up of the Roman Empire made it necessary for the inhabitants of many countries to fight with varying success against destruction by savage invaders and in some cases no doubt by savage animals. But this conflict of necessity involved the gradual loss of acquired civilization. The accounts again of the condition of France during the height of the Hundred Years War or of Germany during or at the end of the Thirty Years War show how easily the necessity for a renewed and lengthy struggle for existence destroys acquired civilization.

society where luxuries, that is to say, things which minister to human happiness and are not like food, clothes, or fire necessary for the support of life, do not exist.

And after all the greatest of luxuries is leisure and one of the most certain notes of a civilized country is that a large number of its inhabitants are, if not absolutely rich, so far free from pressing want that they can, if they choose, enjoy the pleasures of imagination, of thought, and of knowledge. Hence, speaking broadly, it almost follows that wherever there is civilization there is literature, and that a state cannot be considered civilized unless a large portion of its citizens consist of persons to whom is open the enjoyment of art, of philosophy, of science, or of letters, or of their equivalents.[7]

If, then, a civilized society is marked by these characteristics, if, that is to say, it must be an organized body or state, if it must have ceased to be occupied with the mere struggle for existence[,] if it must be a society containing a large number of men of leisure, [and] if, lastly, it must be a society whose members or at any rate whose leading members possess intellectual cultivation and are acquainted with art, science, and letters, we can easily see that all the leading notes of civilization are to be found in classical Athens or Rome, and in modern England, whilst they are not to be found, or at any rate are not all of them to be found, in the England of Alfred the Great.

In ancient Athens as in modern England you find a highly organized political society; it is in fact maintainable that in ancient Greece the state played a more prominent part than in modern Europe. To the Athenians of the time of Pericles as to Englishmen in the reign of Victoria, the periods in which men struggled for existence against wild beasts or savage foes was a mere tradition. True it is that ancient warfare might mean absolute destruction of a conquered city whilst modern warfare means at worst the loss of independence and possibly of political freedom. But speaking generally the citizens of Athens, though they were called upon to fight for independence, did not need to struggle for the right to live. As regards education we may well doubt whether the citizen of Athens was not better off than the Englishman of today. The whole city was full of intellectual energy, and every citizen could share in the life of the city.

Compare now the England of Alfred with the England of today. It is clear that every effort was needed to constitute what we should call a state, and the Saxon state when constituted was a far less organised body than the English nation of the

---

[7] The reason why I have added this expression, 'their equivalents', is that under the conditions of the classical world it was possible for men to obtain a high degree of knowledge and civilization with little or possibly no knowledge of reading or of writing. An Athenian citizen in the days of Pericles who took an active part in the social and political life of Athens may assuredly have attained a very high level of aesthetic, political, and moral cultivation without reading. How far the ordinary Athenian citizen was ignorant of letters I have no knowledge.

It is worth remark, though as I have never seen the observation made it may likely enough be unfounded, that in the time of Christ the Jews appear to have had two advantages which were almost equivalent to general education. The first is that the constant study of the law must generally have implied capacity for reading, and, even where the student was taught by word of mouth, he must have gone through a severe course of intellectual training. The second is that, as far as appears from the Gospels, the Jews did not hold one another as slaves; they seem at any rate in Judea to have been a nation of freemen.

nineteenth century. The struggle for existence was in the time of Alfred by no means over. It is indeed his greatest triumph that his whole life was a constant and in the main successful effort to repel Danish invasion. To compare the literary condition of England in the time of our greatest Saxon King with the culture either of Athens or of modern England savours of unseemly irony. The credit justly attributed to the King for his zeal in learning to read and for his efforts to stimulate among his countrymen some sort of desire for letters is a satire upon the gross ignorance of his time. The simple truth is that the elementary kind of culture involved in capacity for reading and writing was confined to churchmen, and the kind of knowledge possessed even by clerics would have appeared contemptible alike to the educated contemporaries of Socrates and to the educated Englishmen of the nineteenth century. We are accustomed to criticise with severity the attitude of the writers of the eighteenth century towards what they called the 'dark ages'. It is well, however, to recollect that this attitude was not without its justification. They felt, and felt truly, that the Middle Ages were intellectually and in some respects morally a period of retrogression. Ancient civilization had through large parts of Europe perished, modern enlightenment had begun only when the Middle Ages came to an end. The superstitious criticism of men like Voltaire, Gibbon, and Hume gave expression, though in an unsatisfactory form, to the principle insisted upon by Arnold that we are in many respects further removed from the times of Alfred than from the age of Pericles or of Cicero.[8]

III. In the annals of the ancient world, as in the history of modern Europe, you can trace the development of democracy.

It is easy to convince ourselves that there exists a very close analogy between the development of democracy in Greece and Rome and the so-called democratic progress which has at any rate for a century, and according to one class of writers for a far longer period, characterised the life of modern Europe.

The very word 'democracy' is, as already pointed out, inherited from Greece, and it is impossible to read the historians either of Greece or of Rome without seeing that in these states there existed political parties which could be described by the very expressions which we apply to the parties known to ourselves and our fathers. In Greece and in Italy, no less than in England, you find aristocrats, oligarchs, reactionists, moderates, or Whigs, Radicals, democrats, and revolutionists. The political philosophy (may we not say the satire) of Plato anticipates the censures and sarcasms which modern critics direct against the democracies of Paris or New York, and in the writings and speeches of Cicero you meet again and again with the language and the ideas of an English Whig or liberal Conservative. The great orator exhibits the essential merits, combined with the essential defects, of a Parliamentary leader. Of apologies for democracy fewer traces are to be found in classical literature than

---

[8] The barbarism of Saxon England in the time of Alfred is well typified by the tale whether true or invented that Alfred was induced to learn to read by the offer of a beautifully illuminated manuscript. The story implies both that a gentleman need not learn to read and that books were rare. The anecdote would sound as ridiculous with reference to Pericles as with reference to Mr Gladstone.

modern Englishmen might expect owing to the fact, whatever be its importance, that the men of letters and the philosophers whose writings have come down to us were, whether rightly or not, unfavourable to democratic institutions. The deliberate verdict of the ancient world may from one point of view be considered to be in favour of Republicanism. But there are few students who will deny that it is unfavourable to democracy. Still it is pretty clear that ancient democracies, which, as we shall have to notice, were from the universal existence of slavery all of them in a sense oligarchies, were necessarily defended by apologists on the same grounds as those on which popular government is defended by modern democrats.

Then again the phenomena of revolution were as well known to and as carefully observed by the statesmen or philosophers of Athens, of Greece, or of Republican Rome as by thinkers of the nineteenth century. It has become a commonplace with us to remark that democratic excesses lead to military tyranny. But all that could be said on this matter with regard to the career of Cromwell or Napoleon could be said with equal truth with regard to the Dictatorship of Sulla or the despotism of Caesar. Few indeed are the reflections with regard to the close connection between popular license and the growth of tyranny which have not been anticipated by Plato or Aristotle. In truth the revolutionary movement which marked the close of the eighteenth and the beginning of the nineteenth century revealed to thinkers full either of the traditions or the recollections of the French revolution the affinity between classical and quite modern history. The monarchical governments of the seventeenth and eighteenth centuries and even the aristocratic constitutionalism of England did not, on the surface of things at any rate, exhibit marked likeness to the political institutions of Greece or of Rome. The lessons to be learned from the revolutionary movements of classical times had been forgotten. Those outbreaks of popular violence which we term revolutions were in 1789 not only to French but even to English statesmen an astounding phenomenon—a disease so to speak of which they knew neither the cause nor the cure. Hence the strange helplessness of statesmanship, and, when experience at last taught men the arts by which to resist or elude the force of a popular movement, they found to their surprise that they had in reality been engaged in a contest which closely resembled the conflicts which harassed the free states of the ancient world.

To this revelation is curiously enough traceable one of the most patent of the faults in the prevailing treatment of ancient history, namely the tendency exhibited by writers belonging to the most different schools of thought, and many of them men both of genius and of erudition, to carry into the past the principles, the passions, or the prejudices of their own time.

Arnold's historical judgment is disturbed by the keenness of his political convictions. He could not write of Roman conservatism without recollecting the faults real or imaginary of the English Tories. His condemnation of Caesar reflects his detestation of Napoleon. His estimate of Hannibal is warped by the comparison between the resistance of Rome to Carthaginian and the resistance of England to French invasion. Yet surely to anyone who can look at the matter independently of modern associations, it must be apparent that Hannibal was as true a patriot as Scipio: the Carthaginian general fought to preserve Carthage and to destroy Rome. The Roman general fought to preserve Rome and to destroy Carthage. The one failed, the other succeeded, but each is entitled to equal praise or deserves equal condemnation. To consider Hannibal a reckless invader because he carried war into Italy is as unjust as to condemn Wellington because he invaded France. Hannibal at the gates of Rome was defending the independence of his own country as truly as Wellington was maintaining the independence of England when he entered Paris.

Grote, like Arnold, was a man of conspicuous fairness. His whole wish was to present a true and living picture of Greece and especially of Athens. He unfortunately perceived, and perceived truly, a likeness between the position of an Athenian democrat and the position of an English democrat. He was himself a philosophic Radical when Benthamism was a creed which excited unbounded enthusiasm. It is hardly an exaggeration to say that his *History of Greece* is coloured throughout by his Benthamite Radicalism. He defends and almost eulogizes Cleon because in the Athenian demagogue he sees the forerunner of democrats such as Francis Place.

Turn to Mommsen's *History of Rome*. It is the work of a great jurist from whom you might expect something of judicial calmness yet, if you consider his estimate say of Cicero, you see at once that whilst he writes of Rome he is thinking not a little of modern Germany. The follies and the failures of German Professorial Liberals have a good deal to do with his strenuous condemnation of the orator and man of letters who was the greatest Parliamentarian of the ancient world.

The reason why it is worth while dwelling upon the bias which infects modern writers when dealing with the politics of the classical ages is that this bias proves the strength of the analogy between the democratic movements of the ancient world and the democratic movement of our own time.

It is, however, well to produce the direct proof of this likeness. Such evidence is given by passages in which the most profound thinker amongst ancient historians has described the effect of the revolutionary spirit and has told how the whole Hellenic world was thrown into commotion when in every city the leaders of the democracy were struggling to bring in the Athenians and the leaders of the oligarchy to bring in the Lacedaemonians.

> 'When troubles had once begun', writes Thucydides, 'in the cities, those who followed carried the revolutionary spirit further and further, and determined to outdo the report of all who had preceded them by the ingenuity of their enterprises and the atrocity of their revenges. The meaning of words had no longer the same relation to things, but was changed by them as they thought proper. Reckless daring was held to be loyal courage; prudent delay was the excuse of a coward; moderation was the disguise of unmanly weakness; to know everything was to do nothing. Frantic energy was the true quality of a man. A conspirator who wanted to be safe was a recreant in disguise. The lover of violence was always trusted, and his opponent suspected. He who succeeded in a plot was deemed knowing, but a still greater master in craft was he who detected one. On the other hand, he who plotted from the first to have nothing to do with plots was a breaker up of parties and a poltroon who was afraid of the enemy. In a word, he who could outstrip another in a bad action was applauded, and so was he who encouraged to evil one who had no idea of it. The tie of party was stronger than the tie of blood, because a partisan was

more ready to dare without asking why. (For party associations are not based upon any established law, nor do they seek the public good; they are formed in defiance of the laws and from self-interest.) The seal of good faith was not divine law, but fellowship in crime. If an enemy when he was in the ascendant offered fair words, the opposite party received them not in a generous spirit, but by a jealous watchfulness of his actions. Revenge was dearer than self-preservation. Any agreements sworn to by either party, when they could do nothing else, were binding as long as both were powerless. But he who on a favourable opportunity first took courage and struck at his enemy when he saw him off his guard, had greater pleasure in a perfidious than he would have had in an open act of revenge; he congratulated himself that he had taken the safer course, and also that he had overreached his enemy and gained the prize of superior ability. In general the dishonest more easily gain credit for cleverness than the simple for goodness; men take a pride in the one, but are ashamed of the other.'[9]

Every sentiment contained in this passage, and in the masterly analysis of revolution of which it forms but a part, might with the change of a word or two be applied to the triumph of French Jacobinism. Burke, though he saw further into the perplexities of his time than his contemporaries, might have learned a good deal from Thucydides. He might have gathered that revolutionary enthusiasm, violence, and treachery were no new or inexplicable phenomena but the recurrence of a disease which had already afflicted and ruined the free states of the ancient world. It is assuredly no fancy to maintain that the conflict of oligarchs and democrats in Corcyra displayed and anticipated on a smaller stage the savagery of the conflict between moderates and revolutionists, Girondists and Jacobins, in Paris.

The revolution of Corcyra is then, to use Arnold's language, as 'modern' as the Parisian insurrection of June 1848. The Roman civil wars exhibit the same mixture of political intrigue and military violence as the Napoleonic *coup d'états* by which Buonaparte and his nephew each in their turn overthrew the French Republic, and nothing brings into relief the modern character of ancient politics so clearly as a comparison with the barbarous and, so to speak, old-world policy of Alfred or of William the Conqueror. What is there in the England of today which corresponds with the struggle against Danish pirates? How is it possible even to compare the policy of rulers who may be called the makers of modern England with the policy of Ministers who have to govern a country where peace and order have been for centuries established, and where every institution has its roots in the distant past? What has the Englishman of today to do with Barons and their retainers? How are we concerned with the elementary difficulty of introducing the rule of law? Where, above all, are we to find a real parallel for the conflict for supremacy between Pope and King? What has a modern statesman to do with a state of society in which science did not exist, in which the elementary arts of reading and writing were all but the monopoly of priests and monks, and the knowledge of restricted and scanty literature was confined to the clergy? It is all but impossible to realise in imagination

---

[9] Thucydides (tr. B. Jowett), vol. 1, pp 222, 223. Book III, s. 82 (part).

the times in which that 'benefit of clergy', which has till recently existed in England as an astonishing survival of bygone barbarism, might be regarded, not only as a mark of reverence due to the priesthood, but also as a concession by ignorance to the claims of education and culture; it is impossible, do what we will, to identify the disputes which agitated mediaeval society with the political conflicts of today. We have no doubt for bad and good inherited more of the ideas of the Middle Ages than may be at first sight apparent; the continued existence of the Papacy is sufficient evidence of a fact too patent to need proof, but it is nevertheless true that on the whole, and speaking broadly, the politics of the Middle Ages are to us ancient and obsolete. No effort will enable us to identify the questions which agitated the court of Alfred, or of the Conqueror, with the questions which agitate, or have agitated, the Parliaments of William IV or Victoria. The democratic movement of today recalls, if it does not repeat, the democratic movements of the classical ages. It neither recalls nor repeats the efforts to re-establish order and civilization which are the characteristic of the Middle Ages.

A Digression

It is interesting to notice that the division of history into ancient and modern has been attacked on two totally different grounds which, though easily distinguishable and in a sense inconsistent with one another, have sometimes been confused together by writers not in general chargeable with confusion of thought.

The first ground of attack rests upon the doctrine advocated by Arnold that what is called modern history because it is near to us chronologically, as for example the history of the Middle Ages, is really ancient because it has reference to a state of society earlier than and far removed from our own, whilst, on the other hand, much of what is called ancient history, and notably a certain part of Greek and of Roman history, may be rightly called modern because it refers to social and political conditions closely resembling the conditions of the present day, whence it follows that the right way of comparing historical periods is, instead of grouping them chronologically as ancient and modern, to place side by side those portions of every historical cycle which are analogous to one another and to compare, for example, the democracy of modern England or of France with the democratic part of the cycle of Greek or Roman history.

The defect of this view clearly lies in the artificiality inherent in every attempt to represent the history of mankind as a series of recurring cycles.[10] Of this, however, it is unnecessary here to say more; what we ought to note is the exact nature of the objection to the merely chronological division of history. This objection is, in effect, that periods chronologically remote may be really analogous and that eras chronologically near to each other may have no real analogy to one another, and hence that the chronological division into ancient and modern conceals the essential similarities between corresponding periods of history.

---

[10] See Woodrow Wilson, *The State*, s. 1164.

The second ground of attack on the commonly received division is based upon the unbroken continuity of human progress or development.

To fix upon any given point at which ancient history ends and modern history begins is, supporters of this objection argue, an impossibility in the strict sense of that word. How can you divide from each other two aspects of history which, since they are not really distinguishable, are indivisible?

Now, that the unbroken continuity of the development of mankind is a fact of great importance the full meaning of which is often overlooked admits not of denial, and it is easy to see how it happened that writers, such as Mr Freeman, well versed in the annals of English history and much occupied in discovering the links which bound together the Empire of the Caesars with the Holy Roman Empire, should insist strongly upon and indeed exaggerate the delusions produced by the popular habit of supposing that there are real gaps or breaks in history and of believing, for example, that the fall of the Roman Empire was the sudden event which might be compared, say, with the fall of Napoleon the Great and the break-up of the Empire which he had created.

The defects of this view are to an impartial observer pretty obvious. Its advocates in avoiding a popular error have fallen into a peculiar delusion of their own and have certainly seemed in words at least to confuse continuity with identity. It is one thing to assert what is clearly true, that history is in the main continuous, and quite another thing to imply what is certainly untrue, that there do not exist periods which are sharply distinguishable from one another, or changes which, though they may have been produced by the slow operation of causes which have long existed, are at last when they become visible to all men sudden, and the true answer to the objection that you can at no one point divide modern from ancient history assuredly is that continuity is a totally different thing from identity. An old remark often made is of wide application; day, it has been well said, turns gradually into night, and it is impossible to draw with logical precision the line which divides the one from the other, but for all this it is absurd to argue that day cannot be distinguished from night, or that light is the same as darkness.

What is odd is that our two separate grounds of attack coincided with each other. They are in fact totally different, and more than this, they rest upon different not to say opposed views of human progress. The doctrine of Dr. Arnold suggests that the history of every state which has been allowed to accomplish its natural growth may like human life be divided into periods of infancy, of middle age, and of old age.

The doctrine, on the other hand, which may be identified with the name of Mr. Freeman because of the extraordinary vigour with which he advocated it, is that you cannot draw anywhere the line between what is ancient and what is modern. But the emphasis thus laid on continuity is very different from, if indeed it be consistent with, the implied belief in something like the recurrence of historical cycles. However this may be, it is at any rate well to note that the two lines of attack upon the merely chronological treatment of history are distinct and that, while they each embody a good deal of important truth, have each exaggerated the truth which they contain so as to suggest conclusions which if taken strictly are false.

B. Points of Difference

I. *Ancient constitutionalism was based upon the city-state*

The states of the ancient world were not 'countries'; they were towns. Wherever there was a constitution, the rights and the political privileges of the citizen depended upon his being the member of a given city. He might live in the country but his whole position and status arose from his being a citizen or townsman. An Athenian might have his residence in any part of Attica, a Roman citizen might live in any part of the Roman world, but wherever he lived his citizenship or his constitutional rights were the result of his being a citizen and descended from citizens of Athens or of Rome. Even when Roman citizenship was in later ages extended to the whole of the Roman world the theoretical effect was to place every freeman throughout the Empire in the position of a Roman townsman. If we may illustrate great things by comparing them with small, we may explain the status of a Roman citizen by comparing it with the position of a citizen, e.g. John Gilpin, of the City of London. Gilpin remained a citizen whether he lived in Cheapside or at Edmonton, or for that matter wherever he resided, and his children (subject it may have been to the necessity for taking certain steps to retain their citizenship) would remain citizens of London wherever they were born or wherever they lived. Suppose now that an Act of Parliament were to extend to all the inhabitants of the United Kingdom the citizenship of London. This would make an immense increase in the number of persons entitled to exercise the privileges, whatever they are, of London citizenship. But their rights would be rights exercisable only in London and would be the rights of Londoners.[11]

To put the same point in a somewhat different shape, the free states of the ancient world, whose constitutions may be compared with the constitutions of modern Europe, were towns, and the freemen who were members of these states were townsmen. The words 'polity', 'politics', 'citizenship', 'civilization', 'urbanity', and a score more all testify to one and the same thing, that the commonwealths of classical times were towns, or, to use a convenient term, city-states, whilst the commonwealths or monarchies of modern times, such for example, as the French Republic, the English constitutional monarchy, each of the States which make up the United States, are countries. And this difference between the territory of an ancient state, which is a town, and the territory of a modern state which is a country, is essential. It means much more than the mere fact that in Greece and in Rome political rights depended upon a man being the citizen of a particular town, whereas in France or in England a man's political rights depend upon his belonging to a particular country, i.e. being born in or being the descendant of parents born in a territory, such as England or France, which may indeed contain towns but consists to a large extent of rural districts. It means that originally at least political rights depended on a person's living

---

[11] Note too that when Roman citizenship was extended to the whole Roman world the Roman city-state had passed into a very different thing, the Roman Empire. It may be said broadly that the ancient world knew of city-states and empires, but did not recognize what we term countries.

in and being a member of a city community where the townsmen were necessarily linked together by all the ties springing, not only from common descent or race, but from constant association and from sharing the common labours of a common city life. So closely indeed was the idea of a commonwealth connected in the mind of a Greek with the idea of township or citizenship that Aristotle did not believe that a real polity could exist except in a town of a very moderate size,[12] and the idea that countrymen could share in the life of a state except by coming to the city to which they belonged, and there taking part in the assembly of citizens, seems to have been utterly inconceivable either by the statesmen or by the philosophers of the ancient world.

Here indeed, as elsewhere, it is true that the Roman Empire affords transition from classical to modern conceptions. The conquest of the world by Rome led to the formation, not indeed of a country, but of an empire. Even before the end of the Republic the necessity arose for the expansion of the city-state so as to include the inhabitants of districts and towns lying outside the city. The Social War in effect extended Roman citizenship to all the free inhabitants of Italy,[13] but this change, great as it was, did not in reality make Italy into a country, but—a very different thing—made every Italian a citizen of Rome. Hence an Italian living, e.g. at Naples, had the status of a Roman citizen just as St Paul had the status of a Roman citizen though living at Tarsus. But he could not exercise the political rights of a citizen which in 89 BC were a reality without coming to Rome and voting in the assembly of citizens at Rome.

II. Representative government was unknown to the classical world

This fact whatever its explanation is indisputable. The absence of any idea that a citizen could exercise his rights through representatives is seen in cases where according to modern conceptions the use of representation would have been natural and even necessary. In the Social War itself the Italians who allied themselves against Rome saw no other way of asserting their rights than by founding a new Rome at Corfinium, which was rechristened with the name of Italica. All Italians were to be citizens of this new metropolis, and here were to be the place of assembly and the Senate House. A Senate of 500 members and a magistracy resembling that of Rome completed a constitution which adhered closely to the very political conditions which its authors had most reason to abjure:[14] and Rome herself, when forced to open her gates to the Italians, could find no other way of admitting them to citizenship than

---

[12] Rousseau, who was a citizen of Geneva and who attempted to revive ancient ideas of citizenship, held that every state ought to be small.

[13] Pelham, p. 202. The difference between a city-state and a modern country involves an essential difference of political conceptions. In the ancient world township and citizenship were identified, or rather were only two ways of looking at the same thing. Men felt a common patriotism because they were fellow townsmen. Civilization itself was according to ancient ideas the disseminating throughout the country of the spirit of the town. The word 'country', on the other hand, refers apparently originally to the open land: 'the country' in the material sense of the word, and fellow countrymen were people inhabiting not the same town but the same land or territory. The word seems to mark the transition from the classical to the mediaeval idea of a state.

[14] See ibid., p. 201.

to extend the rights of Roman townsmen to the freemen of Italy. If ever again there were circumstances which one might have thought would have suggested representation it was the condition of things which created the Achaean League. For the first time the states of Greece perceived the wisdom or felt the necessity of federation. The members of the League created a sort of federal government yet the assembly of the League was not a representative body. It was constituted of citizens of the several allied states who chose to attend at its meetings.

Why, it may be asked, did the political intelligence of the ancient world fail to grasp that idea of representation which at the present day seems as obvious as it is useful?

The first and most general answer to this inquiry is that in no sphere of thought or in action is invention so rare as in the field of politics, and that in modern Europe 'representation' has not been an invention devised by human sagacity but a notion which has gradually grown up under a course of long and complicated historical development.

The second answer is that the idea of one man being empowered to act for and thus become the agent and ultimately the general representative of another is so far from being a simple notion, or one which is at all easy to grasp, that it has even in the sphere of private law been developed only by degrees, and with great difficulty. The genius of Rome for jurisprudence has excited the admiration of mankind. Yet even the Roman jurists found it hard to work out the conception of representation or agency, and in the law of England you can discover traces of exactly the same difficulty.

To which it may be added that, in addition to the difficulty of realising how one man could represent another, a statesman or thinker of classical times would, had the idea of representative government been suggested to him, have probably rejected it for a reason which, as we shall see, is by no means without force: representation, though it has its conveniences, leads to a diminution in that keen sense of citizenship generated by personal participation in public affairs, which was the life blood of an ancient commonwealth.

III. Ancient constitutionalism, as indeed classical society generally, was based on slavery

Every ancient democracy was, in early days, an oligarchy. Athens was the most democratic of classical states yet in Athens the number of slaves exceeded the number of freemen.

The presence of slavery had, it must be noted, several most important effects.

It allowed the free citizens to devote to public affairs an amount of time and attention which are not at the disposal of men who are forced to labour with their hands for the support of themselves and their families.

It freed statesmen from the necessity of considering what was the position and what were the rights which ought to be conceded to men who, though forming part of the state, could hardly devote themselves to liberal arts and pursuits or in other words to the professions which alone, it was held, became freemen. The existence of slavery further arrested the growth of those general ideas as to human equality which, both as elements of progress and as causes of disturbance, have in modern Europe exerted an immense influence over the course of politics.

Of the economical and the moral evils of slavery it is unnecessary to say much: they are patent and generally recognized. What must here be insisted upon is that every ancient state was a slave state, and that the only parallel to this condition of affairs which is presented by modern times is to be found in the slave states of the American Republic as they existed before and during the War of Secession. There, and there alone, it was possible till not 50 years ago to observe the phenomenon of democracies based upon slavery.

IV. In the classical world of city-states the Church had no existence

Religion, or more strictly religions, of course existed in classical times, and it is quite possible that religious feelings and theological beliefs had a more potent influence than one would suppose from the books which have come down to us from the ancient world. The writings of Cicero, Caesar, Tacitus, Thucydides, and the like, represent the sentiment of highly educated men and of sceptical thinkers. It is almost certain that, even in the age of Thucydides and even at Athens, the masses of the people were far more strongly influenced by religious ideas than were the great classical writers who have given us a picture of Athenian life. Whatever Cicero or Caesar may have thought about the gods, we may pretty safely conclude that in the most cultivated ages of ancient Rome the mass of the people were not sceptics; but, though a writer, fond of stating sensible conclusions in a paradoxical form, has maintained that ancient states owed a great deal of their civilization to churches, this contention, even if it be sound, means nothing more than that in early times community in religious beliefs, the worship of the same gods, and the use of the same sacrificial rites, constituted a strong bond of union. Grant the truth of this doctrine, but remember at the same time that the prevalence of common religious beliefs is a very different thing from the existence of a Church. The notion itself of a Church comes to us from the East. Christianity in giving currency to an Eastern religion introduced into the Western world the conception of a Church, that is to say of a great religious body or corporation to which men belonged independently of their connection with the state, which enforced moral or religious rules which might or might not coincide with the law of the state, which offered rewards different from those given and threatened penalties different from the punishments inflicted by the state, and lastly which claimed from its members an allegiance which might conflict with and override the obedience due to the state. The existence in short of the Church limited the sphere of the state and at the same time created a power which was always a rival and might be the foe of the civil government. With the claims of Church and State, with the attempts to adjust them, or with the efforts which have from time to time been made to identify Church and State and thus make now the one, now the other, absolutely supreme, we need not here concern ourselves. All that need here be noted is that the antithesis between things civil and things ecclesiastical was unknown in Europe before the rise of Christianity had introduced into public life a whole body of new and perplexing problems. Demosthenes or Cicero would we may conjecture have found it impossible to understand that conflict between Church and State which has coloured and still colours in one shape or another the whole course of modern European civilization.

Consider too that the existence of the Church brought with it a whole body of feelings and beliefs which have given rise to political problems which were practically all but unknown to the city-states of the older world. The claim, for instance, which has taken a hundred forms, to obey God rather than man has led at once to a kind of revolt and on the other hand to a kind of persecution which could hardly have been imagined by a Roman or Greek statesman. The extraordinary effect on the imagination of Greece and Rome [of] the death of Socrates is in reality a proof how rare was direct religious persecution, and note that the reason why Socrates, and occasionally other philosophers, came into conflict with the power of the state is that philosophy performed in classical times, though to a very limited extent, the function in later ages of religion and, by advocating a moral standard different from the ideals supported by the state, brought about, though to a very slight degree, the kind of conflict which has raged in later ages on a huge scale between State and Church, or between the state and between men who claim to follow the dictates of their own conscience as revealing to them the will of God. The ancient world produces in the West at any rate no parallel either to the Reformation or to the Thirty Years War.

V. Greece and Rome knew nothing of feudalism

'Feudalism' is one of those vague terms which because of their uncertain and varying significance at once escape definition[15] and at the same time exert an undue influence over the imagination. It gives at any rate expression to a just feeling that mediaeval society contains certain elements which, difficult as they are to define, are not to be found in social life either of classical ages or of the present day. For my present purpose we are happily freed from the necessity for giving a precise definition of feudalism. We may fairly describe it as a social organisation which, though varying greatly in different countries and in different generations, was based on the ownership of land and on personal relations created by or closely connected with the ownership of land. It might be called a state of society in which public relations depended upon private relations and political rights depended on landed rights whilst the ownership of land was concentrated in the hands of a few persons.[16] But a student would do well not to let himself be tied down by any precise definition of feudalism and to content himself with noting that mediaeval feudalism under all its forms and all its varying modifications included certain ideas unknown to the city-states of the ancient world.

---

[15] See 1 Pollock and Maitland, p. [left blank].
[16] See Ramsay on Feudalism, 9 *Encyc. Brit.*, p. 120.

1. Feudalism is the denial of the distinction between public and private law or indeed of public and private rights.

> Just in so far as the idea of feudalism is realised all that we call public law is merged in private law. Jurisdiction is property, office is property, the kingship itself is property, the same word dominion has to stand now for ownership, now for lordship. The king, it is true, is a highly privileged as well as very wealthy person. Still his rights are but private rights amplified and intensified. It would be easy to exaggerate the approach made in any country to the definite realisation of this feudal ideal. But just in so far as it is realised, 'public law' appears as a mere appendix to real property law modified in particular cases by a not very ample law of persons.[17]

2. The property on which rights depended was real property or land.

At Athens or Rome, it has been well said, a man was entitled to a share in land because he was a citizen. In a mediaeval country a man's place as a citizen, or rather as a subject, depended on the holding of land.

3. According to the feudal ideal the members of a country were linked to one another by the personal relation of homage and tenure, that is by relations based at bottom on the personal fealty of A to B arising from his homage or from A's having become B's man in return for land which he received from or held of B.[18]

Some parts of feudalism are, it is said, traceable back to the later institutions of Imperial Rome. It is further credible enough that analogies to feudalism are to be found in the annals of countries which had no relation whatever with mediaeval Europe. Nor would it be at all astonishing should the earlier stages of classical civilization present points of likeness to mediaeval feudalism. What we should as students of law note is that from a legal point of view the essence of feudalism is the dependence of status and rights upon the tenure of land and upon homage, and generally that the ideal of feudalism contained at least three conceptions familiar indeed to Alfred the Great or to William the Conqueror but absolutely unknown to Alexander the Great or to Caesar. These conceptions are, first, the identification of public with private rights, secondly, the close connection of civil rights with the ownership of land and, thirdly, the bond of union arising from the personal relation between tenant and landlord which was based upon homage and fealty and culminated in the conception of allegiance to the King as head of the state, and this allegiance, be it noted, was something very different from, though not unconnected with, the duty of a citizen to obey the supreme power in the state, and was in effect the fealty due to the King as ultimate owner of the national territory.

Now this feudal ideal which became closely intertwined with the ecclesiastical theories of the Middle Ages, whilst it contained notions all of which were foreign to the citizens of the classical city-states and some of which cannot easily be accepted by modern Englishmen, has left its traces upon the whole political and social life of countries such as France, England, or Germany. In some regions its influence is visible or has been visible mainly in the realm of public law. In other countries, and certainly

---

[17] See generally 1 Pollock and Maitland, pp 208, 209.
[18] See ibid. bk. II, ch. I, s. 6, Homage and Fealty. 'Fealty of course is the Latin *fidelitas* but it is interesting to notice that on manorial rolls written by clerks who were no great Latinists the word becomes *feodelitas* or *feoditas* so close is the connection between faith and fee.' Ibid. pp 278, 279.

in England, it has profoundly influenced private law. Our law of real property at the end of the nineteenth century cannot be understood without a careful study of fees, of tenure, and the like, and, if you look at the matter from a general point of view, you will find that from feudalism we derive a body of words and conceptions which be they good or bad are absolutely unclassical. Homage, loyalty, honour—to sum the whole thing up in one word, chivalry—are words for which you cannot find real equivalents in the language of Thucydides or of Livy. The ideas which these words denote have excited the most different emotions in different minds.

> 'But the age of chivalry is gone. That of sophisters, economists, and calculators has succeeded, and the glory of Europe is extinguished for ever. Never, never more shall we behold that generous loyalty to rank and sex, that proud submission, that dignified obedience, that subordination of the heart which kept alive, even in servitude itself, the spirit of an exalted freedom. The unbought grace of life, the cheap defence of nations, the nurse of manly sentiment and heroic enterprise, is gone! It is gone, that sensibility of principle, that chastity of honour, which felt a stain like a wound, which inspired courage whilst it mitigated ferocity, which ennobled whatever it touched, and under which vice itself lost half its evil by losing all its grossness.'[19]

> 'If I were called upon to name', writes Dr Arnold, 'what spirit of evil predominantly deserved the name of Antichrist, I should name the spirit of chivalry—the more detestable for the very guise of the 'Archangel ruined', which has made it so seductive to the most generous spirits—but to me so hateful, because it is in direct opposition to the impartial justice of the Gospel, and its comprehensive feeling of equal brotherhood, and because it so fostered a sense of honour rather than a sense of duty.'[20]

This difference of judgement has immense significance; it means that Burke and Arnold were each aware of a contrast and even an opposition between classical and mediaeval ideals, but Burke unrestrictedly admired whilst Arnold as unrestrictedly condemned the characteristic in which mediaeval society differed fundamentally from the social life of the ancient world. Neither the praise nor the condemnation was just. Prophecy is rarely combined with equity. What neither Burke nor Arnold, though looking at the same matter from an opposite point of view, fully appreciated is the extent to which mediaeval conceptions have become a permanent part of modern civilization.

VI. *Until the rise of the Roman Empire there existed no elaborate administrative system(?)*[*]

In a modern state[,] administration, the action that is to say of the Courts, of government officials, and [of] the like, is really of more consequence and more deeply affects

---

[19] Burke, *Reflections on Revolution in France* [as taken from] *The Wisdom of Edmund Burke*, by E. A. Pankhurst, pp 153, 154.
[20] *Life of Dr Arnold*, by A. P. Stanley, vol. 1. (5th edn), p. 255.

---

[*] In the margin the following later manuscript note was added: 'I rather doubt the historical truth of this assertion though I think it contains a certain amount of real truth. A.V. D. 22 June 1900.'

the happiness of the people than the mere form of the constitution. It is hardly possible to make the same assertion of the strictly city-states of antiquity. The condition of society under which every citizen could take an active part in the management of the city affairs is only conceivable when the state is in fact a town and we must add not a very large town. In classical Athens as in Republican Florence it was possible for a very intelligent and energetic body of citizens each to take an individual part in every kind of public duty. Now that states are countries and the art of administration is a highly technical art which must be entrusted to experts, the most that a citizen can do is to take some indirect part, generally a very indirect part indeed, in appointing the persons who, to use modern expressions, are the civil or military servants of the state. The very idea of a judicial body of trained lawyers, or an administrative body of trained civil servants, is all but inconsistent with the existence of that intensely active civil life which was originally the ideal of the city-state. Here, as in other points, the annals of Rome mark the transition from ancient to modern ideas of government. It was the tremendous administrative system, including in that term both the military and the civil service of the Empire, which for ages supported Roman civilization, and left to the mediaeval world the tradition of Imperial greatness.[21]

C. Results of Comparison

I. If we weigh carefully the resemblances against the differences between ancient and modern constitutionalism we arrive at the conclusion that the differences are essential.

The city-state differs fundamentally from a country. The existence of slavery raised indeed difficulties from which modern politics are free but it also prevented the existence of problems which perplex European statesmanship. Representative government, with which we may combine the creation of a large administrative system, has placed an ordinary citizen in quite a different relation to public affairs from that occupied by an Athenian with regard to the political life of Athens. But above all, the existence of the Church and the traditions inherited from feudalism have in every direction changed the colour of public life. On the whole we are more likely to overrate than to underrate the immediate likeness between ancient and modern constitutionalism. We have inherited the idea of politics and the terms of the political art from Greece and Rome. But the fact that we use the language of the classical ages is

---

[21] In the United States where, in theory at least, all citizens take a part as electors in the appointment of officials of the government of the country, there has always been a distinct prejudice against the creation of a special and skilled civil service; and the popular feeling has been that even judicial appointments ought to be made directly by the people. Bosses or party managers have favoured a prejudice which increases their influence, but it must in candour be admitted that the maintenance of a permanent civil service of persons appointed for their knowledge and capacity is opposed to the essentially democratic feeling that one man is nearly, if not quite, as competent as another to undertake any public function whatever. This feeling is of course in one sense a prejudice due to ignorance, but it certainly falls in with the sound conviction that under a democratic constitution every man ought to take an active part in the management of public affairs.

apt to conceal from us the difference between the ideas which may be covered by one and the same word. Democracy does not mean the same thing in modern Europe which it meant in ancient Greece. Citizenship under the French Republic is a very different thing from citizenship in Sparta. What we may gather from the comparison between ancient and modern constitutionalism is at best a certain number of useful analogies.

II. Here, as elsewhere, an exception illustrates the rule. Certain European countries either retained or revived the conditions of classical times. In the Italian Republics, such as Milan, Florence, or Venice, in the Swiss cantons, and especially in such towns as Bern and Zurich, and in the states which ultimately formed the Dutch Republic, we find city-states where we may see reproduced the phenomena most characteristic of the Republics of classical times. No one can read the annals of Florence, or of Genoa, or of Venice without recalling the history of the Greek Republics. City governments, city conflicts, city civilization, with all its merits and defects, oligarchies, democracies, and, above all, tyrannies, reappear. But for all this the Italian Republics show the influence of circumstances and of ideas for which you will find no parallel in Athens or in Republican Rome.

The Italian Republics flourished in a world which became more and more a world of countries and not of city-states. At the time when Athens and Sparta played a leading part in the history of mankind, civilization, or at any rate European civilization, was represented by cities. The Empire of the Great King menaced, and the growth of the Macedonian monarchy was in the long run fatal to, the Greek system of independent cities. Still, until Rome became the mistress of the world, a city-state was the only known type of civilized government and, long after the Empire of the Caesars was practically accepted as the best form of government for the countries which then made up the civilized world, philosophers, historians, and rhetoricians kept alive the tradition that freedom could exist only in a Republic, that is in a city-state. This was a view of the world which could not be maintained by a citizen of Florence or of Milan.

For the Italian Republics were in theory part of the Roman Empire and their citizens never doubted that Imperial authority, however much they might in fact defy it, was legitimate authority sanctioned by Heaven.

Then again, the Italian Republics, as indeed all the mediaeval Republics, and notably the Swiss cantons, were profoundly influenced in one way or another by feudalism. The nobles of Italy retained a kind of power which did not belong to any of the noble families of Greece or of Rome. The mediaeval noble stood outside the city. He was not like the great Athenian families or the Roman patricians part of the city.* Then too city-states in the Middle Ages, such for example as Bern, were themselves possessed of feudal rights and superiorities. Down to 1798 Switzerland was filled with survivals of feudalism. The *ancien régime* was more markedly feudal in the 13 cantons than in France.

To this ought perhaps to be added that, though trade had more to do with the politics of Greece or of Rome than at first appears, yet that trade and mercantile considerations

---

* The manuscript page has a question-mark in the adjacent margin.

exerted a far more potent and avowed influence in Italy, as also in the states which made up the Dutch Republic, than they ever exerted in the classical world.

But, after all, the most essential difference between the city-states of Italy, and the city-states of Greece and of Rome, lies in the existence of the Church. There is nothing in the ancient world which even faintly resembles the conflict between the Papacy and the Empire, and this conflict created the Italian parties of Guelfs and Ghibellines. Contrast again the career of Socrates and Savonarola. The one is as natural a result of the condition of society in the fifth century BC as the other of the state of society at Florence in the sixteenth century AD. But they each belong to such completely different social, religious, and political conditions that it is impossible even in imagination to transfer the career of Savonarola to Athens or of Socrates to Florence. Place the two men side by side and you may measure the whole difference produced by the existence of the Church. The comparison is the more instructive because the Italy of Savonarola was filled with men zealous for the revival of classical learning and classical ideals, and one may assert with confidence that Christian or ecclesiastical ideals exerted less power in the Italy of Savonarola than in any other so-called Christian country.

III. Our comparison then leads to the conclusion that the states of the modern world differed in such essential particulars from the city-states of classical times as to make it almost inconceivable that in the matters which now concern a constitutionalist much direct instruction can be derived from the experience of Greece or of Rome. No doubt you may find in ancient history analogies with modern constitutional history which are interesting and suggestive, but that, from the annals of the ancient world we can derive anything like the kind of instruction which Arnold and others have supposed that we can find there, is something very like a delusion. The constitutional experience of Athens or of Sparta will not solve any of the problems which present themselves to modern statesmen or thinkers.

And to this conclusion a candid examiner would come without any reservation whatever were it not for a consideration which often escapes attention. It is that some of the ideas which distinguish modern from ancient…

[Missing page of text]*

which[,] at the death of the Archbishop passed like a thrill of emotion over the whole Catholic world, and was stimulated far less by his mere martyrdom than by admiration of the Saint who under his archiepiscopal robes wore a hair shirt and inflicted upon himself all the self-imposed tortures of a true monk. We still admire the Crusaders but we can no more imagine the outbreak of the Crusade than the commencement of another Thirty Years War between Catholics and Protestants. It is certain then that some of the ideas which divide us from the classical ages have lost their potency, and it is at any rate conceivable therefore that the constitutionalism of the twentieth century may in some respects be a reversion towards the constitutionalism of classical times, and in this sense therefore we may possibly find that ancient history turns out to be modern.

---

* For some idea of what is missing, see points III and IV under C in this lecture's Analysis (p. 192 above).

3

Representative Government

Analysis*

Introduction
> *Two questions*
>> 1. What is meant by representative government?
>> 2. What are merits and defects of representative government?

A. What is Representative Government?
> Delegation by citizens of state to their agents or representatives of authority to act for such citizens mainly in matters of legislation
> 1. Invention unknown to classical times
> 2. Invention mainly unconscious, i.e. an arrangement to meet immediate wants
> 3. Degrees of representative authority
> 4. Variation in power of representative legislature or Parliament

B. What are Merits and Defects of Representative Government?
> I. *Merits*
> Makes possible that—
> 1. Inhabitants of large country should take part in political life;
> 2. Legislation should be continuous;
> 3. Legislators should be superior to rest of community;
> 4. (Separation of powers should exist.)
>
> II. *Defects*
> Representative government—
> 1. Cannot be extended beyond the real though indefinite limit;
> 2. Lessens the part taken by individual citizens in government of country;
> 3. Creates a body of representatives with interest or wishes of their own;
> 4. Gives undue authority to parliamentary majorities.

(See Freeman, *Federal Government*, ch. V, s. 3, pp 254–74;
Mill, *Representative Government*.)

---

* Its contents, apart from the suggested reading, have been derived from an undated manuscript attached to the lecture schedule headed 'Easter & Trinity Terms 1900'. The suggested reading has been derived from the title page of the full lecture text.

Representative Government[*]

Introduction

My purpose in this chapter is to consider two questions: first, what is meant by representative government? secondly, what are the merits and defects of the representative system?

A. What is Meant by Representative Government?

The essence of representative government is, that the citizens of a state delegate the right or power to act for them (or, in other words, authority to represent them), in matters primarily of legislation, to their agents or representatives. The body which thus represents them, or, it may be, a portion of which thus represents them, is usually and conveniently called a Parliament.

This conception of representation is at the present day so widespread and commonly received that it is thought to he a simple and obvious idea. As a matter of fact it is a complex and artificial notion which was wholly unknown to the city-states of the ancient world and was in reality foreign to the ideas of citizenship natural to the inhabitants of a town. It seems to us no doubt strange that a political device, with which we are all familiar and which presents obvious advantages, should not have suggested itself either to the thinkers or to the statesmen of antiquity and in modern Europe should have developed itself only by degrees and along a path not very easy to trace. There were, as has been already suggested, at least two causes which delayed, and might well have prevented, the development of this new political invention or discovery.

The most obvious of these causes is that representation is opposed to that active and direct discharge of public duties and that zealous participation in the public life of a state or town which was essential to the prosperity of the city-state. It may well be doubted whether strictly representative assemblies would ever of themselves have come into existence in small independent communities. Switzerland is the one European country where something like the small states of the ancient would still flourish and, though in Switzerland representative bodies now exist, yet it is easy enough to see that even these representative assemblies are not Parliaments of the English

---

[*] The manuscript's title page was dated 3 May 1900, but the lecture text is the product, in places, of what appears to be mainly subsequent alteration. On the implications of Dicey's treatment of representative government for his account of parliamentary sovereignty in *The Law of the Constitution*, see Editor's Introduction, pp xxxvi f. above.

type, and that the Swiss people still retain a preference for non-representative forms of democracy.[1]

The second and less obvious cause is that the notion of agency, that is of *A* being empowered by *B* to act for *B* and bind *B* by his action, is an idea which, familiar though it be to us, even trained lawyers of great ability, and *a fortiori* laymen unaccustomed to legal conceptions, found it at one time very hard to grasp even in the sphere of private law. A very slight knowledge of the law of Rome is sufficient to prove this, and, if in the early law of England lawyers whose mode of thinking was after all indirectly influenced by the civil or canon law were able to accept with ease the idea of agency, a student ought to note that the rules forbidding the assignment of *choses in action* or, in non-technical words, the transference by *A* of his right, e.g. to be paid £20 by *B*—rules which even now complicate the law of England—bear witness to the existence even down to modern times of the same condition of thought as that which originally delayed the acceptance of the idea of agency; in each case people have felt a natural difficulty in admitting that the rights or liabilities of *A* which are personal to him and the result of his own acts could be transferred to *B*, and if it was difficult to adopt the conception of agency and of notions kindred to it in the sphere of private law there was a still greater difficulty in accepting it in the realm of public law. How, it might well have been said by a citizen of Athens or of Florence, can I be bound by the acts of my so-called representative? It is conceivable indeed that I may be bound by a specific act which I acting as a member of the general assembly have told my agent or representative to perform, such for example, as the signing of a Treaty, but I cannot transfer to him my civic rights. I can no more make him represent me in everything than a freeman can agree to be bound in the whole conduct of his life by the action of another man to whom be has given plenary authority to act for him.

It is indeed not sufficiently noted that even in countries where the idea of representation, that is of agency in the sphere of politics, has obtained acceptance there may exist very different degrees of representation, or, to adopt the terms of private law, there may be great differences in the extent of the authority given by the principals, that is the electors, to their agents.

Thus the representative may be, not so much a representative or a general agent of those by whom he is appointed, as a person delegated to do some particular act. This was very much the position of the delegates sent by the cantons to the old Swiss Diet. They were more like ambassadors assembled at a congress than members of a legislative assembly. Each of them was bound to follow the instructions of his canton. If any difficulty arose he was bound to ask for further instructions, and this lack of full authority made the action of the Diet very feeble. The same thing, unless I am mistaken, was true of the body which represented the German Confederation from 1815 to 1866.

A representative again may represent not the whole nation but an order. This was the position occupied by the members of the French States General. They represented each of the three orders or estates, namely the Nobility, the Church, and the

---

[1] It is to be noted that Rousseau objects to the system of representative government.

Third Estate or, as we should say, the Commonalty, and of each of these orders the members of the States General were rather delegates (that is particular agents with limited authority) than real representatives or, if we may use the terms of private law, general agents with unlimited authority.

The matter may be looked at from a different point of view and we may consider what is the extent of the authority conferred not on the individual members of a legislature but on the Parliament itself. We shall then find that this authority may be either unrestricted, or at any rate absolutely indefinite as is the authority of the English Parliament, or else be restricted.

And restriction on the competence of the legislature may take two different forms.

Its competence may be limited by its being authorised under the constitution to deal only with certain definite topics. This is a restriction placed on the authority both of the American Congress and of the Swiss Federal Assembly. Each of these Parliaments can legislate on certain definite subjects but on no others, and this kind of restriction is imposed on the action of many other legislatures.

The competence of the legislature may be limited by the fact that the laws made by it require for their validity the ratification of the electors. An example of this kind of restriction is found in the existing Constitution of Switzerland under which the action of the federal Parliament is made subject in many cases to the referendum or, speaking broadly, to a vote of the people. The Conventions, to give another example, which propose amendments in the constitutions of an American State act almost invariably subject to the approval or ratification of the people. Such a Convention proposes a scheme of constitutional reform. The plan when at last put into formal shape, i.e. after it has been finally voted upon by the Convention, is submitted to the people and does not come into force until and unless it has been approved and ratified by a popular vote. To use again the terms of private law an American Convention is an agent of the people with authority to draft a scheme for amending the Constitution. It has no authority to legislate or to put the scheme into force.

The various methods by which the power of representatives, or the competence of representative assemblies, is limited are at bottom merely illustrations of the fact that, under many constitutions, either the particular men who represent the people or the representative bodies themselves are agents with a merely limited authority.

Turn now to the best and most famous example of an absolutely representative assembly, that is of a legislative body which, whether you consider the position of the individual members or the position of the legislative body itself, is in theory at least the full and absolute representative of the nation. This legislature is of course the Parliament of the United Kingdom. Each individual member[2] of the House of Commons is, though elected by a particular constituency, a person acting not for London, or Middlesex, or Liverpool, etc. but for the whole nation. He is supposed

---

[2] For convenience we may as well confine our attention to the House of Commons, but the other parts of the Parliament, *viz.* the Crown and the House of Lords, each together with the House of Commons represent and are agents of the nation.

in theory to be absolutely free from the necessity for attending to the instructions of his constituents. Not only is he not called upon in theory to resign his seat if he should happen to disagree with the men who elected him, but 'resignation' of a seat in the strict sense of the word resign is unknown to our constitutional law. It is a proceeding which can be accomplished only in an indirect and roundabout manner and which for its accomplishment requires the assent of the Crown. Then too as each representative acts for the whole nation so Parliament collectively exerts during its existence the whole of the national authority. The English constitution knows nothing of popular ratification. The Septennial Act is a conclusive proof that the constitution imposes no limit upon the authority of Parliament. The plain truth is that the doctrine of representation or agency has under the English constitution been carried out to its extreme limit. Parliament may be described as a body [or an agent?]* with unlimited authority to act for its principal—the nation. The nearest parallel to full representation as it exists theoretically in England is to be found in the Constituent Assemblies which in France and other Continental countries have since 1789 been convoked with a view to remodelling the Constitution or to create a new constitution. These Assemblies, such for example as the last States General, which was also the first National Assembly of France, the Convention of 1792, the National Assembly of 1848, or the National Assembly of 1871, have according to the doctrine of French law represented the whole authority of the nation. They have been invested with sovereignty; they have in short been as truly representative bodies as the Parliament of England.

But be it remarked that, though the English Parliament and other Assemblies have in theory been invested with complete sovereignty, this absolute transference of the authority of the nation to its delegates has never really been completely acquiesced in by the electors. An agent after all derives his power from the will of his principal and, just as no man can in private life constitute a universal agent who has the right to act for him and to bind him in all matters whatsoever, so the people of a country never will and never in reality can transfer to a representative assembly absolute, unlimited, irrevocable authority to act for the nation. A representative body must after all represent. Even in England the authority vested in Parliament is rather indefinite than absolute, and it would be simply ridiculous to press the theory of representation to such an extent as to make the people of a country the slaves of the very body which exists to carry out the will of the people. The plain truth is that the theory of absolute representation is of necessity qualified by the tacit assumption, which takes in different times and places very different forms, that the agent or representative is after all subordinate to the electors whom he represents. Still, when every reservation is made and when we have noted the facts, both that very different degrees of authority may be conferred on representative bodies and that representation, being nothing else than agency, involves in its very idea a tacit limit on the power of a representative assembly or, to use current language, a Parliament, it still remains true that political

---

* In later manuscript insertions, 'a body' was underlined and 'an agent?' written in the adjacent margin.

representation is a modern idea which was unknown to the ancient world and which has in many ways given a new character to modern constitutionalism.

B. What are the Merits and Defects of Representative Government?

Some of its merits are obvious.

First, representation makes it possible for the inhabitants of a large country to take a real part in political life. Ancient constitutionalism suited only a town. From the moment that a country became of such a size that its inhabitants could not really attend meetings in the market place of its chief city, the constitution of the city-state broke down. The countrymen who were often the most respectable members of the community were for all practical purposes governed by the inhabitants of the capital. It was impossible in reality to extend the citizenship of Rome effectively even to the inhabitants of the whole of Italy. Every Italian might be turned into a Roman citizen, but an Italian who lived 30 or 40 miles from Rome was politically governed by the Roman mob. The consciousness that this was so accounts for, if it does not justify, the resistance made by Rome to the extension of citizenship to the whole of Italy. It is also one of the many considerations which explain the immense power in practice exercised by the Roman Senate during a period when the Republic was nominally a democracy.[3] But, if it was impossible to confer upon the freemen of Italy the political rights of Romans, it would have been a palpable absurdity to extend the political power of Roman citizens to every freeman throughout the Roman Empire. When Roman citizenship was at last thus extended it had lost its political significance.

We may illustrate by two examples the great gain to large states of the representative system.

Italy and Greece are, as we know by experience, countries by no means too large for union under the form of representative government, but history tells us that it was absolutely impossible to fuse the city-states of ancient Greece into one country and impracticable even to bind them together under a federal government, and that whilst Italians were made in name citizens of Rome it was for want of representative government impossible to give the inhabitants of Italy an effective share in the government of the Roman state.[4]

---

[3] 265–146 BC. Pelham, bk. III, ch. III. The Senate, consisting of persons who had held offices to which they were elected, might in a very indirect and vague sense of the term be considered a representative body.

[4] It has been well said that the two different relations of the City of Rome to the rest of Italy in the absence of representation might be understood if we imagined the City of London to be the ruling power in England and representative government to be unknown. Under such a condition of things London citizenship might be refused to all Englishmen who were not citizens of London. In this case the livery would be the avowed sovereign of the rest of England which would be a dependency governed by the Freemen of London. This was roughly speaking the state of things in Italy before the Social War. London citizenship again might be extended to every Englishman. Under these circumstances every Englishman might if he could and liked attend at Guildhall and vote as a citizen of London on the affairs of the country, but the practical effect would still be that England would be ruled by the citizens who lived in or near London. This was the state of things in Italy when after the Social War the citizenship

The gigantic federations, again, of modern times, such for example as the United States or the German Empire, could never have come into existence but for the representative principle. The best known and largest federation of the ancient world—that is the Achaean League—embraced only a part of Greece and the whole of Greece might in regard either to size or population be included in a single American State.

Secondly, representative government makes it possible that legislation should be at once continuous and popular, i.e. dictated by the express wish of the people.

Legislative continuity may of course exist under a despotic government, but it is hard to imagine that legislation dictated by the will of a popular assembly could, at any rate in modern times, have the merit of continuity without the existence of some form of parliamentary representation. How, we may well ask, could the process of law making be otherwise than spasmodic and irregular if it were in reality and not merely in name confided to the whole body of citizens collected together in one assembly? Nor let anyone suppose that the experience of Rome shows that the difficulty raised is imaginary. Even under the Republic, legislation resulted to a great extent either from the continuous action of continuous officials, such as the Praetors, or from the action of the Senate, and after all the full development of the law of Rome took place after the fall of the Republic. In no case was it in reality due to the intelligent legislation of huge popular assemblies.

Thirdly, the representative system opens a possibility of placing legislative power, and indeed the government of the country, in the hands of persons who are supposed to be superior to the rest of the community in education and intelligence.

In many modern constitutions the attempt has been made in one form or another to create Parliaments which represent the best elements of the state.

The endeavour to achieve this end may take very different forms.

The electorate itself may be a limited and select body making up a class of persons who may represent the influence supposed to be due to property as well as the intelligence or independence for which the possession of a certain amount of wealth is supposed to give a sort of guarantee. In England for example, at the present day, even under a system which is inaccurately described as based on household suffrage, the electors form a more or less select body from which the poorest and therefore on the whole the most ignorant class of the people are excluded. Then again, the persons who are eligible to seats in Parliament may be persons who have attained a certain age, e.g. 30, or who possess a certain amount of property, and in some countries attempts are made to include in the legislature persons who may specially represent education or intellectual eminence.

The representative system, in short, does facilitate the simultaneous maintenance among the citizens of a state of complete civil and of incomplete political equality.

---

of Rome was extended to the Italians. How limited was the size of any territory over which it was possible to extend the citizenship of an ancient town-state may be best brought before our minds when we remember that Athens almost alone among Greek states extended her citizenship beyond the precincts of the city and, at the time of her highest fortune, had already made all the free natives of Attica Athenians. Sparta, to take one example, ruled over Lacedaemonia, and there were doubtless citizens of Sparta living in the country but the inhabitants of Lacedaemonia living outside Sparta were for the most part not Spartan citizens (see Freeman, *Federal Government*).

To achieve this is a matter of some difficulty. It is very hard to say whether, e.g. at Athens, it would have been possible, especially if slavery had been abolished, to give to the poorest man in the state the same civil rights as were possessed by the richest and noblest, and yet deny him an absolutely equal share with his richer neighbour in political power. The representative system therefore is more easily compatible than is any form of non-representative democracy with the existence of a large labouring class, each member of which is in the fullest sense a freeman whilst very few of the members thereof take part in the government of the country. Whether indeed the existence of such a class is desirable is an inquiry to which different thinkers will give different answers. All that is here insisted upon is that representative government falls in with the conditions of modern life under which, slavery being abolished, a large number of free citizens are wholly occupied in earning their livelihood by manual labour. The existence of such a class of labourers was, under the constitution of the ancient world, a menace to the safety of a state. Workmen who were excluded from political rights could not enjoy the complete civil rights of citizens whilst if admitted to citizenship they lacked the qualities needed for the beneficial exercise of political power. The same idea is sometimes expressed under the paradoxical assertion that in the ancient world slavery was the necessary basis of freedom since nothing but the existence of slaves enabled the free citizens to devote the whole of their energies to the government of the state. If there be any truth in this paradox, representative government lessens the need, if it ever existed, for the maintenance of slavery.

Fourthly, representative government favours the separation of powers.[5]

Whenever sovereign authority lies in the hands of a non-elected sovereign assembly there is a natural tendency for this one body to exercise legislative, executive, and judicial authority. In truth, in early times these three modes of expressing the will of the state are separated neither in fact nor in thought. Laws or general rules for regulating the conduct of citizens originate to a great extent in decisions with regard to particular cases. Men first determine, according to their customs, habits, or feelings, that A has committed an offence, e.g. murder, punishable either with death or, as the case may be, by a heavy fine, and only by degrees, after applying the same rule to A, B, C, and D, become conscious of the fact that all murderers ought to be punished with death, or by a heavy fine, and later still it may be lay down the rule or law that murder is a capital offence. The work too of a popular assembly was in the early city-states quite as much to decide what ought to be done in particular cases, whether for example the state was to make war or peace, or whether a given citizen was to be elected Consul or Archon, as to determine whether a particular law was to be passed. It was therefore in strictness impossible that an assembly of citizens should practise, or even conceive, of the separation of powers. No doubt the same thing is to a certain extent true in early times of representative assemblies or Parliaments. Acts of Attainder, Bills of Pains and Penalties, and in a less degree impeachments are in reality the exercise of judicial authority by Parliament, but representative assemblies just because they were not originally a permanent part of the government, because

---

[5] See ch. IV below.

in England at any rate they were distinct from and even opposed to the executive power of the Crown and were quite separate from the ordinary judicature of the country, did not and as a rule could not exercise either judicial or executive authority, and hence by their very constitution favoured and brought into view so to speak the distinction between executive and legislative power. It is worth while even here to remark that the one modern commonwealth in which the exercise of judicial is not clearly separated from the exercise of legislative and executive power is Switzerland, and that Switzerland is the one country in which, though there exist representative assemblies, the constitutions both of the Confederacy and the cantons are to a great extent based on the ideas derived from non-representative democracy.

The defects* of the representative system, though often overlooked, are considerable.

First, representation diminishes the part taken by individual citizens in the government of their country.

In the city-states of ancient Greece, or of mediaeval Italy, the men who had full citizenship did themselves and in their own person discharge all the duties of citizenship; an Athenian or a Florentine was a law maker, an administrator, a soldier, a juryman, and to a great extent a judge. In England hundreds of men who are good average citizens discharge very few public duties except voting every four or five years for a member of Parliament.

Hence several results which to a citizen of a small state where representation was unknown would have seemed almost wholly evil.

An English elector receives little or no training in the conduct of public affairs. The political education of an Athenian in the best days of Athens was, it has been said, better than the political education of an English member of Parliament;[6] it assuredly was incomparably superior to the political education of an ordinary English elector, and the same remark applies, though with considerable reservations, to a citizen of Florence or a burgher of Bern at the time when the Florentine Commonwealth or the City of Bern were independent states.

Nor can it be assumed that where parliamentary government exists all, or anything like all, the electors will take part in the elections. Even in a country like England, where representative government is seen at its best, it constantly happens that many voters abstain from going to the poll. If a man's party have in a particular county or borough a decided majority he feels there is no reason for his voting, since he knows that without any trouble on his part the person whom he wishes to see elected will be returned as a member of Parliament. If on the other hand our elector belongs to a party who in a particular constituency are in a decided minority, he does not care to

---

[6] See Freeman, *Federal Government*, p. [left blank].

---

* Dicey's treatment of the first and second defects appears to have been influenced by his contemporary preoccupation with issues raised by the Bill that became the Commonwealth of Australia Constitution Act 1900: G. Hand, 'A. V. Dicey's Unpublished Materials on the Comparative Study of Constitutions' in G. Hand and J. McBride (eds), Droit Sans Frontières: *Essays in Honour of L. Neville Brown* (Birmingham: Holdsworth Club, 1991), 77–93, especially 84 f.

exert himself to give a vote since he supposes that his vote will in fact have no effect whatever.

In England, however, or in the United States of America, the mass of the people do, at any rate when there is a political crisis, record their votes. But in many countries where parliamentary government exists, the electors notoriously cannot be induced to take even the moderate trouble of coming to the ballot box. Ever since 1789 representative government of some kind or other has existed in France yet the majority of the French electorate are, it is said, profoundly indifferent as to the result of the elections. It is only a minority who in ordinary cases go to the poll at all. The mere trouble of voting is more than the ordinary citizen is prepared to undergo.[7] Hence under a Republican government where every man of full age has a vote, the majority of the people really take no part in and therefore of course receive no training from the government of the country.

Then again representative government in its actual practice leads to the disastrous dilemma. Elections must be rare or frequent. If elections take place only at long intervals it is possible in a country where public spirit is strong, or party feeling runs high, to interest the electors vividly in an election and induce say 80 or 90 per cent of them to vote: but then just because the elections come at long intervals the people are very rarely practised in the discharge of their civic duties. If, on the other hand, elections are frequent then it of necessity happens that a large number of the electorate abstain from voting, and those who abstain in reality give up their share in public life. Nor is this the whole of the evil. The electors who do not vote are apt to he just the quiet, respectable, sensible citizens whose opinions ought to have weight; for such men, being fully occupied in their own affairs as lawyers, doctors, clergymen, merchants, and the like whose time and thoughts are given to the successful discharge of professional duties, will not and, to speak plainly, cannot again and again leave their ordinary avocations for the sake of acting at constantly recurring elections. But the men who are unsuccessful in business, or who have not got professional work of their own, are quite ready to crowd the polling booths. Political managers, wire pullers, loafers, bankrupts, ne'er-do-wells record their votes just when respectable citizens abstain from voting. Such abstention may be a grave political vice. So be it. The student of constitutions must be content to take men as they are and to examine the working of given institutions on the assumption that human nature will remain as it is and that, above all, the majority of mankind at all times and in all countries dislike labour and will certainly not as a rule incur trouble for the sake of the commonwealth when to do so is opposed to their clear interest. If this consideration suggested by the most obvious common sense be borne in mind, we are driven to the conclusion that the representative system does involve this dilemma. If the elections are rare the electors rarely take part in public affairs; if elections are frequent the electors who vote will be few and, what is worse, the electors who abstain from voting will be the men whose judgement ought to have weight whilst the electors who do vote will be the men who,

---

[7] See 2 Bodley, p. 72.

to put the matter in the most moderate form, ought certainly not to possess more influence than they derive from their numbers.

Turn the matter then which way you will, the representative system, as compared at any rate with non-representative democracy, diminishes the part played by individual citizens in public life, and generates all the evils which flow from the habit of leaving to agents business which ought to he a person's own vital concern.

Secondly, the representative system cannot with advantage be extended beyond territorial limits which, though indefinite, are real.

'The great political invention of Teutonic Europe' makes it possible to create political communities not enclosed within the boundaries of a city, but it does not make it possible to create commonwealths of unlimited size.

The limits on the use of parliamentary government are of two kinds: the one is strictly physical, the other may be called moral.

The physical limit may be thus described. No representative assembly or House of Parliament can be a good body for debating purposes if its members exceed a small number of persons. The House of Commons has assuredly reached the number of members suitable for a House of Parliament. We may with some confidence lay down that a Parliamentary assembly ought not to consist of more than 600, and had better not consist of more than 400 or 500, members. Then again the constituencies which return a representative ought to be of such a size that each voter can feel he has a real or appreciable part in the return of a member. But the combination of these two requisites shows that the population which can be adequately represented by an elected legislature is not by any means unlimited, whence it also follows that parliamentary commonwealths, no less than city-states, are in reality limited within certain territorial boundaries. A Parliament of the world is no more a possibility than was in classical times an assembly which should include the citizens not of a town but of a country.

The moral limit though different from is closely connected with the territorial limit and may be thus described. The representative system cannot be applied with success to countries which lack a sentiment of common interest, i.e. which have not the feeling of being one community, and it is difficult [or unlikely],* though not impossible, that such a sentiment can unite the inhabitants of countries which are divided from one another by wide distances of space. No doubt much depends upon the existence or non-existence of easy means of communication. During the earlier stages of the contest between England and the Thirteen Colonies it occurred to political theorists that the principle for which the colonial leaders nominally contended, namely the inseparable connection between liability to taxation and the right to representation, might be wisely conceded, and that the quarrel between England and her colonies might be composed, not by surrendering the title of the British Parliament to tax Massachusetts or Virginia, but by summoning members from the Thirteen Colonies to seats in the British Parliament. Burke met this proposal by arguments from inconvenience which even in 1770 were hardly conclusive and which in 1900, when

---

* The interlinear, later manuscript note 'unlikely?' was inserted above 'difficult'.

New York is in point of time as near if not nearer to London than was Shetland in 1800, have an appearance of futility, yet Burke was in substance right. The proposed innovation was, as he no doubt saw, impracticable: members from New York or from Boston would never have formed a natural or real part of the Parliament at Westminster. There would have been lacking in their case that sense of unity which ought to pervade all the members of a common Parliament. Let us suppose that at this day the Canadian Dominion, the West Indies, the Australian Commonwealth, and the South African colonies were all called upon to send members to the Imperial Parliament.* Would it be possible that such a change should work well? It is difficult to answer this inquiry in the affirmative. The physical distance which divides England's greater colonies from each other and from Great Britain, taken in combination with other circumstances, forbids the existence of that community of sentiment and of that obvious identity of interests among all the countries represented which lies at the basis of successful parliamentary government. The Imperial Parliament would be rendered less effective than it is as a Parliament of the United Kingdom and it would not become a body which gave adequate representation to the colonies no less than to England. But, if a Parliament for the whole British Empire could be constructed only with the greatest difficulty, a Parliament of the world is, to any one who weighs the nature of the representative system, an absolute impossibility.[8]

Thirdly, parliamentary government creates a body of representatives with feelings, wishes, or interests of their own which may be different from or opposed to the will or the interest of the community.

That this is so hardly needs demonstration. It is on the face of things certain that the interests or the desires of an agent do not always coincide with the interest or wishes of his principal. It is further certain that any body of persons is apt to acquire both for bad and good certain common or corporate feelings which belong to them as members of the body whereof they form part and are really different from the sentiments which in many cases individuals would entertain if they were not biassed by corporate sentiment or *esprit de corps*. Consider for instance the position of every member of Parliament in regard to his constituency. He must, in general, have a very strong wish to retain his seat. One obvious and immediate consequence of this is that he desires to retain the goodwill of his constituents or to speak accurately of the majority by whom he was returned, and it is absolutely impossible to suppose that, however honest a member may be, his judgement will not as a rule be biassed by the desire to remain in harmony with his supporters, and of course the wishes of

---

[8] Whether or not some form of federal connection between England and her self-governing colonies can be invented is a point on which it is not expedient to pronounce any opinion. What is pretty clear to anyone who considers the limitations inherent upon the beneficial operation of representative institutions is that the peculiarities and the very excellence of the English colonial system point at present far more strongly towards the formation of a permanent defensive and offensive alliance between England and her colonies under which every country throughout the Empire may contribute something to the defence of the Empire, rather than towards any scheme of federal government.

---

* On Dicey's opposition to federal government for the British Empire, see *The Oxford Edition of Dicey*, i, *The Law of the Constitution*, 66 ff.

a constituency may very well be opposed to the course which would be dictated by a sound view of what is expedient for the nation. Nor is it even certain that under various circumstances the minority of a member's own constituency may not exert a great influence over his conduct or even over his way of thinking. Mr. Jones, we will suppose, has been returned to Parliament by a Conservative majority but by a majority which exceeds the numbers of votes obtained by his Liberal opponent only by 100. Mr. Jones finds that a limited number of his supporters, say 200, entertain a strong feeling against the muzzling of dogs, the closing of public houses, or the enforcement of vaccination, and that the 200 feel so strongly on the particular matter that, unless he adopts their view, they will either vote against him, or at best stand neutral at the next election. He has further a reason to believe that the majority of his supporters are on the whole indifferent as to the question, e.g. the muzzling of dogs, which excites such strong feeling among the minority of 200. Human nature being what it is, Mr. Jones, we may take it, will go a good way to meet the wishes of the 200 enthusiasts. Nor need he act dishonestly: he will persuade himself that their views are right. And what is true of Mr. Jones in one constituency may be true of member after member in other constituencies. It is therefore to say the least conceivable that a very large number of members of Parliament may from their position as representatives be guided by the wishes of a small but energetic minority.

Fourthly, parliamentary government gives undue authority to parliamentary majorities.

The whole system of representation rests on the assumption that a fairly constituted and freely elected Parliament must from the nature of things represent the opinions and wishes of the electors. That this assumption is in a great measure well founded is proved by the success of parliamentary constitutionalism, for the authority and power of a Parliament in the long run depends on the willingness of the electors to ratify the acts of their agents and to treat the voice of the Parliament as the verdict of the nation, or at any rate of that part of the nation which takes an effective part in public affairs.

It has of course always been recognised that the principle that a representative assembly represented the nation could at best be treated as only approximately true and as subject to a good number of limitations.

It is clear, for instance, that it is the majority of an elected Parliament and not the whole of the Parliament which represents the electors, and that what the parliamentary majority represents is at best not the whole of the electors but the greater part of them. It is further hardly disputable that the electoral body may be so constituted that the wishes of the electorate are not of necessity the wishes of the nation. Thus the electors may quite conceivably be a comparatively small body of persons who are themselves influenced by the opinions or prejudices of a particular class, or the electors may from their poverty or from other causes be dependent upon and obedient to the wishes of a limited number of persons and be exposed to corruption and intimidation. Both these charges were brought with plausibility against the electorate which up to 1832 returned the unreformed House of Commons, and the charge of reflecting the opinions and wishes of only one class, and that a limited class, of citizens was brought against the Chamber of Deputies as it existed in France from 1830 to 1848.

But, though it has always been patent that representative assemblies cannot in their action represent more than the majority of a nation and though reformers have always been ready enough to insist upon the possibility of a representative legislature being so constituted as to misrepresent the nation, it was till recent times tacitly assumed by democrats, and even I conceive by the assailants of democracy, that a Parliament fairly and freely elected by all the citizens of a country must, if the electors were protected against every kind of intimidation and corruption, represent more or less exactly the wishes of the nation or at any rate of the majority thereof. The validity of this assumption was hardly criticised even by the severest critics of democracy. Such censors contested the moral right of a majority to govern and intimated pretty clearly that, the majority of the nation being for the most part fools, their representatives would constantly represent human folly and incompetence. But of recent years the validity of the very assumption in which men of opposed political sympathies agreed has become open to question, for one of the lessons most distinctly taught by the comparative study of recent constitutional history is that a fairly constituted Parliament which has been freely elected may on very important matters fail to represent the wishes of its electors. The possibility at any rate of this being the real though paradoxical effect of representative government is proved by patent facts. In Switzerland you have a Republican and democratic commonwealth. The Swiss people stand in education and in intelligence above the level attained by the inhabitants of most European countries. The intelligent people of Switzerland elect the Federal Assembly with perfect freedom. Their choice is not vitiated either by corruption or intimidation. The members elected are a pre-eminently respectable body of men who represent the sound sense and prudence of the country. Yet it is a matter of common knowledge that laws passed by the Federal Assembly have failed on a referendum to obtain the assent of the electors, and that though this has happened the electors have on a new election returned again to Parliament the very men whose legislative proposals the same electors refuse to sanction. And be it noted that what is true of the Federal Assembly is true of the elected legislatures of the cantons. The same phenomenon reappears in a slightly different form in each of the States which make up the United States of America. The people of a State everywhere show distrust of their own State legislature. Its powers are year by year more closely restricted and the legislative body is so to speak placed under the more and more close control of the Courts. The amendment of the State constitutions which is constantly taking place is as a rule taken out of the hands of the ordinary legislature and committed to 'Conventions'—that is to say assemblies elected by the people for the sole purpose of preparing amendments to the Constitution. These Conventions are elected for this one definite end. Their members are far superior in position, character, and intelligence to the ordinary run of politicians. The work they turn out is often very good, yet even these picked Conventions do not always in fact represent the wishes of the people. The Constitutional amendments or the new Constitution which a Convention has drafted frequently failed to obtain the assent of the electors.

Representative assemblies, in short, may fail to represent, and this fault, it should be noted, is a defect peculiar to the representative system; it could not in the absence of fraud or intimidation exist in a city-state where every citizen attended the public assembly.[9] But, when once it is perceived that a representative assembly may fail to represent the will of the electors, a heavy blow is given to the moral authority of a parliamentary majority, since this authority depends at bottom upon the supposition that the voice of the majority is the voice of the nation. No doubt the elected body or Parliament may in many cases be wiser than the electors, but in so for as a Parliament does not represent its electors the representative principle fails. An agent may be a far cleverer man than his principal. An able solicitor, for example, may excel both in judgement and in ability the nobleman for whom he acts, but when such an agent acts against the will of his employer, though the employer may be benefited, the object for which agency exists, i.e. the carrying out of the will of the principal, has not been attained. Nor is it safe to assume in public any more than in private life that it is as a rule desirable that an agent should go beyond his proper sphere. Popular government rests upon the belief that the citizens of a country are in the long run the best judges of their own interests. A Parliament may be wiser than the citizens who elect it, but a Parliament which does not represent its electors is not an assembly which illustrates the benefit of the representative system.[10]

---

[9] The existence of the defect I have been commenting upon is proved by the demand for proportional representation which is at bottom a plan for ensuring that an elected assembly should adequately represent the electors. Whether the plan would attain its object and whether the object is one which, if attainable, is desirable, is a point on which I here pronounce no opinion.

[10] Nor is it any answer to this remark that it is often well that electors should confer wide powers upon their parliamentary representatives and allow their members who are better educated than themselves to determine points, e.g. of foreign policy, which the electors are not competent to determine wisely. Here there is no contradiction between the will of the elector and the will of the MP. The case is the very ordinary one in private life of a layman trusting to an expert. A landlord of no special ability or experience acts wisely when he leaves the management of his estate in the hands of a competent and honest land agent.

4

The Separation of Powers

Analysis (1900)*

Introduction
    Three questions
        1. What is meant by the doctrine of the separation of powers?
        2. What is importance of doctrine?
        3. What attempts have been made to carry out doctrine?

A.   What is Meant by the Doctrine of the Separation of Powers?
    Two points
        1. Legislative, executive, and judicial power may be exercised either by one person, or body of persons (combination), or by different persons or bodies (separation)
        2. Combination of powers fatal, separation favourable, to personal liberty (Montesquieu, bk. XI, chs IV and VI)

B.   What is a Just Estimate of the Doctrine?
    I. *Its importance and partial truth*
        1. Attempt to protect personal freedom
        2. Combination of the three powers unfavourable to personal freedom and to supremacy of law
        3. The most important element the separation and independence of judiciary
    II. *Its defects*
        1. Powers distinguishable rather than absolutely separable
        2. Powers may be kept separate though exercised by same person, if exercised by him in different characters, e.g. case of English Chancellor
        3. Powers not in fact kept separate in England to extent supposed by Montesquieu
        4. The separation between executive and legislature may be an evil
        5. The separation of powers does not fix the limit of each power. Hence
        6. Doctrine admits of and has received different interpretation in different countries

(See Montesquieu, bk. XI, chs I to VI;
Locke, *Civil Government*, chs XI, XII and XIII;
Girons, *Essai sur la Séparation des Pouvoirs*.)

** Its contents have been derived from an undated manuscript attached to the lecture schedule headed 'Easter & Trinity Terms 1900'. On Dicey's treatment of the separation of powers here and in *The Law of the Constitution*, see Editor's Introduction, pp xxxix f. above.*

Analysis (1899)*

Introduction
    Three questions
        1. What is meant by separation of powers?
        2. What is importance of doctrine of separation of powers?
        3. What attempts have been made to carry out doctrine?

A.   What is Meant by Separation of Powers?
    I. *Montesquieu's doctrine*
        1. The existence of three powers
           (i)   Legislative
           (ii) Executive
           (iii) Judicial
        2. The three powers may be exercised by same person, e.g. monarch or assembly, or by separate persons, e.g. legislative body, executive (Crown), judiciary
        3. This separation exists under English constitution
        4. Combination of powers means despotism, separation the only guarantee for freedom
    NB Cf. Locke, *Civil Government*
    II. *Montesquieu's doctrine*
        1. Not inconsistent with any doctrine of sovereignty, i.e. does not mean that there are three separate authorities in state
        2. Does mean what is certainly true that authority of state exercisable in three different ways. The three powers are in effect three functions and that exercise of all functions by one person is unfavourable whilst their exercise by separate persons is favourable to individual freedom.

B.   What is Importance of Doctrine?
    I. *Its partial truth*
    The exercise by one person or body of all three powers promotes tyranny
    – Early despotisms
    – Jewish assemblies
    – Athenian assemblies, e.g. case of Ten Generals
    – Acts of Attainder
    – Impeachments
    – English Long Parliament
    – French Convention
    On the other hand, mere separation, especially of legislative and judicial power, does tend to protect freedom, e.g. English law Courts, French *Parlements*, modern absolute monarchies.
    II. *Its defects*
        1. The three functions rather distinguishable than separable
        2. All three powers to a slight extent exercised by each organ of state

---

* Its contents have been derived from a manuscript dated 11 April 1899. This second, longer, analysis has been provided to complement the first in the absence of a full text for the lecture.

3. May be combined in same person or persons if exercised in different character, e.g. English Chancellor
4. Separation of judicial from legislative and executive power what is really important for freedom

NB The attitude of legislature quite foreign to attitude of judge

5. The doctrine of separation if it means absolute disconnection attempts impossibility. If it means different spheres does not provide rule for limitation of spheres
6. Doctrine not really carried out under English constitution though more nearly in Montesquieu's time than in any other

C. What have been the Attempts to Carry Out the Doctrine?
It has been differently interpreted in England, in France, in USA
 I. In *England* nominal separation, but in reality close connection between legislature (Houses of Parliament) and Cabinet. Subordination of judges to any law passed by legislature (Act of Parliament) but independence subject to this exception both of Parliament and of executive, i.e. the Courts determine rights of individuals as between themselves and as against the executive
 [II.] In *France*, as originally interpreted, meant complete severance of legislature and executive which practically led to exercise of executive power by parliamentary committees, e.g. Committee of Public Safety, but, under later French constitutions, compatible with existence of parliamentary executive.
Judiciary confined wholly to questions between individuals and excluded from all intervention in matters of State
 [III] In *USA* real separation between the three powers. Executive not appointed by and may be hostile to legislature. Powers of legislature, e.g. Congress, limited. Judiciary determines rights of individuals but incidentally may pronounce upon validity of Acts of legislature
NB Election of judges leads back again to confusion of powers

(See Montesquieu, bk. XI, chs VI. and I–V;
1 Laferrière, pp 10–13, bk. III, ch. I, pp 471–513, ch. VII, pp 637–651, and ch. VIII, pp 655–666.)

5

Divisions of Constitutions

Analysis[*]

Introduction
    What are the different ways in which constitutions may be divided?
A.   Written (enacted) and Unwritten (unenacted) Constitutions
        Examples
        Cromwellian Constitution of 1653 (written)
        Constitution of United States (written)
        Constitution of each State of the United States (written)
        Most modern Continental constitutions (written)
        Roman constitution (unwritten)
        English constitution (unwritten)
        Hungarian constitution (unwritten) (?)
        1. Early constitutions or customary [constitutions]
        2. Constitution may be partly written and partly unwritten
        3. In most modern constitutions a written (enacted) and unwritten (unenacted) element
        4. Distinction not the same as distinction between law of constitution and conventions of constitution
B.   Flexible and Rigid
        1. The relation between this division and foregoing division
        2. Varying degrees of rigidity
        3. Modes of maintaining rigidity of constitution
        4. Comparison between rigid and flexible constitutions
C.   Constitutions Responsive to Opinion and Constitutions Irresponsive to Opinion
        1. Nature of this distinction
        2. Apt to be confused with distinction between democratic and non-democratic constitutions
D.   Constitutions in which there is a Parliamentary and Constitutions in which there is a Non-Parliamentary Executive

(See Bryce, *American Commonwealth*, 3rd edn, ch. XXXI, p. 359;
Dicey, *Law of Constitution*, 5th edn, pp 22–25;
Freeman, *Growth of the English Constitution*, ch. III.)

---

[*] Its contents have been derived from an undated manuscript attached to the lecture schedule headed 'Easter & Trinity Terms 1900'.

Division[s] of Constitutions*

Representative governments or constitutions may be classified in accordance with various different principles. My purpose in this chapter is to examine and comment upon four such classifications, and among these to dwell most upon those divisions, not so much which are the most important, but which, being the least known, are it is probable the least understood. It may be well to premise that the divisions here dealt with constitute what logicians call cross-divisions, by which is meant that one and the same constitution may be brought under more than one and it may be under all of the four divisions which are the subject of our consideration.

A. Written (enacted) and Unwritten (unenacted) Constitutions†

This division is a popular one and expressed therefore in rather lax language which is apt to mislead.

A 'written' constitution means not a constitution, the terms or articles whereof have been expressed in writing, but a constitution the terms whereof have been at some time, or times, formally decreed or enacted.

An 'unwritten' constitution, on the other hand, means not a constitution, the terms or articles whereof have not been reduced to writing, but a constitution the terms whereof, as a whole, have originated in custom or habit, and have not been at any moment decreed or enacted.

The distinction, in short, aimed at in the words 'written' and 'unwritten' is in reality the distinction between a constitution which originates in legislation or enactment and a constitution which originates in custom or habit.

Of written or enacted constitutions the modern European world affords a large number of examples. The earliest, or nearly the earliest of such constitutions is the Cromwellian Constitution of 1653 embodied in the Instrument of Government. The most successful and the best known is the Constitution of the United States, of which, the Constitution of the Swiss Confederation, of the Canadian Dominion, and of the Australian Commonwealth may be considered effective, though in various points of view amended and altered, copies. The greater number again if not absolutely the whole of the constitutional monarchies of modern Europe as also the Republican polities of each of the States which make up the American Union are written, i.e. enacted constitutions.

---

* The manuscript's title page was dated 27 June 1900 in a later manuscript note, but the text is the product, in places, of substantial alteration that appears to have been mainly after that date. The full lecture text's title has been slightly changed here to 'Divisions of Constitutions' to conform to its title as this appears in its corresponding Analysis and in the lecture schedule headed 'Easter & Trinity Terms 1900'.

† On the division between written and unwritten constitutions, see Editor's Introduction, pp xlii f. above.

Of 'unwritten', unenacted, or customary constitutions examples may be taken either from the classical times of Greece or Rome or from mediaeval Europe. The truth is that the political institutions, no less than the laws, of a people always originate in custom or habit. Hence customary constitutions precede chronologically written or enacted constitutions, and, just as in the sphere of ordinary law enacted rights supersede customary rights, so unwritten are gradually superseded by written constitutions. The most famous of unwritten constitutions are the constitution of the Roman Republic and the constitution of the English monarchy. The latter is the sole or nearly the sole existing specimen of an unwritten constitution. The Constitutions of Sweden, of Denmark (?), of Spain, of Holland, of France, each of which countries at one time possessed an unwritten constitution, are now written or enacted constitutions.[1]

[Missing page of text]*

Provisions of Magna Carta, of the Bill of Rights, of the Acts of Settlement, of the Acts of Union, and of the successive Parliamentary Reform Acts beginning in 1832 and ending for the moment in 1884. Thus too written constitutions depend for their working on principles or laws which are either not enacted at all, or are certainly not enacted as part of the constitution. The written Constitution of the United States would be absolutely unintelligible to any one who did not bear in mind the principles of the English common law which, so to speak, underlie it. Nor could the scanty and fragmentary *lois constitutionnelles,* which technically make up the Constitution of the Third French Republic, be intelligible unless they were read in combination with the so-called principles of 1789, the Code, and, above all, the tacit assumptions as to the right relation between the executive, the legislature, and the judiciary which are embodied in the doctrine of the separation of powers as interpreted by French jurists and statesmen.

Care must be taken not to confuse the distinction between written (or enacted) constitutions and unwritten (or customary) constitutions with the essentially different distinction between the law of a constitution and the conventions of a constitution. The one is a mode of distinguishing one kind of constitution from another. The other distinction is a mode of distinguishing the different parts of one constitution. The law of a constitution means those parts of a constitution, whether the constitution itself be enacted or customary, of which the Courts take recognition and which can be legally enforced by some recognised legal process. The conventions of a constitution are those constitutional rules on which men act but which are not recognised by the Courts and do not admit of being enforced by process of law. Thus it is a law of the English constitution that the Crown shall descend in accordance with the provisions of the Act of Settlement, and it is a law of the constitution that the King can do no wrong, which means in effect that the King cannot be treated by the law Courts as personally responsible for any unlawful act, whence it follows, according

---

[1] Whether the constitution of Hungary is an unwritten constitution?

* For some idea of what is missing, see the Analysis for this lecture (p. 232 above) under A.

to legal logic, that a wrongdoer, e.g. X who has assaulted or imprisoned A, can never be allowed to defend himself on the plea that he acted under the authority of the Crown. The one rule is to be found in the statute book, the other is a rule to be found in no part of the statute book, but [is] to be deduced from decided cases or from judicial dicta. Each rule is equally a law and part of the law of the constitution. The rule, on the other hand, that a Ministry must resign office if it has ceased to command the confidence of the House of Commons but need not resign office simply because it has lost the confidence of the House of Lords, is a maxim on which modern statesmen constantly act, but it is not a law since it is not recognised by the law Courts, and is assuredly not part of the law of the constitution.[2] Nor again must the distinction be in any way confounded with the distinction between flexible and rigid constitutions.

B. Flexible and Rigid Constitutions[*]

A 'flexible' constitution is one which can be changed by the ordinary legislative body, or Parliament, by the usual process of legislation. Such, to take the best known instance of a completely flexible polity, is the English constitution and such, it would seem, are most constitutional monarchies.

A 'rigid' constitution is one which cannot be changed by the ordinary legislature in the ordinary manner of legislation. Such, for example, was the Cromwellian Constitution of 1653; such is the Constitution of the United States; and such too have been the greater number, though not every one, of the constitutions which have existed in France since 1789.

The happy terms 'flexible' and 'rigid' are due to the invention of Mr Bryce. The idea which these words denote has been well worked out by Mr Bryce and other writers, and is pretty well understood so that the notion hardly requires to be here worked out in detail.

Four observations, however, deserve attention.

First, though this and the foregoing division of constitutions are essentially different there is a real relation between them. A rigid constitution (since *ex hypothesi* distinct limits are placed by law upon the facility of amending or changing it) will almost necessarily be a written or enacted constitution, whilst a flexible constitution may either be written or unwritten. To put the same thing in other words, rigid constitutions are as a rule written or enacted, but a flexible constitution may be either written, i.e. enacted, or unwritten.[†] If all the rules which make up the English constitution were codified and enacted by Parliament the English constitution would not therefore cease to be flexible, but if it were desired to make the English constitution

---

[2] See Dicey, *Law of the Constitution*, [left blank] [See *The Oxford Edition of Dicey*, i, *The Law of the Constitution*, 23 ff, 185 ff].

---

[*] See *Oxford Edition of Dicey*, i, *The Law of the Constitution*, 'Rigidity of French Constitutions' (Note 1, 3rd edn), 250 ff.

[†] In a later marginal note, the suggestion was made that the sentence be omitted as really superfluous.

rigid it would be a natural, and all but a necessary, step to reduce the constitution or at any rate some part of it to the form of a statutory enactment.

Secondly, there may be very different degrees of rigidity in constitutions. The United States, the Swiss Confederation, the French Republic, and the Belgian monarchy are each governed under a rigid constitution. Neither the Constitution of the United States nor the Constitution of Switzerland, nor the Constitution of the French Republic, nor the Constitution of the Belgian monarchy can be altered by the ordinary legislature by the ordinary process of legislation. These Constitutions therefore are all rigid, but it is far easier to amend the Constitution of France or of Belgium than to amend the Constitution of the United States or of Switzerland, and it is easier to amend the Constitution of Switzerland than to amend the Constitution of the United States. The rigidity therefore of a constitution is a matter of degree.

Thirdly, there exist different methods for maintaining the rigidity of a constitution, or, in other words, for preventing legislation which contravenes any article or provision of the constitution.

One, and by far the most effective, of these methods is to allow the ordinary law Courts to treat as a nullity, and therefore in effect as non-existing, any law which they hold to be inconsistent with the terms of the constitution. This is the system which prevails in the United States; it exactly answers its purpose. Any Court throughout the Union is bound to treat as null any law, e.g. an Act of Congress, in so far as it is repugnant to the Constitution of the United States, whence it follows that any citizen can raise the question whether a law contravenes the Constitution or not simply by disobeying it, and leaving to those who are bound to enforce the law, or are interested in the law being enforced, to bring him in some form or other before the Courts for disobedience to it. The Courts then when the case comes before them will decide whether the law is valid or not. It need hardly be added that, if the citizen who disobeys the law is in the opinion of the Courts mistaken in his contention that the law infringes the Constitution and is therefore invalid, he will in some form or other suffer punishment, i.e. according to the nature of the procedure he will incur some penalty or be compelled to pay damages. Thus it was at one time a matter of doubt whether Congress had under the Constitution authority to issue inconvertible paper currency known as 'greenbacks'. Ultimately some citizen or some citizens refused to receive payment in greenbacks and the question came ultimately before the Supreme Court of the USA whether a debtor who tendered or gave greenbacks in payment of his debt had or had not paid his debt. If the Act of Congress making greenbacks currency was within the constitutional authority of Congress and therefore valid, the payment was good; if otherwise, the payment was bad or, in effect, no payment at all. It was at last decided that payment in greenbacks was good payment or in effect that an Act of Congress making greenbacks inconvertible currency was not an infringement on the Constitution and was valid. The Greenback Cases exhibit, however, the one weakness of the American system. No American Court has in strictness authority to nullify any law whatever, and it may well happen that years may pass before a case arises which raises the question as to the validity of a particular enactment which the Courts, when the question comes before them, hold to be unconstitutional and invalid. Thus payments were made and accepted in greenbacks for years before the decision of the Greenback Cases.

What has been here called the American system is in principle borrowed from the common law of England. No Court throughout the British Empire, it is true, ever treats as invalid or unconstitutional an enactment of the Imperial Parliament, and this for the simple reason that the fundamental dogma of our constitutional law is the absolute sovereignty of Parliament. But any Court throughout the British dominions may treat as invalid any law made by a subordinate law-making authority which exceeds the legal limits of its powers, and this whether the law-making authority be the Parliament of the Canadian Dominion or the Corporation of Oxford.[3]

A second method which has been adopted under some foreign constitutions is to empower either some special body or the Courts to nullify in the strict sense of the word, that is to say, when formally applied to, declare null any law which is unconstitutional. Authority of this kind was possessed by the Senate under the First Napoleonic Empire and, unless I am mistaken, is under some circumstances conferred upon the Courts, or a Court, under the Constitution of the Mexican Republic. This power of nullification, however, though it sounds effective, has been found in practice of very little worth. It will only be exercised at a crisis, just at a time, that is to say, when party feeling runs high and when the Courts are likely to have little real power as opposed to the legislature or the executive. In any case it brings the authority called upon to nullify a law into direct conflict with the legislature and in all probability with the executive.

A last method is to treat the articles of the constitution as maxims of political morality which derive the strength which they possess from their being formally inscribed in the constitution and from the support of public opinion. This appears to be the true character of the French constitutional laws and of the provisions which make up the Constitution of Belgium. The Courts have no authority either to nullify or to treat as void enactments of the French National Assembly or of the Belgian Parliament, but it is generally understood that such enactments ought not to violate the articles of the Constitution. On the whole such an understanding is a more real check on unconstitutional legislation than an English lawyer might expect it to be. Assuming that a constitution expresses the deliberate opinion of the nation as to the proper limits of legislation, it may reasonably be expected that public opinion itself will be strong enough to prevent legislation which openly and directly violates the constitution. The defect of this system is that it affords hardly any protection against legislation which while it does not directly violate the constitution violates it indirectly, and thus bit by bit introduces unconstitutional changes of which people do not at first see the bearing.

Fourthly, [there is the] comparison between rigid and flexible constitutions.

---

[3] See *Law of the Constitution*, p. [left blank] [See *The Oxford Edition of Dicey*, i, *The Law of the Constitution*, 54 ff].

In another work I have considered at some length the question whether the rigidity of a constitution secures its permanence.[4]

The answer to this question may be briefly summed up as follows. The rigidity of a constitution, in so far as it can be preserved, tends to check gradual innovation but, just because it impedes change, may, as on various occasions in France, and notably at the time of the *coup d'état* in 1851, provoke or justify revolution. It is certainly curious to note how ineffective have been the constant attempts of statesmen to render a constitution unchangeable and thus give to their work a sort of immortality. The one rigid constitution which has ever existed in England was constituted under the Instrument of Government in 1653; it was changed within four years. Of the excessively rigid constitutions of France not one has had any permanent existence. The truth appears to be that in many cases the precautions taken by constitution makers to render their work unchangeable is itself a sign of a well founded dread that it will not be suffered to exist for any long period. The one great example of a constitution which though not absolutely unchangeable has been rendered almost too rigid to be changed is the Constitution of the United States. But a critic who admires the immutability of the American Republic is bound to observe that[,] whilst the articles of the Constitution have, except as a result of the Civil War, undergone singularly little alteration[,] [t]his immunity from outward change is due in part to the readiness of Americans to alter the spirit whilst leaving untouched the forms of the constitution. The President and the Senate each possess today much the same constitutional rights as they did in the time of Washington. But no one really supposes that the position of Mr McKinley is in reality the same as the position of the first President of the Republic. The Senate itself has grown from a council of 26 members into a second House of 90 members, and its weight has diminished as its numbers have increased. Then too the President, the Senate, the House of Representatives, all exercise their functions subject to the rules of an elaborate and artificial party system which was absolutely unknown to Washington and his contemporaries. The constitution has not been deliberately altered, but it has been by the mere course of events thoroughly transformed.

C. Constitutions with a 'Parliamentary' and Constitutions with a 'Non-Parliamentary' Executive[5*]

Representative governments, with which alone we are concerned, exist in one form or another in most European countries, as well as in countries such as Japan which

---

[4] See ibid., ch. II.
[5] See ibid., Note III.

---

* On the significance of Dicey's treatment of the division between constitutions with a parliamentary executive and those with a non-parliamentary executive here and in *The Law of the Constitution*, see Editor's Introduction, pp xxxii ff, xli above. See also 'Prussian Constitutionalism', p. 116, n., above; 'Comparison between English and Other Executives', app. II, lectures 4 and 5.

have come within the influence of European ideas. There are few civilized states in which legislative power is not exercised by a wholly or partially elected body of a more or less popular or representative character. But representative government does not mean one and the same thing everywhere. It tends to exhibit two different types which are discriminated from one another by a difference in the relation between the executive and the legislature.

Under the one form the executive is a 'parliamentary executive', by which term is meant that the legislature or, it may be, the elective part thereof appoints and dismisses the executive government which under these circumstances is almost certain to be chosen from among the members of the legislative body.

Under the other form of representative government the executive is a 'non-parliamentary executive', that is to say it is an executive which, by whatever name it is called and whether it be an Emperor and his Ministers or a President and his Cabinet, is not appointed by the legislature.

This mode of division leads to several consequences deserving attention.

First, it affords a new principle for the classification of constitutions. Thus if they be tested by the suggested criterion, namely the relation of the government to the legislature, it will be found that, on the one hand, the constitutions of England, of Belgium, of Italy, of France under her present regime belong to one and the same class, for under each of these constitutions there exists a parliamentary executive, whilst, on the other hand, the Constitutions of the United States, of the German Empire, of France in the time of the Second Republic, as well as under the rule of the first and during the greater part of his reign of the third Napoleon, must be placed together in another and different class, since under each of these constitutions there is to be found a non-parliamentary executive.

Secondly, the practical power of a legislative body depends upon its ability to appoint or dismiss the executive. The possession of this right is the source of more than half the authority which at the present day has accrued to the English House of Commons. Until this right or power has been acquired, parliamentary government has not reached its full development and been transformed into government by Parliament.

The distinction, it should be particularly noted, with which we are now concerned does not square with the difference between a constitution under which there exists a sovereign Parliament and a constitution under which there exists a non-sovereign Parliament. In England it is true you find at the present day coexisting both a sovereign Parliament and a parliamentary executive. For the British Parliament can both make and repeal any law whatever, i.e. [it] is in the technical sense a sovereign body and can in reality though not in name appoint the true executive, *viz.* the Cabinet. But this combination of Parliamentary sovereignty with a parliamentary executive is not essential but accidental. The English Parliament has for centuries been a sovereign body, but down at any rate to the Revolution of 1689 the government of England was a non-parliamentary executive, and, on the other hand, while the Parliament of no English colony is a sovereign body, there exist in many English colonies, such for example as the Canadian Dominion, the Australian Commonwealth, and the

States thereof, Cabinets or executives appointed and dismissed, nominally by the Governor, but in reality by the local Parliament, or [there exist], in other words, parliamentary executives. In the German Empire, on the other hand, you find a sovereign legislature, but you certainly do not find a parliamentary executive, and it may be said with substantial truth that the essential cause of the conflict between Bismarck, representing the Crown, and his opponents in the Prussian Parliament was the opposition on the one side to, and the demand on the other side for, the creation of a parliamentary executive. Each party to this contest was from its own point of view in the right. Bismarck maintained that the existence of a sovereign parliamentary legislature was not under the Prussian Constitution inconsistent with the maintenance of a non-parliamentary executive or, in other words, with the retention by the Crown of real executive power. The Liberals were right in contending that, unless there existed in substance a parliamentary executive, the Prussian Parliament did not possess the constitutional authority of the English Parliament which German Liberals undoubtedly thought was the necessary consequence of the introduction of constitutionalism into Prussia. All the world now knows that in substance the King of Prussia and Bismarck were victorious and that the doctrine and practice of Prussian not of English constitutionalism is now accepted under the Constitution of the German Empire. What is true of the German Empire is equally true, paradoxical though the assertion sounds, of the United States. The President is the true head of the executive, but he is neither appointed nor dismissed by Congress. That the German executive, as represented by the Chancellor, is appointed by the Emperor whilst the President is elected by the American people is no doubt a difference of no small importance. All that is insisted upon here is the point, also important, of similarity. The executive neither of the Empire nor of the United States is a parliamentary executive and in each case the consequences of this likeness are in one respect the same. The legislative body has neither in Germany nor in America anything like the authority of the British Parliament.[6]

Thirdly, the difference between a parliamentary and a non-parliamentary executive covers but does not correspond with a distinction insisted upon by Bagehot

---

[6] It may be well to point out that the Irish Parliament under Grattan's Constitution—1782–1800—was a sovereign legislature without a parliamentary executive and, though it is idle to suppose that any constitutional mechanism however ingenious would have enabled Grattan to secure the real Parliamentary independence of Ireland, a critic may without absurdity assert that the combination of a sovereign Parliament with a non-parliamentary executive made it necessary that Grattan's Constitution should either be profoundly modified or else come to an end. From the point of view of historians or Irish patriots who hold that it was desirable in 1782 to establish the practical Parliamentary independence of Ireland, it would seem that Grattan and his followers made a mistake in not insisting in the moment of victory rather upon the creation of an Irish parliamentary executive than upon the absolute legislative supremacy of the Irish Parliament. The experience of the English colonies shows that under favourable circumstances a country may enjoy almost complete independence in all local concerns if its Parliament appoints the local executive, even though that Parliament is not theoretically sovereign. But it is very doubtful whether a Parliament which does not appoint and dismiss the executive can give even local independence to a country in virtue of the mere possession of legislative sovereignty. The error, if mistake it were, made by Grattan, is noteworthy because it is characteristic of his age. Neither in England, nor in Ireland, nor on the Continent, nor, we may add, in the United States had thinkers or politicians at the end of the eighteenth century grasped the fact that the English Parliament did, though indirectly, appoint or control the appointment of the executive, and owed its authority to this real though unrecognised power.

between Cabinet government and Presidential government. One of the few errors in a book so full of important truths as Bagehot's *English Constitution* is the apparent failure of its author to perceive that Cabinet government is only one form, and by no means the necessary form, of a parliamentary executive, whilst Presidential government is even more certainly only one form and not by any means a necessary form, of a non-parliamentary executive.[7]

Fourthly, the merits and defects belonging to each kind of executive are pretty obvious.

A parliamentary executive cannot from the nature of things exhibit independence as against the Parliament by which it is appointed except indeed in the rare case of its being able by a dissolution of Parliament to obtain the support of the electors, and speaking generally a Cabinet appointed by Parliament will show itself excessively sensitive to parliamentary feeling which in its turn will be greatly influenced not only by the permanent opinion, but also by the transitory sentiment or wishes, of the electors. A non-parliamentary executive, on the other hand, may exhibit a considerable amount of independence but is liable to come into conflict with the legislature, and no one can doubt that such conflict is in itself an evil and in many ways injurious to the nation. The experience not only of America but of France under the Second Republic shows how serious the inconvenience and under extreme circumstances how great the perils imposed upon a country by the quarrels almost certain to arise between a Parliament and a non-parliamentary executive.

Fifthly, the founders of constitutions have more than once tried, but not with great success, to constitute a government which should combine the merits whilst avoiding the defects both of a parliamentary and of a non-parliamentary executive. But French experiments, of which there are several, have in this matter not been successful. The last of them is exhibited by the present French Republic under the Constitution of which the President, though elected by the Assembly, is chosen for a fixed term of seven years and cannot be removed. He is given the nominal power of choosing his Ministers. In practice the part played by the President has become more and more insignificant and the Ministry are more completely dependent for their existence on the will or the caprice of Parliament than is an English Cabinet. In France in short, a parliamentary executive which was intended by its creators to possess a certain amount of independence has through the course of events turned out to be a poor imitation of the English Cabinet system and is far more dependent on the will, the caprice, or the intrigues of Parliament than is an English Ministry.

The attempt again, made during the later years of Napoleon III, to establish, according to the political cant of the day, a liberal Empire was nothing but the endeavour

---

[7] An English Cabinet is in reality a parliamentary executive, but it is a parliamentary executive which as a matter of history was originally a non-parliamentary executive, i.e. a body of servants of the Crown who were really and in truth appointed not by the Houses of Parliament but by the King. Here as elsewhere throughout English constitutional law and practice the maintenance of old names conceals the growth of new institutions. It is a matter of curious speculation whether a general election may not by degrees become something like the equivalent to the popular choice of a given statesman as Premier. Should this at any time become the constitutional rule the result would be that our executive would cease to be a parliamentary executive for it would no longer in fact be appointed by Parliament.

to transform a non-parliamentary executive which owed its existence to the will of the Emperor into a sort of semi-parliamentary executive which though appointed by the Emperor should nevertheless represent the predominant opinion of the French Chambers. The experiment was cut short by the German War, the defeat of Sedan, and the consequent revolution at Paris. Whether it could in any case have succeeded is open to grave question. The steps taken by Napoleon III towards liberalizing the Empire point to a conclusion, confirmed by the whole history of parliamentary government, that a Ministry which in any way depends for its power on the will of an elective assembly will ultimately become dependent upon, and the representative of, the Assembly, or, in other words, will turn into a completely parliamentary executive. The truth is that the Napoleonic system, at any rate among a people so sensitive to opinion and to oratory as the French, absolutely required for its maintenance the subordination of the legislative body and the complete separation of the legislature from the executive. This was secured by the original Constitution of 1852 which made the Ministry absolutely, entirely, dependent on the will of the President, who later received the title of Emperor. The mere constitution of a Ministry the members of which might belong to, and take part in the debates of, the Parliament,[8] introduced an essential change in virtue of which parliamentary speakers, such for example as Thiers, however small their numbers, began to exert great influence over the public. The executive tended to become in spirit, if not in form, the representative of Parliament.

The one modern example of the successful creation of an executive which may be called semi-parliamentary is to be found in Switzerland. The Swiss Council or, as we should say, Cabinet is directly elected by the two Houses of the Federal Assembly sitting together at their first meeting. It holds office for three years, i.e. until the next meeting of the next Federal Assembly or in English phraseology of the next Parliament. The Council has proved an admirable board for the administration of public affairs. It is not in the English or French sense of the word, a Ministry. It does not strictly represent a party and it has never come and is never likely to come into collision with the Assembly. Part at any rate of the explanation of the success in Switzerland of an experiment which has failed elsewhere is that the power of the Assembly itself is limited by the existence of the referendum, that the Swiss people by this means keep the management of affairs, or rather the determination of the principles on which such affairs are to be managed, very much in their own hands, that the people of Switzerland are better educated and more intelligent than the inhabitants of most countries, and that the party system is very imperfectly developed among them. Politics, in short, in Switzerland become a matter of business and are treated on business principles. But when everything is taken into account the marked success in the transaction of national affairs of the Swiss Council is a very curious phenomenon and proves that under very favorable circumstances it is possible to create a parliamentary executive which shall be free from some of the defects, and especially from the instability, of Cabinet government. It must, however, in fairness be added

---

[8] See Decree of the Senate, 8 Sept. 1869.

that if the Swiss Council is as a board for the management of affairs far superior to a Ministry under the Third French Republic, and as regards certainty in the tenure of office surpasses an English Cabinet, yet the Council lacks one at least of the merits which may with some fairness he ascribed to Cabinet government in England. It gives little scope for the leadership of one statesman who represents the wishes of the nation. A man such as Pitt, or Peel, or Palmerston, or Gladstone would have been out of place in such a national council as guides the affairs of the Confederation at Berne. And while the Swiss Council constitutes a more intelligent and business-like executive than is in general formed by an American President and his Cabinet, neither the Council nor any member thereof could presumably exert at a great crisis the kind of personal influence which in the hands of Abraham Lincoln saved the American Commonwealth from destruction.

Whatever be the differences between and the varying merits or demerits of various kinds of executives, the foregoing observations do, it is submitted, establish at least thus much, *viz.* that the character of a constitution is essentially affected by the relation between the legislature and the executive and that a parliamentary differs in points of vital importance from a non- parliamentary executive.[9]

D. Constitutions Responsive to Opinion and Constitutions Irresponsive to Opinion[*]

This distinction, though real, is not much noticed and is not easily expressed in language which is free from objection.

A constitution responsive to opinion may be conveniently termed a 'responsive constitution' and means, as here used, a constitution under which expression can be rapidly and easily given to the wishes, feelings, or opinions of the citizens of a given country, or rather of those citizens who as a class enjoy full political rights.

A constitution not responsive to opinion may be conveniently termed an 'irresponsive constitution', and means a constitution under which expression cannot rapidly or easily be given to the wishes, feelings, or opinions of the citizens of a country.

The best example in existence and perhaps which has ever existed of a 'responsive constitution' is the modern constitution of England. It is so to speak an instrument which responds easily and immediately to the wishes of Englishmen. The Houses of Parliament, and especially the House of Commons, can constitutionally and do in fact give effect to the real or supposed wishes, one might even say, to the whims of the electorate. This is so in matters of legislation, in matters of policy, in matters of

---

[9] It is worth notice that the Cromwellian Constitution of 1653 was not only a rigid constitution but a constitution under which the executive was all but completely independent of Parliament. This at the time did not appear to be an innovation, for down to the Revolution of 1688 the Ministry, to use modern terms, consisted of Ministers who were in reality as well as in name the servants of the Crown.

[*] On the notion of a constitution's responsiveness, absent from *The Law of the Constitution*, and on the division between responsive and irresponsive constitutions, see Editor's Introduction, pp xli f. above.

administration. No one who knows what modern England is can believe that any law can be carried to which the majority of the electors are opposed, or that the passing of any law can long be delayed which the majority of the electors distinctly desire to see passed. That the policy of the country agrees and varies with the sentiment of the country, i.e. of the electorate, does not admit of reasonable denial. If anyone for example looks at the history of domestic policy during the nineteenth century, and especially during the last quarter of the century, he will find in every department that the work of statesmen has almost unconsciously corresponded with the flow of public opinion. No better example of this can be found than the course of law making with regard to trade and labour. The free trade legislation from 1845 to 1860 exactly reflected the average beliefs and wishes of the day. The Factory Acts, which have really developed into a whole code for the regulation of labour by the state, have exactly reflected the development of opinion or the tendency of popular wishes during the latter half or latter third of the nineteenth century. But in nothing whatever is the responsiveness of the modern English constitution better seen than in questions of administration. No one even dreams that a government could hold office which had distinctly lost popular support. At every turn the administration of the law is, as many persons would think, to a disastrous degree subordinated to the sentiment of the moment. To muzzle dogs, to enforce vaccination laws, to hang a murderess who has succeeded in exciting the interest of the public, to tax cyclists, or to impose a match tax, may well be administrative efforts beyond the strength of an English Ministry. The existence of a strong Cabinet may be imperilled through the hasty arrest by an indiscreet policeman of a young woman whose character is distinctly not above reproach. Whether the way in which our institutions foster in every part of the government extreme sensitiveness to each varying and, it may be, transitory phase of public opinion is a question which need not here be brought into discussion. My aim is only to insist upon and illustrate the fact that responsiveness to popular feeling is a marked characteristic of the English constitution as it now exists.

Nor is it really necessary to confine this statement to the existing constitution. The unreformed Parliament no doubt represented a limited class of Englishmen or, to put the same statement in another form, the Englishmen who before 1832 possessed the full rights of citizens were a limited body, and the same remark holds to a considerable extent true up to the Reform Act of 1867 and even of 1884, and it was therefore far more possible, up at any rate till 1866, than it is now, that the government of the country should not correspond with the immediate wishes of the majority of the people. But even when this was the case, the constitution was responsive as regards the electorate though the electoral body itself was an inadequate representation of the country. And (what is more important) Parliamentary history affords good ground for supposing that the electoral body—the 'legal country', to adopt a French expression—has in England always far more nearly represented than one might perhaps have expected the opinion, so far as any opinion existed, of Englishmen who took any real part in politics. It is curious to note how even before the Reform Act of 1832 public opinion told upon the action both of Ministries and Parliaments. Sir Robert Walpole's Excise Bill was, as most historians think, a statesmanlike measure.

It could not be carried in the face of popular dislike. The difficulty in abolishing tests which excluded Dissenters from power lay not in the prejudice of statesmen, but in the widespread dislike of Dissenters and in the popularity of the Church. It is easy to find cases where the disposition of the House of Commons or of the House of Lords was during the last century more liberal than the popular feeling which Parliament was in effect compelled to obey. The immediate repeal of an Act passed to facilitate the naturalization of Jews (1753) is a curious monument to the influence in the middle of the last century of popular prejudice. There is every reason to believe that public sentiment and opinion inside and outside of the electoral body supported the war with the American colonies, and whatever may be said against the opposition by George III to Catholic Emancipation no one can seriously allege that he in this matter opposed himself to the will of the people. It may indeed well be doubted whether the passing of the Catholic Relief Act in 1829 must not be noted as a rare instance in which statesmen under the pressure of national peril overrode rather than carried out the will of the people. The overthrow of the Coalition Government, possessed as the Ministry were of a large parliamentary majority, the carrying of the Reform Act itself, which was hostile to the interest of every owner of close boroughs, are singular proofs even in an unreformed Parliament of the way in which or the degree to which* the influence not only of the electors but of numbers who desired to become electors told upon Parliament. Birmingham was a power in the land, when Birmingham sent not a single member to the Home of Commons.[10]

The most striking example of a constitution which is not responsive is, paradoxical though the assertion sounds, to be found in the Constitution of the United States of America.

It would be extremely difficult by any constitutional means to change any article of the American Constitution and indeed the only changes which have been carried out of recent years were the result of a civil war, and were carried through by means which, though morally legitimate, partook to a great extent of force. No one supposes that the majority of the whites in the States which had made up the Southern Confederacy really approved of the Thirteenth, Fourteenth, or Fifteenth Amendments,

---

[10] The difficulty of carrying through changes either admittedly or possibly beneficial will be urged either by reformers or innovators as a proof that the English constitution is far less responsive to opinion than is here maintained. The evidence tendered for this want of responsiveness is utterly inconclusive. Its value depends upon the assumption that the majority of English people counted by the head, or what is popularly called the people, always desire, and have always desired, the adoption of laws or the following of policies which intelligent reformers maintain, often rightly enough, to be expedient and beneficial. But this assumption is itself utterly groundless. If we look at the past, of which alone we are at all fair judges, there is no reason to suppose that the views of the wisest statesmen or of the most far-sighted innovators have generally commanded popular approval. It is pretty certain that, during the half century which dates, roughly speaking, from about 1780, the dislike of change which stopped both innovation and reform was shared by the mass of the people and the real obstacle to carrying out after 1832 the proposals of Radical reformers was that the electors had little desire for radical changes. During periods of legislative inaction quite as truly as during periods of legislative activity, the English constitution has exhibited its responsiveness to public opinion.

---

* In a later marginal manuscript note, either/both 'of the way in which' and 'the degree to which' were noted for insertion.

or that under a normal state of things it would have been possible to obtain for these Amendments that ratification by three-fourths of the States constituting the United States which is required by the Constitution. The difficulty, it may be added, of effecting constitutional changes or, in other words, the rigidity of the Constitution has, combined with other circumstances, checked the tendency or disposition to agitate for such changes.

But the irresponsive character of the American Constitution is not by any means wholly due to its rigidity. It is due, at any rate in part, to that system of checks and balances, in short to that elaborate distribution and division of powers which is an essential feature of the constitution erected by the founders of the Union. Thus the sphere of the President, of the Houses of Congress, of the judiciary is strictly limited, but, on the other hand, each of these three authorities have a certain independence within that sphere and can check the action of each of the other two. The result therefore certainly is in many cases that public opinion cannot tell as directly and immediately upon the action either of the government or the legislature as in England. No doubt a President may be, and often has been, intensely anxious to follow public opinion, though the opinion to which he is likely to look is rather the opinion of his particular party than of the country. But if a President is a man of a strong will who either does not desire, or has no chance, of re-election he assuredly can act with an independence of public opinion within his sphere which is impossible to an English Prime Minister or even an English Cabinet. There are assuredly one or two known instances, and there may be others not so well known, on which President Lincoln carried out by his own authority acts of policy which it is probable neither Congress nor the people of the Northern States at the moment were prepared to sanction.[11] On the other hand, the other authorities in the state may make it impossible for a President to carry through a policy which he may well suppose to command popular support. He is hampered by the really independent legislative authority of Congress and by the administrative power of the Senate, to which one ought to add, though here a critic goes beyond the strict limits of the constitution, that the elaborate party system, which in reality though not in name forms part of the constitution as it really exists and works, prevents the direct action of public opinion in matters both of legislation and of policy[,] in any case where such action is inconsistent with the normal working of party mechanism[s] or, to adopt an American expression, of the machine.

With regard to the distinction between a responsive and an irresponsive constitution two points require careful attention.

First, the distinction is not the same though it has sometimes been confounded with the distinction between a democratic and a non-democratic constitution.

This becomes apparent in a moment if we put side by side the British monarchy and the American Republic. On the one hand, the monarchical constitution of England is obviously far less democratic than the Constitution of the United States. In the one country we have both a monarch and a powerful nobility; in the other you

---

[11] One or two of President Cleveland's acts were apparently done wholly on his own responsibility.

have a President elected in effect by universal suffrage, and you have no nobility of any kind whatever. In the United Kingdom you have a scheme of voting which is best though not quite accurately described as household suffrage; in the United States you have universal suffrage. On the other hand, the monarchical constitution of England is a far more responsive constitution than the Constitution of the United States. So markedly is this the case as to lead an observer struck by the rapidity with which public opinion controls the government and the legislature in England to assert that our institution are more democratic than those of the United States. The assertion is for the reasons already given obviously inaccurate, but it rests on the perception of the fact that the constitution of England is responsive to opinion in a sense in which the Constitution of the United States is not, whence it follows that changes desired by the people can be more readily effected in England than in America.

The difference between the responsiveness and the democratic character of a constitution may be illustrated by another comparison. The United States and the Swiss Confederacy are both democracies; they are both federal governments; they each in several points bear a very strong resemblance to one another, yet it is quite certain that the Swiss Constitution is far more responsive than the American. Changes in deference to popular will are frequent and easy. The Confederacy in its present form dates from 1848; it has existed that is to say for 52 years. The Constitution of the United States dates from 1787; it has existed, that is to say, for 113 years. The Constitution of Switzerland has been at least once remodelled or amended, and is at any moment susceptible of easy alteration should there be a wide demand for a change. The Constitution of the United States was slightly altered within some 17 years of its creation, but the amendments then made were not of a searching character. In consequence of the Civil War three amendments were carried with a view to the complete abolition of slavery. With these exceptions the Constitution remains unchanged, and to amend it is admitted to be a matter of the greatest difficulty. The Swiss Ministry or Council again is a governmental board which though not dismissible is appointed for three years by the Federal Assembly. It is a board of capable business men which does not pretend to the kind of independence exercisable by the American President. It is, in short, like the Parliament by which it is created amendable to public opinion.

Secondly, the distinction between a 'responsive' and an 'irresponsive' constitution is not the same as the distinction between a 'flexible' and a 'rigid' constitution.

A flexible constitution is one under which every law of every description, including in that term the laws or articles of the constitution, can legally be changed with the same ease and in the same manner by one and the same body. A rigid constitution is one under which certain laws, generally known as constitutional or fundamental laws, cannot be changed in the same manner as ordinary laws.[12]

A responsive constitution is one under which public opinion easily and immediately finds its expression either in acts of legislation or in acts of administration.

A rigid constitution it is true can, in so far as it is rigid, hardly be so responsive as a flexible constitution for the object of its rigidity is to prevent the too easy or rapid

---

[12] *Law of the Constitution*, 5th edn, pp 119, 120.

change of fundamental or constitutional laws. But a rigid constitution may allow the administration of affairs to be under the direct control of the legislature. In this case, if the Parliament fairly represents the people of a country, the constitution may be in all administrative and in many legislative matters freely responsive to public opinion. A flexible constitution, on the other hand, need not be a particularly responsive constitution. The constitution of England has for centuries been a flexible constitution, for it has been impossible to point to any definite law or laws which Parliament could not alter or pass by a duly enacted statute. This is the necessary result of Parliamentary sovereignty. On the other hand, no one can doubt that the existing constitution of the United Kingdom is a far more responsive constitution than was the same constitution in 1801 or *a fortiori* than was the constitution of England in 1660.

Here we pass to a somewhat curious:—

Question—What are the conditions which are favourable to the responsiveness of a constitution?

If by responsiveness we mean responsiveness to the general public opinion of the majority of the nation, the conditions favourable to its existence may be thus summed up.

The constitution must be a flexible constitution for, as already pointed out, the rigidity of a constitution is merely a term for the existence of legal obstacles in the way of changing the fundamental laws of a country.

The executive must be a parliamentary executive. The very essence of such an executive is that it is elected by and amenable to the opinion of the legislature and therefore as a rule responsive to the opinion of the persons by whom the legislature is elected.

The electorate must either be the whole body of citizens or fairly represent the feelings and opinions of the whole body of the citizens. The defect or at any rate the characteristic of the English constitution before 1832 was that, while it was thoroughly responsive to the predominant opinions of the electorate, including in that term the owners of nomination boroughs, the electorate itself did not on some points at least represent or respond to the opinion of the nation. Hence if we have in our eye public opinion in a general sense, we may say that during the existence of the unreformed Parliament the constitution was not responsive or did not give full expression to the predominant opinion of the country.

If then, to sum the matter up, a constitution is flexible, the executive is a parliamentary executive, and, lastly, the legislature fairly represents the feelings and opinions of the electorate, you have a combination of the conditions which, as far as the form of a constitution is concerned, will create a responsive constitution or, in other words, a constitution under which the opinion and the wishes of a given people readily and immediately find expression in the legislation, in the administration, and in the policy of their country.

6

The Judiciary in Relation to the Executive and Legislative Powers

Analysis (1900)*

Introduction
    1. In every civilized country judiciary 'independent'
    2. Difference under different constitutions as to limits of judicial authority in respect of acts of
        (i) Legislature
        (ii) Executive

A. What are Limits with regard to Legislature?
    I. In *England*
        1. Judiciary have no authority to pronounce on validity of Act of British Parliament
        2. Judiciary have authority to pronounce on validity of laws passed by subordinate law-making bodies
        3. Judiciary never in strictness annul a law
    II. In *United States*
        1. Judiciary have authority to pronounce on validity of Acts passed by any legislature
        2. Judiciary have no authority to pronounce on validity of Constitution of United States, or of duly passed amendments thereto
        3. Judiciary cannot annul laws
    III. In *France* and on *Continent* generally
        Judiciary have no power to treat as invalid any law passed by national legislature and duly published

B. What are Limits with regard to Executive?
    I. In *England* and *United States*
        Judiciary have authority to pronounce on legality of any act done by any person
        Question. How far are acts of State done out of England, e.g. during course of war, legally justified by order of Crown?
    II. In *France* and on *Continent* generally
        1. Acts of State in proper sense of term beyond [the] jurisdiction of any Court whatever

---

* Its contents have been derived from an undated manuscript attached to the lecture schedule headed 'Easter & Trinity Terms 1900'.

2. No remedy in ordinary Courts for official or governmental acts which violate rights of individuals
   3. Remedy in administrative Courts for such acts
   4. Limits to jurisdiction of ordinary Courts fixed ultimately by *Tribunal des Conflits*
III. *General comparison* between *English* and *Continental* doctrine

Analysis (1899)[*]

Introduction
- 1. In every civilized country judiciary in theory independent, i.e. judge is intended to act independently of non-judicial considerations, i.e. to do justice
- 2. Great difference in different states as to extent of judicial authority, i.e. what are the questions which can be submitted to the ordinary Courts for decision
- 3. The limits of judicial authority may have reference
  - (i) to the acts of the legislature
  - (ii) to the acts of the executive

  Two questions
  - (i) What are limits of judicial authority in regard to legislation?
  - (ii) What are limits in regard to acts of executive?

A. What is Judicial Authority in regard to Legislation?
   I. *English (and American) doctrine*
      NB Really [the] same though application [is] different.
      Judges have no power to pronounce on validity of laws passed by sovereign legislature, but have power to pronounce on validity of laws passed by any subordinate legislature. Hence,
      - (i) No English Court can treat Parliamentary statute as invalid, but an English Court may treat bye laws of corporations or Acts of colonial legislature as invalid
      - (ii) American Courts may treat any Act of Congress as invalid if inconsistent with Constitution of United States and Act of State legislature as invalid if inconsistent with Constitution of United States or of State

      No American Court can treat duly passed amendment of US Constitution as invalid
   II. *French and, in general, Continental doctrine*
       The Courts cannot question the validity of any law passed by national legislature, even if it violates the Constitution.
       This in principle applies even in Switzerland, (Austria), and German Empire.
       NB Question in theory open as regards German Empire

B. What is Judicial Authority in regard to the Executive?
   See Dicey, *Law of Constitution*; 1 Laferrière, bk. III, ch. I, pp 7–9
   I. *English and American doctrine*
      Authority of executive does not justify acts otherwise illegal and every individual responsible civilly and criminally for breaches of law and subject to jurisdiction of ordinary Courts.
      Question—How far are acts of State, e.g. acts done in course of war, beyond jurisdiction of Courts?

---

[*] Its contents have been derived from a manuscript dated 13 April 1899. This second, longer, Analysis has been provided to complement the first Analysis in the absence of a full lecture text.

NB No remedy gives to Crown [immunity], i.e. in some cases no available remedy for wrongs done by state
II. *French and Continental doctrine*
   1. Acts of State in proper sense of term lie quite beyond the competence of ordinary Courts
   (Compare 1 Laferrière, p. 471)
   2. For official or governmental acts which infringe upon the rights of individuals no remedy before the ordinary Courts, i.e. Courts have no jurisdiction in respect of administrative matters
   3. There is remedy before administrative Courts which give effect to administrative law
   4. The limits of the jurisdiction of the ordinary Courts is ultimately fixed by *Tribunal des Conflits*
III. *Comparison between English and Continental doctrine*
   1. English doctrine does not recognise administrative law, i.e. at bottom does not recognise difference between public law and private law. Continental doctrine treats public law as particular kind of law regulating the rights of the state
   2. Under the English doctrine the ordinary Courts determine the limits of their own jurisdiction, under Continental doctrine the Courts are forbidden to determine their own jurisdiction and cannot trench on the rights of the administration
   Under English doctrine wrong done by administration within jurisdiction of ordinary Courts; under continental doctrine within jurisdiction of administrative Courts
IV. *Why the French consider their system of administrative law as a peculiar excellence of French institutions?*
   Answer
   1. As contrasted with the English system it ensures the rights of state and further gives individual remedies which he does not possess in England
   2. As contrasted with administrative principles of other Continental states it has developed a real system of *law* in place of arbitrary administrative power and a system advantageously administered by special Courts
   On French view in short *droit administratif* good
   Thus as compared with England it is 'administrative' as compared with other Continental countries it is 'law' and not arbitrary authority

(See Montesquieu, bk. XI, ch. VI and chs I–V;
1 Laferrière, pp 10–13, bk. III, ch. I, pp 471–513, ch. VII, pp 637–71,
   ch. VIII, pp 655–60;
Brinton Coxe, *Judicial Power and Unconstitutional Legislation*;
1 Lowell (France), pp 47–65;
2 Lowell (Austria), pp 83, 84, 399;
2 Lowell (Germany), pp 281–6;
2 Lowell (Switzerland), pp 214–20.)

7

Local Government and Centralization

Analysis (1900)*

Introduction
    1. Meaning of 'local government' viz. management of local affairs by local authorities
    2. 'Centralization' means management of local affairs by central government or agents thereof

A.   Contrast between Constitutions which favour Local Government and Constitutions which favour Centralization
    Illustrations—Local Government
      United States, especially New England
      Switzerland
      England
    Centralization
      France (i) under *ancien régime*
               (ii) under modern administrative system

B.   Merits and Demerits of Local Government
    Merits
      1. Persons living in locality most likely to understand their own affairs
      2. Local government may under favourable circumstances stimulate interest of citizens in public life
    Defects
      1. Local government may tend to parochialism
      2. Matters of local government may be of general interest and require control by central government
      3. Local government requires active interest in local affairs by inhabitants to whom confided
      4. Local government not necessarily opposed to state interference

C.   The Relation between Local Government and
    I. *Self-government* and
    II. *Personal freedom.*

(See Mill, *Political Economy*, bk. V, ch. XI;
Tocqueville, *Democracy in America* (transl.), vol. 1, p. 189;
Tocqueville, *L'Ancien Régime*, bk. II, chs II and X; and,
as to English local government, 1 Blackstone, pp 110–120; 351–4;
'Local Government', 7 *Encyc. Laws of England*, p. 49;
Blake Odgers, *Local Government*, especially pp 201, 202, 204 (Citizen Series).)

---

* Its contents have been derived from an undated manuscript attached to the lecture schedule headed 'Easter & Trinity Terms 1900'. See also the Notes on self-government and local self-government, app. III below.

Analysis (1899)*

Introduction
> Meaning of self-government ambiguous
>> 1. Administration of local affairs by local bodies. In this sense it is 'local' government or the exercise of powers of state through local bodies as contrasted with centralization or exercise of powers of state by central government, e.g. in England by governmental offices in London, or in more general terms by officers dependent upon central administration or executive
>> 2. Management of individual's own affairs either independently or in combination with others without state interference. In this sense self-government or personal freedom of action is opposed not to centralization but to state interference
>> 3. Tacitly assumed that the two meanings coincide, i.e. that where there is local self-government as contrasted with centralization there will be individual liberty as contrasted with state interference

A. Contrast between Constitutions which favour Local Government and Constitutions which favour Centralization
   Examples
   Local Government
   > United States, especially New England
   > Switzerland
   > England

   Centralised government
   > France
   >> (i) under *l'ancien régime*
   >> (ii) Modern administrative system

B. Merits and Defects of Local Government
   Merits
   > 1. Persons living in locality are most likely to know and understand their own affairs
   > 2. Local government tends under favourable circumstances to stimulate interest of inhabitants in public life and to increased self-reliance
   > 3. Local self-government tends (?) to foster individual freedom as contrasted with state interference

   Defects
   > 1. Local government means narrow-minded or parochial government
   > 2. Matters of local government may be of general interest and require general regulation, e.g. education. Hence in England constant increase for last 50 years of centralization
   > 3. Local government answers only where inhabitants in reality take part in local affairs
   > 4. Local government not necessarily opposed to state interference

C. The real Relation between Local Self-government and Personal Freedom in England

---

* Its contents have been derived from a manuscript dated 1 May 1899. This second, longer, Analysis has been provided to complement the first Analysis in the absence of a full lecture text.

8

Federal Government

Analysis*

A. What is Meant by Federal Government?
   I. *Conditions and Aim* of federalism
   Conditions
   1. Existence of separate countries (states) capable of forming one common country
   2. Existence of federal sentiment, i.e. desire for union without desire for unity

   Aim
   Formation of union under which states shall for some purposes, and especially in regard to foreign powers form one country, and yet shall, as between themselves and for many purposes remain independent states

   II. *Principles* of federalism
   1. Federal or common government and each State to have independent authority within its own sphere
   2. The maintenance of this division of spheres to be maintained by each State as such, having a share in the sovereign power.

   Hence, distinction between
   (i) Federalism and extended local self-government which may exist in unitary state [and]
   (ii) Federalism and Home Rule (i.e. the position of dependencies with large powers of self-government)

   III. *Characteristics* of federalism
   1. Federal constitution based on distribution of powers
   2. Federal constitution must in general be a written and a rigid constitution
   3. Federal constitution may lead to increase in authority of Courts

B. Merits and Defects of Federalism
   Merits
   1. Substitutes union for separation
   2. May encourage growth [of] common national sentiment

---

* Its contents have been derived from an undated manuscript attached to the lecture schedule headed 'Easter & Trinity Terms 1900'. There is not a longer, second, Analysis available in the Dicey Papers with which to complement it. On the subject of this Analysis and the next, see also *Oxford Edition of Dicey*, i, *The Law of the Constitution*, 'Swiss Federalism' (Note VIII, 5th edn), 304 ff, 'Australian Federalism' (Note IX, 6th edn), 329 ff.

Defects
1. Federal government is weak government
2. Federal government tends to be conservative government, and in Anglo-Saxon countries fosters legalism

C. Questions
1. Does federal government reconcile existence of political unity with recognition of separate nationalities?
2. Does federal government tend towards beneficial separation between general legislation and State legislation?

(See Freeman, *Federal Government*, chs I and II, pp 1–122;
Dicey, *Law of Constitution* (5th edn), ch. III, p. 130;
Mill, *Representative Government*, ch. XVII.)

9

Federal Government (continued) The Australian Commonwealth

Analysis[*]

A. Points in Australian Commonwealth Common to all Modern Federal Governments
   I. *Distribution of powers*
   II. *Share of States in sovereign power*
      1. Representation of States by Senate
      2. Amendment of Constitution
   III. *Two Houses representing States and population respectively*
B. Peculiar Points in Australian Commonwealth
   I. *Legislative power of Commonwealth Parliament definite, of State Parliaments indefinite*
   II. *Cabinet government part of Constitution*
   III. *Special position of Senate*
      1. Permanence combined with liability to dissolution
      2. Direct election of Senators by population of State
      3. Number of Senators to be half number of Representatives
      4. Special share in legislation
   IV. *Important position of law Courts*
   V. *Amendment of Constitution subject to referendum*
C. Questions
   1. Whether Cabinet system suitable to federal government?
   2. Whether Senate or House of Representatives the more powerful?
   3. Whether Constitution not too rigid?

---

[*] Its contents have been derived from an undated manuscript attached to the lecture schedule headed 'Easter & Trinity Terms 1900'. There is not a longer, second, Analysis available in the Dicey Papers with which to complement it. Dicey's inclusion of this lecture in *The Comparative Study of Constitutions* course appears to have been influenced by his contemporary preoccupation with the bill that became the Commonwealth of Australia Constitution Act 1900: G. Hand, 'A. V. Dicey's Unpublished Materials on the Comparative Study of Constitutions' in G. Hand and J. McBride (eds), Droit Sans Frontières: *Essays in Honour of L. Neville Brown* (Birmingham: Holdsworth Club, 1991), 77–93, especially 84 f.

APPENDIX

COMPARATIVE CONSTITUTIONALISM

I

Memorandum on English Party System of Government[*]

A. Nature

Under all forms of popular government there must be political parties. Englishmen assume that the existence of political parties involves the existence of our system of party government. This assumption is both historically and logically unsound. Our present system is of recent growth and under many forms of popular government it has no existence.

The modern English system is marked by the following characteristics:

First, the executive is a Cabinet or committee nominally appointed by the Crown, but in truth indirectly elected by the party which possesses a majority in the House of Commons. By the same party it is kept in power and (indirectly) dismissed.

The indirectness of the method under which a Cabinet is removed from office deserves notice because it has some important practical effects. A Cabinet may indeed be dismissed by a direct vote of want of confidence. In recent times it has more often been displaced by the refusal of the House of Commons to pass some measure or to adopt some policy recommended by the Cabinet. As to the amount of opposition on the part of the House which may justify or necessitate the retirement of a Ministry no definite rule can be given. The ruling principle is that a Cabinet should retire whenever the House shows by its acts that Ministers have lost its confidence, or in other words that the House wishes for their retirement.

Secondly, the members of the Cabinet are collectively and personally responsible for the conduct of legislation, for the management of the administrative business of the government, and for the whole policy of the country both in its general outline and in its details.

Thirdly, the Cabinet represents and guides the party, e.g. the Liberals, who have a majority in the House. This party are supposed to possess a coherent body of principles which influence the whole of their policy and which are opposed to the principles of their opponents, i.e. the minority of the House, or in other words the Opposition.

Fourthly, in theory at least the Opposition are supposed to be prepared, on the Cabinet losing the confidence of the House, to undertake the business of governing the country in accordance with the party principles of the Opposition.

---

[*] The manuscript was dated 6 August 1889 but is the product, in places, of what appears to be mainly subsequent alteration. On Dicey's severe early criticism of the party system and innovative advocacy of the referendum in the English context, see Editor's Introduction, pp xix, xxx f. above. See also 'Party Government' (pp 122 ff above).

Fifthly, the Cabinet has the power, within certain limits, of dissolving a Parliament from which they do not receive support and of appealing to the country to determine whether the views of the Cabinet or the views of the House are to be adopted.

Sixthly, the Cabinet has at its head a Prime Minister, who chooses his colleagues among the principal men of the party to which he belongs and who, if he and a colleague disagree, can require the colleague, if the disagreement be vital, to retire from office.

Seventhly, the Cabinet is expected to place at the beginning of every session before the country a programme of legislation and more or less takes the credit of the Ministry on carrying this programme into effect.

The general result is that the government of the country is placed in the hands of a committee which represents a predominant party and which is created by and at every moment depends for its existence upon the will of the House of Commons. A Cabinet has neither in theory, nor often in fact, any certainty of existence for a definite period. It is a temporary body which represents not the nation but a party and (subject to the possibility of a dissolution) may at any moment fall from power, either by ceasing to command the support of the party, or from the party itself ceasing to be predominant in the House.

Three considerations modify the action of the party system and have hitherto made the Cabinet in reality a more permanent and independent body than might be expected from its characteristics.

The Crown, in the first place, has had till historically very recent times a considerable part in the appointment of Ministers. They have been more or less 'servants of the crown'. Circumstances might even now easily be conceived under which the choice of a Premier, or the exclusion of a particular politician from a Cabinet, might depend on the choice of the Crown.

Hitherto, in the second place, an idea has prevailed that at any national crisis, e.g. during a war, a time of disturbance, and the like, the leaders of the Opposition should support the executive as representing the country, and should, as the expression goes, see that 'the Queen's government was carried on'.

In the third place, the non-parliamentary members of the civil service are all but irremovable except for misconduct. A permanent Under Secretary of State is supposed never to let his private views interfere with his public duties and may with perfect honour serve every Minister with equal zeal.

These three considerations ought carefully to be weighed. They have hitherto modified in practice the evil results of entrusting the government of a country to a picked body of partisans whose tenure of office depends on their success in guiding their party.

B. Evils

Party government, as it exists in England, demands for its working the existence of two, and not more than two, opposed parties.

Even assuming these conditions to exist—and as to this assumption more will be said later—this plan of government has several obvious vices—and vices it must be added not by any means necessarily inherent in the existence of political parties.

First, party government through a Cabinet must sacrifice good administration to party exigencies. This occurs in at least two different ways. Leaders are selected for their skill as parliamentary tacticians and not for their skill as administrators. Half at least of the ablest statesmen are at any given moment excluded from office. No one can honestly doubt that it may well happen that the most competent Foreign Minister is a Conservative, the most competent Chancellor of the Exchequer a Liberal, the most competent Lord Chancellor a man who might just as well be termed a Liberal as a Conservative. Yet it is absolutely impossible to bring these three men together into one Cabinet.

Secondly, the essential vice of party government is that it is government by and for a party, and not by and for the nation, and moreover it is a scheme of government under which successful administration or legislation by the executive defers the return of the Opposition to power, or, to look at the same thing from the other side, under which every failure of the government is *pro tanto* a gain to their opponents. The inevitable result is that politics become a game in a way in which no other serious pursuit of life is turned into a game by men of character. The constant effort of Government and Opposition must be to trip one another up, or in effect to injure one another at the cost of the nation. Every year there is brought forward Bill after Bill on the general principles of which men of good sense are pretty well agreed. They could easily be carried were it not that successful legislation strengthens the Cabinet. They are not carried because an Opposition exists to oppose. The same tendency displays itself in matters of administration even in matters affecting judicial proceedings. Whoever reads the Maamstrasna debates, the discussions about Miss Cass, the questions asked, or motions raised, about the treatment of political offenders in Ireland, and the like will see in a moment how the nation suffers because party success depends upon impeding the action of the national government. The harm which is visible is not one-half as great as the harm which is unseen. Any knowledge of human nature will convince us that the members of a modern English Cabinet are always trying to avoid offence. Things are left undone which ought to be done, because the doing of them might incur immediate unpopularity. Lincoln saved the United States from danger, if not ruin, by surrendering the men taken on board the *Trent*. Few English Premiers would act as boldly, but Lincoln's tenure of office did not depend on a vote of Congress.

Thirdly, Cabinet government of the English type stimulates the demand for constitutional changes while it gives no guarantee that these changes shall be carried out by experts, or be the result of mature deliberation.

This almost of necessity results from the way in which parties bid against one another and from the fact that in England no difference is recognised between fundamental and other laws.

There are very considerable evils in making a constitution what is called 'rigid', but the world has never till recently seen what is likely to be the result of letting the fundamental institutions of a nation be changed at any moment by a party vote.

Persons who totally disagree as to the policy or impolicy of Home Rule will yet on reflection admit that such a matter as the Union between England and Ireland, ought not to have been determined by such haphazard legislation as that proposed in 1886. There was a precedent to be found for it in the Jury Reform Bill of 1866, but the precedent was as vicious as the imitation. The vice here signalised is, it may be said, inherent in the English constitution. The remark is formally true, in substance it is misleading. Till a period of not more than 60 years ago large legislative changes in the constitution were practically unknown, and even 30 years ago no one dreamt that they could be carried out without lengthy deliberation.

Fourthly, the party system undermines the belief in the duty due from citizens to the nation. The idea that the state or community has moral rights, to which men of all parties ought to defer, is perishing.

For the spread of this moral disease the party system is responsible. In order that men who in any way respect themselves may act with vigour as partisans, by which I mean as members of a regularly organised body of persons who support the Government or the Opposition, as the case may be, it is necessary for them to persuade themselves and others that the differences between themselves and their opponents are vital, and that they differ on fundamental principles. As moreover the weakening of the Government is the reason for which an Opposition exists—and in England a government can be weakened by attacking both its administration and its legislation—it follows that the Opposition for the time being are under the constant and practically irresistible temptation to misrepresent both to themselves and to others every act of the Government.

As regards nine out of ten of the legislative proposals, or the administrative acts of a government, there is, in England at the present moment, little difference in point either of honesty or of capacity between the conduct of Liberals or Conservatives. On points especially of administration the best men of both parties are substantially agreed. Such men when in office, to whatever party they belong, transact the business of the country to the best of their ability and, whatever their good intentions or capacity, never avoid a large number of blunders. Yet each party, when in opposition, attack the conduct of the government both as a whole and in details. Men actually engaged in politics soon come to believe that their opponents cannot do right on any point whatever. Hence further the Government of the day is considered not as the government of the Crown or of the country but as the government of a faction, and what the government is considered to be, that it is likely in fact to become. This tendency to look upon the government as in some way opposed to the nation of which it is really the organ is in England stimulated by historical causes. Modes of thought and feeling appropriate to the time when the country was really engaged in a contest with the Crown have survived to a period when the authority of the Crown is only a name for the authority of the state.

Fifthly, the party system may well have the effect that half the policy pursued by the Cabinet is not the policy approved by the nation. The majority of the electors wish, say, to maintain the Union and for a pacific foreign policy. The Conservative leaders advocate the maintenance of the Union and a warlike foreign policy, the Liberals, a peaceful policy abroad and Home Rule in Ireland. Neither party when in power carries out the will of the nation.

Sixthly, the party system, if it is to work even tolerably, depends upon the existence of conditions which can as a matter of fact be found only under exceptional circumstances.

These conditions are the existence of two parties, and of no more, each of which is held together by belief in a more or less complete and coherent political creed and each of which disbelieves in the creed of its opponents.

In a very rough way this state of affairs has existed in England, and in some other countries[,] as long as there was a *bonâ fide* contest between the advocates and opponents of democratic government. But the establishment of popular government has, in England at any rate, obliterated this broad line of division between two leading parties. This want of a real division which has been often felt in other countries as well as in England has two effects. It induces political leaders to find out or invent causes of division. In other words it gives a factitious stimulus to agitation; it further is favourable to the rise of groups or factions. These may be bodies which are united by belief in the supreme importance of some particular principle or measure. Such are the anti-vaccinationists, the temperance party, the Irish Home Rulers. These groups again may be real factions, that is knots of men allied together for the sake of promoting the political interests of themselves or their followers. The appearance of these groups or factions is fatal to the existence of a strong Government and a strong Opposition. In France where this modern Parliamentary disease shows itself in its worst form any Ministry can be turned out by a temporary coalition of factions. But the groups which have for the moment coalesced are unable to lay the foundation of a strong government. The national executive is placed at the mercy of intriguers. This malady of modern Parliaments prevails, be it noted, in every part of the civilized world. In France, in England, in the United States, in Switzerland, men suffer from the evils of 'Parliamentarism' though it is only in one or two of these countries that the infliction has as yet obtained a name (see especially Bryce's account of American State legislatures). It is only, however, where the Cabinet system of party government prevails that Parliamentarism can, as in France, reach its full development. Where the executive does not depend from day to day for its existence on the vote of the legislature the divisions of the legislative body need not necessarily weaken the executive.

C. Mitigations or Remedies

The object of all the mitigations or remedies proposed for the lessening or the removal of the bad results of the party system is in the main to restore the nation to control over its own destinies by placing the national executive and the fundamental institutions of the state so far at any rate out of the reach of Party that the one cannot be overthrown, and the other cannot be suddenly changed, by the sudden whim either of the House of Commons or of the electors whom the House of Commons represents.

Under a system of popular government, such as does exist and practically must exist in England, it is vain to suppose that any constitutional devices can make it impossible for the nation, that is for the distinct majority of the electors, to get rid of any government or institution which the nation deliberately condemns. What, if any, may be the means of checking the progress of democracy, or what, if any, the methods of overthrowing a democratic form of government are questions with which this memorandum has no concern whatever. They are enquiries, it may be added, with which no sensible Englishman will at the present day trouble his head. What this memorandum is concerned with is how far, in a democratic state like modern England, it is possible to get rid of the modern system of party government or to mitigate the evils which it entails. That such removal or mitigation is possible is proved by the experience of other countries, notably of the United States, (of Germany?) and of Switzerland.

I. *Remedies which might be introduced without a formal change in the constitution*

1. **The authority of the Crown as standing outside and above the conflicts of Party might be considerably increased and this without any change in the form of the constitution**[1]

Suppose, for example, (and the supposition is not in itself by any means inconceivable) that the mass of the electors were to feel that a King more nearly represented their general and permanent wishes than did a Cabinet or a Premier appointed by a fluctuating party, and were therefore to allow the King considerably more authority than the Queen now exercises in determining the constitution and the conduct of the Cabinet. Such a state of feeling would, it is clear, modify the whole working of the constitution. There are many circumstances, not necessary here to work out, which suggest that a democracy might be far more willing than were the aristocracy of the last century to constitute the Crown a kind of arbitrator among parties. The Constitution of the French Republic embodies an attempt though not a very successful one to create a head of the executive who, without coming into conflict with the Parliament, should stand above the Ministry of the day. Nor is there any reason in the nature of things why a King who shared popular sentiments or prejudices should not, like George III in the later part of his reign, represent the national will more truly than any Minister. Even as it is a King could at present probably exert, on one or two matters, a kind of influence upon opinion to which for sixty years Englishmen have been quite unaccustomed. It is further possible though far less probable that the miscalled 'veto' might be revived in regard to great constitutional changes as a 'suspensive veto'

---

[1] There are one or two administrative functions which even now were better left in the hands of the Crown than of the Ministry. Such are the 'pardon', in the strict sense of the term, of offences, the appointment of military or naval commanders, and (under conceivable circumstances) the conduct of foreign affairs (?). Of course by 'pardon' I do not mean the reinvestigation of a prisoner's guilt; what is meant is the determination whether under certain circumstances, the legal guilt being established, punishment is to take effect. I doubt whether any modern Ministry would venture to hang a clergyman as popular as Dodd.

which could be used in place of the 'final veto' which is unusable. Any plan, however, for increasing the influence of the Crown is at the present moment not worth discussion. It depends upon having on the throne a King of at any rate more than average capacity who should have gradually acquired as did George III weight and authority among the mass of the people.

2. The House of Lords might constitute itself the guardian of the constitution

Taking warning by the fate of the Royal veto the House might while there is still time transform its nominal power of finally rejecting Bills into a real and valuable suspensive veto on constitutional innovations.

To achieve this end no formal change in the constitution is absolutely necessary.

It would be attained if the leader of the majority among the Peers announced, with the consent of followers who were prepared to act on the announcement, that henceforth any Bill affecting the foundations of the constitution, from whatever side it proceeded, would be rejected by the House in order that its provisions might be submitted to the electors on a dissolution of Parliament, and that any Bill would, after being so submitted and having again passed by a decided majority through the House of Commons, be passed by the Peers.

The announcement may appear vague; almost all constitutional understandings are in their nature vague. They are not the less easy to act upon by politicians who honestly mean to give effect to them.

Such an announcement as has been suggested would (little as MPs believe this) give no offence to the electors, whose authority it would distinctly acknowledge and increase. It would raise the power of the Lords, for a rejection of a Bill would thenceforth cease to mean a threat of thwarting the popular will. As things now stand a rejection of a measure involving large changes has in reality pretty much the effect that the proposed announcement ascribes to it. But the formal surrender of a right of final veto which cannot be exercised would take away all offence from the actual exercise of a suspensive veto, which entails nothing but a referendum to the people. The House of Commons would be the loser, but to anyone who wishes to reform the present party system the House of Commons is the enemy.

No changed action, however, on the part of the Lords would be really effective without a change in the constitution of the upper House.

3. The older practice might be revived of a Ministry retiring only after a formal vote of want of confidence by the House of Commons

It lies in the hands of any government to proclaim its resolution to take this course. The change may seem a small one, but it would give a not inconsiderable check to attacks on measures which are assailed, not because really objected to in themselves, but because the rejection of any measure always damages and often may turn out a government. It lies rather beyond the scope of this paper to consider the various methods by which the 'debating', so called, of the House of Commons may be cut short, the waste of time in a debate on the address be curtailed, frivolous questions be put an end to, and the like. It will some day be worth consideration whether an annual Queen's Speech is of any good whatever: the harm it works is much more clearly manifest than the benefit. These details are mentioned here only because to diminish the possibilities of parliamentary obstruction is indirectly to check the development of the party system.

4. **By a change in constitutional understandings, which is also something like a return to an older system, certain members of the Cabinet might be treated as in the main departmental Ministers, and not be expected as an invariable rule to retire with their colleagues**

Such for example might be the Chancellor, the Minister of Foreign Affairs, the Secretary at War, and the First Lord of the Admiralty. Of course there are many cases in which one or all of these Ministers might fairly be expected to retire, but there is in the nature of things no reason why a Lord Chancellor, or a head of the Admiralty, should have any special views upon say Home Rule or the right policy to be pursued in Afghanistan. And the foreign policy of the country ought as a general rule to be so continuous, and so clearly based upon plain facts which statesmen of opposite sides may recognise, that the same Foreign Minister might, one would suppose, pursue his proper work in spite of a change of colleagues, caused say by the rejection of a Bill for the reform of the Poor Law. Of course such an arrangement would involve the result that these permanent Ministers would take comparatively little part in the general policy of the Cabinet. It would be curious to ascertain what part they even now take as a rule in matters not concerning their own department. It would, however, be compatible with the rule that any of these departmental Ministers should retire whenever the Cabinet was defeated on a subject concerning the department of such Minister, or whenever his views as to the conduct of his department disagreed with the views of the Cabinet. Even in France where parliamentary control has been fatal to the stability of Ministries the advantage of a continuous foreign policy has led to an effort to keep foreign affairs in the hands of a Minister not changing with successive Cabinets. Were it not for the influence of party customs it is difficult to see why, for example, Lord Rosebery or Lord Herschel should be incapable of discharging their appropriate duties in Lord Salisbury's Cabinet simply because they disagree with the Premier on the matter of Home Rule. One advantage of retaining departmental Ministers in office would be that statesmen who are eminent specialists in particular lines would not be called upon either to form or express decided opinions upon questions as to which they speak with no special authority whatever. The existence, however, of departmental Ministers depends upon, or is closely connected with, the possibility of giving 'rigidity' to the constitution and thus restricting the sphere of Parliamentary legislation.

II. Remedies which involve a formal change in the constitution

1. **The introduction of some form of Presidential government, combined as it almost inevitably would be, with the establishment of a written constitution containing fundamental laws**

This 'Americanising' of the English constitution would not of necessity be incompatible with the formal maintenance of the Crown. There might indeed be some gain in separating the ornamental part of the constitution from the office of elective Prime Minister or President. Still the plain truth is that, things being as they are, the nominal authority of the Crown makes it extremely difficult to establish a really fixed executive, not depending on the vote of the House of Commons. Moreover it is all but inconceivable that such a change as that suggested could be brought about without a revolution.

2. The appointment by Parliament of a Cabinet which shall hold office for a definite period, namely until the convocation of a new Parliament

This innovation may, it is likely enough, be in fact though not in theory introduced without any legal change in the constitution. The experience of the last 20 years suggests that a Ministry gains nothing by a dissolution. If this be the fact a Cabinet once secure of a parliamentary majority will as a rule continue in office for at least the length of each Parliament.

If, however, the fixity of the executive is to be secured, changes both of law and of custom are requisite. Probably the duration of each Parliament ought to be fixed so that irregular dissolutions should be altogether avoided. This in its turn would, it may be suspected, necessitate the shortening of the period for which each Parliament should exist to a time, say, of three or four years.

This alteration in the tenure of office is almost inevitably connected with other alterations in the constitution such as the introduction of the distinction between 'constitutional articles' and ordinary laws.

3. The rendering [of] the constitution more or less 'rigid' by providing special modes for changing fundamental laws

It would be comparatively easy to mark off certain topics, e.g. the rights of the Crown, the constitution of Parliament, the Acts of Union, and the like, which should be held to be, or be made the subject of, 'fundamental' or 'constitutional' laws, and to provide that these articles of the constitution should be altered by Parliament only in a special manner, e.g. by a two-thirds majority of both Houses, or after the proposal to alter any of these articles had been made in one session and adopted in another.

Nor is it certain that such a provision might not have a considerable practical effect in ensuring deliberate procedure in the making of constitutional changes. Still it is more likely than not that the effect of these provisions would be small and that they would fail just at the times when it was most desirable that they should have effect, i.e. at periods of momentary popular excitements. Artificial devices, of the kind suggested, encourage violent methods of forcing through changes approved by public opinion and, what in England is of more consequence, foster political intrigue, and even corruption.

The only means (as far as experience guides us) for placing the foundations of the constitution beyond the reach of the ordinary legislature or Parliament is to provide for their change by some body which may carry greater moral weight than Parliament itself and whose commands may be treated by the Courts as superior to the commands of Parliament, i.e. to an ordinary statute.

The sole body which in a modern democratic state, such as England, which carries greater moral weight than Parliament itself is the people or, in other words, the majority of the electorate.

It is idle for the present purpose to discuss whether the deliberate voice of the majority ought to command this moral weight. All that is necessary, for the present purpose, is the admission that in a modern democratic state the will of the electors is finally and in the long run decisive, and that there is no other power of which the influence can as things now stand conceivably overbalance that of Parliament.

If therefore it be desirable to place certain fundamental articles on a different basis from that of ordinary Acts, this can be achieved only by, in some form or other, obtaining for these fundamental articles a popular sanction not directly given to other laws.

Let me, to illustrate and explain my meaning, assume that it is thought desirable to make the Acts of Union, either as they at present stand, or after being remodelled, fundamental articles of the constitution.

The following is the sort of method to be pursued.

An Act of Parliament—the Constitutional Statute—should be passed enacting that the Acts of Union should not be changed except in the manner therein provided, which manner should provide, in some shape or other, for submission of the change to a popular vote.

The Constitutional Statute should also enact that the Constitutional Statute itself should not come into force unless within a certain time it was sanctioned by a popular vote and should not be changeable except by an Act itself sanctioned by a popular vote, and that any Act of Parliament or portion of an Act either directly or indirectly contravening the Constitutional Statute should be, and should be held by the Courts to be, void.

The possible methods for submission of the Constitutional Statute or of changes therein to a popular vote are, speaking roughly, twofold.

First, [there is] the Constitutional Convention, such as prevails in the United States and such as, in effect though not in name, drafted the Canadian Constitution.

Such a Convention being elected *ad hoc* and consisting as it ought to do, and might, of persons who have special qualifications as legislators and are not ordinary party politicians is likely both to excel Parliament in legislative skill and to carry weight with the public. In order moreover to give additional force to the resolutions of the Convention they should before they became laws obtain the sanction of a direct popular vote and (perhaps) of a Parliamentary vote (which should be confined to passing or rejecting the Bill as it came from the Convention).

Secondly, [there is] the referendum,* such in substance though not of course in details, as it exists in Switzerland.

---

* On Dicey's innovative advocacy of the referendum in the English context, see Editor's Introduction, pp xix f., xxxi above.

The essence of this system is that the electors should be called upon to decide sometimes on one of two and sometimes on two points, namely, first, whether there be a constitutional change at all, and, secondly, whether the constitutional change prepared by the legislature is to be accepted.

If the system of the referendum were adopted (which it is apparent is combinable, and in America is in reality combined, with that of the Convention) then the Constitutional Statute could never be changed unless the change were approved after deliberation by the majority of the electors.

All this constitutional machinery, it may be objected, would be futile because Parliament might of its own authority by a subsequent Act alter or repeal the Constitutional Statute.

The objection is plausible, but at bottom futile. It implies that a sovereign power can never surrender its sovereignty, which really amounts to saying that the acts of men can be tied by the forms of logic and in this case by a misapplication of such forms. The plausibility of the objection arises from the known fact that Parliament has altered the apparently unalterable provisions of the Acts of Union. The essential difference between these Acts and the supposed Constitutional Statute is that they did not receive, and the Statute would receive, a sanction beyond that of Parliament. The Acts of Union moreover instituted no other body than the United Parliament, capable of changing them. It therefore became absolutely necessary that the United Parliament should exercise or assume the power of amendment or repeal.

Grant, however, for the sake of argument, that the Imperial Parliament *could* by a subsequent Act repeal the Constitutional Statute. There is no reason to suppose that in fact Parliament would do so. Such a repeal would be a direct defiance of the real sovereign authority, namely a majority of the electors, and would therefore hardly be attempted by men who certainly do not err by want of deference to electoral opinion.

Of the two methods by for the best from a jurisprudential point of view is that of the 'Constitutional Convention'. The alteration of the constitution by a body, elected *ad hoc* and which undertakes no other business than that of preparing a special scheme of legislation, is in itself a great improvement on what may be called the parliamentary or 'constituent' method of constitution making. It happily separates legislation on most important points from the question what men and what party are to remain at the head of the administration.

The referendum is, on the other hand, by far the most easy method to pursue. It might even, as already pointed out, be indirectly imported into the constitution without the necessity for legislative change by the mere action of the House of Lords. This perhaps is a convenient opportunity for adding that, for the proper carrying out of any change which shall correct the evils of the party system, the reform of the House of Lords is all but essential. It is now for all practical purposes a party body. In order that it may represent national conservatism it must cease to be an instrument of the Conservative party. It should be greatly lessened in numbers; it should become, in great part at least, representative; it should admit all Ministers to its debates, and if possible, force on the House of Commons the admission of all Ministers to debates in that House. The one policy of the House should be to become the guardian of the constitution by representing the permanent wish of the nation against the factitious combination of parliamentary groups or factions.

To the Constitutional Convention, and still more to the referendum, it is objected, and with truth, that they each tend to decrease the importance of the House of Commons and of parliamentary debate. This is undoubtedly their bad side. They are, however, either alone or in combination, essential parts of any scheme for diminishing in England the evils of the party system of government. Take, however, the referendum, which is the most open to theoretical objection, and consider the great advantages which might counterbalance its admitted evils.

First, the very charge, though not I think fully made out, that the referendum impedes salutary reforms is only another way of admitting that it prevents legislation which goes much beyond popular opinion. This in some cases is a great advantage. It would have been a great gain could the policy of the Contagious Diseases Acts have been originally submitted to a popular vote. If the policy had been approved a reform would have been secured. If the policy had been disapproved a futile attempt at reform would have been avoided as well as disgraceful concession to a very damaging agitation.

Secondly, the referendum brings clearly before the nation that the law is the decree of the people for which they are responsible and not a rule made by the oppressors of the people which lawbreakers can defy in the name of the people.

Thirdly, the referendum makes it possible for statesmen honourably and honestly to conduct the affairs of the country even though on some points the policy of the nation does not agree with the views held by some of the executive.

Thus, if it were possible to decide by an honest popular vote that the great majority of the electors did or did not approve of Home Rule, it would be possible without any sacrifice of principle for Lord Salisbury or Mr Gladstone, as the case might be, to hold office even though his policy were not adopted. There is nothing disgraceful in carrying out to the best of one's ability the business of an employer who in some respects pursues a course of which his possibly better instructed agent does not approve. What is disgraceful is for the agent to surrender his own opinion or to pretend that he agrees with his employer. The truth is that the referendum would lead quickly to that kind of decision which even now when it is obtained after years of party contest every sensible man admits to be final. No one ever blamed Peel for accepting the Reform Act after opposing the Reform Bill.

Fourthly, the referendum separates in the mind of the people the question of measures from the question of men. It prevents the inextricable confusion between the effect of a proposed law and the effect of keeping certain persons in power. At this moment half the Home Rule electors would, it may be suspected, give up Home Rule if without Home Rule they could have Gladstone as Premier.

Thus the referendum cuts at the very root of the English party system and[,] when difference of opinion is not needed to support distinctions of party[,] differences of opinion become far less common and far less important. It is, moreover, quite one thing to say that the mass of the electors are incompetent to pronounce on legal details and quite another to assert that they are incompetent to pronounce on general lines of policy. Their real or supposed competence in this respect is the essential basis of modern popular government, and what can be said against the referendum may be urged in the main against democracy itself.

I am quite aware, however, of the evils, actual and possible, of this institution. All I urge is that in some modified form it may be used as a corrective to the English party system.[2]

---

[2] NB To the referendum is, I suspect, due the stability of the Swiss Council or Cabinet. Its members, though elected every three (or four?) years, are constantly re-elected. It is, as every executive ought to be, a permanent body of trained officials. Contrast this with the Ministries of England, France, or Italy, and even with the Presidential government of America. The contrast with France is particularly instructive, because, if it be objected, as with some plausibility it may, that the stability of Swiss administration arises from one party (the Liberals) having been permanently in power, it should be observed that in France also one party, namely the Republicans, have been in power since the fall of Macmahon.

It may further be noted that the suggestion that Ministers may under the referendum creditably carry on the administration even though the people refuse to sanction some part of the Ministerial policy is no more than suggesting that the heads of the executive may, in the case supposed, occupy a position similar to that filled with the highest honour by all permanent civil servants in England.

II

Lecture 4
Comparison between English [Executive] and other Executives
OR
Parliamentary and Non-Parliamentary Executives

Analysis*

A. Parliamentary Executive
   Two kinds
   I. *Government by committees*, e.g. Long Parliament, French Convention
   II. *Cabinet government*
      English Cabinet
      Form—government by Crown
      Substance—government by members of Parliament
      NB Stages of development
         English Cabinet
         French Cabinet

B. Extra-Parliamentary Executive
   I. *Presidential*
      1. American Presidency
      2. French Republic, 1848
   II. *Monarchical*
      1. French Empire
      2. German Empire

---

* Its contents have been derived from an undated, detached, manuscript page, which has been used as the source for two reasons. First, its contents resemble those of the text of Lecture 4. Secondly, it was seemingly written at the same time and by the same hand as the Analysis for the accompanying Lecture 5, p. 286 below. The lecture titles have been slightly altered so as to be consistent.

Comparison between English [Executive] and other Executives*

Parliamentary government in a wide sense of that term has during the last hundred years become common to almost all civilised states. For in every European country, except Turkey and Russia, there exists an assembly more or less elective which exercises more or less of legislative authority. In England, further, parliamentary government in this sense of the term has existed for centuries, let us say roughly from the time of Edward I. But though all civilized governments are now in a sense parliamentary it has not been enough noticed that under the general head parliamentary government are included two distinct types of government which are differentiated from one another according to the relation between the executive body and the legislative body.

The executive may consist of a person or body of persons which are in fact appointed and dismissible [by] the legislature. This may be termed a parliamentary executive. The executive again may be a person or body of persons not appointed or dismissible by the legislature. This may be termed an extra-parliamentary executive.

If we divide constitutions according to the relation between the executive and the legislature we obtain a classification which gives curious results because it exhibits the point of likeness between constitutions apparently dissimilar from each other and the point of difference between constitutions in which may be traced a strong family likeness.

Under constitutions with parliamentary executives we may bring the modern British constitution and, subject to some limitations, all constitutional monarchies, all the constitutions of such British colonies as enjoy representative government, and also the existing French Republic, which curiously enough was intended by its founders to possess a more or less extra-parliamentary executive whilst the course of events has turned the government of the Republic into one of the extremest forms of parliamentary executive. In the same class we must number the Republic of France during the existence of the Convention and the English Commonwealth from the death of Charles I until the creation of the Protectorate.

Under constitutions with extra-parliamentary executives we must bring the United States, the German Empire, [and] the Napoleonic Empire under all its different forms prior to 1815 and again between 1852 and 1870. Under the same head ought to be classed the old monarchy of England till certainly as late as 1688, and in truth till a later period, and also the government of the Protector from 1653 to 1658.

---

* The manuscript was undated. It would seem to have been written sometime before the completion of the 6th edn of *The Law of the Constitution* (published in 1902) and after the completion of the 5th edn (published in 1897) because the 5th edn's Note III was cited on the lecture manuscript's title page. See *The Oxford Edition of Dicey*, i, *The Law of the Constitution*, 'Distinction between a "Parliamentary Executive" and a "Non-Parliamentary Executive"' (Note III, 4th edn), 290 ff. On Dicey's treatment of the distinction between parliamentary and non-parliamentary executives—its significance and background—here and in *The Law of the Constitution*, see Editor's Introduction, pp xxxii ff, xli above; 'Prussian Constitutionalism', p.116, n., above.

For reasons which will become more apparent in the course of this lecture, we shall find more than one constitution as to which it may be a fair question whether its government is to be counted as a parliamentary or an extra-parliamentary executive. This is true, for example, of the Swiss Confederation and possibly of some nominally constitutional monarchies. In this lecture I propose first to consider what is meant by a parliamentary executive, to exhibit to you its two main types, and to show you how the British constitution, in this as in other instances, has preserved throughout centuries an almost unchanged form whilst in reality it has gone through an extraordinary transformation so as to have passed from the class of constitutions whereof the executive is extra-parliamentary into the class of constitutions whereof the executive is more strictly parliamentary than the government of any country except possibly that of modern France. I shall then commence the examination by way of contrast and comparison of polities whereof the government has an extra-parliamentary character.

It is always well to vary from time to time the phrases in which a doctrine or fact is expressed. This course guards us to some extent against the danger of being the slaves of names. I therefore will sum up, before proceeding further, the result of the distinction on which I am insisting in the following form. In England, France, etc there exists not only parliamentary government but also government by Parliament. In the United States and the German Empire government by Parliament does not exist though there does exist parliamentary government.

A. Constitutions with a Parliamentary Executive

An elective legislative assembly or Parliament has often in different countries and times attempted with more or less success to get into its hands the functions of the executive government.

Experience seems to show that practically such a legislative assembly which aims at exercising executive functions must take one of two courses. It must either directly appoint committees from among its own body or else, whilst not attempting directly to carry on the administration, obtain a more or less predominant voice in the appointment of executive officers who when appointed may carry on the work of administration without constant reference to Parliament. To put the same thing in other words, government by Parliament may either mean administration by committee, or what we in England call Cabinet government.

I. Government by committees

The simplest and, as it would at first sight appear, the most effective form in which an assembly too large to form of itself an executive body can carry on the administrative business of a great nation is to appoint committees of its own members for the management of different affairs. This was the course taken on two celebrated occasions by two celebrated legislatures. The Long Parliament after the defeat of the King and the French Convention during the whole time of its existence governed through committees. This system, though natural and to appearance effective, has at least two defects. The first is that it does not tend to produce good and successful administration. Government by a body of committees means government through rival and clashing authorities. Unless, as happened during the Reign of Terror, a small body of men concentrate the authority of the ruling legislature in their own hands, government by committees must almost of necessity be weak and ineffective government.

A second defect is that government by parliamentary committees violates the soundest part of Montesquieu's doctrine enjoining the separation of powers. It is plain that when a supreme legislature tries to govern directly through the agency of committees legislative, judicial, and executive powers are blended together. The legislature is law-maker, judge, and executioner in one, and is all but certain to exhibit in a short time all the worst features of a tyrant.

This point is well illustrated by Paley.

'For the sake of illustration', he writes, 'let it be supposed, in this country, either that, parliaments being laid aside, the courts of Westminster-Hall made their own laws; or that the two houses of parliament, with the King at their head, tried and decided causes at their bar; it is evident, in the first place, that the decisions of such a judicature would be so many laws; and, in the second place, that, when the parties and the interests to be affected by the law were known, the inclinations of the law-makers would inevitably attach to one side or the other; and that, where there were neither any fixed rules to regulate their determinations, nor any superior power to control their proceedings, these inclinations would interfere with the integrity of public justice. The consequence of which must be, that the subjects of such a constitution would live either without any constant laws, that is, without any known pre-established rules of adjudication whatever; or under laws made for particular cases and particular persons, and partaking of the contradictions and iniquity of the motives to which they owed their origin.'[1]

The history both of the Long Parliament and of the Convention exactly confirms the truth of the doctrine laid down in this passage. The experience of other countries tells the same way. Direct government by Parliament through committees, and it is the only way by which a large assembly can attempt direct government, is certain to promote injustice.

II. Cabinet government

The second method by which an assembly can exercise executive power is by leaving large powers to the executive to be exercised by it at its own discretion but at the same time keeping in the assembly's own hands the means of appointing, controlling, and criticising the executive.

---

[1] Paley, *Moral Philosophy*, bk. VI, cap. VIII.

This is the course of action which by a sort of instinctive policy the British Parliament has for centuries pursued. Neither of the Houses singly, nor both of them acting together, have ever except during revolutionary periods affected to give direct commands to any executive officer. Neither the House of Commons nor the House of Lords can appoint or give directions to either a judge or a policeman. What the Houses have done is, at first in fact and then more or less nominally, to leave the executive in the hands of the King and his officers and to leave the Ministry or government the exercise of all the royal prerogatives, but at the same time to obtain by degrees, first, the right of controlling the policy of the government, secondly, the right that Ministers should as a rule be members of the Houses of Parliament, thirdly, the right of dismissing Ministers who were not supported by the House of Commons, and lastly, in effect, of designating to the Crown by an indirect process who should be appointed Ministers.

In the modern British executive one must therefore carefully distinguish *form* from *substance*.

In *form** the Cabinet are the servants of the Crown through whom the Crown's prerogatives are exercised and who are appointed and dismissed by the Crown.

In *fact* the Cabinet are a body chosen from among the members of the two Houses, who though in constant consultation with the Crown are really in the main the servants of Parliament. The Cabinet exercise the royal prerogatives in accordance with the general wish of Parliament. They are, speaking generally, both appointed and dismissed by Parliament or in fact by the House of Commons.

The system of government by Parliament has in the course of its development passed through several stages:

First, the establishment of Parliament's exclusive right of *legislation*;

Secondly, the establishment of the right of Parliament to criticise and *control* the acts of the King's *servants* or Ministers;

Thirdly, Parliament's right in extreme cases to *drive a Minister from power*;

Fourthly, the principle that Ministers must be *members* of one or other of the Houses of Parliament;

Fifthly, Parliament's right, or in effect the right of the House of Commons, to dismiss and lastly to *appoint* or *elect* the Ministry.

I have tried to give the development of these rights or powers in their historical order. You will observe that the right of *appointment* is placed subsequently to the right of dismissal; this is because the logical and the historical order of things differ. The House of Commons could in substance dismiss Walpole. The House of Commons could not determine who should be Walpole's successor. One of the points contested between George III and the 'Orthodox Whigs', if so we may call them, represented by Rockingham and inspired by Burke was the right of appointment, especially to the Premiership. The King maintained and to a certain extent made good

---

* Editor's emphasis to correspond with emphasis upon 'fact' in manuscript.

his right to choose, if not the party who should hold office, at any rate the member of that party who should be Premier. The Rockingham Whigs maintained that the party or connection had the right to nominate the Prime Minister.

Let it be remarked that even down to the present day the right of indirect appointment or even of dismissal by the House of Commons is not absolutely established by constitutional custom.

This right is subject to one more or less *formal* and to another very *real* check.

The *formal** limitation is that the Crown can exercise a certain though indefinite amount of choice in the selection of the Premier. Nor can anyone who recalls to his mind the events of 1839 deny that under peculiar circumstances the Crown can keep in office Ministers who hardly command the support of the House of Commons.

The material and very *real*† check consists of a Cabinet's power, with the assent of the Crown, of appealing by means of a dissolution from Parliament to the constituencies. In 1857 Parliament condemned but the electors supported the government of Lord Palmerston. In 1874 Parliament still supported, but the electors, or, as the expression goes, the country, did not support the government of Mr. Gladstone. In each case the will of the country was decisive.

An English Cabinet therefore is a strictly parliamentary executive indirectly appointed and dismissed by the vote of the House of Commons subject, at any rate as to dismissal, to more or less formal control by the Crown and to real control by the electors or the country.

The oddity of the thing is that, if you look to matters of form, the English Cabinet is an extra-parliamentary executive. If you look at the substance it is all but a completely parliamentary executive. I purposely use the words 'all but' in order to impress upon you that authorities external to the Houses of Parliament do exercise a certain control over the executive, namely the Crown and the country or the electors.

This control, you will say, is inherent in the nature of things. The remark is plausible but unsound. We can see before our eyes, if we look across the Channel, a more thoroughly parliamentary form of government than that of England. In France you have an executive dependent all but entirely for its existence and its power upon the Chambers, and the authority of the Chambers is nearly freed from the checks which exist under the English constitution.

The matter is well worth a moment's attention. The French President of the Republic is elected for seven years by the two Houses of the National Assembly sitting together as what is called a Congress. The President was meant according to the theory of the constitution to hold his office for his seven-years term without any risk of dismissal by Parliament. He, like an English King, appoints the Ministry; he further, unlike an English King, often if not always takes part in the meetings of the Cabinet. But the French President can no more than an English King carry on the government unless his Ministers have the support of Parliament. He further is, as the experience

---

* Editor's emphasis to correspond with emphasis on 'formal' and 'real' in the introductory sentence.

† In the manuscript (here and elsewhere seemingly written in haste), this sentence was written as the first in a series of closely related, single-sentence paragraphs. They have been compressed here into one paragraph on the topic of the material check on the Cabinet's power.

of President Grévy proved, in fact though not in theory dismissible by the legislature. The French Parliament is therefore free in the appointment or dismissal of Ministers from such control as may be exercised in England by the authority of the Crown.

A French Parliament is also all but free from the control which is exercised in England by the country when appealed to by means of a dissolution. In order that the French National Assembly may be dissolved the assent both of the President and of the Senate must be obtained. The President, be it remarked, is a nominee of the Assembly, and the Senate is one portion of the Assembly. Parliament therefore can determine whether it be dissolved or not, and the right of dissolution may thus be refused to a Ministry who on appeal to the country could undoubtedly secure the support of a parliamentary majority. Gambetta's chance of remaining and becoming head of the government of France and probably to have become the most powerful Minister of the time was lost because neither the President nor the Senate would allow him to dissolve Parliament. It is true that in France Parliament lasts for a period only of four years. It is likely therefore that a public man who, say in 1890, commands the confidence of the country will, by or before 1894, find himself at the head of a parliamentary majority. This likelihood, however, is no certainty. Who can say whether, if in 1783 Pitt had been prevented from immediately consulting the country or if in 1857 Parliament had been unable to dissolve, either Minister would ever have been in command of a parliamentary majority.

In any case the point to be noted is that in France the Cabinet system of government by Parliament has advanced a stage beyond the point which it has reached in England. A newly elected Assembly has the all-but-unlimited power of appointing and dismissing Ministries. Foreigners cannot say whether this right be or be not abused. It is assuredly employed with great freedom.

Under the French Republic a form of government which may be nominally termed Presidential turns out on examination to be in reality an extreme form of government by Parliament, which gives the appointment of the executive more completely into the hands of an elective legislature than is the case under the constitutional monarchy of England.

In many, on the other hand, if not all of the constitutional monarchies which exist or have existed on the Continent, it will be found on examination that the copy of English constitutionalism (at any rate as it at present exists) is imperfect and that the Cabinet is not so truly a parliamentary executive as it is with us.

Naturally enough the imitators of the English constitution have adopted its form more easily than its essence: a monarch who reigns but does not govern is a ruler hardly suited for countries going through or emerging from revolutions. Hence Continental constitutionalists have always been met by the difficulty of fixing the true share of a constitutional monarch in the appointment of the Cabinet and in the acts of the executive. Look for a moment at France between 1815 and 1848. Neither Louis XVIII, nor Charles X, nor Louis Philippe were constitutional monarchs of the modern English type. Of these the first and the last never disputed the exclusive authority of Parliament in matters of legislation. Louis Philippe at any rate never denied that a Ministry could not last which lacked the support of a parliamentary majority. But the head of the Orléans dynasty was no more inclined than either of his predecessors to admit that he was not himself a part, and we may say a predominant part, of the executive government. Louis XVIII and Louis Philippe each were present at Cabinet meetings; each of them was a real head of the government, Louis Philippe perhaps more truly than his cousin. He occupied in reality under very different circumstances and by the use of very different means much the position claimed for himself by George III. He acquiesced in parliamentary institutions but he remained as long as he sat on the throne a real head of the executive. George III used to say of himself that he was a Revolution Whig. The dictum had in it more truth than perhaps it was intended to contain. His Majesty's effort throughout his reign was really though unconsciously the restoration of the Crown to the position it occupied in the time of William and of Anne. The legislative authority and the political control of Parliament was then fully admitted. But the staunchest Revolution Whig would not have denied that the King or Queen was the head of the government. That the executive of England was the King was the theory of Blackstone; in the time of William or of Anne constitutional theory and constitutional fact coincided. Mr. Morley's recent studies have made clear to all the world, what everyone before knew vaguely, that Cabinet government, i.e. the supremacy of a parliamentary executive, did not exist, even in outline, till the accession of the House of Hanover.

B. Constitutions with an Extra-Parliamentary Executive

Governments which are not parliamentary executives have all one negative quality in common: they are none of them appointed by the legislature of the country where they exist.

They may, however, be roughly divided into two classes.

They may be popular executives, i.e. governments appointed not by the legislature but by popular election; such for example is the American Presidency. They may be governments consisting of, or appointed by, some monarch; such for example is the Imperial Executive of Germany, or the royal Cabinet of Prussia.

The fact, it may be noted, which makes it possible for an extra-parliamentary executive to exist, is that, even in countries where there is an elective legislature, the people or the classes who in the last resort guide the people will on some matters and within certain limits either by their votes or their arms support the executive, be he President or Emperor, against the legislative body. This is a point which Englishmen of the 19th century find it hard to understand. They can easily conceive of an absolute monarch who combines in his own hands the authority of a legislator and of the head of the executive or, to put the thing plainly, of a Commander-in-chief. They can understand, for they live under the rule of a practically sovereign legislature, but what they find it extremely difficult to understand is that, side by side with a King or President who is the real head of the state and who exercises real executive powers, there shall exist a true legislature with real legislative powers or, in other words, with real authority to make laws. Englishmen cannot believe as regards executive and legislative authority in any real 'separation of powers'. The difficulty is caused by two circumstances—first, the want of experience of a constitution where this kind of division is clearly drawn—secondly, a logical puzzle of the following kind: a legislature, it is argued, which can pass laws and can really legislate and *a fortiori* a legislature which under the form of law making imposes taxes can always, either by means of direct legislation or by cutting short the supplies, obtain command of the executive government. Wherever therefore there is a real Parliament there is also, under one name or another, a parliamentary government. The fallacy of this argument is twofold. Its formal flaw is that a real legislature, such for example as the American Congress, need not under the articles of the Constitution have unlimited legislative authority. Its laws may be invalid when they touch the sphere of the executive. The more serious or substantial error is that a nation may without any inconsistency be prepared to obey the legislature whilst acting within a particular sphere and be prepared to obey the executive whilst acting within another sphere. There is no logical inconsistency in the American people being willing to obey the President as regards appointments to office and the like, and being willing to obey Congress as regards laws within the competence of Congress. The distinct sphere of the two powers which are established in the United States by a written constitution may exist and have existed in other countries by virtue of custom. No doubt it is impossible, either by law or custom, so to discriminate between executive and legislative powers that the authority of the government and the legislature shall never clash. Who, it may be asked, will the nation then obey? No rule can be *a priori* established. Half the nation may obey the legislature, half the government. What in a civilized country is even more probable is that the nation will obey the authority which in the judgement of sensible men is least responsible for the collision. In any case the nation are extremely likely to insist, in a country where the separation of powers is an accepted feature of political life, that the separation shall be preserved, and directly or indirectly to punish the authority, whether legislative or executive, which has violated a fundamental constitutional principle. All this may savour of digression; it is a digression, however, necessitated or excused by the importance of bringing home to Englishmen the often neglected fact that there is no reason in the nature of things why a true Parliament or legislature should not co-exist with a true extra-parliamentary executive.

As such [an] extra-parliamentary executive may be either elective or hereditary [and] we may roughly divide governments belonging to this class into—first, Presidential governments—secondly, monarchical governments. The best type of the one is found in the United States; a good if not the best type of the other is found in the German Empire.

I. *Presidential executive*[2]

The Presidency of the United States is the type of Presidential government.

---

[2] See 1 Bryce, pt. I. ch. V, pp 45–125.

The President is, under a complicated system with which we need not trouble ourselves, in effect elected by the people of the United States. This is not exactly what you will find written in the Constitution, which will tell you that each of the States elect certain electors and that the electors select the President. But the electors are now nothing better than ballot balls; they are every one of them elected to choose a particular man, say Cleveland or Harrison, as President, and it would be the grossest breach of public honour which a man could commit to vote for any other person than the presidential candidate whom he was chosen to elect. Under certain exceptional circumstances a President might be chosen by Congress. But these circumstances have never arisen since the foundation of the Union and are not very likely to arise. Dismiss from your minds therefore all idea that the President is nominated by Congress. He is chosen by the people, not by the legislature; he represents the nation as truly as Congress, perhaps more truly.

The President is elected for four years; during his tenure of office he cannot be dismissed. No vote of Congress can deprive him of his position. He is re-eligible. He may be, and as a matter of fact sometimes is, re-elected at the end of his term for a second Presidential period. Not a word in the Constitution forbids or discourages constant re-election. But a custom which has now the force of law prohibits a President from being re-elected more than once. A President's tenure of office, in short, is a certain four years and a just possible four years' tenure. But no man ever has [held], and we may safely say that as things now stand no man ever will hold, the Presidency for more than eight years. The immediate point, however, for you to notice is not so much the length of time for which, but the conditions on which, he holds power. The creation and the connivance of his authority [are] absolutely independent of Congress. The President may be a free trader; Congress may be filled by protectionists. The President may favour an aggressive foreign policy; the majority in Congress may hold that no national triumph is worth the sacrifice of peace. But whether the Congress and the President differ or agree they must somehow get on together. Disagreement is not only possible but highly probable. The President and Congress in America have more than once carried on with each other war to the knife, in so far as war was possible within the limits of the Constitution.

The President is a real head of the government. He has been called a George III elected for four years. He has, be it added, many powers which George III claimed in theory but could only occasionally exercise in practice.

(i) The President is in a real and effective sense the head of the executive; he appoints officials subject to the approval of the Senate; he is Commander-in-chief in the sense that he can really appoint the general in command and can give directions as to what the general shall do.[3] He has power to grant pardons, and in matter of fact Lincoln's power of pardoning military offenders during the Civil War was at times exerted in a way which the generals thought inconsistent with army discipline.

---

[3] Constitution of the United States, Art. 1, s. 2.

(ii) He has a suspensive veto on legislation. He may send back a Bill for reconsideration by the two Houses and unless it again passes each House by a two-thirds majority the Bill does not become law. This veto is not an obsolete prerogative but an increasingly exercised power.[4]

(iii) He can make treaties with the assent of the Senate.[5]

(iv) He is irremovable except on impeachment for treason and other high crimes and misdemeanours.

(v) The exercise of his power is not impeded by the necessity of having a parliamentary Cabinet.

The so-called Cabinet is a body of seven Ministers appointed by the President, subject to the assent of the Senate which is never refused. They are simply departmental officers who have no seats in Congress, and cannot address Congress. They are in no sense parliamentary leaders. None of them is a Premier and they do not act collectively. A seat in the Cabinet is not now, as it once was, a stepping stone to the Presidency. The President is responsible; the Minister is practically irresponsible.[6]

> In America the administration does not work as a whole. It is not a whole. It is a group of persons each individually dependent upon and answerable to the President but with no joint policy, no collective responsibility.[7]

NB The President can no more dissolve Congress than Congress can remove the President.

The French Presidential Republic of 1848 was, as regards the executive, modelled to a certain extent on the American Constitution.

The President was elected by the whole French people for four years; he was not re-eligible.

(i) He had the ordinary powers of a constitutional King except in regard to legislation.

(ii) He had no veto but had the right of sending back a law to the Assembly for reconsideration.[8]

(iii) He had the power to appoint and dismiss Ministers as well as Commanders-in-chief, and

(iv) His acts needed Ministerial counter-signature.

(v) The Ministers had a right to enter and speak in the National Assembly. Hence the Ministers might either be, or not be, members of the Assembly.

(vi) (The Ministry was a Cabinet in the English sense of the term, but I conceive that the President could take part in the Cabinet meetings.)

---

[4] Ibid. Art. 1, s. 7.
[5] Ibid. Art. 2, s. 2.
[6] See 1 Bryce, p. 118.
[7] See ibid. p. 121 for contrast between English and American Cabinet.
[8] Constitution of 1848, Art. 59.

NB The French Republican Constitution constituted a curious and inconsistent mixture of the system of Presidential government and of Cabinet government.*

[The] authority of the President rivalled [the] authority of the legislature. In so far he was an extra-parliamentary executive. The President's Ministers, on the other hand, were practically, if not members of, dependent upon, the Assembly, and therefore constituted a parliamentary executive. [The] only consistent plans would have been either to make [the] President appointed by [the] Assembly, as under [the] present Republic, or to keep Ministers outside the Assembly, as in America.

[II. Monarchical executive][†]

Under French Imperial government whatever its form, an essential feature was that the Emperor should be the real head of the executive and that the executive body should be in the strictest sense extra-parliamentary.

There were Ministers but there was no Ministry or Cabinet[9] for:

(i) the Ministers are each responsible to the President;
(ii) they are each departmental Ministers;
(iii) they have no joint responsibility;
(iv) they are not members of the legislature;[10]
(v) the Ministers do not, as such, defend laws before the Assembly;[11]
(vi) the President is responsible to the French people.

These provisions are noteworthy as they constitute the exact negation of Cabinet government.

It should be noted that the gradual modifications of the Imperial government, e.g. by the Decree of 19 January 1867, are all approximations towards Cabinet government, and at every step there became apparent the contradiction between the parliamentary and the extra-parliamentary system, especially the law of 8 September 1869. The plain truth is that the two systems [are] logically and practically irreconcilable. Of their respective merits and demerits, I hope to say something in the next lecture.

Meanwhile let me take a last example of an extra-parliamentary executive from the German Empire. The real and effective head of the Imperial government [is the Emperor as King of Prussia, whose Ministers are in reality as well as in name the servants of the Crown.][‡]

---

[9] See, e.g., Constitution [of] 1852, Tit. III, Art. 13.
[10] Ibid. Art. 44.
[11] Ibid. Arts 50, 51.

---

* What follows in the manuscript was written as a series of closely related, single-sentence, paragraphs in the manuscript. They have been compressed here into a single paragraph on the topic of the system of government under the French Republican Constitution.

† This heading has been introduced to complement the first heading and has been derived from the Analysis (p. 274 above).

‡ The lecture text ends at 'Imperial government', i.e. with an incomplete sentence. The gist of how it might have been completed has been suggested here on the basis of Dicey's lecture, 'Prussian Constitutionalism', pp 105 ff above.

II (continued)

Lecture 5
Comparison [between] English Executive [and] other Executives (continued)

Analysis*

A.   Cromwellian Constitution, 1653
       I.   *The Protector*
       II.   *The Council*
       III.   *The Parliament*
       [IV. *Constitutional ideas of the Puritans and of the age*]†
           Light thrown by Constitution of 1653 on constitutional ideas of Puritans
           Light thrown by Constitution of 1653 on ideas of [the] age as to
               relation between Crown and legislature
    Questions
         1. Is it possible that a real legislature should co-exist with the really
            independent executive?
         2. Is it possible for executive to be independent of legislature if members
            of executive take part in legislative debates?

B.   Comparative Merits of Parliamentary Executives and of Extra-Parliamentary Executives
       I.   *Merits and demerits of parliamentary executive (Cabinet government)*
       II.   *Merits and demerits of extra-parliamentary executive*
           (Presidential government)

(See Gardiner, *Documents of Puritan Revolution*, pp 271, 314; 4
Masson, *Life of Milton*, pp 7, 542.)

---

    * Its contents have been derived from an undated, detached, manuscript page, which, although separated in the Dicey Papers from the Analysis for Lecture 4 (p. 274 above), seems to have been written at the same time and by the same hand. The lecture titles have been slightly altered here so as to be consistent.
    † The heading has been inferred from the content of the full lecture text and that of the Analysis, and has been added to complement the existing headings.

Comparison [between] English Executive [and] other Executives (continued)[*]

In my last lecture I explained the exact difference between constitutions which have a parliamentary executive and constitutions which have an extra-parliamentary executive.

As types of the one kind of polity I selected the monarchical constitution of modern England and the Republican Constitution of modern France.

As types of the other kind of polity I selected the United States, the French Republic of 1848, and the existing German Empire.

I further pointed out in the course of my lecture that the English constitution had at one time been a constitution with an extra-parliamentary executive and still was so in form, but that under a curious process of development it had at last become a constitution with a more completely parliamentary executive than any existing commonwealth unless it be the French Republic.

I propose tonight to carry the system of comparison on which this course of lectures is based a step further and compare the position of the executive in England of the 19th century with the position of the executive under what we may call the great Puritan Constitution of 1653 or, in other words, with the Constitution embodied in the so called Instrument of Government.

[A. Cromwellian Constitution of 1653][†‡]

Whilst, however, my main object is to contrast the extra-parliamentary executive created by the Instrument of Government with the parliamentary executive or Cabinet which taken in combination with the Crown forms the true executive government of modern England, I shall avail myself of this opportunity to bring out as clearly as I can the essential differences between the Cromwellian Constitution of 1653 and the Victorian constitution of 1890.

For the present purpose you need not trouble yourselves with the steps by which historically the Constitution of 1653 came into being. It was in fact influenced as is supposed to a great extent by the ideas of Ireton. It was framed by Cromwell and what we may call the Cromwellian Republicans, after the so-called Barebones Parliament had resigned its authority to Cromwell.

Let us examine and criticise the Constitution of 1653 not as historians but rather as legists just as we should criticise, say, the Constitution of the United States.

---

[*] The manuscript for this lecture text, as for the previous lecture text, was undated, but see p. 275, n., above.
[†] This heading has been added because it was included in the Analysis and was the first of the two headings that were written on the lecture manuscript's title page. The second heading on the title page corresponds with heading B in the Analysis and in the lecture text below.
[‡] See 'Constitutionalism of the Commonwealth' lecture (pp 29 ff above).

The Constitution of 1653 possesses besides its inherent merits the special interest that it is the earliest of that long series of written constitutions of which, during the last hundred years, so many have been created and so few have stood the test of time.

For our present purpose this Constitution has the further claim to our attention that it is an elaborate attempt to create for the government of England at once a real legislative assembly or Parliament and also a strong extra-parliamentary executive.

Let us note the following features in the Constitution of the Protectorate. They have curious points both of contrast and of similarity with the parliamentary constitution of today.

I. *The Lord Protector*

The Protector, Oliver Cromwell, is appointed for life, but the Protectorship, unlike the Kingship, is elective, and not hereditary. After Cromwell's death, succeeding Protectors are to be elected for life by the Council.[12] He is to be the real head, the real executive power. All writs run in his name, all honours and offices are at his disposal. He has the right of pardon except in case of murder and treason. He has with the consent of Parliament the control of all military and naval forces. He is to govern by the advice of the Council in accordance with the Constitution (i.e. with the Instrument itself) and with the laws. A revenue is secured from customs for the maintenance of a standing army of 10,000 horse and 20,000 foot, and also a revenue of £200,000 for the necessary expenses of government. This whole revenue cannot be taken away or diminished but with the consent both of the Protector and Parliament.[13] This revenue being secured, no other tax or charge can be imposed but by common consent in Parliament.[14] The laws, it is provided, are not to be altered, suspended, abrogated, or repealed, without the consent of Parliament.

The Protector is therefore under the Instrument a ruler who holds his office for life but who must rule in accordance with law. He is, however, a real ruler. The powers given him, and the revenues secured to him, place him beyond that indirect control of Parliament, which has gradually transferred to the House of Commons the prerogatives of the Crown.

His position has a close resemblance to that of an American President. It is in substance though not in form like the position of a German Emperor. The Protector, like the Emperor, is a real ruler whose authority is protected against parliamentary encroachment. But the Protector like the German Emperor is a ruler bound by the Constitution and by the law of the land. Neither one or the other has independent power of legislation though both are in effect part of the legislature. Protector and Emperor alike, though possessing large executive powers, are under the Constitution bound to respect the legislative authority of an elective assembly or Parliament.[15]

[12] See Instrument of Government, Arts 3–6.
[13] Ibid. Arts 27, 28, and 30.
[14] Ibid. Art. 6.
[15] Compare 4 Masson, p. 542.

II. The Council[16]

The Council are a permanent body, named by the Instrument itself[17] of 15 persons, and as many more, not exceeding 6, as the Protector and the Council should add before the meeting of the first Parliament.

1. The members of the Council are appointed for life, but may be removed for misconduct, e.g. corruption.
2. New members are appointed from *six* nominated by Parliament out of which, Council elect *two* and from these [the] Protector selects *one*.
3. The Council advise [the] Protector on points of government.[18]
4. [The] Protector with the consent of the Council has power of temporary legislation (Ordinances).[19]
5. [The] Council on [the] death of [the] Protector elect [a] successor and until [such] election carry on [the] government.

The Council seems to be the Privy Council with larger and more definite powers especially of legislation than were possessed by the Privy Council. It rather resembles the American Senate which originally consisted of only 26 persons. It was not a Cabinet, for it could not be dismissed nor directly elected by Parliament. But owing to its indirect connection with Parliament it could not have ultimately failed to represent Parliamentary opinion.

Masson notes that Cromwell had never any difficulties with his Council.

[III. The Parliament]*

The Parliament consists of one House of 400 members for England and Wales and 30 each for Ireland and Scotland. *Semble* it was intended that Jersey and Guernsey should be also represented.[20]

1. Parliament is triennial, i.e. to meet every third year.
2. [The Parliament] [c]annot be adjourned, prorogued, or dissolved without consent, during five months from [the] day of meeting.[21]
3. The seats are distributed under the Instrument.
4. The electors are all persons possessed of estate real or personal to the value of £200 and not, within certain exceptions, all of which are temporary except that excluding Roman Catholics.

---

[16] Instrument of Government, Arts 2–5, 25–7, 30, 32.
[17] Ibid. Arts 4, 25, 26.
[18] Ibid. Art. 5.
[19] Ibid. Art. 30.
[20] Ibid. Art. 10.
[21] Ibid. Art. 8.

---

* The heading has been derived from the Analysis (p. 286 above).

5. Parliaments may be summoned at intermediate periods by [the] Protector with [the] advice of [the] Council, and Parliament must be summoned in case of war with [a] foreign power.
6. All Bills agreed to by Parliament [are] to be presented to [the] Protector for consent. If within 20 days he does not consent, or satisfy Parliament, they become law.
7. Certain matters are beyond [the] legislative authority of Parliament.

The Constitution is what is now called a rigid constitution, but the degree of rigidity is rather uncertain.* According to Gardiner, the Instrument contains no means for its own legal alteration. This conclusion is based on Article 24. The inference seems to me doubtful.

The Instrument, criticised from a merely legal point of view, may, it is submitted, be interpreted as dividing laws into three classes.

(i) [There are] laws which may be passed by Parliament without the consent of the Protector. Under this lead come all laws which do not affect the Instrument of Government, or as we should now say the articles of the Constitution.

(ii) [There are] laws which may be passed by Parliament with the consent of the Protector, i.e. laws which affect the Instrument of Government generally.[22]

(iii) [There are] laws which cannot be passed at all, i.e. laws which affect Christian liberty as provided for in Articles 35–38, or which affect the sale of lands, the security of the public debt, etc provided for by Acts of Parliament and referred to in Article 39.

If this view be correct the Constitution is by no means excessively rigid. Parliament has complete control over ordinary legislation. Parliament, with the consent of the Protector, can alter most parts of the Constitution. The only things made unchangeable are the provisions securing the right of religious liberty, sales, etc carried out under the authority of Parliament.

[IV. The constitutional ideas of the Puritans and of the age]†

We have therefore in the Cromwellian Constitution of 1653 a form of government which throws a curious light on modern English constitutionalism from two points of view.

First, it shows that the constitutional ideas of the Commonwealth men were in some respects essentially different from the ideas of the Whigs who in 1689 finally

---

[22] Ibid. Art. 24.

---

* This sentence was the first of four closely related, single-sentence, paragraphs in the manuscript. They have been compressed here into one paragraph on the issue of the Constitution's rigidity.

† The heading has been inferred from the content of the lecture text and of the Analysis (p. 286 above) and has been added to complement the existing headings.

expelled the Stuarts and ultimately laid the foundation of our modern Parliamentary system.

These are some of the chief points of contrast.

1. Under the Protectorate the executive was a body which though slightly connected with Parliament was in the strict sense extra-parliamentary.

The Protector and his successors were not appointed by Parliament. Neither the Protector nor the Council could be removed by Parliament.

A fixed revenue moreover was secured to the executive and also an army which were placed beyond Parliamentary control.

2. The Council formed a body of highly paid officials—the salary, according to Mr. Masson, of each Councillor was equivalent in our money to about £3,500 a year— who were to a certain extent independent at once of the Protector and of Parliament. I know of no constitutional body which the Council so nearly resembles as the American Senate. But the power and the independence of the Councillors exceeded that of the United States Senators. The Council and the Protector had moreover authority to issue, in the absence of Parliament, what we may call Ordinances which remained in force unless in some way revoked by Parliament.[23]

3. The Legislature, on the other hand, is an independent legislative body, at once more powerful and less powerful than the Houses of Parliament under the Stuarts.

The legislature is more powerful than the Houses in the 17th century because the Cromwellian Parliament must be convoked at least once every three years, cannot for five months be dissolved without [its] own consent, has an indirect share in [the] nomination of [the] Council, and can, except on certain topics, pass laws by its own authority.

The Cromwellian legislature is, however, less powerful than the two Houses because the Protector and [the] Council are an independent government, are provided with revenue and an army, and are disconnected with the legislature, and because the legislature's power to change the Constitution either does not exist or is at any rate limited in regard to certain topics. The legislature, in short, is bound by the Constitution.

The Constitution is, to use modern expressions, based on a separation of powers.

4. The Constitution recognises fundamental and unchangeable laws[24] and possibly (makes the whole Constitution unchangeable by any recognised process).[25]

It is worth notice that the Constitutional Bill of Cromwell's first Parliament, in so far as it deviates from the Instrument, is all in favour of Parliamentary power. Thus:

The Constitution is made amendable by Parliament;[26] the election of [the] Protector is, if Parliament be sitting, placed in the hands of Parliament; the approval of persons nominated to the Council is placed in the hands of Parliament; it is further not quite clear whether any articles whatever of the Constitution are placed beyond the competence of Parliament to deal with them.

[23] Ibid. Art. 30.
[24] Ibid. Art. 24.
[25] Ibid.
[26] Ibid. cap. II.

The differences between the Instrument of Government and the Parliamentary Constitutional Bill strike a reader at first sight as comparatively trifling. There is, however, one essential difference which it is easy to underrate. Under the Instrument of Government the Parliament is the creature of the Constitution; under the Bill the Constitution is the creature of Parliament. To have passed the Bill would have been in effect a denial of Cromwell's authority under the Instrument.

Both the Instrument of Government and the Constitutional Bill rest, however, on ideas foreign to the Whig notion of parliamentary government. They both substitute a written for an unwritten constitution; they both place a strong and non-parliamentary executive side by side with a real legislature; they both create a constitution far more like that of the United States or the German Empire than the constitution of modern England.

It is curious to note the analogy* in some points between the Cromwellian Constitution of 1653 and one at least of the Napoleonic constitutions. In the *Acte Additionnel* of 1815 there is an attempt to combine a strong executive under Napoleon with a real legislature. The Emperor retains most of the powers which are given him by earlier Imperial constitutions, but he also creates a legislature and nominally concedes ministerial responsibility. It is, however, to be noted that certain things, e.g. the recall of the Bourbons, the re-establishment of the feudal nobility, interference with the rights acquired under the sale of the national domains, are positively prohibited by the Constitution.[27]

Secondly, the Instrument of Government is a record of the opinion of the age as to the relation between the Crown and the legislature.

The Puritans were in one sense rather conservatives than innovators. The object of the Instrument of Government was to give to the one person, or Protector, the authority exercised by an ideal English monarch, e.g. Elizabeth.

Hence the Constitution is to be parliamentary in the sense that there is to be a Parliament which meets at no long intervals and legislates. The government is to be according to law; the government, further, is to be carried on by a Council just as the old Tudor administration was carried on by the Privy Council. But while Parliament is to be a regular part of the Constitution there is no intention of subordinating the Protector, especially when acting with the concurrence of his Council or to use the old formula as King in Council, to Parliament. He is to be the powerful head of a powerful executive, and, though it is hoped that the executive and Parliament will act in harmony, it is certainly not intended that the government shall be a parliamentary executive like a modern Cabinet. The notion, in short, of the time was the same which had always prevailed in England up to that period, namely that while the head of the government, whether King or Protector, should pay attention to the advice of the legislature, and should legislate only in concurrence with the legislature, yet the

---

[27] Acte Additionnel, Art. 67.

* This and the following three sentences were each written in a separate paragraph in the manuscript but have been included in one paragraph here because they are all about the analogy.

monarch, or 'one person', should be a real, independent power or, to use modern phraseology, a non-parliamentary executive.

This, be it added, was the idea both of William III and Anne. It could not be carried out by the [first two] Georges, but it was within certain limits revived by George III.

As already pointed out there are two possible conceptions of parliamentary government.

According to the one conception the executive and the legislature each exercise a real and independent power, though when the head of the executive is wise and the legislature patriotic they ought each to act together. This conception, which involves the existence of an extra-parliamentary executive, prevailed in England in the 17th century and was not entirely expelled by the other view until at any rate the accession of the House of Hanover.

According to the rival conception which now prevails in England, the legislature indirectly appoints, controls, and dismisses the executive body. This view when fully developed leads inevitably to a parliamentary executive, whereof the now prevalent form is a 'Cabinet' chosen by the legislature from among its members. This is in essence the form of government existing in England, in the British colonies, in France, and in various constitutional kingdoms.

Englishmen find it difficult to understand the position of a legislature or Parliament which does not appoint or control the executive government.* A legislature they assume must either be powerless or in reality all-powerful. A Parliament which *bonâ fide* does not appoint the government must, they fancy, be like the Assemblies of the First French Empire really subordinate to the executive even in matters of legislation and be no better therefore than a sham legislative body. A legislature on the other hand which has *bonâ fide* legislative authority must, they conceive, be or soon become like the English Parliament, the controller and elector of the government.

This view rests in the main on the supposed lessons of English history, but it is sometimes supported by a line of *a priori* reasoning which may be thus summed up: a Parliament, it is argued, which has real power to make laws must gain control of the executive; for the government is bound to obey the laws made by the legislature, and Parliament may always indirectly use its legislative authority so as to curtail the power of action, and therefore ultimately to control the policy, of the government.

The doctrine, however, that a legislature cannot possess real power of law making without becoming all-powerful or sovereign is, though plausible, erroneous.

Its unsoundness is shewn by experience. The President of the United States cannot control the legislative authority of Congress, nor can the Houses of Congress control except to a very limited degree the President's choice of his Ministers, or the President's action as head of the government. No vote of the Houses could have prevented President Lincoln from surrendering to England the Confederate envoys

---

* This sentence and the next two sentences were written in separate paragraphs in the manuscript but have been included in one paragraph here because of their common topic.

taken from the Trent. It would have been impossible for the Houses to dictate either directly or indirectly the terms in which President Cleveland should refer in his Message to the question of free trade. No doubt the party by whom an American President is elected can exert influence over his policy; the Senate can refuse Senatorial approval to some of his appointments. But the influence of partisans is not the same thing as interference by the legislature, and the Senate's opportunity of imposing a veto upon appointments arises from the Senate possessing under the Constitution a certain amount of executive authority. Nor does English history support the notion that a Parliament if not powerless must of necessity become supreme. Under the Tudors, under Charles II, under William, and under Anne, Parliament was a real legislature. No laws could be passed which were not sanctioned by Parliamentary authority. But under none of these monarchs was the government a really parliamentary executive. A singular but most instructive example of the possible separation between legislative and executive power is found in the annals of Ireland during the existence of what is called Grattan's Constitution, i.e. between 1782 and 1800. The Irish Parliament was the only legislature which existed in Ireland. No man, Tory or Whig, denied its absolute and exclusive authority to legislate for Ireland, but the Parliament which could legislate could not, either in theory or in fact, control or appoint the executive. In modern Germany we see the same phenomenon. The Diet is a true Imperial legislature; the Emperor cannot pass laws without the Diet's assent, but the federal Parliament which can reject Bismarck's proposed legislation could neither remove Bismarck from office nor, were Bismarck dismissed by the Emperor, reinstate him in power.

Nor let anyone have recourse to the empty form of words that the doctrine of the necessary supremacy of any real legislature is unsound in practice but true in theory. The *a priori* argument by which it is maintained is unsound. The contention that a true legislature can always make itself supreme over the executive rests on the assumption that a legislative body may not possess equally with an executive a real though limited power, and this again rests on the further assumption that it is impossible for two authorities in the same state to be each supreme in a different sphere. Such supremacy depends at bottom on the capacity of each authority to command popular obedience, and those who maintain the necessary supremacy of a real legislature in reality contend that, in a conflict between the legislature and the executive, the people or the mass of them will always obey either the one or the other and that that one which commands obedience is in reality supreme or sovereign. This dogma rests on no satisfactory basis for it does not allow of the possibility or probability of the people rendering obedience to the legislature on one class of subjects and to the executive on another. The citizens, that is to say, believe in and wish for the division of powers and, as long as this is the sentiment of the nation, this division of powers will, whether prescribed by the constitution or merely upheld by custom, in general exist. Whether, if the legislature or the executive encroach upon the sphere of the other, the encroachment will receive popular support is a question which admits not of an *a priori* answer; the contest beginning in 1862 and lasting till 1866 between Bismarck and the Prussian Parliament ended in a drawn battle. Whatever may be the verdict of a constitutionalist on the point of law at issue between the Minister and the parliamentary majority, a philosophic historian will without difficulty perceive the true lesson of the struggle. The Prussian people wished for a parliamentary government, they did not wish to be governed by Parliament. Their ideal was the rule of a strong King co-existing with the authority of a real legislature. The King was to reign and the legislature was to make laws. This ideal, which was also that of English Parliamentarians down to 1689 and to a certain extent of American Republicans in 1789, found its realisation first in Prussia and then in the German Empire.

The dogma that a real legislature of necessity controls the executive can be established neither by experience nor by theory.

A fact, however, of great importance is often confounded with the doctrine of Parliamentary supremacy. This fact is that an executive which consists of members of the legislature or which is called upon to explain or defend its action before the legislature is apt to become more or less under legislative control and therefore under whatever form to turn into a parliamentary executive.

Hence under most constitutions framed with a view to maintain the separation of powers the rule has generally been laid down that the members of the government shall not be members of the legislature. This is the principle rigorously maintained in the United States. It has been embodied in many French constitutions as, for example, the Monarchical Constitution of 1791, the Directorial Constitution of 1795, the Consular Constitution of 1799, the various succeeding Imperial Constitutions down to 1814, and the revived Imperial Constitution of 1852. Note further that, with a view to maintain the independence of the executive, Ministers have under many of these Constitutions been unable to take part in the debates of the legislative assemblies. Experience shows that both these precautions are if not necessary at any rate highly expedient for the maintenance of an extra-parliamentary government. When Ministers *can be* appointed from among the members of a Parliament, it is hardly possible without a direct quarrel with the legislature to maintain a Ministry not consisting of parliamentary notabilities. A government again which must defend its acts in parliamentary debate is apt to become far more rapidly than could *a priori* have been expected amenable to the sentiment of Parliament. A singular example of this tendency is to be found in the later history of the Second French Empire. The Opposition was at no time formidable in numbers, yet a very small body of hostile critics made their influence felt in the Imperial legislature from the moment that Ministers were allowed to take part in debate and were forced either to endure in silence, or to answer in argument, the criticism of opponents. Men are at least so far rational that when once debate is opened they feel it almost intolerable to admit that their acts cannot be defended by reasoning. The experience of Ireland during the 18th century tells in the same direction. That Parliament possessed limited legislative authority and no executive power, yet its debates influenced the opinion of the country and the action of the government.

B. Comparative Merits of Parliamentary Executives and of Extra-Parliamentary Executives

[I. Merits and demerits of a parliamentary executive (Cabinet government)]*

A Parliamentary executive possesses at least four great merits.

1. Its connection with Parliament obviates, or tends to obviate, conflicts between the legislature and the government.

When an assembly dismisses, controls, and appoints the executive, it is all but impossible that there should be any lengthy conflict between the legislature and the government.

Such contests have no doubt occasionally arisen in England, but the reason of this is that the Cabinet has been, or is, to a limited extent appointed by authorities outside the legislature and has not been, or is not, a thoroughly parliamentary executive. The greater the control of Parliament the less the chance of conflicts between Parliament and the Cabinet.

A contest is an undoubted evil. It always produces a waste of national strength; it may produce danger of revolution. President Johnson's disagreement with Congress involved the United States in new risks of commotion and, it is quite possible, lost to the nation some of the advantages gained by the War against Secession. The conflicts and intrigues which characterised the Presidency of Louis Napoleon were terminated only by the *coup d'état*.

2. Cabinet government which is the best developed form of a parliamentary executive immensely facilitates the easy transaction of business.

The contrast drawn on this point by Bagehot between the procedure of Congress and the procedure of the English Parliament, confirmed as it is in every respect by Mr. Bryce, is decisive.

3. Cabinet government leads to the selection for executive functions of men whose character is personally known to the electors, i.e. the House, by whom they are appointed.

The House of Commons know as a body the qualities, good or bad of Lord Salisbury or Mr. Gladstone, of Lord Hartington, or of Sir William Harcourt, in a way in which these qualities cannot possibly be known to outsiders.

Cabinet government again puts, or ought to put, in power men who have gained reputation in Parliament and through their parliamentary reputation are known to the nation. Cabinet government means or ought to mean government by known statesmen.

It is hardly conceivable that a man should become Prime Minister in England whose name and antecedents were unknown to the English people.

---

* This heading has been derived from the Analysis (p. 286 above) and has been added to complement the other headings.

Lord Bute was hardly known to an English elector till George III created him to be the most unpopular of England's Premiers. When Mr. Polk was installed in office as President of the United States a man in the crowd shouted 'who is Mr. Polk?' and the question elicited roars of sympathetic laughter.

The tendency of Cabinet government to place known men in power is probably its greatest recommendation; unfortunately, since the day when Bagehot wrote his defence or eulogy of this system of administration, experience has taught us that Cabinet government need not of necessity mean the rule of notable persons. Of the constantly changing French Ministries few persons outside France know the names. Frenchmen themselves, it is said, often know little of the Ministers who hold office. The most noticeable fact of modern French politics is that the best known among Republican statesmen is banished from Parliament and is said to be permanently excluded from office.

4. Cabinet government facilitates a change in the system of administration.

A Minister is in power well suited for the conduct of home affairs; he is a man of peace and has come into office during a period of general tranquillity. A war or a rebellion breaks out. Everyone feels that the pacific Premier is not the man for the time. He can at once be changed by a vote of the House of Commons, and the man whom the nation deem most suited for the emergency be put in his place. All that can be said on this advantage of Cabinet government has been said so well by Mr. Bagehot that it were useless to repeat and impertinent to alter what he has written.

The defects of Cabinet government are so to speak the seamy sides of its merits.

1. Legislation is hopelessly mixed up with the question of a Ministry's tenure of power. Laws in the English Parliament are never discussed on their own merits. As, further, office depends upon success in administration, all who wish to gain office, in other words the Opposition, try to make the administration of the Government end in failure. The administration of the government is, however, nothing but the management of national affairs. The object therefore of every Opposition is more or less consciously to prevent the successful management of national business. This need not argue want of patriotism. If A's accession to power and the success of the political principles which A advocates depends upon showing that B's management of public business is a succession of blunders, the best known laws of human nature make it a certainty that A will *bonâ fide* think B a disastrous blunderer.

2. Cabinet government means government which, because it is easily changed, is apt to become changeable.

    The success of a policy depends upon a series of accidents; a Ministry dare not be even for a moment unpopular, and a Ministry which never dare be unpopular cannot always follow its own ideas of wisdom.

Turn now to the characteristics of an extra-parliamentary executive.

[II. Merits and demerits of an extra-parliamentary executive (Presidential government)]*

Its demerits are a constantly recurring and dangerous tendency to conflicts with the legislature, a great want of pliability in the transaction of any affairs wherein cooperation between the legislature and the executive is desirable, and lastly the possibility of its producing the rule of an unknown man.

This last is probably the worst of the evil results which may fairly be attributed to the existence of an executive not under the control of the legislature. If the real head of the government be an hereditary monarch then at any moment the holder of supreme authority may be a man whose qualities are either unfitted for government or quite unknown to people he is going to govern. Frederick the Great when he came to the throne was thought a sentimentalist. Few are the persons who can pronounce decisively on the talents and disposition of the German Emperor or the Russian Czar. If he be appointed by popular election the apparent securities for his being either known or capable are on the whole illusory. 'I should be a good President,' said an American, 'but I should be the worst of candidates for the Presidency.' Louis Napoleon was elected by 5 millions of votes at a time when not one Frenchmen in 10 thousand knew whether Louis Napoleon was a fool or a genius.

An extra-parliamentary executive possesses, or may possess, two merits.

First, questions of legislation may under such a government be to a certain extent separated from questions of administration.

Where the rejection or passing of a Bill does not involve the existence of a Ministry, Bills may possibly be discussed on their own merits.

Secondly, an extra-parliamentary executive, such for example as that planned by Cromwell, ought to be far more independent than a parliamentary Cabinet of temporary terms of popular opinion. A man, whether Emperor, Protector, or President, who knows that a blunder or the appearance of a blunder will not entail a fall from power, may especially in administrative matters do what seems to him best or most just independently of the popularity of his acts. No one can doubt that Cromwell and Lincoln were each able to act with an independence of immediate popularity which is all but forbidden to any modern Premier.

---

* This heading has been derived from the Analysis (p. 286 above) and has been added to complement the other headings.

III
Note 2[*]
Self-Government

The term, brought into vogue by Tocqueville, is ambiguous.

1. It may mean the right of individuals, whether acting singly or collectively, to manage as they please affairs such as trade, religious worship, and the like which directly and immediately concern mainly the individuals interested, e.g. in a particular kind of trade or in the promotion or practice of certain religious views or rites.

Self-government is, in this sense, in the main a form of individual freedom, i.e. of liberty in the sense in which the word is used by Mill. It is opposed to state interference whatever form it may take, whether the authority of the state be exercised by the central government or by a local body, such as a municipal corporation. It is, in short, the management of men's own affairs by themselves.

At the time when Tocqueville wrote, self-government, as the negation of state interference, was a marked characteristic of England and still more of the United States as contrasted with France. Tocqueville was struck by the fact that Englishmen or Americans were allowed to manage their own affairs and especially to associate together for the promotion of any purpose not in itself illegal. He contrasted this both with the laws and with the habits of the French. The contrast still exists. The law as to associations, the law as to recognised creeds, and the like imply the existence of a theory in France as to the rights of the state and individuals totally unlike the theory which has hitherto governed the law of England and of America. As regards at any rate the collective action of citizens the difference may be thus summed up: under the Common Law Englishmen may do, either alone or in combination with others, anything which the law does not distinctly forbid, though this prohibition may be expressed either in a statute or in some recognised principle of common, i.e. customary, law.

2. Self-government or, as it is better called, local self-government may mean the right of the inhabitants of different localities, e.g. of a county, a borough, or a parish, to manage for themselves their local affairs without being interfered with or directed by the central government.

Local self-government is, in this sense, opposed, not to the interference of the state, for it is itself a form of state interference, but to interference by the central power or, in the technical language of English law, of the Crown, or, in other words, to centralization.

The distinction between the two meanings is vital.

---

[*] The manuscript was not dated but this Note, together with the following Note, in the Dicey papers is attached to and following Note 1 (a typical list of headings for lectures/chapters on the comparative study of constitutions) which does not refer to self-government but was dated 22 March 1899. See also the 'Local Government and Centralization' lecture (pp 253 f. above).

Local self-government or, in other words, the government of individuals by local bodies, may interfere with the freedom of individual men or women as much as centralization. If the County Council imposes taxes upon me, if the County Council determines whether my house shall be built in one way rather than another, if the County Council decides at what hours, if at any, I can buy a glass of beer or a glass of spirits, if the County Council like the local authorities of some American towns can determine at what hours my children, if below the age of 15, are to go home for the night, and the like, my own choice of action or, in other words, my individual freedom is fully as much curtailed as it would be if the same powers were exercised by say the Local Government Board at Whitehall. Interference, whether expedient or inexpedient, does not cease to be interference because it is carried out by a county council or a vestry.

Tocqueville, when he analysed English and American institutions, was impressed, especially when he came to observe the United States, with the great amount of local self-government and the small amount of centralization which existed in both countries. He noted that in England the country gentlemen in their country of magistrates had the control of local affairs and exercised functions which in France fell to officials of the central power. He noticed that in New England all the smaller and more ordinary functions of government were exercised by town meetings. He therefore seems to have believed that self-government in the second sense of the term, which he did not very carefully distinguish from the first, was a special characteristic of English, no less than of American, institutions.

Herein, as regards England at any rate, he made, as many persons following have also made, one or two natural errors.

(i) He did not observe that you cannot, as already pointed out, identify local self-government with individual freedom.

(ii) He did not observe that in England, at any rate in the English country districts, there was a marked want of organised local bodies capable of carrying out local self-government in accordance with the wishes of the inhabitants e.g. of a parish or a county. Hence, when he wrote, there was less local government in England than in many Continental countries, notably in Prussia and in Switzerland.[1]

(iii) He did not note that, while in the counties unpaid magistrates, that is country gentlemen, exercised local authority, the mass of the inhabitants took no part in local government.

(iv) He fail[ed] to notice that in the England of his day it was not so much the case that many duties discharged in France by the central government were with us performed by local bodies as that they were not performed at all.

---

[1] Tocqueville's speculations are much vitiated by his having studied the institutions of France, England, and the United States without, as it would seem, having paid much attention to the local institutions of Continental countries such as Switzerland, Prussia, or Norway.

The decay of an old administrative system, combined with the influence of Benthamite individualism, established in England during the period when Tocqueville studied the country (1835–1860 (?)) a system of practical *laissez faire*.

These confusions are partly due to inadequate acquaintance with the working of English institutions, but their ultimate source is that there is a real connection between 'self-government' in its two different senses. Nothing is more difficult than to keep apart ideas which though perfectly distinct in themselves are nevertheless interconnected.

The relation between self-government as a form of individual freedom and self-government as meaning a special form of governmental interference with individual freedom, or in other words the control of individuals by local authorities, is this: if these local authorities are the inhabitants of a district, e.g. the parishioners of a given parish or the townsmen of a given township, or are persons elected by such parishioners or townsmen, it is possible for, e.g., the parishioners to determine to a great extent at their own will, which by the way only means the will of the majority of such parishioners, what are called their own affairs, that is the business of the parish, and [to] further the habit of taking part in the management of parochial affairs[,] [which] when once formed gives to individuals that kind of vigour and energy the exercise of which is the real safeguard of individual freedom. Nay more—though the minority of a parish do not under a system of local self-government really control the affairs of the parish, yet the man who is in a minority on one question may well be in a majority in another and, at lowest, he may make known his opinion about parochial matters and may exercise a limited kind of influence over them, whilst he could not with effect do either one or the other if the affairs of the parish were regulated by a permanent Under Secretary of State sending out his decisions from the Local Government Board in London. There may therefore be a real and very important connection between individual freedom and the existence of local self-government. But, be it noted, this connection exists only when it can be assumed that the inhabitants of a locality take an active and effective part in the administration of its affairs. In Tocqueville's time this was the case in the townships of New England as it is probably still the case in the *communes* (*Gemeinde*) of a Swiss canton. But the existence of such energetic interest, which implies the taking of a good deal of trouble, is no matter of course. A London vestry is a local body; it exercises important powers, but the vast majority of the inhabitants of London do not know the names of their parochial vestrymen and take no effective part whatever in the management of parochial affairs.

When this is so, local self-government is the negation of individual liberty. It means that the majority of Londoners are, in many of the minor matters of daily life, governed by an unknown authority whose action they do not, or cannot, control.

III (continued)
Note[*]
Self-Government and Local Self-Government

'Self-government' means the power of an individual person, A, to pursue, as regards matters which mainly and directly concern himself, the course of conduct which he prefers to follow.

'Local self-government' means the power of the inhabitants of a locality to pursue, in regard to matters which mainly and directly concern the interest of such locality, the course of conduct which the majority of such inhabitants prefer to follow.

The 'self' referred to in self-government is an individual man or woman, and the matters which he governs are matters primarily concerning the interest of such man or woman.

The 'self' referred to in the expression 'local self-government' consists of the majority of the inhabitants of a given locality, e.g. a parish, and the affairs which this 'self' governs are not affairs which primarily concern the interests of one individual man, or even of a majority of the parishioners, but which primarily concern what is called the locality, i.e. all the parishioners.

Note that we are constantly misled by the identification of the majority with the whole of a body of persons. When it is assumed that a parish with wide rights of self-government will in the main pursue at any rate the apparent interest of the parish, we are in reality confusing two different propositions. The one is that the majority of a parish will pursue what appears to such majority to be the interest of such majority. This proposition, though really subject to some limitations, may plausibly be deemed self-evident. The second proposition is that the majority of a parish will always pursue the apparent interest of all the members of the parish.

This proposition is so far from being true that, if we may assume the truth of the first proposition, this—the second proposition—is palpably false, since the apparent, if not the real, interest of the majority of a parish may well conflict with the apparent, if not the real, interest of a minority. A parish, for example, is inhabited by four wealthy landowners and 100 labourers receiving each wages of 15s. per week. The apparent interest of the labourers at any rate is so to impose and spend the rates that the payment of them may fall upon the landowners and the spending of them be for the advantage of the labourers. This is assuredly not the apparent interest of the wealthy minority.

---

[*] The manuscript was not dated, but see p. 299, n., above.

IV

Modes of Changing or Amending a Constitution

Analysis*

Introduction
    Three typical methods of amending constitutions
        1. The English method, ordinary Parliament
        2. The French method, Constituent Assembly
        3. The American method, Constitutional Convention, and popular ratification

A.   The English Method
    I. *Its essential characteristic*—no real distinction between constitutional and other laws and constitution therefore changed by ordinary process of Parliamentary legislation
    II. *Its merits and defects*
        1. Change easy and unrevolutionary
        2. Change may be too easy and made without due consideration
        3. Evils of party government increased by making constitutional changes depend upon immediate party interests

B.   The French Method
    I. *Essential characteristics*
        1. Constitution distinct from ordinary law
        2. Constitution can be changed only by sovereign Assembly representing distinct will of people
    NB This result partly of theory and partly of position of States General and example set by States General of 1789
    II. *Results*
        1. Change of a constitution is in effect a revolution
        2. Has all defects of English system and other defects of its own
        3. Change of constitution dictated by political interests of time
    NB Position of Ministry determined by jealousy of Mirabeau.
    Position of President—1848 by jealousy of Cavaignac, desire for Restoration, ambition of Bonapartists.
    Present constitution—a Republic framed with view to Royalist restoration

C.   The American Method
    I. *Essential character*—Convention a body appointed solely to draft constitution, and no authority for any other purpose. Constitution does not come into force till approved by people

---

* Its contents have been derived from a manuscript dated 4 May 1899 and attached to the manuscripts from which Analyses for lectures 4, 6, and 7 above have been derived.

II. *Results*
   1. No disturbance of ordinary administration or government
   2. Constitutional debates independent of immediate party interest
   3. Members of Convention much superior in character to members of ordinary legislature
   4. Attention of members directed to business of constitution making
   5. Ratification or disapproval of people corrects errors
   NB Swiss system to a certain extent combination of English and American methods

(See,
for English method,
   Dicey, *Law of Constitution*, 5th edn, pp 22–5;
   and, generally, Ibid. pp 118–29, App. Note I, p. 403;
   Bryce, *American Commonwealth*;
   Freeman, *Growth of English Constitution*, ch. III;
   Raleigh, *Elements of Politics*, ch. VI;
for French method,
   Revision des Constitutions;
for American method,
   Bryce, *American Commonwealth*, vol. 1, 3rd edn, pp 667[–9] and chs XXXVIII and XXXIX.)

V*

Authorities and Questions
Comparative Study of Constitutions

Authorities

(NB These should be read with a special view to the subjects of my lectures and to the questions hereinafter suggested, but the student would do well to read more of the works enumerated than the passages to which special reference is made.)

> Lowell, *Governments and Parties in Continental Europe*, especially the chapters as to France, Prussia, and Switzerland;
> Paley, (on the British constitution) *Moral Philosophy*, bk. VI, chs V–VII;
> Dicey, *Law of the Constitution* (5th edn), especially as to Rigid and Flexible Constitutions, ch. II, and as to *Droit Administratif*, ch. XII;
> Bryce, *American Commonwealth*, (3rd edn), pt I, chs XXIII, XXIV–XXXIII, and Appendix, Note to ch. III;
> Mill, *Representative Government*, pp 1–6;
> Mill, *On Liberty*;
> Montesquieu, *L'Ésprit des Lois*, bk. XI, chs I–VI;
> Locke, *Civil Government*, chs X–XIV;
> Stephen, *Lectures on the History of France*, i, Lecture VIII, p. 259;
> as to French *Parlements*,
> Chéruel, *Institutions de la France*, ii, '*Parlement*' p. 943.

Questions

(NB These questions are intended to provide students with subjects of investigation as to which they may with advantage write short essays.)

I. What is meant by an 'historical Constitution' and what are its merits and demerits? (See Mill, *Representative Government*, pp 1–6.)

II. How far are the political and constitutional ideas of ancient (classical) times applicable to modern states? (See 1 Arnold, *Thucydides*, Appendix I.)

III. What is meant by feudalism? (See Pollock and Maitland, *History of English Law*, bk. I, ch. III, pp 66–73; bk. II, ch. I, s. 6, pp 296–307.)

---

* The manuscript was not dated but was indicated as having been 'sent out 11 May 1899' in a later manuscript note.

IV. Give an account of modern political and social ideas derived from classical and mediaeval sources respectively.

V. What is meant by representative government? What are its merits and defects? Why was the representative system unknown to the statesmen and thinkers of Greece and of Rome?

VI. What is meant by the doctrine of the separation of powers? (See Montesquieu, *L'Ésprit des Lois*, bk. XI, chs I–V; Locke, *Civil Government*, chs XI, XII, and XIII.)

VII. Compare the views of Locke and of Montesquieu on the separation of powers.

VIII. What is the difference in the mode in which the doctrine of the separation of powers has been applied
1. in France, and
2. in the United States?

IX. What is meant by local self-government, and what is its relation to
1. the political freedom of a nation,
2. individual freedom?

X. Give an account of and criticise Burke's views as to party government.

XI. What is meant in the United States by a Constitutional Convention? How does it differ from a Constituent Assembly? (See *Cyclopaedia of Political Science*, vol. I, 'Convention', p. 626.)

XII. Examine any (or all) of the following statements.

(i) 'Pour qu'on ne puisse abuser du pouvoir, il faut que, par la disposition des choses, le pouvoir arrête le pouvoir.' (Montesquieu)

(ii) 'The largest part of that history which we commonly call ancient is practically modern, while, on the other hand, most of what is called modern history is practically ancient.' (Arnold)

(iii) 'Another kind of political reasoners regard [a form of government] as a sort of spontaneous product, and the science of government as a branch (so to speak) of natural history.' (J. S. Mill)

(iv) 'Party is a body of men united, for promoting by their joint endeavours the national interest, upon some particular principle in which they are all agreed.' 'Certain it is, the best patriots in the greatest commonwealths have always commended and promoted such connections.' (Burke)

'The best party is but a kind of conspiracy against the rest of the nation.' (Halifax)

VI

Note 17*
Conclusions as to French Droit Administratif

A. Nature of

French administrative law rests upon [the] following principles.

1. The rights of the state and its officials as against individuals and of individuals as against the state are determined by a special body of law different from the law regulating the rights of individuals between themselves. This body of law is droit administratif or administrative law. It includes [the] rights of a state against officials or private individuals and of either private individuals or officials against the state, as well as the rights of individuals against officials as of officials as such against individuals.

    This *droit administratif* is according to French ideas a special branch of law.

2. Questions of administrative law in so far as they give rise to any legal proceedings whatever are to be determined by administrative Courts, of which the principal are the Conseil d'État and the Prefect's Council. They are not to be determined [by,] i.e. are not within the jurisdiction of, the ordinary courts (whether civil or criminal) which for the sake of convenience may be termed civil as contrasted with administrative tribunals.

3. Certain acts of State, i.e. direct acts of public power or authority, are not within the jurisdiction of any Courts whatever whether they be civil Courts or administrative tribunals. It is very difficult to ascertain from French authorities what are precisely the acts which, as acts of State, are beyond the jurisdiction of any Court whatever.

4. In virtue of the doctrine of the separation of powers the civil Courts have no right to interfere with the action of [the] government or of the administration, and

---

* The manuscript was not dated but is attached to Note 16 (a list of references to other notes on French administrative law, which are not in the Dicey Papers and, presumably, have not survived), which was dated 25 May 1899. Both Note 16 and Note 17 were bound in a bundle headed 'Rough Notes' at the start of which they were listed last. Furthermore, a citation of *The Law of the Constitution*'s 5th edn on p. 314, n., below is evidence that Note 17 preceded the 6th edn's publication in 1902. Notes 16 and 17 may have been preparatory work for Dicey's new Notes on *droit administratif* in the Appendix of *The Law of the Constitution*'s French edn and that of its 6th English edn, which he incorporated in ch. xii of later editions: *The Oxford Edition of Dicey*, i, *The Law of the Constitution*, 'English Misconceptions as to *Droit Administratif*' (6th edn, Note X), 337 ff, 'Evolution of *Droit Administratif*' (6th edn, Note XI), 343 ff. On the significance of Note 17 for our understanding of Dicey's attitude to *droit administratif* and his conception of the rule of law, see Editor's Introduction, pp xix f., xxxviii f. above.

therefore in case any person is injured by an administrative act his remedy (if any) is by proceedings in the administrative tribunals.

5. The question whether an act is an administrative act is not determinable by the civil Courts, but is ultimately determinable by the Conflict-court, (Tribunal des Conflits) which consists partly of members of the Conseil d'État and partly of members of the Cour de Cassation. It is, in effect, a Court consisting in part of officials in part of judges for determining the limits to the jurisdiction of the civil Courts and the administrative tribunals respectively.

6. Officials enjoy as to acts done in pursuance of their official duties a threefold protection.

   (i) An official who has acted under the orders of his superiors in a matter lying within their sphere of action is thereby exempt from punishment, i.e. the order of an official's proper superior in matters within the latter's province is a defence against proceedings for a wrongful action.[1]

   (ii) An official cannot for an official act (acte administratif) be proceeded against in any but an administrative tribunal.

   (iii) An official cannot be made personally liable for [an] administrative act, i.e. an act done in pursuance of his official duty, unless either by acting maliciously or with gross negligence he has deprived the act of its administrative character; the remedy for harm caused by an administrative act is against the state and not against the official.

To sum up: the essential characteristics of administrative law as understood in France are [as follows].

First—The existence of a special body of law regulating the relation between the state and its officials, on the one hand, and individuals, on the other.

Secondly—The determination of all questions of administrative law by administrative tribunals.

This excludes the jurisdiction of the ordinary civil Courts.

Thirdly—The determination of the limits to the jurisdiction of the civil Courts and of the administrative tribunals respectively by the Conflict-court.

Fourthly—The special protection extended to officials acting, even though illegally, in pursuance of official duties.

B. Misunderstandings as to Nature of *Droit Administratif*

These are of two kinds.

The first error is to suppose that *droit administratif* is merely the same thing as rules of law regulating the conduct of officials or, to put the thing somewhat differently, it is the same thing as official law.

---

[1] *Code Pénal*, Art. 14.

Such law must exist though the amount of it may greatly differ in all civilized countries, in England and in the United States no less than in France or in Prussia: and it is of course easy to point out rules of English law, mostly it may be added to be found in statute or in regulations made under statutable authority, which determine the special duties and rights of officials. It is also true that, though to a very limited extent, officials, such as judges, Justices of the Peace, constables, and others, are specially protected when acting in discharge or in pursuance of their official duties. To this it may be added that the tendency of modern civilization is in England and even in the United States to throw more and more duties upon the state and upon the state officials, and hence to increase the amount of official law. At the time, for example, when Blackstone wrote, the state or, at any rate, the central government in no way took charge of education, the inspection of factories, or even, strange as the assertion sounds, of the provision of a police force for the protection of citizens. At the present day education is a national affair. Factories and workshops are liable to state control. A body of police constituting in the case of London a sort of civil army is raised and governed by the state. The result is the growth of a whole body of official law embodied in Education Acts and Codes, in regulations for the inspection of factories, in rules for the government and the direction of the police. But the increase of state intervention is not the same thing as the growth of administrative law. No men or body of men, not even the army, are in England or in the United States exempt from the law of the realm. There does not exist in either country such a thing as administrative jurisdiction: for every breach of law an appeal can be made to the ordinary Courts. Above all the ordinary Courts determine what are the limits to the legal powers of government officials, or indeed of any existing body of persons. There is no authority known to the law of England, like the Conflict-court, which can set a limit to the jurisdiction of the ordinary Courts. It is a mere error to confound official law with administrative law, and the idea to which it has given rise, that *droit administratif* has come into existence in England, is utterly without foundation.[2]

The second error is the belief that *droit administratif*, as it exists in France, is not in reality law at all but is a system under which the claims of individuals against the state or its officers are determined in accordance with the discretionary authority of officials.[3]

For this view which prevails among the limited body of Englishmen who have examined the character of French *droit administratif* there exists, or rather there existed, a good deal of justification. Up till 1870 no proceedings could be taken by a private person against an official for acts done in discharge of his public duties without the license of the Council of State; with 'acts of State' (a wide and indefinite term) French judges are incompetent to interfere; redress for official misdoing must be obtained, if at all, from an administrative or, as we should say, an official tribunal, and at the beginning at any rate of this century, or later, the Ministerial powers and

---

[2] For an example of this error see 1 Goodnow, pp 6–9, and contrast 1 Laferrière, p. 106.
[3] See my *Law of the Constitution*, ch. XII, where the extent to which *droit administratif* has developed into a regularly administered body of law is not sufficiently recognised.

the judicial authority of a French Minister were so strangely mixed together that it was hardly an exaggeration to assert that the decision of a question at issue between a private person and the state was left to the discretion of Ministers. The *Conseil d'État*, moreover, was more of a Ministerial than a judicial body, and its decisions, when delivered, were in reality what by the way the judgments of our Privy Council are in form, advice tendered to the executive rather than judgments, and might be rendered ineffective for years simply because [they were] not signed by the proper Minister.[4]

But, though there is much to suggest the notion that administrative law is in France not 'law' at all in the sense in which the word 'law' is used in England, this idea is as regards the present day erroneous and is grounded on ignorance of a gradual change which has taken place during the course of this century.[5]

From about 1800 to the present day there has been gradually developed in France a body of real administrative law. It has been the creation in the main of the administrative Courts. It rests upon precedents and is in reality judge-made law. But this transformation of discretionary governmental authority into a set of legal principles administered by bodies which have at last become Courts has been aided by direct legislation.

In 1800, or about that date, administrative suits, if one may use the term, were hardly separated from other governmental business and were in reality ultimately determined by Ministers in accordance with their discretion. The Council of State was at once an executive and a judicial body. Its judicial and its executive functions were hardly separated, to which must be added that the Council of State or *Conseil d'Etat* was itself the final Conflict-court. The state of things which then existed in France bore some analogy to what would be the condition of matters in England if there were little or no distinction between the Cabinet as a part of the Privy Council and the Judicial Committee of the Privy Council, and the Cabinet determined judicial questions with a general reference to political expediency.[6]

Reforms, however, carried out at different periods, e.g. 1828, 1831, 1845, 1848, 1870, and 1872, gradually separated off the judicial from the administrative functions of the *Conseil d'État* (which is hereinafter in this note called the Council). Litigious administrative business (*contentieux administratif*) was assigned to a particular committee or section, and became in general the subject of argument and of judgments as would have been the case if it had been determined by a regular Court. The decisions moreover were reported and on this point great stress must be laid. The

---

[4] See 1 Laferrière, p. 273.
[5] Ibid., bk. 1, chs I–IV, pp 139–283.
[6] See Note 12, Book III, p. 21. The *Conseil* originally exercised three different functions—

(i) the final decision of questions of administration
(ii) the hearing of appeals in all administrative suits
(iii) the determination as a Conflict-court of all questions of jurisdiction.

[The reference to Book III would seem to be a reference to one of Dicey's own, presumably lost, four notebooks, which he refers to on the first page of the manuscript headed 'Comparative Study of the Constitution: List of Papers etc' (see pp xiii, n., p. 307, n., above).]

reporting of the decisions or judgments led to the growth of precedents or of case law. The character too of the Council in its judicial character was changed and, after various alterations, the Council was ultimately made[7] into a real tribunal, though an administrative tribunal, and its decisions were given by law the force of judgments. As the final result of the same tendency, there was at last created a real Conflict-court consisting of nine members, four of them Councillors, and four of them members of the Court of Cassation; the ninth is the Minister of Justice who was technically President. The members are elected by the Court itself.

What ought to be impressed upon Englishmen is that, by a process bearing a curious analogy to the way in which in earlier times Courts were formed out of the King's Council, the *Conseil d'État* has within the last 60 or 70 years been changed, as regards administrative suits, from a part of the executive into a real and effective tribunal. It has in one sense an official character because the Councillors are members of what we should call the civil service, but these Councillors, though having administrative experience, act judicially, and the Court which ultimately determines the limits which bound the jurisdiction of the administrative Courts and the civil Courts respectively or, in other words, the Conflict-court consists in part of Councillors, but it also consists in great part of trained lawyers taken from the highest Court of Appeal. It is in character a judicial body.

One other change ought to be mentioned. A decree of the Government of National Defence made on 19 September 1870, and virtually ratified by the National Assembly of 1871, repealed Article 75 of the Constitution of the Year VIII and thereby did away with the necessity of obtaining the authorization of the Council for proceedings against officials.[8] But this change produced less effect than an English lawyer might have expected from it. He would be inclined to interpret it as subjecting officials to the jurisdiction of the ordinary law Courts, and he would conclude that it to a great extent made the ordinary Courts competent to decide matters of administrative law. This is not the interpretation which after some hesitation has been put upon the decree by French Courts. They have held that, while the repeal of Article 75 makes it possible to take proceedings against an official without obtaining the leave of the Council of State, the repeal does not in any way change the jurisdiction of the civil Courts and of the administrative Courts. The civil Courts remain incompetent to pronounce judgment in regard to administrative acts. These remain subject to the jurisdiction of the administrative tribunals. It of course may and indeed must happen, when proceedings are taken against an official for an alleged wrong, e.g. what we should term a trespass, that the question should often arise whether he is being proceeded against for an act of personal wrongdoing, over which the civil Courts have jurisdiction, or for an act done in pursuance of or in connection with his official duties, over which the administrative tribunals have jurisdiction. It occurs to an Englishman that here at least the authority of the civil Courts must come in, for [the reason] that it must be within their competence to determine what is the character of

---

[7] See especially Law of 24 May 1872.
[8] See 1 Laferrière, bk. III, ch. VII, p. 637.

the act complained of. But this conception of judicial authority, natural as it seems to us, is foreign to French law. The character of the act is ultimately to be determined not by the ordinary civil Courts, but by the Conflict-court. The ordinary Courts have[,] then, since as before 1870[,] no jurisdiction in respect of administrative suits.

An English critic then who weighs carefully the character of French *droit administratif* will perceive two things.

[*First*]—It is accurately called administrative law.

It is '*administrative*' or official and it is therefore a kind of law regulating the rights and duties of individuals in regard to the state or government, which is quite unknown to England, and which is administered by a special body of Courts independent of, to use English terms, the common law Courts.

But it is '*law*'; it makes up a body of distinct rules created in the main by judicial legislation and enforced by the authority of the state. These rules moreover are administered by bodies which, though consisting of officials, act judicially and are real Courts.

[*Secondly*]—*Droit administratif* is judge-made law.

This point is worth notice. We have nothing in England like *droit administratif*, yet it is the only portion of the law of France which has been created after the same manner as the better part of the law of England.

The law of England is built up to an immense extent on judicial decisions; it has its roots in precedents or, to use a current expression, it is judge-made law. Now this is not the case with the greater and most noticeable part of French law. It rests upon the Codes; it is, as we should say, statute law. The Codes no doubt have been explained and annotated by the Courts, but the decisions of French Courts are in theory at least determinations of isolated cases. They are not precedents nor are they binding decisions as regards later cases. We may sum up the difference between the mass of English and the mass of French law in language which is not quite accurate but which is intelligible. English law is in its origin at least, for the most part, common law. French law is for the most part statute law. But with the particular department of French law known as *droit administratif* it is otherwise. Little or nothing is to be found about *droit administratif* in the Codes. It has grown up, almost-unnoticed, outside them; it is the fruit of decisions given by the administrative tribunals. Its sources are reported cases; it rests on precedent; it is judge-made law. It is this characteristic which gives it an expansiveness and flexibility unknown to the Codes and has fostered its growth. One of the reasons why a foreigner finds it difficult to appreciate the nature of *droit administratif* as it now exists is that like the common law of England it changes and grows from generation to generation. Vivien, at one time a leading authority, published his work on *droit administratif* some fifty years ago. Compare it with the authoritative treatise of Laferrière, and you see at once that the branch of law of which they each treat has passed rapidly through a course of development, amounting almost to transformation. An English critic who relies upon Vivien for his picture of modern administrative law stands much in the position of a foreign critic who relied for a picture of English law as it exists in 1899 on the pages of Blackstone.

C. The Demerits and Merits of *Droit administratif*

Demerits

An English lawyer when he has come to realise the true nature of *droit administratif* easily enough perceives what from an English point of view are its defects.

It is part of a system which under the name of the division of powers lowers the position of the civil Courts. The theory and the practice of French law is that these courts should confine themselves to the decision of questions between individuals. Their criminal jurisdiction, it is true, forms a considerable exception to this principle, but even in criminal matters the action of French judges is, as far as an Englishman can form an opinion, restricted within narrow limits. Any inquiry involving a question of State lies outside their competence. They can neither determine liability for any administrative act nor have they jurisdiction to declare whether an act has or has not an administrative character. They do not in short themselves fix the limits to their own jurisdiction, and this one fact is enough to make the situation of the French judiciary different from and in truth inferior to the position of the English or American Courts. Then again it is natural to assume (though the correctness of the assumption admits of some doubt) that a private individual who seeks a remedy in an administrative Court may suffer from the official bias of his judges. Administrative tribunals are Courts but they are Courts made up of administrators.

Merits

Yet *droit administratif* has real merits whether we compare it, on the one hand, with the English system or, on the other, with the systems existing in Continental countries outside France.

Comparison with English system

From this point of view *droit administratif* has at least two recommendations.

First—It gives a person damaged by the act of the state an acknowledged remedy or claim for compensation against the state. Now this an Englishman as a rule does not possess.[9] If, for example, a ship of the Royal Navy runs down a ship belonging to a shipowner, if a post cart runs over a person on foot, and the like, the legal remedy of the person injured is confined to an action against the wrongdoer, who probably would be in the one case the captain of the ship, in the other the driver of the mail cart. The person aggrieved has no remedy against the Crown.[10] Then too, what is a valuable part of the French system, a person has in many cases it would appear a

---

[9] There exists a limited exception in those cases in which a petition of right lies.

[10] This grievance is to a certain extent only theoretical. The Admiralty, it is presumed, would in most cases pay the damages recovered from a naval commander for any act done strictly in pursuance of the orders of the Crown.

right to get administrative or official acts annulled which are *ultra vires* even where they have not caused him actual pecuniary damage. As far as I can discover no similar power exists under English law. If, for example, the Home Office were to issue an order or notice which was *ultra vires*, i.e. which went beyond any right possessed by the Secretary of State either in virtue of the prerogative of the Crown or under a statute, any man might, if he chose to risk doing so, treat the notice as a nullity. But there does not appear to be any way in which he could get it withdrawn or nullified.[11]

Secondly—The official character of administrative tribunals makes it easier than in England to enforce laws passed in the interest of the state but not commanding much public sympathy.[12]

Comparison with systems of other Continental countries

French writers treat the *droit administratif* of France as a peculiar creation of French genius and hold that it compares very favourably with systems existing in other countries, such as Germany, Italy, or Belgium.

As far as an outsider can form an opinion it would appear that the French view is right. In most, if not in all, Continental countries some kind of *droit administratif* exists but, in very few, has it been reduced to the condition of a regular branch of the law of the land, which, as we have seen, it now is in France. Moreover in Germany at any rate, administrative law (*Verwaltungsrecht*) tends apparently to give servants of the state, whether civil or military, independent rights and an independent position which the civil service of France does not possess. On the whole it appears to be true that if administrative law is to exist it is seen at its best as French *droit administratif*.

---

[11] It is in several ways a defect of English law that it affords very little means of testing the legality of anyone's action until actual damage has been caused by it.

[12] See, as to the powers of the Board of Trade under the Maritime Safety Acts, *Law of the Constitution*, 5th edn, pp 329–30.

VII[*]

Why Universal Suffrage Suits France

The establishment of universal suffrage in France was the result of a political accident.

It was unknown to the French constitutional monarchy. Under the Orléanist dynasty from 1830 to 24 February 1848, the right to elect members of the Chamber of Deputies was confined to a very limited class of more or less well-to-do citizens. In France, in short, under the Charter of 1830, the parliamentary franchise was exercisable by a narrower class than in England under the Reform Act of 1832. It is indeed fairly maintainable that in 1830 the unreformed English House of Commons more fairly represented the English people than under the Charter of 1830 the French House of Deputies represented the French people. Nor were the Radicals, who in 1847 agitated France with the cry for Parliamentary reform, advocates of universal suffrage. Their demands were moderate: they asked not that every Frenchman should have a vote, but that the number of Frenchmen entitled to the parliamentary franchise should be somewhat increased. French Liberals of 1847 did not even claim the household suffrage which English Conservatives introduced into England in 1866, and extended from the towns to the country districts in 1884.

The Revolution of February was, as it was termed, a 'catastrophe'. It banished the Orléanist dynasty and destroyed the constitutional monarchy. The Provisional Government forthwith established universal suffrage. Their action was suggested by the circumstances of the moment; it met the wish of the Parisian mob who had vanquished Louis Philippe; it promised some benefit to, though it did not in fact greatly strengthen, the Republican party; it was in accordance with the principles of a French politician Ledru-Rolin who, though a conspicuous member of the Provisional Government, was absolutely unknown out of France, and has apparently long been forgotten by the French people.

We might have expected that an immense constitutional change which had never been ardently demanded by the nation, and which was the result of accidental and transitory circumstances, would itself have passed away with the influence of the men by whom it had been introduced. This expectation has been entirely falsified by the event. The Revolution of 24 February turned out a complete failure. The Provisional Government fell from power in less than five months. The Republic of 1848 was, odd as the assertion sounds, created and governed by reactionists who regretted the fall of the monarchy. The *coup d'état* of 1851 swept the Republic away—it perished all

---

[*] The manuscript was dated 23 June 1900 on its first page. It was thus written during the period when the full lecture texts in Part II above were being written but is not referred to in those texts or elsewhere in the Dicey Papers. In this text, Dicey dealt extensively with a topic he covered briefly in his 'French constitutionalism' lecture, p. 96 above.

but unregretted—and the Empire which then typified reaction was sanctioned by the voice of the French nation. With one exception all the changes introduced by the Revolution of 1848 have passed away. The one exception is universal suffrage. No one protested against it. No party in the state has ever ventured directly to attack it. One French legislature, filled as it was with reactionists and royalists, tried by a measure, which we should call a Registration Bill, to limit, in effect though not in name, the universality of the parliamentary vote. The endeavour was fatal to the legislative body. It afforded the plea, if not the justification, for the *coup d'état*, and the President, who violated his oath and the law of the land, put forward the apology that if he overthrew the Constitution he in reality restored the right of every Frenchman to full political citizenship. The moral of the President's success has not been forgotten. Even reactionists, who in 1871 contemplated a restoration of the monarchy, have treated universal suffrage as the one unassailable institution which forms the foundation of every French government.

These facts are worth notice. They show that for some reason or other universal suffrage meets the needs of France.

What then is the cause of the suitability of this particular institution to the condition of France?

The answer, in general terms, is that the right, now fully established of every French citizen who is not under some special disability (such e.g. as want of full age or condemnation for crime) to vote for a parliamentary representative, is the natural outcome of French history and harmonises with the sentiments or convictions of which French history is, in the main, the cause.

In the countries which make up modern France the feudal system originally prevailed as in the greater part of modern Europe. One essential characteristic of that system was to constitute in every country separate orders, ranks, or classes, each of which possessed their different rights or rather privileges. These privileges, it is true, were, according to the feudal ideal, inseparably connected with the liability to discharge public duties; but it is hardly an exaggeration to assert that the tendency of mediaeval society was to substitute the idea of privilege for the idea of right. One immediate result of this state of things was that a nation or country came to consist of orders, such as the nobility and the Church, corporations such as were in England the parliamentary boroughs, the trade guilds, and the like, and generally of bodies which foreign writers are apt to describe by the vague but convenient term as moral persons. These moral entities, such for example as the Church or the universities, had each a separate life, power, and moral authority of their own. In England, where feudal notions have survived just because they were, owing to the great and early-acquired power of the Crown, cut down so as to be compatible with the development of national life, these moral persons or, as we should rather say, corporate or quasi-corporate bodies have always played and still play a great part. The English Parliament itself, though happily only to a slight extent representing orders, was in reality until quite recent times rather the representative of bodies than of the individuals who make up the nation. The House of Commons represented the boroughs and the counties rather than the people of England. The Commons themselves were a class. The House of Lords represented, if the term may be used, the Church and the nobility. The Houses themselves were rather organised bodies with their own special rights than the mere representatives of the nation. It is a fact not without significance that Parliaments in their conflicts with the Crown claimed the rights of Englishmen never the rights of men;[1] the claim for the privileges of Parliament was the response to the assertion of the prerogative of the Crown. In France the course of events was different. The ancient French monarchy, it is true, was in the eyes of its admirers, such for example as Montesquieu, a feudal and even in one sense a parliamentary monarchy. It was surrounded by public bodies; it was founded on the recognition of a hierarchy of privileges, of prerogatives, of franchises, of individual rights which held the place of public rights; it was in short a monarchy of a constitutional character which rested on the foundation of fundamental laws and which was supported by intermediate authorities subordinate indeed but independent and possessed of a real power of their own.[2] But this temperate and feudal monarchy was always more or less of an idea which hardly corresponded with actual fact. The annals of France are down to the Revolution the record of the gradual increase of the royal power at the expense of every other independent body. The growth moreover of the monarchy which welded together the different countries which constitute modern France created the unity of the nation, and the Crown was in the long run invariably supported in its assaults upon all those moral persons or classes which could claim to stand between the central government, which represented the nation, and the people. The result as the Revolution approached was very perplexing to Englishmen in the eighteenth century but is now, in consequence of the labours of Tocqueville and others, pretty well understood. The Crown or the central government had stripped every class in the community of independent power. The nobility had lost their legal rights and moral authority and retained nothing but immunities which were universally detested by the majority of their countrymen. Add to this that, while the oppressiveness and the cumbersomeness of the feudal system survived, its real merits were dead, and that a society legally divided into hostile classes irritated against one another by the existence of iniquitous privileges was in the way of thought and feeling singularly homogeneous so that civil or political inequality was artificially maintained in a nation which consisted of individuals who were intellectually and morally equals. There existed but one authority in the state which still claimed to balance the unrestricted sovereignty of the Crown. This body was made up of the *Parlements* represented in a sense by the *Parlement* of Paris and claiming to combine the exercise of judicial functions with the exertion of something very like a veto on royal legislation. The prerogatives, however, of the Parliaments were hateful to the Crown; they did not habitually command the support of the people; they were defied with success by Louis XV, and, though at the crisis just preceding the convocation of

---

[1] Contrast the attitude of the French States General during the 14th and the 15th centuries. Their language and their acts constantly anticipate the phrases and the policy adopted by the revolutionary assemblies of the 18th century. See especially Stephen's *History of France*, vol. 1, chs 10–12.

[2] See Janet, vol. 2, p. 362.

the States General in 1789 the *Parlement* of Paris was for a moment popular because it opposed the King, yet revolutionists and reformers were at least as hostile to the authority of the law Courts as had ever been the most despotic of the Bourbons. Before 1789 the Crown had deprived nearly every independent order or body of real power. The Revolution swept away surviving privileges and destroyed the few corporate bodies which could still lay any claim to independence. And here it is well to remember that the statesmen of the Revolution were from a certain point of view individualists. Thus they limited the right of association in matters of trade as strictly as did English Tories, and would not have objected in principle to the great Combination Act of 1800, provided that the law had been as stringent in restricting combinations of masters as in restricting combinations of workmen. Revolutionary statesmen looked with jealousy on the right of association and specially condemned every kind of trade guild, both because guilds or unions might balance the authority of the state and because guilds or unions interfered with individual liberty as it was understood by Rousseau and his disciples. In this matter Napoleon was the child and the organiser of the Revolution and the maxims of Napoleonic administration still formed the basis of the French administrative system.

The net result then of the history of France has been the creation of a strong central power which represents and is brought face to face with the nation. Hence the one authority outside the actual government which still possesses moral force is the nation itself, consisting not of orders or corporations but of so many million individual Frenchmen.[3]

Of such a condition of things universal suffrage is the logical and natural expression, to which we may add that the body of peasant proprietors, which according to all observers forms the most solid portion of the French social system, could receive its due political weight only under a scheme of representation which confers upon every man of full age the right to vote. And it is curious to observe how, as is apt to happen in the world of politics, current theories and general opinion have conformed to historical facts. It is only too easy to point out the fallacies of Rousseau's theories, but it is equally easy and more instructive to note that his doctrines are in perfect harmony with French detestation of the *ancien régime* and of all the institutions which, whether good or bad, were survivals of feudalism,[4] and that the kind of equality advocated by Rousseau necessarily involved the establishment of universal suffrage. In any case the French nation has certainly as a whole gradually adopted the view that by nothing else than the votes of all male citizens can the will of the nation receive authoritative expression. This has always been avowed not only by French revolutionists but also by the representatives of the Napoleonic regime. The *plebiscites* by which Napoleon I and his nephew sought to ratify constitutional changes, carried out in many cases by brute force, were to a great extent, though not so entirely

---

[3] The overthrow of Protestantism, of which the revocation of the Edict of Nantes was the outward and visible sign, was due at least as much to the national desire for unity and dislike for aristocrat privilege or independence as to theological passion. French Protestantism was more or less of an aristocratic creed.

[4] See *Contrat Social*.

as many Englishmen believe, shams; but they were also the theoretical acknowledgment of the deference due to the voice of the whole people. The idea again that a Constituent Assembly elected by the whole nation could rightly exercise the whole sovereign power of the people is really an expression of belief in the moral authority of universal suffrage. If we ask why Louis Philippe's government, which secured eighteen years of peace and material prosperity to France, never commanded the hearty allegiance of even that limited class of citizens who between 1830 and 1848 were possessed of full political rights, a partial answer to a difficult question certainly is that Louis Philippe was called to the throne by a Parliamentary body elected by a limited number of electors and that the Orléanist regime never, either directly or indirectly, received the sanction of popular vote. But the most curious illustration of the superstition of universal suffrage, as a hostile critic might call the prevalent French sentiment, is that a sensible and moderate Republican, such as is Monsieur Borgeaud, who is not ill satisfied with the constitutional laws of the existing French Republic, maintains in the very face of the words of the Constitution that amendments to the Constitution lack moral validity unless they are submitted to and approved by a vote of the people. The admission of this doctrine will be, according to our author's creed, the renewal of a fundamental tradition of French public law which has only been interrupted by peculiar political circumstances.[5] With the worth of a dogma which condemns on the ground of moral invalidity every French constitution (except oddly enough Napoleonic constitutions) which has existed since the beginning of the 19th century, we are not here concerned. For our purpose the existence of the dogma is important only as proving the tendency of French opinion to treat universal suffrage as the only legitimate foundation of political authority. That this tendency is supported by arguments the force of which is open to question is in the highest degree probable. But the very weakness of the abstract reasoning in support of an institution which a powerful nation practically accepts, is a strong proof that this acceptance is due not to the power of logical reasoning but to a far more potent cause—namely the suitability of the institution to the circumstances of the nation.

---

[5] Borgeaud, *Adoption and Amendment of Constitutions*, Eng. trans., p. 257.

VIII*

Scheme of Lectures, 1906

Easter & Trinity Terms 1906†
Comparative Study of the Constitution
(*Six Lectures*)

Daily at 9 a.m.

			Number present
Lecture I	Characteristics of English Parliament during XVIIIth Century	Wed. Apr. 25	47
Lecture II	Scottish Constitution—Nature of the Parliament	Th. Apr. 26	40
Lecture III	Scottish Constitution—The Union	Fri. Apr. 27	37
Lecture IV	Irish Constitution—Nature of Parliament	Sat. Apr. 28	30
Lecture V	Irish Constitution—Union	Tu. May 1	26
Lecture VI	Conclusions	Wed. May 2	24

---

* This 1906 lecture scheme and the 1908 lecture scheme below (app. IX) have been included to illustrate both the variability of Dicey's schemes of comparative constitutional lectures and two variants later than those schemes from which the lectures in Parts I and II have been derived. The earlier, 1905 lecture scheme has not been included because of its similarity to the 1906 scheme (although the 1905 scheme also included an 'English Constitutionalism under George III' lecture).

† The dates stated on a few of the pages below were added in later manuscript notes. They correspond with the dates in this lecture schedule, but both the dated and undated Analyses may have been copies of those that were previously used.

I

Characteristics of English Parliament during the XVIIIth Century

A. The Parliament an **Historical** Parliament
  I. An *historically* developed Parliament
     (Contrast French, Italian, or Belgian Parliaments)
  II. A *continuously* developed Parliament
     (Contrast German Empire, Swiss Confederation)

B. Power of Parliament Not Controlled by **Written** Constitution
  I. Constitution not to be found in any *document*
  II. Constitution the result of *legal decisions* or conflicts
  III. Working of constitution depends on *conventions*

C. Parliament a ***Sovereign*** Parliament
  I. *Legislative* sovereignty
  II. *Parliamentary* executive
  III. *Undivided* sovereignty (i.e. no federalism)

D. Parliament an English Parliament

(See Bagehot, *English Constitution*;
Boutmy, *Études de Droit Constitutionnel*;
Boutmy, *Le Développement de la Constitution*;
Gneist, vol. 2, *History of English Constitution*, chs 44–57.)

Dates in Scottish Constitutional History

1184	Great Council of King, Prelates, etc. Barons, great and small
1326	Parliament (at Cambuskenneth) contains representatives (?) of Burghs (Rait. p. 31)
1367	Lords, or Committee of Articles (Terry, p. 102; Rait, p. 40)
1455–	Burgesses (Commissioners for Burghs) from this date to be found in every Parliament (Rait, p. 30)
1469	Election of Commissioners placed in hands of town council, which is elected by outgoing council, and members of outgoing council combined with members of new council elected Burgh officers, including Parliamentary Commissioners (Terry, pp 56, 57)
1567	Barons of Shires made really representatives
1603–	Union of Crowns
1604–	*Calvin's Case*
1607–	Bill for Union between England and Scotland rejected by House of Commons
1651	Charles II crowned King of Scotland
1653–59	Union of England and Ireland during Protectorate
1660–1	Reaction—end of Union and restoration with Lords of Articles
1666–	Scots wish for Union
1670–	Proposals rejected by England
1689–90	Revolution—Proclamation of William and Mary—Claim of Right—Abolition of Lords of Articles—Legislative independence of Parliament
1690–	Increase in number of representatives of Shires
1703–4–	Hostility between England and Scotland. Act of Security, Scotland. Alien Act, England
1706–	Commissioners to treat for Union
1707	*Treaty of Union*
1712–	Bill to repeal Union nearly carried in House of Lords

II

Scottish Constitution—Nature of the Parliament

Th. 26 Apr 1906

A. Points of Likeness between English and Scottish Parliaments
  1. A natural constitutional growth
  2. A national Parliament
  3. Almost a continuous development
  4. Power greatly increased by Revolution of 1689
B. Essential Differences between English and Scottish Parliaments
Formal
Scottish Parliament:—
  1. was a one-House Parliament
  2. contained different classes of members
     (i) Officers of State (nominees of Crown) (Terry, pp 1–9; 2 Porritt, pp 78, 79)
     (ii) The clergy (bishops and abbots) (Terry, p. 11; 2 Porritt, pp 92–6)
     (iii) The nobility (Terry, pp 14–18; 2 Porritt, pp 93, 94)
     (iv) Barons of Shires (county members) (Terry, pp 17–46; 2 Porritt, pp 73–91)
     (v) Commissioners of Burghs (borough members) (Terry, pp 47–62; 2 Porritt, chs 33, 34)
  3. was not a representative body in same sense as English House of Commons
     (i) Limited number of electors (Terry, pp 39 and 58)
     (ii) Presence of officials
     (iii) Elected members not appointed through general election (Terry, pp 27–30)
  4. was a comparatively small body never much above 200 (Terry, p. 3)
Difference of Character
  1. Delegation by Parliament of legislative power to permanent committee (Lords of Articles) (Terry, pp 103–20; 2 Porritt, pp 27, 28, 76, 77, 85–7, 107–8; Rait, pp 40–55)
  2. Down to 1689 Parliament neither a legislative nor a debating body but rather an official body
  3. From 1689 Parliament possessed legislative sovereignty without control of executive, i.e. without parliamentary executive (compare Scottish Constitution 1689–1707 with Irish (Grattan's) Constitution, 1782–1800)

4. Parliament never the centre of Scottish history, nor, to 1689, anything like the main representative of national sentiment

(See Rait, *The Scottish Parliament before Union of Crowns* (1603);
Terry, *The Scottish Parliament, 1603–1707*;
Porritt, *The Unreformed House of Commons*, vol. 2, pt. V, chs 31–9;
Mackinnon, *Union of England and Scotland*)

III

Scottish Constitution—The Union

Fri. Apr. 27, 1906

A. The Union of the Crowns
   I. *Its effect in Scotland*
      1. Increase of royal power (Rait, p. 38)
      2. Government removed, to great extent to London
      3. Decline in Scottish trade (?)
      4. Scotch cease to be aliens and hold offices in England
      5. Disorder on Border diminished, but no freedom of trade
   II. *Desire of Kings and some statesmen for complete Union*
      1. James, 1607
      2. Charles II, 1666–70
      3. William III, 1702

B. Actual Union during Protectorate
   I. *A union in reality of conquest*
   II. *Union meant free trade throughout united commonwealth*
   III. *The essential difference between this Union and Union of 1707*

C. The Restoration

D. Scottish Parliamentary Independence
   I. *Only period of true parliamentary government in Scotland. Extension of Parliamentary power*
   II. *Relation between English and Scottish Executive and Parliament difficult*
      1. Presbyterian intolerance
      2. Darien Scheme
      3. Judicial murder of Captain Green (Mathieson, pp 102, 103)
      4. Open hostility between Scotland and England
         Act of Security (Scotland)
         Alien Act (England)

E. The Union
   I. *Circumstances which made for Union*
      1. Economical needs of Scotland
      2. Impossibility of maintaining existing arrangements
      3. Interest of Kirk in Protestant succession, and security given by Union against Jacobite reaction
      4. Parliament not associated in Scotland with Scottish nationality
      5. Influence of statesmen greater than at any other period of British history
   II. *Characteristics of Union*
      1. A distinct bargain
      2. An incorporative as contrasted with a federal union
      3. Freedom of trade throughout the whole of Great Britain
      4. Church establishments, laws, and institutions of each country left, as far as possible, untouched

F. Effect of Union
  I. *Immediate* effects (2 Porritt, chs 31, 32)
   1. System of political management
   2. Combined action of Scottish members in Scottish affairs
      (i) To lighten Scottish taxation
      (ii) To obtain office for Scottish members and Scotsmen
   3. Absentee nobility
   4. Corruption of Scottish electors
   5. English jealousy of Scotland
   6. Scotsmen in Colonial Service
   7. Scottish members increase influence of Crown
   8. Breach of spirit of Union and desire for its repeal
      Patronage Act, 1712
      Toleration Act, 1712
      Christmas Vacation Act, 1712
      Attempted repeal 1713
  II. *Ultimate* effects
   1. Free trade throughout Great Britain
   2. Union or free trade relieved Scottish distress?
   3. Complete moral union before 1789

(See especially Mackinnon, *Union of England and Scotland*.)

Dates in Irish Constitutional History

1295	Members for counties sent to Parliament
1341	Burgesses appear in Parliament
1494–	Poynings' Law
1613	Creation of Boroughs by James I
1654–60	Union with England under Protectorate
1692	Exclusion of Roman Catholics from Parliament and members raised to full number (300)
1698	Molyneux's book on independence of Irish Parliament
1719	Act (6 Geo. I. c. 5) declaring Ireland subject to English legislation
1724	Swift's *Drapier's Letters*
1727	Disfranchisement of Roman Catholics
1748–	Lucas's agitation for parliamentary independence
1767	Octennial Act
1769	Contest about Money Bills
1779	Agitation in favour of freedom of trade
1782	Legislative independence (Grattan's Constitution) 1782–1800
1793	Enfranchisement of Roman Catholics
1795	Arrival of Lord Fitzwilliam as Viceroy, and recall
1798	Rebellion
1799	Opposition to Union
1800	Act of Union—39 & 40 Geo. III. c. 67

IV

The Irish Constitution—Nature of the Parliament during the XVIIIth Century

A. Points in which the Irish Parliament Resembled the English Parliament
    I. *The Irish Parliament was in form an imitation of English Parliament*
        1. House of Lords and House of Commons
        2. Electoral franchises like those of England
        3. The Privy Council
    II. *Large number of nomination boroughs and of constituencies subject to influence of Crown or of patrons*

B. Essential Differences between the Irish Parliament and the English Parliament
    I. *The Irish Parliament was 'made' rather than 'grew'*
    II. *The Irish Parliament was a colonial and never a really sovereign Parliament*
        1. Subject to legislation of English Parliament
        2. Subject to restraints imposed by Poynings' Law, 1494–1782
        3. Extensive power of Irish Privy Council
        4. Under Grattan's Constitution (1782) Irish Parliament possessed legislative independence, but did not possess control of executive
    III. *Irish Parliament not the Parliament of the Irish Roman Catholics and therefore not the Parliament of the majority of the Irish people*
        1. Roman Catholics excluded from seats in Parliament, and from parliamentary franchise
        2. From 1793 to 1800 Roman Catholics admitted to parliamentary franchise but not to seats in Parliament
    IV. *Irish Parliament needed support of England*

C. Irish Parliament became the Centre of Irish Political Life

(See Porritt, vol. 2, pt. VI, chs 40–57;
Ball, *Irish Legislative Systems*;
Lecky, *Hist. England XVIIIth Century*, vol. 2, pp 412–37; vol. 4, ch. 16; vol. 6, chs 24 and 25.)

V
Irish Constitution—The Union

A. Constitution of 1782 (Grattan's Constitution)
   I. *Constitution the result of a revolutionary movement* (Volunteer Movement, 1778–83)
   II. *Characteristics of Constitution*
      1. Legislative independence of Irish Parliament
         Repeal of 6 Geo. 1, c. 5 (by 22 Geo. 3, c. 53—English)
         Renunciation Act, 1782–3 (23 Geo. 3, c. 28—English)
         Repeal of Poynings' Law (22 Geo. 3, c. 47—Irish)
      2. No appeal from Irish Courts to English House of Lords
      3. Irish Parliament does not obtain control over Irish executive
      4. No reform of Parliament
      5. No extension to Roman Catholics of parliamentary rights
      6. No diminution of influence exercisable by executive
B. The Union
   I. *Circumstances which made for Union*
      1. Difficult relation between Great Britain and Ireland under Constitution of 1782
         Simple repeal question
         Act of Renunciation
         Impossibility of Parliamentary Reform
         Failure of attempt to carry through commercial treaty (6 Lecky, pp 388–403)
         Different theories as to Regency
         Enfranchisement of Roman Catholics—1792–3
      2. The Rebellion of 1798 and foreign war
      3. The desirability for Ireland of free trade
      4. The success of the Union with Scotland
   II. *The provisions of the Union*
C. Apparent Similarity and Real Dissimilarity between Union with Ireland and Union with Scotland
   I. *Apparent similarity*
      1. Union of Parliaments
      2. Establishment of free trade
   II. *Dissimilarity*
      1. Union with Scotland an elaborate bargain—Union with Ireland a legislative *coup d'état*
      2. Union with Scotland the consequence of several previous attempts at union whilst Union with Ireland the result of pressing dangers
      3. Union with Scotland in no sense compelled by England

4. Union with Scotland gave security to the Church of the majority of the Scottish people. Union with Ireland gave security to Church of minority of Irish people
5. The Scottish Parliament did not, whilst the Irish Parliament did, represent feeling of nationality

(See Ball, *Irish Legislative Systems*, chs 10–13;
Lecky, *Hist. Eng. XVIIIth Cent.*, vol. 4, ch. 17; vol. 6, chs 24, 25, esp. pp 313–19.)

VI

Conclusions

I. *Different forms of parliamentary government*
   1. A Parliament with legislative authority and with control of the Executive (England)
   2. Parliament with very incomplete legislative authority and hardly any control of executive (Scotland, 1603–1689/90, and Ireland, 1700–1782)
   3. Parliament with legislative authority, but without control of the executive (Scotland 1689–1707, and Ireland 1782–1800)

II. *The essential distinction between different forms* of parliamentary government is the existence or non-existence of a parliamentary executive

III. *The doctrine of Parliamentary sovereignty has in England prevented the foundation of any federal system*
   This illustrated by—
   1. history of Union with Scotland and of Union with Ireland
   2. failure of attempts under Protectorate to place limit on Parliamentary authority

IV. *A bad system of representation may nevertheless in fact represent the wishes of a nation* (Scottish representative system, 1689 to 1832)
   NB Note the two different objects of representative government, *viz.*
   1. The attainment of good government
   2. The attainment of government in accordance with the wishes of the governed

V. *Why Union with Scotland much more successful than Union with Ireland*
   1. Union with Scotland originated in a bargain, Union with Ireland in necessities of moment
   2. Union with Scotland did not, whilst Union with Ireland did, destroy a Parliament round which national feeling centred
   3. Union with Scotland secured position of Church of Scottish people. Union with Ireland brought no benefit to Church of majority of Irish people
   4. Union with Scotland left no great questions unsettled which required immediate settlement. Union with Ireland left at least four such questions unsettled, *viz*—
   Position of Roman Catholics
   Position of the state Church
   Parliamentary Reform
   Land tenure

VI. *Relation in case of both Unions between law and opinion*

Scottish Union
      1. No nationalist or democratic theories
      2. Decline in religious dogmatism and increasing enthusiasm for the promotion of material interests
      3. The fear of a Restoration

Irish Union
      1. Prevalence of revolutionary and, to a certain extent, of nationalist theories
      2. Misconceptions as to the political tendencies of Roman Catholicism

IX

Scheme of Lectures, 1908

Easter & Trinity Terms 1908[*]
Comparative Study of the Constitution
Eight Lectures

Daily at 9 a.m. (Saturdays excepted)

			Number present
Lecture 1	General Characteristics of Existing English Constitution	Tu. 5 May	34
Lecture 2	English Constitutionalism under George III	Wed. 6 May	35
Lecture 3	French Constitutionalism	Th. 7 May	36
Lecture 4	The Constitution of 1653 (Instrument of Government)	Fr. 8 May	33
Lecture 5	Constitution of 1653 (cont.)	Mon. 11 May	28
Lecture 6	Scottish Parliament	Tu. 12 May	25
Lecture 7	Scottish Parliament (cont.)	Wed. 13 May	28
Lecture 8	Party Government	Th. 14 May	26

[*] The manuscripts for the lecture Analyses below are attached to the 1908 lecture schedule manuscript in the Dicey Papers but were not dated and may have been inserted later or copied mainly or exactly from those used for earlier lecture schemes. The Analysis for the fifth lecture of the 1908 scheme is certainly an exact copy of that for the second lecture of the 1906 scheme and has therefore been omitted here. Further, this 1908 lecture schedule is the product of various amendments. The schedule and the Analyses below, although derived from manuscripts attached together in the same bundle, do not correspond closely in content, sequence, or numbering. Presumably, Dicey changed or did not adhere to his initial schedule, and the Analyses below were then not consistently renumbered.

I

General Characteristics of Existing English Constitutionalism

A. Constitution an **Historical** Constitution
    I. An *historically* developed constitution
       (Contrast French, Italian, or Belgian Constitutions)
    II. A *continuously* developed constitution
       (Contrast German Empire, Swiss Confederation)
    III. Constitution the product of *historical conditions*

B. Constitution an **Unwritten** Constitution
    I. Not to be found in any *law* or *document*
    II. Result of *legal decisions* or conflicts
    III. The working of constitution depends on *conventions*

C. Constitution a *Parliamentary* Constitution
    I. Parliamentary *sovereignty*
    II. Parliamentary *executive*

D. Constitution a **Democratic** Constitution

E. Constitution a **Unitary** Constitution

F. Constitution an **Imperial** Constitution

G. A Constitution which in practice Recognises the System of **Party** Government

(See Bagehot, *The English Constitution*;
Boutmy, *Études de Droit Constitutionnel*;
Boutmy, *Le Développement de la Constitution*.)

II

The Constitution of 1653 (Instrument of Government)

A. General Character of Puritan Constitutionalism
   I. *Both a revival and a revolution*
   II. *Different types of Puritan constitutionalism*

B. Constitution of 1653
   Revival
   1. Protector (Instrument of Government, Arts 1–6, 24, 30)
   2. Council of State (ibid. Arts 2, 21, 23, 25, 26)
   3. Parliament

   Revolution
   1. Abolition of monarchy and House of Lords
   2. Written and rigid constitutions (Arts 24, 35–9)
   3. Union with Ireland and Scotland (Arts 1, 9, and 10)
   4. Religious toleration (Arts 35–8)
   5. Standing army (Arts 27–9)
   6. Relation of executive to legislature

C. Comparison between Constitution of 1653 and
   I. *Democratic ideals of XVIIth century, and democratic institutions of XXth century*
   II. The *Constitution of 1908*

(See Act declaring England to be a Commonwealth, *Gardiner's Constitutional Documents*, p. 297;
Instrument of Government (Constitution of 1653) ibid., p. 314;
Agreement of the People, ibid., p. 270;
Masson, *Life of Milton*, iv, pp 10, 542;
Gardiner, *History of the Commonwealth*, ii, ch. XXVIII;
Gneist, *History of English Constitution*, ii. (English translation), p. 257.)

III

English Constitutionalism under George the Third

A. Outward likeness to Modern Constitutionalism
    1. Forms similar
    2. Government parliamentary in full sense
    3. Government national
    4. Absence of arbitrary power

B. Differences from Modern Constitutionalism
   I. Difference in **form** of constitution
      1. Parliament a *British* Parliament
      2. Parliament a *Protestant* and (practically) a Church of England Parliament
      3. Parliament an *unreformed* Parliament
   II. Differences in **working** of institutions
      1. The influence of the Crown
      2. The influence of the aristocracy
      3. The position of the Cabinet
   III. Differences in **spirit** of the constitution
      1. Form of constitution practically unchangeable
      2. Constitution rested on predominance of certain classes
      3. Constitution neither in theory nor in practice democratic
      4. Executive supported by Crown had considerable independence
      5. Public life might be a professional career
      6. Limited sphere of state's activity

(See 1 Porritt, *Unreformed House of Commons*, chs 1–19 & 28–30;
Paley, *Moral Philosophy*, ii, bk. VI, ch. VII;
Lecky, *Democracy*, i, ch. II, especially pp 202–16; 253–313;
Lilly and Wallis, *Law Specially Affecting Catholics*, pp 1–33;
Boutmy, *Études de Droit Constitutionnel*.)

IV

French Constitutionalism

A. Relation between French History and French Constitutionalism
    1. The Crown
    2. The States General
    3. The Parliaments

B. General Ideas Governing French Constitutionalism
    I. The *nature of a constitution*
    II. The *sovereignty of the people*
        1. Nothing between the state and individual citizens
        2. Universal suffrage
        3. Constitution cannot be changed by ordinary legislature
    III. *Separation of powers*
    IV. *Authority of executive*

C. Existing Constitution
    1. Universal suffrage
    2. Absence of judicial control
    3. Executive
    4. Parliamentary government

D. Comparison between French Constitution and English Constitution
    1. In both parliamentary government
    2. In French Constitution no direct connection with historical development
    3. In France basis of Constitution is will of individual citizens
    4. In France the sphere of the judges is wholly non-political
    5. In France attempt has been made to form a non-parliamentary executive, but has failed

(See Lowell, *Governments and Parties in Continental Europe*, i, chs I & II;
Boutmy, *Studies in Constitutional Law* (translation), pp 141–75;
Hélie, *Les Constitutions de la France*, Constitutions of 1791 and 1875;
Borgeaud, *Établissement et Revision des Constitutions*, bk. II, pp 249–307;
I Chéruel, *Institutions Moeurs et Coutumes de la France*, art. 'Constitution',
    art. 'États Generaux', and 2 Chéruel, art. 'Parlement';
I Stephen, *Lectures on History of France*, Lects X–XII, pp 343 & following.)

V

Scottish Constitution—Nature of the Parliament*

VII

The Treaty of Union

Introduction—Circumstances which Led to Treaty of Union
1. Near approach to permanent separation or civil war
   Act anent Peace and War (Scottish)
   Act of Security (Scottish)
   Alien Act (English)
2. Necessity of Union for power of England
3. Necessity of free trade with England and share in colonial Empire for prosperity of Scotland
4. Necessity for both countries of maintaining Revolution Settlement and Protestantism
5. Predominance of secular interests
6. Merits and defects of Scottish Parliament

A. Steps by which Treaty of Union Carried
B. General Principles Underlying Treaty of Union
   1. Absolute political unity (Arts I–III)
   2. Complete freedom of trade, partnership in commercial advantages, and common system of taxation, etc. (Arts IV–XVIII)
   3. Security for Revolution Settlement and the established Churches of each Kingdom (Art. II, and Art. XXV, ss 2–11)
   4. No interference with institutions or law of either country, except in so far as necessary for above objects. (See especially Arts XVIII–XXI.)
   NB Note the existence of belief in unchangeable laws (See Art. XVIII and especially Art. XXV)

(See Mackinnon, *Union of England and Scotland*, especially chs IV, VI–IX; 8 Burton, *History of Scotland*, chs 86, 87.)

---

* The Analysis for this lecture was copied exactly from that for the second lecture of the 1906 lecture scheme and has therefore been omitted. See pp 323 f. above. No Analysis available in the bundle of manuscripts was numbered as the sixth. See p. 333, n., above.

Dates in Scottish Constitutional History

1184	Parliament consisting of King, Prelates, Barons, great and small
1326	Parliament at Cambuskenneth contained representatives of Burghs
1367	Origin of Lords of Articles
1455–	Burgesses to be found in every Parliament
1469	Election of Commissioners for Burghs placed in hands of town council which was itself elected by outgoing council. The members of outgoing council, combined with members of new council, elected Burgh officers, including Parliamentary Commissioners, i.e. MPs
1567	Barons of Shires made really representatives
1585–87	Acts establish residential qualification for county representatives and also property qualification
1603–	James VI Scotland, and James I England—Union of Crowns
1604–	*Calvin's Case*
1606–	Bill for Union between England and Scotland rejected in Commons but the Hostile Border Laws repealed
1641	Lords of Articles abolished and other reforms carried
1651	Charles II crowned
1654	Union of England and Scotland under Commonwealth—establishment of free trade between the two countries
1661	Restoration—Lords of Articles and Episcopacy restored. Extension of county franchise
1669	Residential qualification of county electors and representatives abolished
1681–	Extension of county franchise and mode of election regulated
1689–	Revolution. Abdication of James VII. Claim of right. Proclamation of William and Mary
1690–	Lords of Articles abolished. County representation. Additional representation of counties, i.e. voting power increased by 26 members
1699–	Failure of Darien Scheme
1702–	Commissioners to treat for Union, but no agreement
1704–5	Hostile feeling between England and Scotland
1706–	The Union Commission
1707	Act of Union
1712	Rights of patronage restored
1713	Bill to repeal Union
1715	Stuart Rebellion
1736	Porteous Mob
1745	Last Stuart rebellion
1832	Reform Act

VIII

Party-Government or Party System

Introduction
    1. Party government not essential to popular or parliamentary government
    2. Inconsistent views as to party system

A.   What is Meant by Party System

B.   Conditions Requisite for Existence, or at any rate Beneficial Working, of Party System
    1. Loyalty to constitution
    2. Party divisions dependent upon real differences of principle
    3. Existence of two, and if possible of not more than two, parties

C.   Merits and Demerits of Party System
Merits
    1. A check on dominance of private interest
    2. Production of qualified leaders
    3. Critics of government policy
Demerits—Inherent
    1. Measures not considered on merits
    2. Policy of Government maimed by Opposition
    3. Waste of capacity
    4. Exaggeration of differences
Demerits—Owing to failure of necessary conditions
    Summed up in transformation of parties into factions

D.   Mitigation of Evils of Party System
    I. *Party system not the essence of parliamentary government*
    II. *Mitigations*
        1. Separation from party system of judicial and administrative bodies
        2. Politics not made a lucrative profession
        3. Questions of policy kept as far as possible outside party system

E.   Explanation of Inconsistent Views with regard to Party System

(See Lowell, *Governments and Parties*, vol. 1, pp 69–108;
Bodley, *France*, vol. 2, pp 75, 76, 163–5; 297–306;
Ostrogorski, *Democracy and Organization of Political Parties*.)

Index

American constitutionalism
see also **United States**
ancient constitutionalism,
and 211 n21
Constituent Assembly,
distinguished 86
Constitution as supreme
law 80
Constitutional
Convention 86–8
advantages of xxviii,
86–7, 153
amendment of the
Constitution 86
Constitutionalism of the
Commonwealth
similarities
between 87–8
democratic
constitutionalism 72,
158–9, 246
English constitutionalism,
distinguished 80–8
English ideas, based
on 76–9
form of the
Constitution 79
rule of law 78
undeniable historical fact,
as 76
extra-parliamentary
executive 275, 282,
296, 297
federal government, as 76
Governor of State
election 81
powers 81
legislature, independence
from 81
historical constitution 178,
183
judiciary
position of 83–5
legislature
congress 82
executive, separation
from 282
powers, limits to 87
primary law-making
body, as 82
prohibited laws 82–3

State legislatures 82–3
subordinate law-making
body, as 82–3
Montesquieu
influence, of 79
non-parliamentary
executive
Governor of State 81
President 80–1
parliamentarianism 265
parliamentary
government 276
President
Congress, relationship
with 81
election 80
executive 282–4
powers 80–1
Puritan
constitutionalism 48,
59
representative
government 220, 223,
227
Republican government,
as 76
rigid constitution 235, 236,
238
self-government 299, 300
separation of powers 79
unresponsive
constitution 245, 247
written constitution 233,
234
'Analyses'
meaning, of xix
ancient constitutionalism
administrative system
absence pre-Roman
Empire 210–11
ancient and modern
historical division 202–3
Church
non-existence, of 207–8
city-states
basis, of 204–5
country,
distinguished 205 n13
differences between
ancient and
modern 212–13

terminology 204, 205
township,
distinguished 205 n13
civilized society
common traits 196–7
democracy
development of
198–202, 212
feudalism
definition 208
non-existence of 208–10
introduction 193–4
modern constitutionalism
differences
between 204–11
proof of
similarities 200–1
similarities with
194–203
representative government
non-existence of 205–6
slavery
basis of 206–7
social development
resembling modern
life 196–8
sovereignty 195
'state'
concept of 194–6
terminology 195, 204
Arnold, Dr
ancient constitutionalism
relevance to modern
times 193
chivalry
condemnation of 210
cyclical approach to
history 202, 203
historical judgment affected
by modern bias
199–200

Bagehot
Cabinet and Presidential
government,
distinguished 240–1
Belgium
constitutional articles as
political maxims 237
droit administratif,
compared 314

Belgium (*cont.*)
   historical constitution 17
   loyalty to the constitution 130
   parliamentary
      constitutionalism 158
   parliamentary
      executive 11, 239
   party system
      Civil Service
         independent, from 134
      judicial and
         administrative bodies
         independent, from 134
   rigid constitution, as 236
   written constitution 22
Bentham
   Utilitarianism 152
Bishops of the Restoration 30
Bismarck
   'blood and iron' policy 107
   constitutional conflict
      (1862–1866) 116–19
Blackstone
   analytical method of study 4
Bogdanor, Vernon
   Dicey Papers
      discovered, by xiv,
         xiv n14
      notes xvi
Boutmy
   constitution
      'type' of 95
   universal suffrage 176
Bryce, James
   flexible and rigid
      constitutions 235
   letters to xii, xiii
Burke
   institutions governing
      character of
      nations 152
   party system 126, 136
   professional politician,
      as 68, 69

Carlyle
   constitutions
      diminution in
         importance 153
   parliamentarianism
      140, 141
civic virtue
   legal transplantation,
      and xxvi–xxvii

Cobden
   Prussian government 108
Comparative Constitutional
   Lectures *see also*
   methods of study
   constitutional
      principles xxxv–xl
   context
      reflection of xl–xli
   historical context xi–xii
   implications and
      significance of xx–xlv
   institutional focus xxx–xxxv
   method xxi–xxx
      analytical, comparative
         and historical method,
         distinguished
         xxii–xxiii
      comparative
         method xxi–xxii, xxiii,
         xxix–xxx
      educational mission
         xxi–xxii
      historical method xxii
      legal transplantation
         xxvi–xxvii
      spirit xxiv–xxvi
comparative
   constitutionalism
   difficulties facing
      parliamentary
      government
      moral authority of
         representative bodies 160
      parliamentarianism
         160–1
   general conclusions 156–65
   institutions as the embodiment
      of a nation 161–5
   origin of the term xii
   parliamentary governments
      exhibit essential
      differences
      democratic
         constitutionalism
         158–9
      monarchical
         constitutionalism 159
      parliamentary
         constitutionalism 158
   similarity between modern
      constitutions
      democratic
         foundations 157

      elected houses or
         chambers 156–7
      written or enacted
         constitutions 157
'**Comparative Study of the**
   Constitution' xvii,
   xxiii, xxvi, xxix
   text 4–165
'**Comparative Study of**
   Constitutions' xii, xviii
   text 169–257
Constitution of 1653
   army
      Parliament, independence
         from 51
      provision for standing
         army 50–1
   Council of State
      appointment 54–5
      election of Protector 55
      executive, as part of 54–5
      nature, of 289
      Privy Council,
         compared 42, 54, 289
      US Senate, compared 55,
         61
   executive
      creation, of 53
      constitution 54
      Council of State 54–5
      judicial body 57–8
      Parliament 55–7
      Protector 54
      relation between
         constituent
         bodies 54–8
   general character 39, 288
   House of Lords
      abolition of 43
   Instrument of Government
      contained, within 41
   Parliamentary
      Constitutional Bill,
      compared 292
   record of relation between
      Crown and legislature,
      as 292–3
   judicial body
      arbiters of
         constitutionality, as 58
      executive, as part of 57–8
   laws (amending the
      Constitution)
      void nature, of 47

laws (in violation of the
    Constitution)
  classification 45–6
laws (ordinary)
  Parliament passing
    without consent of
    Protector 46–7, 290
  Protector compelling
    reconsideration by
    Parliament 46–7
laws (touching the
    fundamentals)
  liberty, restrictions
    to 47–8
  religious freedom,
    restrictions to 47–8,
    290
modern constitution,
    compared 58–9
monarchy
  absence of hereditary
    monarch 43
Parliament
  army independence 51
  distribution of seats 48,
    49, 289
  executive, as part of 55–7
  form and character 42–3,
    289–90
  franchise 48, 49, 289
  legislative authority 55–6,
    57
  Members of Parliament,
    numbers 50, 289
  ordinary laws passed
    without consent of
    Protector 46–7, 290
  powers 56–7
  reform 48–50
  Reform Act 1832, and 49,
    50
  rotten boroughs,
    abolition of 48, 49
Protector 288
  appointment for life 42,
    54
  executive, as part of 54
  monarch, compared 42,
    54
  'one person' 37, 43, 55
  ordinary laws, power to
    compel reconsideration
    by Parliament 46–7
  powers 42

revenues 42
religious freedom
  conflicting laws deemed
    null and void 53
  nature of 51
  penalties removed 53
  persecution
    forbidden 52–3
  Protestants guaranteed
    toleration 53
  restrictions, to 51–2
revival
  Council of State 42
  Parliament 42–3
  Protector, position of 41–2
revolution
  executive and judicial
    body, relation of 53–8
  House of Lords, absence
    of 43
  monarchy, absence of 43
  Parliament, reform
    of 48–50
  religious freedom 51–3
  standing army 50–1
  union incorporative of
    Scotland and Ireland 48
  written and rigid
    constitution 43–8
union, Scotland and Ireland
  with England 48
written and rigid constitution
  intended
    immutability 44–5
  original nature of 43–4
constitutional statutes
  rigid constitutions, and
    43–8, 57–8, 235–8,
    269–71
constitutionalism *see also*
    particular contexts eg
    Constitutionalism of
    the Commonwealth
  capacious constitutionalism
    xlv–xlvii
Constitutionalism of the
    Commonwealth
  see also **Constitution**
    of 1653; Puritan
    constitutionalism
  capaciousness of Dicey's
    thought xlv–xlvii
  Constitution of 1653
    general character 39

historical background
  to 30–2
legislative authority
  'one person' 37, 43, 55
paradox between reaction
  and innovation
constitutionalism 31–2
foreign policy 30–1
law reform 31
theology 30
United States
  development in 61
constitutions *see also*
  historical
  constitutions
classification 233–48
flexible
  meaning 235
  rigid, compared 238
  unwritten 235
imitation
  cause of evil, as 153
law of a constitution 234–5
opinion, responsive
  to 243–8
  conditions favourable,
    to 248
  democratic character of
    constitution 246–7
  examples 243–5
  flexible constitution 247
  irresponsive constitution,
    distinguished 246–8
  responsive constitution,
    as 243
opinion, unresponsive
  to 243–8
  democratic character of
    constitution 246–7
  examples 245–6
  flexible constitution
    247
  irresponsive constitution,
    as 243
  responsive constitution,
    distinguished
    246–8
  rigid constitution 247
parliamentary executive,
  with 238–43
  Cabinet government,
    correspondence
    with 242
  demerits 241

constitutions (*cont.*)
  legislative power and
    power to appoint or
    dismiss 239–40
  meaning 239
  merits 241
  principle of classification,
    as 239
  prosperity, creating
    bad institutions,
      hindering 154–5
    relationship,
      between 152–6
  non-parliamentary
    executive, with 238–43
  meaning 239
  merits and demerits 241
  Presidential government,
    correspondence
    with 241
  principle of classification,
    as 239
  responsiveness of xli–xlii
  rigid
    constitutional articles as
      maxims of political
      morality 237
    constitutionally
      inconsistent law a
      nullity 236
    degrees of 236
    flexible, compared 238
    meaning 235
    methods for maintenance,
      of 236–7
    nullification by
      courts 237
    Puritan constitutionalism,
      characteristic of 33
    written 235
  semi-parliamentary
    executive 242–3
  spirit, of xxii n39, xxv n68
    concept, development
      of xxiii–xxiv
    definition, difficulty
      of xiii n8, xxiii, 70
    subjective, importance
      of xxv
  unwritten xlii–xliii
    customary 234
    examples 234
    flexible constitutions 235
    meaning 22–3, 233

unenacted 233
written,
  distinguished 233
written
  enacted 233
  examples 233
  meaning 233
  Puritan constitutionalism,
    characteristic of 33
  rigid constitutions 235
  unenacted principles or
    laws underpinning 234
  unwritten,
    distinguished 233
**conventions of the
  constitution**
  constitutional principle,
    as xxxiv, xxxix, 234
  effect xxxi
  innovation of constitutional
    thought xxx
  ministerial
    responsibility xxxii
  parliamentary
    executive xxxiii
  unwritten constitution xlii,
    22, 157, 234
Cosgrove, Richard
  Dicey's abandonment of
    historical research xxii
  Dicey's Papers
    unawareness of xiii n9,
    xiv
Cromwell, Oliver
  constitutional government
    failure to overturn 179
  constitutional king, as 61
  foreign policy 30–1
  Lord Protector 288
  rule of law
    desire to establish 61
*'Development of English Law
  during the Nineteenth
  Century in connection
  with the course of
  Public opinion in
  England'* xii
Dicey Papers
  Bogdanor, Vernon
    discovered by xiv,
    xiv n14
  notes xvi
  consultation xiv

Cosgrove, Richard
  Dicey's abandonment of
    historical research xxii
  unawareness of xiii n9,
    xiv
  dictated form xv
  disordered state xvi
  editorial approach,
    to xvi–xx
  Hand, Geoffrey
    description xvi
    initial unawareness
      of xiii n9, xiv
    notes xvi
  heterogeneity xv–xvi
  Library of All Souls
    presentation, to xiv
  nature of xi, xiii, xv
  publication xv
  revision
    variation of the degree,
    of xvi
  rule of law xxxvii
  value of xv
droit adminstratif
  administrative law
    development of 310–11,
    312
  admiration for xxxviii–xxxix,
    313–14
  Continental European
    countries,
    compared 314
  demerits 313
  English system,
    compared 312, 313
  judge-made law, as 312
  merits 313–14
  misunderstandings, as
    to 308–12
  official law, and 308–9, 312
  officials, proceedings
    against 311
  nature of 307–8
  system of claims, as 309–10

English constitutionalism
  see also **Constitution
    of 1653; English
    constitutionalism of
    George III; Puritan
    constitutionalism**
  characterization xxiv,
    xlii–xlv

continuity xliii–xliv, 18,
    20
democratic 26
generally 17–28
historical xliii, 17–22
parliamentary 23–6
spontaneity xliv–xlv
Unitary 26–8
unwritten xlii–xliii, 22–3
comparative constitutional
    thought, and xl–xlv
continuous character
    xliii–xliv, 18–20
democratic character 26
existing
    constitutionalism 17–28
flexibility 23
general
    characteristics 17–28
historical character xliii,
    17–22, 172
'almost perfect'
    continuity 178
antiquity 175
continuous
    development 18–20,
    176–82
historical
    development 18
meaning of 22
originality 183–6
spontaneity 182–3
work of native
    production 20–2
institutions as the
    embodiment of
    nation 161–2
monarchical
    constitutionalism 159
parliamentary
    character 23–6, 158
government a
    parliamentary
    executive 24
Parliament a sovereign
    law-making body 23–4
Parliament at the
    centre of political
    institutions 25–6
responsive constitution,
    as 243–5
spontaneity xliv–xlv
Unitary character 26–8
unwritten xlii–xliii

meaning 22–3
English constitutionalism of
    George III (c1787)
Cabinet
    independence when
        supported by the
        Crown 73
    position of 70
corruption 67 n8
Crown
    influence, disappearance
        in modern era 67
    influence, exercise of 67
    influence, results of
        existence 67–9
    position of 66–7
differences between
    Georgian and Victorian
    constitutionalism
    form in 64–6
    spirit of the
        constitution 70–4
    working of the
        constitution 66–70
forms
    Parliament 64–6
    parliamentary
        sovereignty 70–1
Georgian and Victorian
    constitutionalism,
    compared 62–70
historical context 61–2
House of Lords
    position of 69–70
'legal country' 71
modern constitutionalism
    (c1897), compared 62
Parliament
    Great Britain, of 64
    independence of 73
    landholders,
        representing 66
    membership 64, 66
    Protestant 64–5
    unreformed 65–6
Peerage
    position of 69–70
politics as a professional
    career 68–9
predominance of certain
    classes 71
similarities between
    Georgian and Victorian
    constitutionalism

arbitrary power
    unknown 63
Cabinet government 63
constitutional
    monarchy 62
nation, supremacy of 63
Parliament, annual
    meetings 63
parliamentary
    monarchy 62
spirit of the constitution
    definition,
        difficulty of 70
state activity
    limited sphere, of
        73–4
undemocratic nature of the
    constitution 72–3
English party system *see also*
    party system
Cabinet
    appointment for specified
        duration 269
    collective and personal
        responsibility of
        members 261
    dissolution of
        Parliament 262
    executive, as a 261
    indirect election and
        dismissal by party 261
    Prime Minister as head,
        of 262
    programmes of
        legislation 262
    representation and guide
        of party, as 261
    characteristics 261–2
Constitutional Convention
    merits 271
    nature of 270
Constitutional Statute
    methods for
        submission 270–1
    nature, of 270
Crown
    arbitrator among parties,
        as 266–7
    demerits 262–5
    citizen's duty to
        the nation,
        undermined 264
    constitutional change
        demanded 263–4

English party system (*cont.*)
  factions, development
    of 265
  good administration
    sacrificed 263
  politics becomes a
    game 263
  remedies 266–73
  will of the nation
    unfulfilled 264–5
  House of Lords
    guardian of the
      constitution, as 267
  Ministers
    permanent appointment
      in certain roles 268
  Ministries
    retirement on
      formal vote of no
      confidence 267–8
  mitigations to
    demerits 265–73
  Opposition preparedness for
    government 261
  Presidential government
    introduction of 268–9
  remedies to demerits
    formal change in
      constitution,
      with 268–73
    formal change in
      the constitution,
      without 266–8
    generally 265–6
  referendum
    demerits 272–3
    merits 271–2
    nature of 270
  rigid constitution
    modes to change
      fundamental
      laws 269–73
  two opposed parties,
    requirement for 262
executives
  Cabinet government 241 n7,
    277–81
    appointment and
      dismissal, indirect 279
    development 278
    form 278
    substance 278
  committees
    French Convention 277

    Long Parliament 276–7
  extra-parliamentary
    executive 281–5
    character of 11, 281–2
    demerits 298
    merits 298
    monarchical
      executive 285
    Presidential
      executive 282–5
  introduction to 275–6
  legislative authority
    compared 293
    distinguished 24
  meaning 239
  monarchical executive
    French Imperial
      government 285
  non-parliamentary
    executive xxxii, xxxiii,
    116, 238–43
  parliamentary
    executive xxxiii,
    238–43
  Cabinet
    government 277–81
    character of xxxii, 11,
    276
    committees, government
      by 276–7
    demerits 297
    France, compared
    279–81
    government of England,
      and 24, 279
    merits 296–7
    non-parliamentary
      executive,
      distinguished xxxii,
      xxxiii, 116
  Presidential
    executive 282–5
    French Presidential
      Republic 284–5
    United States 282–4
  responsibility
    constitutional principle,
      as xxxix
  semi-parliamentary 242–3

France *see droit*
    ***administratif*; French**
    constitutionalism
Frederick the Great

    benevolent and intelligent
      despotism 107–8
  Voltaire, influence of 107–8
Freeman
  ancient and modern history
    no division, between 203
  historical method of study 4
French constitutionalism
    see also ***droit administratif***
  ancien régime
    Crown 92
    effect on
      constitutionalism 91–4
    historical constitution,
      and 188–9
    Parliaments 93–4
    States General 92–3
  anciens textes 91
  arrêts 91, 93
  characterization xxiv–xxv
  constitution
    nature, of 94–5
    'type', of 95
  Constitution of Year VIII,
    Article 75 103–4, 311
  Crown
    effect on
      constitutionalism 92
  droit administratif 103–4
  English constitutionalism,
    compared 101–3
  historical
    development 102
  judiciary 102
  parliamentary
    executive 102
  parliamentary
    government 101
  sovereign
    legislatures 101–2
  will of the people 102
  executive
    authority, of 98
    Republican Constitution,
      under 100
  garantie des
    fonctionnaires 103–4
  Great Revolution
    effect on historical
      development 90–1
  general ideas,
    governing 94–8
  historical character 17, 18,
    90, 172–4

discontinuous
  development 18–19,
    90–4, 102, 181–2
institutions as the
  embodiment of
  nation 162–3
legal authorities 90–1
monarchical
  constitutionalism 159
monarchical executive 285
parliamentarianism 139,
  160–1
parliamentary
  constitutionalism
  158
parliamentary
  sovereignty 97, 102
Parliaments
  Chambers as sovereign
    legislature 100
  effect on
    constitutionalism
    93–4
Republican Constitution
  duration 99
  executive 100
  form 99
  judicial control, absence
    of 100
  parliamentary
    government 100–1
  singular polity 99
  universal suffrage 99
separation of powers
  doctrine 97–8
sovereignty of the people
  concept 95
  constitutional change
    effected by will of the
    people 97
  no intermediate power
    between state and
    citizen 95–6
  universal suffrage 96
States General
  effect on
    constitutionalism 92–3
universal suffrage 93, 96,
  99, 315–19
  establishment 315
  suitability, reasons
    for 316–19
Fuller, Lon
  implicit law xxvi

German Empire
  see also **Prussian
    constitutionalism**
  historical character 18, 174
  discontinuous
    development 18, 19,
    178
  monarchical executive 285
  patriotism 107
  political unification 107
  Prussia
    most powerful state,
      within 107
    King as Emperor 107
Germany
  Dicey visit in 1862 116
Gneist
  historical method of study 4
Greenback Cases 236–7
Grote
  ancient constitutionalism
    historical judgment
    affected by modern
    bias 200

Hallam
  historical method of
    study 4, 5
Hand, Geoffrey
  Dicey Papers xiv, xvi
Harvard University
  Dicey lectures 1898 xii, xiii
historical constitutions
  antiquity 175
  continuity, unbroken 176–82
  defects 188–91
  examples 172–4
  features
    antiquity 175
    continuity,
      unbroken 176–82
    originality 183–6
    spontaneity 182–3
  meaning of 172–5
  merits 186–8, 190–1
  non-historical constitutions
    compared 175–86
  meaning, of 172
  originality 183–6
    meaning 183
  Roman
    constitutionalism 172,
    184–5
  spontaneity 182–3

Instrument of Government
  see **Constitution of
    1653**
Ireland
  Government of Ireland Bill
    1893 xxxi
  institutions as the
    embodiment of
    nation 164–5
  legislative independence 71,
    73
  parliament
    membership 64, 66, 289
    reform 50
  Parliament of Ireland 15,
    164, 240
  party system, affecting 127,
    135, 263, 264, 265
  union with England 4, 5,
    18, 28, 48, 164, 165
  unitary constitution,
    and 27, 28
  united Kingdom 176
Italy
  ancient constitutions 198,
    205, 206, 212
  city states 212–13
  droit administratif,
    compared 314
  establishment of the
    constitution 175
  historical constitution 185, 186
  parliamentary
    constitutionalism 158,
    160
  parliamentary executive 11,
    239
  parliamentarianism xxxii,
    139, 143, 144, 149,
    160–1
  party government 124, 130,
    131
  representative government 206,
    219, 222
  unitary government 27
  written constitution 22

Jewish law 194–5
Jowett, Benjamin
  'a Republic without
    Republicans' xxvi n74,
    xxxiv, 35
  Dicey's tutor at Balliol
    College xxvi n74

judges
  comparative study of 9–10

Kahn-Freud, Otto
  legal transplantation xxvii–xxviii

Laud, Archbishop William
  supremacy 30
'Law of the Constitution'
  canonical text, as xi
  capaciousness xlv–xlvii
  tool-kit, as xlv–xlvi
Ledru-Rolin
  universal suffrage 173
legal culture
  comparative approach, to xxv–xxvi
legal transplantation
  obstacles to xxvi–xxviii
legislatures
  executive, control over 295
  supremacy of 294–5
London School of Economics
  Dicey's lectures 1897 xi, xii n3
Lowell Institute, Boston
  Dicey lectures 1898 xii, xiii

Maine
  party government 124
  referendum 148
Mill
  government as a spontaneous product 186
methods of study
  analytical method 4
  comparative method 6–15
    clarity to English constitution, giving 7–11
    discovery of new affinities and dissimilarities between constitutions 11
    general conclusions, derivation of 13–14
    meaning of term 6
    parliamentary government, and 11–13
    supplementary to other methods, as 6–7

historical method 4–5
  defects of method 5
Mommsen
  ancient constitutionalism
  historical judgment affected by modern bias 200
Montesquieu
  American constitutionalism influence, on 79
  institutions governing character of nations 152
  legal transplantation xxvi
  l'esprit des lois xxiii, xxiv, 70
  separation of powers xxxix–xl, 97–8

non-historical constitutions *see* **historical constitutions**

Paley
  committees, government by 277
  constitution
    continuity 180
    nature, of 94
    spontaneity 182–3
  House of Commons
    unreformed nature, of 66
    representation, within 71
Parliament, English
  absolutely representative assembly, as 217–18
  comparative study, of
    right to extend authority by refusal of supplies 8–9
    right to levy taxes and pass laws 7–8
  continuous development 18–20
  Georgian Parliament (c1787)
    Great Britain, of 64
    landholders, representing 66
    membership 64
    Protestant 64–5
    unreformed 65–6
  political institutions at centre of 25–6
  reform

  Constitution of 1653 48–50
  sovereign law-making body 23–5
  Victorian Parliament United Kingdom, of 64
Parliamentarians *see* **Puritan constitutionalism**
parliamentarism
  'disease of modern Parliaments', as xxxii, 139
  groups, development of 142–3
  introduction, to 139–40
  justification 142–3
  nation's will misrepresentation, of 143
  parliamentary government, decline of
    constructive legislation, absence of 141
    effective administration, lack of 141–2
    reasons for its discredit 140–2
    public discussion 140–1
  remedies
    proportional representation 144–7
    referendum 147–9
parliamentary executive *see* **executives**
parliamentary government
  constitutionalism
    parliamentary constitutionalism 11–12, 158
    non-parliamentary constitutionalism 12
  parliamentary executive, as 24
parliamentary sovereignty
  see also **representative government**
  absolute nature, of xxxv, xlvi, 23–4, 218
  constitutional principle, as xxxv
  definition 70
  inherent limits, to xxxvi, xxxvii, xlvi
  popular sovereignty as limit, to xxxvi

practical limits to xxxvi,
xxxvii, xlvi, 222–8
'theoretically boundless'
practical and
political actuality,
distinguished xxxvi,
xxxvii
party system *see also* **English party system**
administrative bodies
separation from 134–5
advantages 125–7
conduct kept in harmony
with conscientious
belief 16–7
curb on selfishness
or treachery of
individuals 125–6
promotion of well known
leaders to office 126
ambivalence, towards 124,
135–6
Civil Service
independence,
from 134–5
conditions required for
beneficial action
nation must take real
interest in politics 133
parties not kept
together by personal
interest 131–2
party distinction based
on differences of
principle 130–1
party loyalty to
constitution 129–30
two important
parties 132
consequences of failure of
conditions 133
criticism, of xxx–xxxi
demerits (c1832–1845)
consideration of
measures on merits
impossible 127, 128
exaggeration of party
agreement and
opposition 128
government policy
thwarted by
Opposition 127
wasted capacity 127
disloyalty to the constitution

consequences of 129–30,
131
general policy
independence from 135
judges
appointment
militating against
meritocracy 134 n8
judicial bodies
separation from 134–5
meaning of 125
parliamentary government,
and 134
party government
facilitated by 125
inconsistent feelings,
towards 124
patriotic statesmanship,
and 135–6
purifying agent of party
government, as 124
Tories 125
Whigs 125
political parties
Tories 125
Whigs 125
politicians
professional career, as 68–9
Pollock, Frederick
'*The Law of the Constitution*'
political use made of xlv
popular government
success
good citizens a
requirement for 150
proportional representation
parliamentarianism
as remedy for 144–5
rejection of xxxii
representative government
remedy of defect,
as 228 n9
prosperity
constitution
as determinant of
152–6
Prussia
'blood and iron' policy 107
German Empire
most powerful state
in 107
Prussian King as
Emperor 107
military success 107

Prussian constitutionalism
see also **Bismarck**;
Frederick the Great;
German Empire
administration
strength of 108, 109
army
monarch as true
commander-in-
chief 111
characterization xxv
civil service
monarch as head of 111
constitutional conflict
(1862–1866) 116–19
constitutional powers
principle underpinning
exercise 115–19
Dicey's interest in 116
English constitutionalism,
compared 119–21
similarities 119
executive
parliamentary and
non-parliamentary,
distinguished 116
historical context 107–9
institutions as the
embodiment of
nation 163
military
constitutionalism 109,
121
Ministers
position of 112–13, 120
monarchical
constitutionalism 159
monarchy
absolute monarchy 109
appointment of
Ministry 111–12
hereditary civil list 113
hereditary revenues 113
legislative powers
independent of
Parliament 113–14
true head and governor
of the country 110–11,
120
true head of the
executive 111–13
Parliament
legislative powers
114–15, 120

Prussian constitutionalism (*cont.*)
   parliamentary sovereignty 117
   prerogatives of the Crown 114
   public law
      fundamental principles 110–14
      legislative powers independent of Parliament 113–14
      Ministers, position of 112–13
      monarch, powers of 110–13
   Royal ordinances types of 113

Puritan constitutionalism
   see also **Constitution of 1653**
   Agreement of the People nature of 37–9
   characterization 32–41, 290–5
   common elements 327
   differing forms 37–41
   common characteristics
      exclusion from political rights 35–6
      fixed or written constitution 33
      parliament meeting at regular intervals 33–4
      religious freedom or toleration 34–5
      respect for the foundations of society 36–7
      rigid constitution 33
      union of England and Scotland 37
   conservatism of revolutionists 37
   Constitution of 1653 general character 39
   Cromwell rule of law, and 61
   Cromwellian constitutionalists 39
   Democrats nature of 37
   oppositions to 40
   differing forms
      Agreement of the People 37–9
      governmental or Cromwellian constitutionalists 39
      Parliamentarians 39–41
   electoral disqualifications 35–6
   fundamental laws 33
   guaranteed rights 33
   monarchical constitutionalism 159
   paradox between reaction and innovation
      constitutionalism 31–2
      foreign policy 30–1
      law reform 31
      theology 30
   Parliamentarians aims 40, 41
   parliamentary reform
      franchise, improvements to 34
      meeting at regular intervals 33–4
      redistribution of seats 34
   religious freedom or toleration
      direct persecution, abolition of 34–5
      Protestants given absolute freedom 35
      restricted toleration 35
   Republican Parliamentarians opposition, to 40
   respect for the foundations of society
      common law, respect for 36
      traditions, maintenance of 36–7
   union of England and Scotland 37

Puritanism
   theology 30

Rait, R.S.
   Dicey literary executor xi
   Dicey Papers recommendation not to publish xiv, xv

referendum
   advantages of 147–8
   advocacy of xxxii
   disadvantages of 148–9
   English party system, and demerits 272–3
   merits 271–2
   remedy for inadequacies, of 270
   'first English advocate' xix, xix n32, xxxi
   members of Parliament diminution of independence 149
   'new constitutional idea', as xxxi
   Parliament diminution of importance 149
   parliamentarianism as remedy for xxxi, 147–9
   parliamentary intrigue, combatting 148

representative government
   absolutely representative assembly 217–18
   agency
      analogy with delegated representation xxxvi, xxxvii, 216–17
      delay development of representation 216
   defects
      diminution in participation by individuals 222
      morally limited 224–5
      parliamentary minorities given undue authority 226–8
      representatives in opposition to will of the people 225–6
      territorially limited 224
   delegation of right or power by citizens 215
   direct participation in public life
      delay development of representation 215
   legislatures restrictions on competence 217
   limits
      external and internal xxxvi
   meaning of 215–19

merits
  legislation continuous and popular 220
  legislative power in hands of superior class 220-1
  participation in political life 219-20
  separation of powers 221-2
  moral right of majority to govern 227, 228
  parliamentary sovereignty xxxvi, 218
    inherent limits to xxxvi, xxxvii
    practical limits to xxxvii, 222-8
  popular sovereignty xxxvi
  representation
    agency, as xxxvi, xxxvii, 216-17
    concept of 215
    limit on power of representative assembly xxxvi
    modern development, of 215-16
  representative
    role of 216-17
  separation of powers 221-2
Roman Catholics
  Georgian Parliament exclusion from 65
  religious freedom restrictions on 52
Rousseau
  institutions governing character of nations 152
rotten boroughs
  abolition 48
  Reform Act 1832 65
  reinstatement 65
rule of law
  constitutional principle, as xxi, xxxiv, xxxv, xxxix
  Dicey's formal view, of xxxvii-xxxix
  droit administratif, distinguished xxxix, 307

English and American constitutionalism, compared 78
judicial independence, and xl
limitations of xl-xli

Sabbatarianism
  doctrine upheld by Puritans 30
Savoy conference 30
Scotland
  Church
    representative of the nation 163-4
  constitutionalism
    development of 20-1
    French constitutionalism, compared 21-2
    institutions as the embodiment of nation 163-5
  parliament
    membership 50, 289
  Parliament of Scotland 15, 72, 163, 165
  parliamentary representation (c 1787) 66, 72
  rule of law 163
  Scotch constitutionalism 21-2
  union 4, 5, 18, 28, 31, 37, 48, 71
  unitary constitution, and 27, 28
self-government
  local self-government distinguished 300-1
  meaning 299, 302
  meaning 299
separation of powers
  constitutional principle not qualifying, as xxxix-xl
Sidgwick, Henry
  friend to Dicey xiii
Swiss Confederation
  ancient constitutions 212, 215
  democratic constitutionalism 13, 14, 130, 131, 158-9, 247

establishment of the constitution 175
executive
  judicial and executive functions 10-11, 222
federal constitution 26, 247
historical character
  discontinuous development 18, 19, 177-8
historical constitutions 189, 212
local self-government 300
loyalty to the constitution 130
parliamentarianism 143, 147, 160-1, 265
party system, and 134, 136
prosperity dependant on constitution 154-5
Puritan constitutionalism, compared 39, 52
referendum
  constitutional change, and 270
  parliamentarianism, and 143, 147
  stability of government, and 273 n2
religious freedom
  Salvation Army 52
representative government 217, 227
responsive constitution 247
rigid constitution, as 236
semi-parliamentary executive 242-3
universal suffrage 99
Stephen
  analytical method of study 4
Stephen, Caroline Emilia
  cousin to Dicey xv
Story
  analytical method of study 4
Stubbs
  historical method of study 4

Taine
  ancien régime
    modern French institutions, and 91-2

Thucydides
  history of ancient states 193, 200–1
Tocqueville
  ancien régime
    modern French institutions, and 91–2
  self-government 299, 300

Unitary constitution
  English constitutionalism 26–8
  federal constitution, distinguished 26–7
United States *see also* **American constitutionalism**
  constitutional transplantation xxvii
  Dicey's visits to xii

federalism 26, 27
foundation 155–6
irresponsive constitution, as 245–6
parliamentarianism 147, 160–1
Presidential executive 282–4
referendum parliamentarianism, and 147
religious freedom Mormons 51
spirit of the constitution xxv
standing army 54
Supreme Court 10
universal suffrage
  French constitutionalism 93, 96, 99, 173–4, 315–19

Ledru-Rolin 173
parliamentary government 140, 143
United States, in 79

Voltaire
  Prussian constitutionalism influence on 107–8

Wales
  unitary constitution, and 27, 28
Walpole
  bribery 132
  Parliament historical description of anomalies 65–6